toward love

D1714319

CHANGE

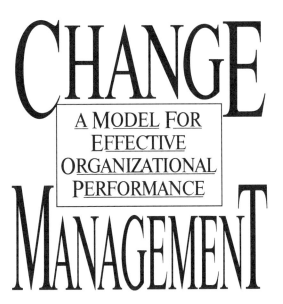

A MODEL FOR
EFFECTIVE
ORGANIZATIONAL
PERFORMANCE

MANAGEMENT

CHANGE

A MODEL FOR EFFECTIVE ORGANIZATIONAL PERFORMANCE

MANAGEMENT

Patricia K. Felkins
B. J. Chakiris
Kenneth N. Chakiris

591553

QUALITY RESOURCES ®
A Division of The Kraus Organization Limited
New York, New York

Most Quality Resources books are available at quantity discounts when purchased in bulk. For more information contact:

Special Sales Department
Quality Resources
A Division of The Kraus Organization Limited
902 Broadway
New York, New York 10010
800-247-8519

Copyright © 1993 Patricia K. Felkins, B. J. Chakiris, and Kenneth N. Chakiris

All rights reserved. No part of this work covered by the copyrights hereon may be reproduced or used in any form or by any means—graphic, electronic, or mechanical, including photocopying, recording, taping, or information storage and retrieval systems—without written permission of the publisher.

Printed in the United States of America
   97 96 95   10 9 8 7 6 5 4 3 2

Quality Resources
A Division of The Kraus Organization Limited
902 Broadway
New York, New York 10010

The paper used in this publication meets the minimum requirement of American National Standard for Information Sciences—Permanence of Paper for Printed Library Materials, ANSI Z39.48—1984.

Library of Congress Cataloging-in-Publication Data
Felkins, Patricia K.
Change management: a model for effective organizational performance/Patricia K. Felkins, B. J. Chakiris, and Kenneth N. Chakiris.
      p. cm.
Includes bibliographical references and index.
ISBN 0-527-91723-0
1. Organizational change.   2. Total quality management.   3. Work groups.
4. Management—Employee participation.   I. Chakiris, B. J.
II. Chakiris, Kenneth N.   III. Title.
HD58.8.F437   1993   93-6989
658.4′06—dc20   CIP

*This book is dedicated
to the
leaders and teams who
will manage global
change.*

Contents

List of Figures

Preface

Change is a way of thinking, communicating, and acting to create new relationships and structures to reflect the way an organization defines itself, the way it responds to customers, and the way it does business now and in the future.

This book focuses on managing change through a process of consultation and teamwork rather than through traditional hierarchy and control. Managers and professionals from a wide variety of organizations can apply the concepts in this book to involve people in meeting new challenges and implementing change.

Change Management uses process skills to develop competence and improve performance in changing roles and structures. Even though managers and leaders have authority, they can practice facilitation, teaming, and collaboration that extends throughout the organizational system to support change. Employee participation, self-directed teams, group clusters, and fluid structures are pushing managers into new roles that require effective communication, coordination, and consultation skills. Employees and other stakeholders are being given greater freedom for participation and responsibility. From the CEO to the manager, from the line supervisor to the employee team leader, from the supplier or customer to special interest groups, many people within organizational systems are finding themselves in situations or contexts in which change is best managed through collaborative inquiry and cooperative action in reaching common goals.

The change management model provided in this book, integrates both innovative and practical ideas for cooperative learning in which individuals, groups, and organizations coordinate diverse agendas and cultural differences to accomplish effective organizational performance. We want our readers to appreciate change management as an effective process for learning and doing. Ultimately, it is the quality of collective action that will have the greatest impact on organizations and communities in the 21st century as people create, interpret, and implement change.

In **Part I, Dynamics of Change,** we establish the groundwork for understanding different views about change. This section discusses the key concepts of change management and defines action research teams as a foundation of that process.

Chapter 1, Nature of Organizational Change, describes directed, nondirected, and integrated change as part of a continuous organizational process. Without integration of directed and nondirected elements, change may be contradictory as the organization works only with formal plans, policy guidelines, and controls while ignoring the underlying complexity of individual and group attitudes, goals, and interrelated work practices. Change is interpreted through the perceptions, cultural norms, and interactions of people. Dialogue and collaborative inquiry in data collection and analysis are encouraged as the basis of effective change management.

Chapter 2, Defining Change Management, illustrates the key components of context, consultation technology, coordination, and results. Competencies are built on a foundation of consultation skills to facilitate effective performance through ongoing information gathering, assessment, feedback, planning, and action. Consultation, the process for managing and integrating change is discussed in greater detail in Chapters 5 through 11 covering these six phases: (1) need and opportunity in change initiatives, (2) agreements for establishing working relationships, (3) data collection and analysis, (4) feedback, decisions, and action planning, (5) applications and results measurement, and (6) continuity and renewal.

Chapter 3, Change Perspectives and Pragmatics, suggests a framework for understanding how people interpret change from various mindsets or worldviews. These perspectives determine the way organizational members create expectations and boundaries, and make decisions for action related to change. Building on the analytical psychology of C. G. Jung, we explore some dominant functions of these four perspectives of change: 1) rational/behavioral, 2) systems, 3) cultural/interpretive, and 4) critical humanism. Organizations are made up of diverse and sometimes conflicting viewpoints. A shared understanding of and appreciation for different change perspectives brings better coordination and more realistic application to help integrate directed and nondirected change.

Chapter 4, explains Action Research Teaming (ART), a strategy and a process aimed at system-wide learning and participation for effective performance and results. ART methods involve individuals and stakeholders such as employees, suppliers, customers, or community in a data-based change process. It is a systematic way to confront and respond to business challenges, legitimize concerns, and coordinate action. Two case studies are used to illustrate the ART application.

Part II, A Context for Integrated Change, furnishes application tools for beginning the process of change management based on the six-phase consultation model.

Chapter 5, Need and Opportunity in Change Initiatives, introduces Phase 1 of our mode and explores the formation of cooperative relationships, without expert or imposed control. This chapter includes a diagnostic checklist to assess the system's readiness, and to clarify goals, roles, and expectations. This is useful when preparing for entry into a group or organization to initiate the change management process.

Chapter 6, Agreements: Establishing Working Relationships presents Phase 2 and offers a foundation for establishing accountability by using collaborative inquiry to form effective relationships among business units, managers, consultation resources, and teams. Need validation, action roles, results, relationships, and cultural norms and values are defined as a part of the agreement. Sample formats are presented as pragmatic tools to focus shared goals, needs, and results.

Chapter 7, Teamwork as a Structure for Change, provides teamwork competencies to facilitate change management through diversity, commonality, renewal, communication, confirmation, and coordination. The interactive "eye" of this teamwork model is diversity which gives energy and new possibilities to the teaming process. Teamwork emphasizes group learning and collective inquiry in understanding issues, taking action, and meeting organizational challenges related to continuous change.

Part III, A Data-Based Change Process, describes implementation and application in the remaining four phases of consultation in the change management model.

Chapter 8, Data Collection and Analysis, covers Phase 3 to begin a collective process of action learning. Effective managers know the value of data in planning, coordinating, implementing, and evaluating change. Data collection approaches for change management are summarized. Factors affecting data collection and analysis are examined to help managers make appropriate choices from a range of sources and data collection methods. The case study in this chapter illustrates the way one organization obtained market information using multiple data collection methods.

Chapter 9, Feedback, Decisions, and Action Planning, explains Phase 4 and emphasizes ongoing use of feedback to involve people in the interpretation of data and action planning to help integrate both directed change at the formal level, and nondirected change at the informal level. Methods are provided for developing agendas for feedback sessions, futuring activities, forcefield analysis, and action planning facilitation. The case study in this chapter illustrates the use of feedback resource groups within an action learning conference to invite constituent participation, interpretation, and validation of ideas during a strategic planning process.

Chapter 10, Applications and Results Measurement, in Phase 5 focuses on intervention applications to improve the performance of the organization. A model of evaluation and measurement tools are illustrated to assess interventions, audit change management consultation practices, and evaluate programs. A planning questionnaire for designing performance measurement is also provided. The case study describes an intervention assessing the customer service system of distribution centers using action learning methods and system-wide change to improve customer responsiveness and satisfaction.

Chapter 11, Continuity and Renewal, concludes with Phase 6 and creating continuity and renewal in change management. Tools include a diagnostic method for assessing the "career" of the organization, and an audit for obsolescence monitoring of roles, tasks, functions, organizations, and industries. Benchmarking questionnaires are provided as an essential method for renewing the organization.

Part IV, Competency Development, deals with the personal and professional development of managers, team members, and staff professionals. This section defines core competencies for change management, describes how to create action learning environments in organizations through exchange of practices, and explores global contexts and ethics.

Chapter 12, Change Management Competencies, begins on a personal and professional level of competence, as managers learn to facilitate the six phases of change consultation. Career development is recognized in the core competencies. Application of action roles for managers and team members are described in this chapter.

Chapter 13, Exchange of Practices, encourages action learning through practicums of academic, corporate, and nonprofit institutes and universities, individual and group sharing at team meetings, and professional colleague cluster networks. Suggested formats provide a plan for organizing and involving professionals in an exchange of knowledge, experience, and action. We invite managers, change facilitators, and teams to design and share practices of change management.

Chapter 14, Global Contexts, focuses on understanding cultural differences and contexts, applications of diversity in the team model, and the need for developing global change perspectives. We review a proposal for assessing the competencies required for global career development and encourage the involvement of geographically local resources in change management programs, activities, and consultation processes. This is illustrated in a case study of a multinational training program developed by a global electronics firm.

Chapter 15, Ethics, discusses issues and challenges related to developing a responsive, reflective view of change management in an ethical context. The dilemmas of change management are examined, including expertise, intent, consequences, equity in relationships, freedom of choice, and openness and truth. Some working definitions and approaches to ethics, and a general statement regarding ethical practices in consultation and change management are provided as resources for managers.

The ideas and work of outstanding theorists, practitioners, and professionals in business, communication, psychology, philosophy, and sociology have influenced this book. Many of these sources are included in the bibliography. However, we do want to acknowledge the pioneering work of Gordon L. Lippitt and Ronald Lippitt.

We recognize the contributions of our clients in facilitating our understanding of change and in achieving their own excellence in quality, productivity, and service through change management.

We also express appreciation to the talented professionals at Quality Resources, especially Michael Shally-Jensen. We thank our many colleagues and friends who have over the years provided insight, support, and inspiration.We want to acknowledge the time our dedicated staff and Sylvia Chakiris spent in computer work and revisions. Dr. Irvin Goldman provided valuable assistance in reviewing the theoretical aspects of change management. Ken M. Chakiris, Sr. supported our work with patience, humor, and encouragement.

We hope this book will serve as a resource for effective change management in a global world and help organizations become more responsive to the challenges and opportunities of continuous change.

P.K.F.
B.J.C.
K.N.C.

PART I

Dynamics of Change

1

Nature of Organizational Change

As momentous changes are occurring in social, political, and economic systems throughout the world, many organizations also are experiencing a transformation. Yet some of the opportunities that could bring organizational learning and renewal are lost in the stress, conflict, and contradictions related to change. Understanding how to manage change can help executives, managers, staff professionals, and team members to seize these powerful opportunities.

Organizational changes are both subtle and dramatic. On the surface many organizations appear to be stable, unified, and generally efficient in day-to-day operations. Yet just beneath the cover of orderly operations and structured hierarchical relationships, the effects of continuous change are creating new patterns and structures and changing the way organizations define themselves, how they respond to customers, and how they will do business now and in the future. Planned changes may involve new products and services, work redesign, technological innovation, response to competitive challenges, customer and stakeholder demands, and financial challenges. However, other changes are more elusive, hidden in the interactions of formal meetings, hallway discussions, electronic memos, daily problem solving, confrontation of new challenges, and unspoken agreements about how things really do work or should work. In continuing formal and informal processes, change quietly alters and at other times powerfully transforms the organizational system. Some changes are more dramatic and focused toward strategic goals; others are created through routine practices, slowly and subtly testing and modifying organizational structures and values.

From economists to psychologists, the experts try to help us understand change. Modern scientists attempt to measure natural change processes, from turbulence in the atmosphere to the evolutionary development of life and the complex behavior of simple systems. However, exploring the nature of change is not a new challenge. Around 500 B.C., the Greek philosopher Heraclitus was thinking about perpetual change and the contradictions in nature when he speculated that a person could not step twice in the same river because the river was continuously flowing and changing. Recognizing and understanding change is not an easy task since, as Heraclitus reminds us, "Nature loves to hide." Indeed, some of the most powerful change opportunities are embedded in daily work practices, shifting structures, and new management roles within the informal organization.

While the dynamics of change can be elusive, the basic components and rules of change are an integral part of the system itself. Change has been characterized as a "crystallization" of new actions and possibilities based on "reconceptualized" patterns of organization (Kanter 1983). Just as change requires new ways of thinking, it also involves a rethinking of the "architecture" of organizational structures and relationships (Nadler, Gerstein and Shaw 1992). These new paradigms are transforming and reinventing concepts of organization.

This presents many challenges, yet the power to understand and influence change is within every organizational system. Whether information and resources are applied or left to their routine patterns is dependent on the capacity of leaders, managers, and staff professionals to understand change dynamics and align both formal and informal change processes in organizational practice. Often the underlying energy and pattern dynamics related to nondirected informal change in everyday activities and attitudes are not recognized and coordinated. Thus these resources remain in the background, segmented, and isolated from the formal planned change efforts which attract all of the attention and interest. Yet without informal support and integration, formal change efforts may not be successful.

Change is ultimately a way of thinking, interpreting, and acting within the organizational system. Consider the worldview of the entrepreneur who "searches for change" and seizes opportunities (Drucker 1985). This perspective is important in recognizing the options for change in everyday organizational functions. Managers and employees begin to manage change as they become more aware of the routine interpretations and responses in daily work practices and plan and implement change in a positive, proactive, and creative way. This "shift of mind" is evident in the "learning organization" (Argyris and Schon 1978; Senge 1990) as people continually learn from their experience and transfer this knowledge to new situations so that the system expands its capacity and resources to create and influence its own future. The facilitation of change is a continuous process of group learning, negotiation, and coordination to increase competence, reduce conflict, align resources, and reach organizational objectives for quality, productivity, and service within a responsive and effective system.

DIRECTED AND NONDIRECTED CHANGE

Successful change depends on an appropriate integration of both formal and informal change processes. Managers must recognize the nondirected change processes in daily work practices and apply them to support focused directed change to achieve specific results and performance goals.

Directed change is intentional and consciously initiated, managed, and evaluated in relation to current and strategic organizational objectives. Major change may be announced by the CEO and supported in meetings, employee publications, and training programs. It may be publicized in a news release or launched with an elaborate public ceremony. This change might be triggered by research for innovation in new products and structures or the need to more effectively control operations and cost, improve quality and productivity, grow competitive resources and market share, and increase employee involvement in customer focused service.

Directed change is implemented through a definite plan and is assumed to be largely under the control of designated boards, executives, managers, or employee teams. This change is often a proactive move to prepare for challenges and deal with issues that will affect the organization. Directed change is likely to be carefully monitored with regular feedback reports, performance measurements, assessment, and necessary adjustments to meet overall objectives.

The continuous process of nondirected change, on the other hand, is often in the shadows, largely out of the conscious awareness of most organization members. Yet this dimension may reflect a more accurate picture of organizational culture in core values and group norms related to change. Practices at this level include the implementation of routine procedures, the interpretation of rules and policies, and the results of daily decisions that are often automatic and unobtrusive. It is also in the hidden agendas, unconscious bias, and cultural norms that subtly influence and reinforce these policies. Not only line employees and support staff but also managers and boards fall prey to the taken-for-granted reality of organizational structure and function. Organization leaders can influence change by paying attention to what is happening to individuals, groups, units, and systems at the nondirected informal level.

The greatest impact of nondirected change may be in the information that is lost and the activities that are not coordinated with directed change. A lack of accurate information and feedback at this informal level may contribute to conflict, boredom, burnout, low productivity, and poor work quality. Other issues such as corruption, cultural insensitivity, and sexual harassment can also be affected by what happens or does not happen at the nondirected level. Lack of training and information gaps may further separate and isolate nondirected change. Decreased employee motivation and management frustration are amplified by perceptions and feelings that often remain at the nondirected level, unacknowledged by organization leaders. These conflicts and distortions can grow unnoticed in the shadows of nondirected change.

Nondirected change involves the preprogrammed decisions and routine policies that are interpreted daily by organizational members in relation to specific problems and situations on the job. Many of these rules are followed without question and never reviewed for continuing viability. Old procedures may be applied to new problems that may not fit the assumptions or context in which the initial policy was made. The different interpretations of routine practices may result in small segmented shifts that may appear to be within tolerances. Yet the sequences of these interpretations may slowly modify or mutate the rules. People may also create new and innovative rules or norms to meet daily challenges. Nondirected change is a natural and often practical sequence that should be recognized and integrated as part of a continuous improvement process supporting overall competitive goals.

Integrating nondirected change with directed change has many benefits.

FIGURE 1.1 Directed and Nondirected Change.

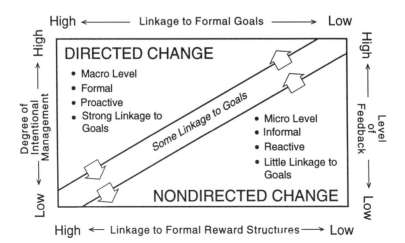

This alignment can help energize a static system with little innovation, or improve coordination in a culturally diverse, fragmented system in the midst of rapid change. There is a continuum connecting directed and nondirected change. This is illustrated in Figure 1.1. As people in an organization experience more feedback through collaborative inquiry and teamwork, many of the variations in activities that would usually be considered "nondirected change" start to become more linked to overall organizational goals, thus crossing over into the "directed change" category. This is indicated in the figure by the arrows crossing over from nondirected change into the region of directed change. Similarly, as the degree of intentional management and awareness decreases, activities that were linked to an overall strategic plan of change become unlinked and cross over into the region of nondirected change. If they are not integrated, organizational goals and actions may not be consistent.

In many cases, the difference between directed and nondirected change lies in the organizational context in which it takes place. Consider two scenarios:

> *Case A:* A purchasing manager, who formerly shopped around for prices at four different suppliers, decides to develop a long term relationship with one of them based on a shared commitment to quality and service.

> *Case B:* A purchasing manager, who formerly purchased materials from four suppliers, now decides to buy from the one with the easiest credit terms.

In case A, the decision was taken as a result of a corporate-wide quality initiative. In case B, the manager was reacting to the fact that only one supplier would tolerate his organization's slow payment policies. In both cases the action is essentially the same, selecting a single supplier from the existing four. Case A would be classified as directed change, while case B would clearly be an example of nondirected change, which may not support quality objectives.

Substantial discussion, planning, and rewards are associated with directed change. Yet the innovation and distortion that occur in the social interaction and interpretation of events at the level of nondirected change are not always recognized. Those who seek to influence change should consider the processes of group interaction in information gathering, problem solving, and decision making as the daily building blocks of change and renewal. The least obvious aspects of organizational life in processing information, making routine decisions, and interpreting procedures and rules are often the most critical elements in understanding and managing change (Weick 1979).

Obviously not all change can be continually monitored and controlled. The integration of directed and nondirected change moves some aspects of change to a more nondirected routine with periodic monitoring and assessment. This requires increased awareness of daily practices through involvement in group data collection, analysis, and planning for needed changes. Task forces and employee involvement groups can help organization members pay attention to interrelationships and integrate directed and nondirected change efforts.

Coordination of directed and nondirected change processes is a critical goal in change management. Without some integration of formal directed change and informal nondirected processes, change may be a generally chaotic process because the organization is only working with formal plans, policy guidelines and controls, and not benefitting from the structures of individual and group attitudes, perceptions, and interlocking work practices.

For example, assessing a quality program at the nondirected level of attitudes, values, and perceptions reveals the informal influence of daily interactions and practices on quality and productivity. A directed effort such as a human resource audit, employee involvement groups, quality teams, or focused assessment and training can integrate activities and knowledge from the nondirected level with a common directed focus. Integration occurs through team data collection, group feedback and analysis, collaborative action planning, and cooperative alliances.

FIGURE 1.2 Directed, Nondirected, and Integrated Change.

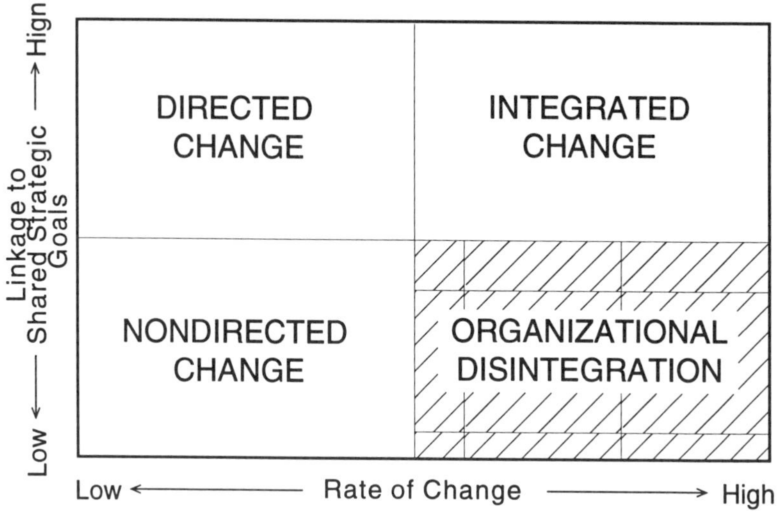

Figure 1.2 illustrates the integral relationship among nondirected, directed, and integrated change. Integrated change is characterized by both a high rate of change and a high linkage to strategic goals. Directed change has a high linkage to these goals but, in many cases, a low rate of change. This could reflect a gap between the group that creates the goals and the group that implements them. It may also reflect unacknowledged contradictions in the planned change, contradictions that cannot be confronted due to a lack of integration between the different resources and critical data.

When the rate of change is high and the linkage to communicated goals is low, members of the organization begin to regard the changes as arbitrary. They start to lose their sense of the organization as a cohesive entity. This can create disintegration which affects quality, productively, and service.

CHARACTERISTICS OF CHANGE

Both directed and nondirected change are affected by the basic characteristics of change itself. An understanding of these concepts creates the foundation for managing complex developmental processes throughout the organizational system. The following are the basic characteristics of change:

- Organizational change involves contradictions.
- Organizational change is a continuous process.
- Organizational change is interpreted through the perceptions and interactions of people.
- Organizational change can be facilitated through collaborative inquiry and teamwork.

Change Involves Contradictions

For both individuals and organizations change begins with a recognition of contradictions between intentions and actions, between "where we are" and "where we want to be." The process of trying to understand and deal with these contradictions in order to influence change is a significant learning experience for individuals, groups, and organizations.

Understanding and managing the seemingly contradictory aspects of change will be one of the most critical developmental skill for managers and professionals in 21st century organizations. Some of the most successful business leaders have understood and integrated these contradictions to make their businesses more responsive and innovative. For example, Sam Walton's Wal-Mart success is based on a seemingly contradictory concept, "Think small and grow big" (Walton with Huey 1992).

There are powerful competitive opportunities in the integration of contradictions in technical and social systems, objective and subjective perspectives, and formal and informal aspects of organizational life and practice. Yet in the midst of change, organizations may experience an identity crisis as they seek to balance the contradictions—stability and innovation, individual and group, and global and local. By understanding and coordinating the contradictory and complex aspects of change into a unified and yet differentiated whole, both individuals and groups can learn to see the organization in new ways and recognize opportunities for learning and development. Through this integration process, the organization becomes more effective and organizational members develop a clearer sense of a shared vision, increased knowledge of system operations, greater determination of their own actions, and an expanded sense of responsibility for results.

Empowerment and employee involvement—from conventional quality teams to clusters and self-directed teams—have brought the contradictions in the structure, policies, and roles of the traditional organization into sharper focus. For example, the executive who *demands* that there must be participation and involvement is creating a contradictory situation that threatens the basic values of the program. On the other hand, organizations say they are customer-driven, but don't listen to their customers and the employees lack cooperation with the next department that is their internal customer.

In the changing context of authority and participation, organization members should be more aware of the impact of the roles they play, the meanings of their conversations and actions, as well as the sometimes contradictory organizational contexts in which they work. In an objective, seemingly rational, approach to the world, managers and employees alike may be surprised to find the existence of a subjective "constructed" reality in the values, norms, and unwritten rules of everyday organizational life that they have helped create and endorse in their routine practices. This might include accepting minimal expectations and standards for quality, maintaining informal power networks that serve hidden agendas, and creating innovative workarounds that are not documented or shared with other units. When this information moves into general awareness, some organization members might feel as if they are "suddenly awakened" in a place that they only thought was familiar (Mills 1959). For example, one executive group was astounded to find from the results of a human resource audit that their employees cared about quality, but thought that management was not concerned with quality because managers put emphasis on high production quotas. As one employee wrote, "All they want is for us to get the product out the door. They don't support our ideas."

Even when we recognize the contradictions and double binds in organizational life, it may still be difficult to change old habits and negative attitudes.

There also are contradictions based on positive actions. For instance, the organization concentrating all of its energies on winning a prestigious national award may not realize the point at which the award itself becomes the goal rather than the standards of excellence and quality that it represents. There are many other examples in negative economic contexts. In one context, the president of a manufacturing firm finds it difficult to close plants and consolidate operations. The results are working contradictions. In a small town whose economy depends on one manufacturing plant, more than 300 employees are producing a product for which there is no longer a viable market. Resolving these contradictions is not easy for this executive or for these plant workers.

Yet the effective management of the change process starts as organizations begin to recognize their strengths and weaknesses, the contradictions and gaps, as well as the dysfunctional aspects of their systems and cultures that might serve as barriers to growth and development. As Deming (1986) has reminded us, most problems are not in individual people but in the interrelated system of people and resources and the processes of how these people relate to one another, gather information, and solve problems. The emphasis on organizational "architecture" and "reengineering" recognizes systems problems in the formal and informal relationships, structures, and processes of organizations. Systems are balanced by contradictory forces.

Much of directed change is assumed to be based on a rational model. This can also present contradictions because of the nondirected elements of change. Focusing on the "myth of rationality" in organizations, Cohen, March, and Olsen (1972) present this provocative definition of organizational contradictions and possibilities: "An organization is a collection of choices looking for problems, issues and feelings looking for decision situations in which they might be aired, solutions looking for issues to which they might be the answer, and decision makers looking for work." This perspective reflects some of the paradoxes and contradictions of organizational activities in relationship to change. The possibilities for collaboration that are overlooked, the important questions that are never asked, the solutions that are not sought, the problems that are ignored, the untapped potential of people not used, and the failures and successes that are not explored as opportunities for change—these are too often lost in the routine of informal nondirected change. Yet the myths of rationality are also evident in planned directed change, such as an assessment program designed to recognize and reward "effective" managers that results in the dismissal of several "ineffective" managers. In another case, members of an organization say they want to improve teamwork, but add that they don't have time to work as a team.

Contradictions can both energize and distort the change process. When people in organizations realize that faster could be slower and that solutions can create more problems, the contradictions associated with change are remarkably clear. The balance between control and innovation, cost and profit, competition and cooperation—these elements of organizational life motivate many everyday dramas in a continuous, sometimes subtle process of change, playing somewhere between order and chaos.

Much of the scientific work that attempts to understand and measure chaos and turbulence in nature reinforces the same contradictory interrelationships: stability mixed with instability, entropy moving toward equilibrium, and simple systems exhibiting complex behavior. Feigenbaum, who discovered the universality in chaos, explained the need for a new way of looking at the world—to "reassemble" how we think about what is "important" in what happens in the world (Gleick 1987). Nondirected change may be the most critical base for managing directed change. Contradictions can require this kind of "upside down" thinking (Handy 1989).

Most employees care about quality. Organizational audits show that the challenge to produce quality work is one of the highest motivating values for all levels in the organization. If this is true, then why don't more organizations produce higher-quality work? By recognizing the natural contradictions within the system—from the relationship between productivity and quality to the problematic contradictions in traditional structures, roles, hierarchy, and expectations—organization members can learn to reduce the gaps and conflicts that confuse, distort, and undermine quality and effectiveness.

Imagine a sign on a door that reads "In or Out." Depending on individual perspective and needs, that sign can have opposite meanings at the same time. Organizational change can bring learning and development or chaos and decline and all the options in between. Managers, staff, and other organization members who have the responsibility of influencing and managing dynamic change processes can learn to appreciate the opportunities for knowledge, development, and innovation in these apparent contradictions.

Change Is a Continuous Process

From philosophers and physicists to harried managers and strategic planners, there is some agreement that nature never allows us to get too comfortable or to remain static. Just when executives, managers, and boards might be feeling some sense of satisfaction with the order and certainty in overall operations, something happens that dramatically shifts the system. Change also comes from more subtle nondirected actions that have been building up without notice over time in small decisions and conflicting interpretations of procedures and rules. Managers and staff professionals cannot become too content with the current order of things; they need to be aware of the impact of continuous change processes and the value of collaborative inquiry in data collection, analysis, action planning, and monitoring the results of both directed and nondirected change.

Any discussion of organizational change illustrates the paradox of attempting to explore and define a complex, dynamic system with static words, numbers, and diagrams. The reality of continuous change is not in a clever phrase or a new vision but in the interpretation and impact of *change* in relation to *no change*. The negative splits the idea and the image (Burke 1966). The idea of no change helps us to rationally understand continuous change in terms of its contradictions and continuity. This positions change as a conscious goal as well as a living reality.

Change is not a stop-and-go process; it is constant. Change is both fast and slow, conscious and unconscious, negative and positive, visible and invisible in every aspect of organizational life. To paraphrase a common communication axiom, "You cannot not communicate," (Watzlawick, Beavin, Jackson 1967) we might also conclude that, "An organization cannot not change." Just because change is nondirected or people are unaware of its progression doesn't mean change does not occur. The organization is always changing in some way on different levels. If continuous change is not integrated with strategic goals, then disorganization and chaos can occur. As Peters (1987) warns, "There is no place to stand anymore." Everything seems to be shifting and there is no stable ground or quiet place to observe or ignore the changing world.

Change cannot be squeezed into an organizational chart or captured in elaborate computer projections. Change cannot be completely controlled, no matter how hard some may try. In a healthy organization, change is a continuous, dynamic process based on information, conversations, relationships, and activities that are always nudging, modifying, and changing the boundaries and concepts of organization.

Even though executives, managers, boards, and staff professionals cannot control all elements of continuous change, they can influence and direct some aspects of the process within the social and technical systems of the organization. Other objectives and results including market share, cost-profit margins, and technological leadership depend on understanding continuous change in a larger context. Organizations can benefit from a broad interpretation of change as well as a specific awareness of how daily decisions and practices affect this process.

The parable of the boiled frog illustrates that survival depends on being aware of continuous gradual change processes (Senge 1990). Since a frog responds to sudden and not gradual changes in environment, a frog may sit in a pot of water with slowly increasing temperatures until it is boiled. Continuous change requires a clear comprehension of both directed and nondirected processes. The interpretation and ultimate meaning of change is in the awareness and influence organizational members have in relation to that change.

Effective change management helps members view themselves as part of this continuous process, always "arriving" in creating their reality, renewing their commitment, and celebrating their success, and always changing in relation to environmental information and performance measurements. As organizational members accept continuous change, they become more aware of the implications of their own actions and the need for collaborative inquiry and continuous learning to create the future of the organization.

Change Is Interpreted Through the Perceptions and Interactions of People

Integration of directed and nondirected change requires some shared interpretations and coordinated actions in relation to change. Yet organization members in their interactions and practices make individual and group decisions about what change means to them. In a realistic analysis, the significance and value of change is determined by the people in an organizational system — board members, leaders, managers, employees, suppliers, distributors, stockholders, and customers. Through their perceptions, conversations, and actions, they establish the meaning of change and feel its consequences most directly. In many ways the real impact of directed change cannot be completely known until people create and interpret that change in terms of their own needs and actions throughout the organizational system. This is why the impact of change may be most evident at the informal level where employees feel change most acutely.

A specific directed change effort is more effective if the perceptions and expectations of that change for individuals and groups within the organization are discussed, evaluated, and clearly understood by all members. Recognizing different perspectives toward change can help to reduce potential conflict and improve the results of collaborative inquiry in managing issues and solving problems related to change. Identifying the contradictory meanings and the conflicting attitudes that might exist in the minds of employees, managers and others can help prevent some future problems.

These are some of the key questions people should ask to better understand the unique perceptions of change in their organization:

- What does change mean to the CEO, the board, and the senior officers of the organization?

- What does change mean to individual and team members who will implement a directed change?
- What are the organizational conversations about change?
- What are the activities and behaviors related to change?
- What are the objectives of directed change efforts?
- How do people get information and feedback about change?
- How is change aligned with organizational vision and mission?
- What is the level of awareness of informal nondirected change?
- How are directed and nondirected change related in organizational practices?

Resistance to change as well as readiness for change are evident in everyday organizational interactions, decisions, and attitudes. These questions help to identify supporting and resisting forces as well as specific attitudes and conflicting perceptions that might affect implementation and performance measurement.

If change is extensive and imposed, it can bring uncertainty, anxiety, and frustration for people throughout the organization. Changes such as major job redesign, technological innovation, or mergers and downsizing can produce substantial stress. Change imposed by competition and diversity, and the desire of organizations to become more customer-oriented and quality-driven at lower costs, may require an adjustment of cultural norms and practices at the informal level. In this context, attention must be paid to the nondirected changes that will eventually support or undermine formal change efforts.

From a psychological perspective, change is both exciting and frightening. Yet even if change is focused and directed there still can be a substantial amount of uncertainty and ambiguity. For the individual and the organization, changes and adjustments to new ways of doing business can bring growth and, with this, some sense of loss for the familiar, even if the familiar is no longer effective or appropriate. For employees, new products and technological development may require additional skills, knowledge, and retraining. For managers, a change such as the creation of self-directed teams signals a reallocation of authority and a new consultation role. For many organization members, change can bring "a trapeze feeling" (Ferguson 1980) as the performer must leave one safe place to leap toward another that is uncertain.

The meaning of change, on both a directed and nondirected level, is created in the interaction of organizational members in processing information, making judgments, taking action, and evaluating that action. Sometimes the leaps that change requires are difficult for people to make. From new facilities and complex technologies to mergers, takeovers, and rightsizing, directed changes can eliminate people and routine ways of working and bring a conflict in values and divided loyalties and priorities. Rules and norms have to be continually assessed and renegotiated as part of managing the changing culture.

Organization members create the meaning of change as they experience it in their conversations, interactions, and work practices. For many managers this is the unknown area of nondirected change that may be undervalued or ignored. One communication expert suggests the development of "subtle managers" who are sensitive to the multiple ways organization members interpret their organizational realities, and who manage meaning, processes, contexts, choices, and coalitions with greater understanding (Trujillo 1987).

Organization members make their own meanings in relation to change. Without collaboration, shared information, and a unifying vision these meanings may stand in opposition to organizational objectives. Both directed and nondirected change processes should be considered in assessing individual and group interpretations of the "reality" of the change process. The meaning of change may be reflected in many different and conflicting voices.

Change Is Facilitated by Collaborative Inquiry and Teamwork

Organizational change is a group activity best understood from a "we" rather than an "I" perspective. It is difficult to isolate change in one department or unit, or delegate change initiatives to a few strategic executives or managers. An effective response to change may demand a dissolution of artificial barriers among departments and units as well as the elimination of rigid boundaries between the formal internal system and the external environment and community in which it exists.

From suppliers to customers, from finance to operations, from sales to human resources, there are many natural linkages throughout the organization that have been broken and fragmented within a formal bureaucratic structure. Functions and roles are progressively changing as organization members recognize the contradictions and limitations of traditional approaches and seek alliances and partnerships that link organizational resources in different ways. There are substantial untapped human resources existing in most organizations, sometimes unnoticed and often not utilized. A consultative approach, as advocated in this book, focuses on interaction and collaborative processes in gathering data, maximizing resources, and managing change throughout the organizational system. In most cases, employees can best answer questions about how routine work practices relate to organizational competence and competitiveness, but they need some systematic process to gather and apply this information. Managers and staff professionals may have valuable knowledge and insights that are not transferred to others. They can benefit from collaboration and networks to integrate knowledge and competencies for effective change management.

The consultative approach involves people in needs validation, data collection and analysis, feedback and interpretation, decisions and actions, and applications and monitoring. These are at the core of the group learning and integration required for facilitating organizational change in a dynamic system. Yet consultation skills often are underdeveloped at all levels. Employee involvement, self-directed teams, and empowerment require that managers and staff professionals work effectively with colleagues, employees, customers, and community to implement and influence change. Facilitation, communication, feedback, confrontation, and negotiation are some of the most essential consultation competencies needed by managers because they can encourage participation and provide the opportunity for shared dialogue and information to help manage change.

Change can be managed best when the process is coordinated through the energy and resources of people at every level of the organization, informed and motivated, working as a cooperative team to gather and process data, make decisions, and take action toward organizational goals and results. An interactive or consultative approach accepts change as a continuous natural process of organizational development and team learning. The organization is seen as part of a constantly changing environment that has been created through interaction and collaboration both within the formal organization and in an extended network of distributors, suppliers, customers, stakeholders, and community.

While this book deals with many aspects of change, it focuses most on collaborative and data-based change management that moves organization members from reactive to proactive perspectives. This involves recognizing contradictions and barriers, reducing threats, optimizing resources, and building on opportunities to integrate directed and nondirected change. Such collaboration may include managers and staff professionals as well as internal and external consultation teams, boards of directors, task forces, clusters, employee teams, and special project groups that may involve customers, suppliers, and community leaders.

Sometimes organization members lack the knowledge and opportunity to see the organization as a cooperative, interdependent system. Many employees don't know how information and products move within the organizational network. They may not consider the next person in the process as their "customer." In a traditional worldview, both managers and employees may maintain rigid internal and external boundaries. Yet internal and external components such as suppliers, customers, production, and sales are interrelated and often indivisible in determining the success of a seamless competitive system. These natural linkages and alignments can bring renewed energy and direction to the organization.

Rather than being controlled by distinct internal and external forces, change can be better understood and influenced by proactive organizations that use collaborative inquiry and process consultation skills to develop resources and take advantage of opportunities for innovation and development in an interactive holistic system within a changing economic and social environment. Change management is an essential component of effective performance and ultimate survival.

Effective organizations choose options and influence results rather than simply responding to someone else's agenda. Only by continuously confronting information and learning together can organization members facilitate change and renewal in a world of increasing competition and diminishing resources. People throughout the organizational system can be involved in gathering information and integrating directed and nondirected change in their areas and units. Employees will be more committed to change if they had access to information to understand and implement change as a continuous process. This communication also helps to promote a shared vision and facilitate cooperation in achieving strategic goals and improving organizational performance.

Uncertainty is one of the most difficult aspects of change for all those who are involved. There is often high equivocality in the information available about directed change. This information can be incomplete or obscure. Shared information processing and involvement can help individuals and groups learn about the changing organization as they gather and interpret data, solve problems, and plan together.

Organizational structure and culture are created by the people who participate in that system of interrelated activities. These members may or may not be aware of the kind of organization they are creating. In the effective organization, members work as a cooperative and integrated team, sharing information and utilizing total organizational resources in planning, implementing, and assessing change as they create their collective future together. This does not happen without efforts; it requires managerial insight and training in consultative skills and technologies to support strategic outcomes.

DEVELOPING A CHANGE ORIENTATION

A proactive change orientation means that the organization looks toward change with vigilance and celebrates change as an opportunity for continuing learning and development. Change orientation is both attitude and action, it is both a way of understanding change and a set of competencies to manage change. With this change orientation, people in organizations are talking and thinking about change as a positive force rather than a threat.

FIGURE 1.3 Approaches to Change.

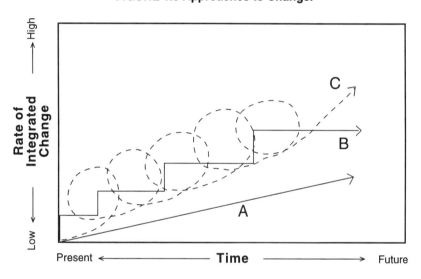

Figure 1.3 illustrates some approaches to change as a way of getting from the present to the future. It shows three approaches and plots the rate of organizational change as a function of time.

Approach A moves toward the future with directed change, deliberate speed, and intention. This approach may have some competitive advantages, but problems arise because change is contradictory, continuous, interpreted by organization members, and best facilitated through collaborative inquiry. The present and the future are changing, and the race may be lost if organizational members do not recognize that they must continually monitor and create their present and future in both planned change and informal work practices. A direct line toward the future may not take adequate time to gather information and feedback to integrate directed and nondirected processes. Because of this, change may be misdirected and total cycle time increased.

Approach B is also deliberate, but with specific interim objectives and regular opportunities for analysis and planning throughout the process. This approach recognizes the transitional states and steps as the organization develops through directed stages in an incremental process that moves from the present to the future. Lewin's (1951) model of progressive development through intentional "stops" analyzes change movement and process in order to integrate nondirected elements. Within each cycle the organization improves its competency and rate of change. Using this approach, the future becomes part of a developmental process for individual, group, and organization.

Approach C is usually perceived as taking more time and resources. While this may be true initially, the long-term results are more positive. This approach acknowledges both directed and nondirected change processes and involves people throughout the organization in interpreting and creating their collective future. The cyclical model reaches toward the future with continuous feedback, monitoring, and assessment in a data-based change process. The cyclical approach is illustrated by the looping behavior of the graph. Each loop illustrates data collection and feedback processes used to interpret and reinterpret the past, present, and the future to meet changing needs. The contradictions and complexity of change can be dealt with more effectively in this manner. A strong developmental focus emphasizes a high level of involvement and innovation in change management. There is also a recognition of the reality of a changing present and future. This approach must be flexible and responsive to maximize resources, measure results, and improve performance within a competitive timeframe.

CHANGE INTEGRATION THROUGH CONSULTATION

This book is about managing change through the process of team consultation to help people within organizations to get from the present to the future. This process integrates directed and nondirected change to more effectively respond to organizational needs and performance objectives. This book provides executives, managers, staff professionals, boards, consultation teams, employees, and community leaders with a competency-based model for change management.

Many people within organizations talk about the certainty of change but fewer are certain about how to change. Through the insight and energy of people and the process of teamwork and collaborative inquiry, the strategic goals and vision of the organization can be achieved. Consultation skills can help managers and team leaders to facilitate change and integrate and align organizational resources to make the organization more responsive to all stakeholders including employees, customers, suppliers, boards, stockholders, and community. This helps support performance and profit.

Since change is continuous, contradictory, and interpreted in multiple ways, it is essential to optimize organizational experience, knowledge, and resources in managing change. Consultation competencies help managers and team leaders achieve these change management objectives:

- Integrate directed and nondirected change processes;
- Create awareness of contradictions and close performance gaps;
- Facilitate change as a continuous improvement process that requires ongoing information gathering, assessment, monitoring, and feedback;
- Increase organizational competency to seize opportunities for innovation and competitive advantage;
- Support cooperative relationships and teamwork and motivate employee involvement and commitment to change;
- Improve communication and feedback in processing information and understanding perceptions and attitudes toward change;
- Involve people in collaborative inquiry to understand and implement successful data-based change;
- Encourage organizational learning and high performance.

These results are accomplished by using influence rather than control to develop commitment and empower people throughout the organization to work together in improving quality, productivity, and service at both the directed and nondirected level. The consultation relationship establishes a partnership between a client system and a facilitating system to integrate technical and process skills and develop individual, group, and organizational competencies for effective change management. Teamwork and collaborative inquiry create a continuous cycle of learning and participation for all organization members in moving from the present to the future. Chapter 2 defines this model of change management and the new consultative roles and interactive processes that are at the core of effective organizational performance.

2

Defining Change Management

Organization leaders must find effective ways to deal with the profound changes that are redefining structures, redesigning work, changing relationships, transforming cultures, and creating new roles for boards, managers, staff professionals, team members, and employees. Leaders must take on more facilitative roles, as competencies in *change management* become critical to creating and sustaining effective organizations.

Increasingly, much of management is concerned with the *process* of coordinating resources and performance, and supporting learning within a dynamic, interconnected system. This coordination operates under many constraints. Managers are increasingly asked to respect and integrate individual, group, organizational, and community perspectives in improving performance and reaching mutually beneficial goals. Change management should be an interactive process that links daily work practices with strategic, directed change programs and performance goals.

In our model, change-management competencies are built on a foundation of *consultation skills*. With consultation skills, managers learn to facilitate change as a continuous process that requires ongoing information gathering, assessment, feedback, and action planning. Consultation helps organization members recognize the nondirected contradictions and gaps related to change, and involves people in collaborative inquiry to understand the meaning and application of change at both formal and informal levels. The results are evident in improved quality, service, and productivity, as well as in individual, group, and organizational learning.

Our definition of consultation focuses on the competencies that help individuals and teams understand, plan, integrate, implement, and monitor complex change processes as part of overall organizational strategy. In this definition, the consultation relationship plays a key role. The key players and the basic elements of this relationship are illustrated in Figure 2.1.

FIGURE 2.1 Elements of The Consultation Relationship.

FACILITATING SYSTEM
- Manager
- Change Facilitator
- Expert Resource
- Team Leader
- Staff Professional

Consultation Relationship
- Voluntary commitment
- Give and receive help
- Process facilitation
- Transfer of competencies
- Focus on results

CLIENT SYSTEM
- Client
- Sponsors
- Customers
- Suppliers
- Employees
- Teams
- Board

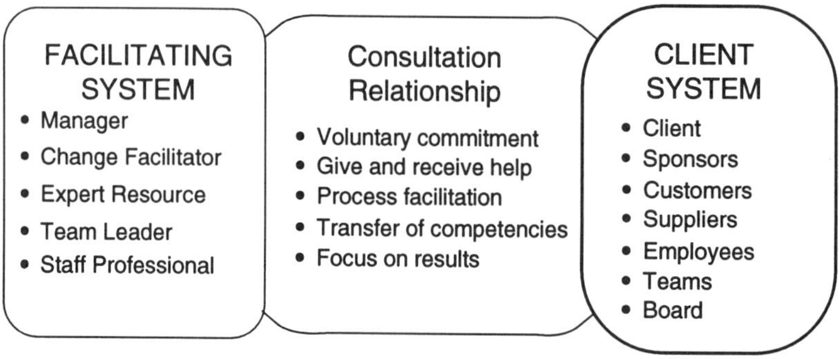

First, consultation starts out as a *voluntary* relationship between a client and a change facilitator with a high degree of commitment and communication in which value is perceived by all parties. They share both technical and process knowledge and develop competencies in supporting organizational objectives. This expands into a relationship between a client system and a facilitating system. Second, consultation is an *attempt* by a facilitating system *to give help to* a client system working on a current or potential business challenge, need, or opportunity. The intention and results of the consultative relationship are grounded in unified goals that develop individuals and groups as well as organizations. This interdependent relationship, whether temporary or ongoing, builds organizational competencies and the capacity for managing change. Initial working agreements should allow the parties involved free choice to enter into this relationship because each person sees the benefits of working together toward specific shared goals. Consultation relationships are built on commitment, communication, and perceived value.

Not all consultation is successful. There is no magic formula. Even the best change facilitator or consultation team cannot help if the client refuses to recognize gaps, take responsibility or make a necessary decision. People who are not ready to accept a major directed change can sabotage the best change management effort. The authority for decisions and actions ultimately remains with the client.

The third defining characteristic is that this relationship focuses on *influence rather than control*. Even though managers or supervisors have legitimate authority, they can choose methods of consultation as they teach, listen, advocate, and inspire. They can coordinate information gathering, align resources, and encourage individual and team development through cooperation and communication. Effective consultation teams facilitate through influence and interaction rather than control. In this context, managers and team members practice new leadership competencies.

The fourth characteristic is that the consultation relationship *encourages the transfer of competencies* to the client system, which gains knowledge and practice in collecting and analyzing data and managing change. If the client depends on experts for answers in the relationship, the client system becomes passive over time and does not expand the capacity for managing change. The consultation team should encourage building the capacity of the client system by developing the skills and confidence of people within that system.

The fifth characteristic is that the consultation relationship requires the change facilitation team to work within defined boundaries in a *temporary* structure focused around specific outcomes or results. However, the relationship may have continuity even though the project is completed. Each project has new roles, expectations, and outcomes.

In developing and sustaining an effective cooperative relationship, all of these concepts should be clarified in agreements and working contracts among people made at various points throughout the consultation process. This view of consultation points toward an expanded definition based not only on an expert individual resource, but also on specific consultation skills and competencies for managers, leaders, staff professionals, project teams, boards, and other groups within the organization to manage change and integrate directed and nondirected processes.

Even though this chapter is entitled "Defining Change Management" we will spend most of our time discussing consultation, because we believe that the core competencies in change management are found in consultation.

REDEFINING THE ROLE OF MANAGEMENT

Managers are being given increased responsibility for facilitating organizational change. Employee involvement, self-directed teams, and decentralized structures are creating new roles for managers (see Figure 2.2). However, the manager's traditional position can be precarious within current organizational structures. "Involvement-oriented" organizations (Lawler 1992) give employees greater freedom, participation, and responsibility. This shifts the position of an imposed expert and may threaten traditional perceptions of management authority, but it also opens a critical new area for management development in consultation. This is a role that has been neglected in the classic view of "management as control." The bureaucratic model of the manager's role in producing change is based on authority and expertise.

FIGURE 2.2 Changing Role of the Manager.

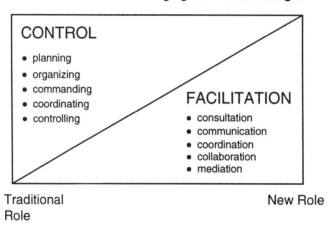

Traditional Role   New Role

Indeed, the classic functions of the manager are often defined as planning, organizing, commanding, coordinating, and controlling (Fayol 1949). Yet managers today often mediate and facilitate more than they control and command. Control is based in a formal structure of bureaucratic hierarchy and a tightly regulated system of reward and punishment. That implies an objective, often impersonal authority. Influence, on the other hand, is more subtle and difficult to quantify. The characteristics of influence include open communication, mutual trust, and respect that comes from direct interaction and voluntary acceptance. Influence is based on facilitation and shared values and goals, which increase cooperation and commitment to change.

Mintzberg (1973, 1990) divides the manager's roles into three categories: interpersonal roles (figurehead, leader, liaison); informational roles (monitor, disseminator, spokesperson); and decision-making roles (entrepreneur, disturbance handler, resource allocator, negotiator). However, many of these roles still contain elements of both control and facilitation. Managers are caught between two conflicting paradigms. Traditional perspectives give them the power to maintain order and efficiency in everyday operations; at the same time, employee involvement transfers increasing authority to employees through participation and empowerment.

Organizations are changing and the result of change is often conflict

(McWhinney 1992). Today, managers may be primarily concerned with "organizing conflict" (Deetz 1992) in a sometimes chaotic organization. While conflict cannot be eliminated completely, the manager must seek new ways to reduce and direct this energy through coordination and influence as individuals and groups working on various tasks compete for limited resources and rewards. This new managerial role demands process skills in conflict management, problem solving, and resource development.

Crisis, ambiguity, and conflict can become opportunities for development and growth as managers lead the organization on a path of empowerment toward a more humanistic, responsive, and productive culture (Vogt and Murrell 1990). The empowered manager is a change facilitator, consultant, coach, advisor, teacher, and partner to a variety of clients within the organizational system, from colleagues and senior executives to line employees and customers.

Fluid structures, work redesign, employee involvement, and empowerment are also changing the roles and practices of employees. A more flexible, flatter organizational structure provides an opportunity for an increasing number of people to take on management, leadership, and consultative functions within a more creative and risk-oriented system. Understanding and facilitating change within the organization requires a new approach to management based on developing and coordinating all the resources of the organization through a collaborative, consultative model.

People are the greatest resource for effective change management. Kotter (1990) suggests that many people within the organization act as leaders with a little "*l*." He states that as much as 50 percent of all jobs might involve leadership roles, depending on how much the organization needs to change. According to Kotter, dialogue, adaptation, and collaboration are key elements in developing "thick networks of informal relationships" with communication based on trust, credibility, and shared values. Encouraging and facilitating coordination among people is a central aspect of consultative management practices.

While the traditional approach to change management is prevalent in many organizations, the realities of a diverse workforce, a reduction in the number of middle managers, complex technologies, new alliances and coalitions, and a highly competitive global market are creating a need for leaders, managers, staff professionals, and team leaders to be competent in facilitating organizational change.

From the CEO to the manager and the line supervisor, many people within organizations are finding themselves in a consultation context in which they are facilitating and managing change. They are providing information and coordinating resources and personnel, and influencing others without exerting direct control even if they do have the power to exert such control. As these new roles emerge, the competencies required of managers and other staff professionals are also expanding. A major priority will be developing skills in change consultation to work with and through others to develop organizational capacity to manage complex change.

CHANGE MANAGEMENT MODEL

This chapter explores the process and context of consultation and presents a model (see Figure 2.3) that illustrates the essential elements of change management. The basic components of this model are:

- Context
- Consultation Technology
- Coordination
- Results

The following four sections introduce each element of the change

FIGURE 2.3 Change Management Model.

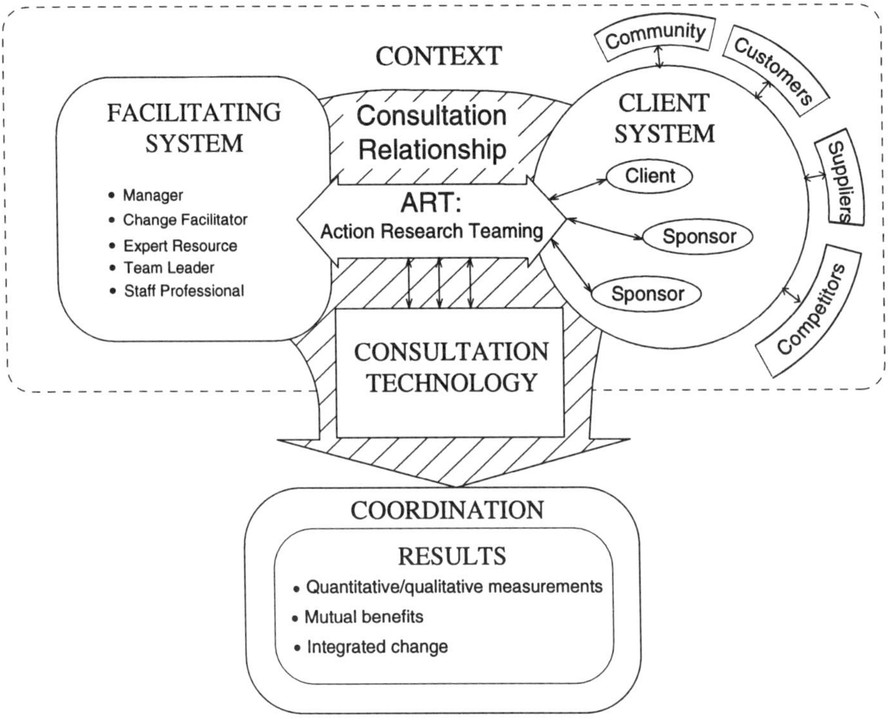

management model in some detail. Other issues concerning the model are expanded in later chapters. This is a pragmatic model driven by performance goals and results, coordinated relationships, and consultation technology in a context that integrates directed and nondirected change.

Our model of change management uses action research teaming (ART) to link the facilitating system with the client system. The ART model will be discussed in greater detail in chapter 4. The basic elements of the ART model are summarized in Figure 2.4. This collaborative process is at the heart of effective change management.

FIGURE 2.4 ART: Action Research Teaming.

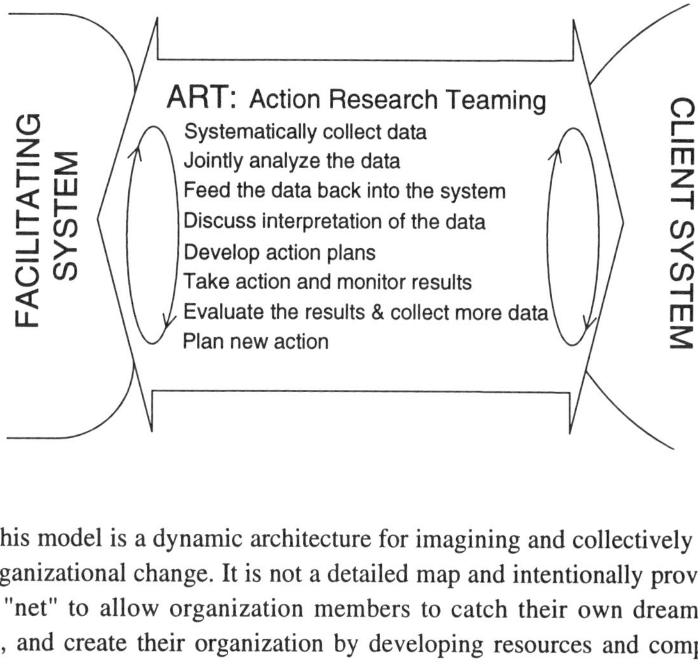

This model is a dynamic architecture for imagining and collectively creating organizational change. It is not a detailed map and intentionally provides a loose "net" to allow organization members to catch their own dreams and vision, and create their organization by developing resources and competencies for effective change management. As an interactive construction through which organizations can plan, implement, facilitate, and monitor change, this model encourages an understanding of change on both a directed and a nondirected level, in both grand plans and in everyday work. These goals are centered around effective performance.

Organizational *effectiveness* is a judgment influenced by the surrounding context of economic and social conditions as well as individual and group judgments on the meaning of effectiveness. This interpretation and judgment may be based on quantitative or qualitative data depending on the norms and needs of the organization and agreed-upon measurements for quality and service performance. For example, effectiveness may mean gaining lost market share, being more responsive to customers, implementing a total quality program, or serving the needs of the community.

Performance is a negotiated interpretation of individual, group, or organizational effectiveness. It is both a way-of-being and a way-of-doing within a system bounded by specific cultural norms and expectations for roles and actions. Performance is a joint process of interpretation that often involves an audience or customer. This audience may be management, boards, employees, consumers, community representatives, or stockholders. In most cases, effective organizational performance is assessed through collective interpretations of quality, trust, service, and cooperation. This shared creation of performance is an important contextural component of change management.

CONTEXT

The first component of the change management model is the context of change which includes both organizational culture and relevant environment . Context influences the interpretation, implementation, and evaluation of change. Context is defined as the set of circumstances, conditions, and "rules" existing at any particular time that can affect the organization in relation to current and strategic goals. Context may be viewed in the narrow sense by looking at the specific aspects of culture in the organization that serve as "control mechanisms" (Geertz 1973) and that unify the system by establishing and maintaining a set of shared norms, rules, values, and behavior for members of that culture. However, context is also a broader environment that affects organizational change in relation to economic circumstances and market conditions, innovation, and technological development, global perspective, and social responsibilities.

The organization changes and develops as part of its environment, not distinct from that environment. Organizational leaders and change facilitators need to understand how the organization relates to this larger system. Increased awareness and integration of context brings greater organizational alignment and self-determination in anticipating, planning, facilitating, and implementing complex, continuous change.

The cultural aspects of directed and nondirected change are evident throughout this book. The following sections focus on the organization in a broad economic, social, and political context. This includes cycles of economic development, sources of innovation, global perspectives, and organizational obligations and responsibilities.

Cycles of Organizational Change and Development

Cycles of development focus on obsolescence as well as renewal in relation to customers and community. Economic circumstances establish the context that may determine the creation, development, and life of an organization. Organizational evolution is a broad concept focusing on the dynamics of organizational systems and structures in adapting to changing environmental conditions. Several factors affect organizational change and development over time (Winter 1990):

- The culling of less fit organizations;
- The growth of more fit organizations;
- Improvement of skills and routines through learning;
- Availability of models of successful representatives for imitation;
- Historical trends favorable to a particular type of organization.

It is useful to consider the developmental pattern of organizations in relation to specific changes. Adizes (1988) characterizes organizational lifecycles of growth and development in relationship to flexibility and controllability. Young organizations are more flexible, but also more difficult to control. Older organizations are more controllable but less flexible. He suggests that an organization can stay in its "prime" with balanced growth and rejuvenation by changing organizational cultures, goals, and leadership styles to insure a clear, institutionalized vision and creativity. Increasing structure and control moves the organization into a stable position and establishes a rigid bureaucracy. While this process can be reversed, this is essentially a linear model of development and change. We characterize change as a dynamic cyclical process of renewal through all stages of development.

The process of continuing organizational change can be viewed from several perspectives. Those who study organizational evolution place substantial emphasis on "founding" characteristics and how they "imprint" the organization with a lasting context for thought and action (Singh 1990). Mintzberg (1989) takes a broader environmental perspective in describing the characteristics of organizational development. He suggests that the age of the industry as a whole may influence organizational structure and response to change, no matter how old the specific organization is.

Lippitt (1982) looks at the growth stages of an organization using a more cyclical model that integrates renewal and change through an organization's consistent efforts to seek uniqueness and adaptability, and develop and share organizational resources. Lippitt's overview of the growth stages of an organization helps in understanding how organizations change and develop, and the key issues and decisions at each developmental stage.

The first stage of growth, according to Lippitt, is the *creation* of a new organization. The key issues at this stage revolve around risk and the investment of money, resources, and time.

The second stage is *survival,* which often requires some tough choices related to profit, allocation of time, retention of key players, and products.

The third stage is *stabilization.* The focus is on how to organize and set formal job functions and procedures. The key decisions center around diversification, reassessing the mission, developing potential talent, creating marketing strategy, and making alliances and coalitions to strengthen long-term growth and results.

The fourth stage is building *a reputation and developing pride.* The basic concerns are establishing image, quality benchmarks, and a code of ethics. At this stage the key performance measurements are related to quality, productivity, customer service, human resource development, and economic factors.

The fifth stage is the *achievement of uniqueness and adaptability.* The basic issues focus on what to change and how to respond to diverse market segments as well as internal publics. Recognizing unique selling propositions and being creative in developing new products and refining existing products and services are essential to continuing success.

The sixth stage is to *contribute to society,* to the industry, or profession and to the community and nation. Decisions must be made as to how to share organizational resources and contribute to international, national, and local economic development. Organizations at this stage have a greater concern and involvement in community and social issues.

These six stages outlined by Lippitt show how the organization changes as part of responsiveness to a total environment. Many organizations find themselves cycling through these stages and constantly growing and trying to define their uniqueness within a larger social, economic, and political context. This is a part of the context of change management. Renewal only takes place if the organization confronts issues and concerns. If they are no longer responsive and relevant, organizations cease to exist.

Innovation and Change

In managing change, organizations must balance stability and innovation. In meeting customer and community needs. Drucker (1985) lists the contextual sources for change as they foster innovation and entrepreneurship: the unexpected; incongruity; innovation based on process need; changes in industry or market structure; demographics; changes in perception; and new knowledge. According to Drucker, the first four sources lie within the enterprise and the last three involve changes outside the organization or industry. However, as an organization moves toward becoming more flexible and permeable, any of these could be both internal and external sources of change. Sources of innovation and change come from many sources throughout the organizational system, both inside the formal organization and in the complex environment surrounding and interacting with the organization. For example, employee demographics such as more working mothers with small children or the increased diversity of employees, can encourage innovation in workplace practices, training, and personnel policies just as surely as shifts in consumer demographics change marketing plans.

According to Drucker, one major source of change is the *unexpected*. Even though organizations may try to direct all change efforts, there are many nondirected processes occurring both in the formal organization and in the surrounding environment. These may go unnoticed until they produce some unexpected results. Drucker describes incongruities as the difference between reality as it actually is and reality as it is assumed to be or as it "ought to be." An expressed *need for process innovation* in "how the job is done" is clearly a need for directed change. After the need is adequately understood, information can be gathered and an appropriate solution can be found that meets the needs of the job and the people who do that job. *Changes in industry and market structures* from the global market to minimarket segments and "consumer sovereignty" have transformed the way many organizations do business. This is a major opportunity for innovation.

Demographics present a significant source of change and innovation in any industry or organization. Diversity in the workforce and increasingly segmented markets demand continuous monitoring and demographic analysis to serve changing markets and capture new markets. Changes in demographics are generally objective measures, while *change in perception*, moods, or meaning are more subjective and difficult to measure in a precise way. These changes are related to both demographics and societal values and the symptoms might show up as an unexpected success or failure. While *new knowledge*, both scientific and nonscientific, might seem to be a major directed source of innovation and change, it is, according to Drucker, one of the most difficult to actually implement. Innovation and change based on new knowledge depend on timing and finding a "window of opportunity" and receptivity in the market.

With rapid development and the need for continuous change and innovation, some organizations may be experiencing "organization shock" (Harris 1983) as they find themselves in a new economic, technical, and social environment. In a complex, "informated" (Zuboff 1988) organization in the process of continuous change and reorganization, innovation and participation can be lost in the sheer volume of data that must be processed and in the increasing dependence on sophisticated computer systems. This context demands a more open, flexible, and creative way of thinking about organizational operations and options. Even Peters has modified his perspective on "excellent" organizations after the prescriptions of his earlier work (Peters and Waterman 1982). He begins *Thriving on Chaos* (Peters 1987) with the statement that there are no excellent companies. He explains that organizational change has not been rapid enough and that organizations must learn to thrive in a context of chaos and continuous change with responsiveness, innovation, and flexible leadership. The management of change becomes a major priority.

Global Change Perspectives

Whether we recognize a "borderless world" (Ohmae 1990) based on an interlocked economy or work within a more domestic framework, the change toward a global context cannot be ignored. The growth of technology has created global managers and technical resources who can work effectively "anywhere on the planet" with people of different nationalities and disciplines (Harris 1983). This has already been extended to collaborative efforts in science and technology.

Ohmae (1990) applies a global perspective to marketing and other operations with the "equidistant manager" who sees all key customers as the same distance from the corporate center. This perspective changes organizational worldviews and eliminates the idea of "overseas" operations or "foreign" markets. Today materials, production, and products are integrated across borders. For example, parts may be produced in one country, assembled in another, and sold in yet other countries.

In this time of rapid and continuous change, organizations cannot afford "learning disabilities" (Senge 1990) with mindsets that are unable to recognize strategic patterns or get out of negative routines. From a global perspective, organization members must be prepared to deal with the contradictions and the continuity of change processes within complex systems. The organization changes as individuals and groups learn and apply that knowledge to new situations. The organization also changes in response to the specific economic, political, and social environments of which it is a part. "Global localization" and other terms have been advanced to try to integrate local and global perspectives. This is a contradiction that can be resolved through the development of local nationals within multinational corporations and the creation of strategic alliances and agreements that support shared technology and research in a way that benefits everyone involved. Change management competencies are critical to achieving these goals. Global perspectives are covered in more detail in Chapter 14.

Organizational Obligations and Social Responsibility

Consumer power and issues coalitions have forced organizations to change and to recognize their obligations and social responsibilities within a broad context of concerns. Some individuals and interest groups are demanding increased responsiveness and equity toward employees, stakeholders, and the community.

There are change management issues related to organizational obligations and responsibility. Issues that may affect the organization can be identified by collecting and analyzing information from the various components of the system as well as from the relevant environment. By identifying issues that will impact the organization and determining the time frame and intensity of that impact, organizations can anticipate, plan, and manage change in a proactive way.

Issues management has several major goals: issues monitoring and prioritization; continuing analysis of the correspondence between public expectations of corporate behavior and the implementation of corporate codes of social responsibility; and internal and external communication efforts to discuss public policy issues (Heath and Nelson 1986). Issues and public expectations can create a powerful context for organizational change.

Some of the issues that determine the social and economic context of change are documented by Naisbitt and Aburdene (1990) as "megatrends" in their assessment of the new directions for the future: a booming global economy, a renaissance in the arts, emergence of free-market socialism, global lifestyles and cultural nationalism, privatization of the welfare state, rise of the Pacific Rim, women in leadership, age of biology, religious revival, and the "triumph of the individual." These show an increased awareness of an expansive environment that reaches around the world and points toward a more culturally responsive and critical approach to change processes. They also reflect the contradictions of a changing world.

Consultation skills in change management help the organization increase information exchange and feedback, confront sensitive areas, and reinforce commitments to employees, customers, and the community as part of a broad context of organizational renewal and collaborative learning.

CONSULTATION TECHNOLOGY

The second component of the change management model is consultation technology or competencies for change management that integrates specific
knowledge, experience, methodology, theories, and interventions related to the
process of consulting (see Figure 2.3).

Some of the best-known definitions of consultation reflect specific technologies for helping organizations deal with change. Lippitt and Lippitt (1986)
characterize consultation as two-way interaction in "a process of seeking,
giving, and receiving help" to mobilize resources to deal with problem
confrontations and change efforts. Schein (1987) focuses on process consultation and emphasizes the psychological aspects of the relationship between the
client and the change facilitator and the importance of helping the client to
perceive, understand, and act on "process events." Argyris (1970) emphasizes
data collection as well as helping the client decide how to use the data and
building commitment to this decision. All of these definitions include gathering and using data and building relationships through some systematic
process. They acknowledge elements of directed and nondirected change in
individual and group perceptions and actions as integral to success.

Consultation is the process of helping people within a formal or informal
organization to work together in managing change to more effectively meet
organizational needs while also developing individual and group resources.
Consultation technology can include a learning design, an intervention
approach, data-collection methods, planning technology, or transferring
competencies from change facilitator to the client system. Other strategies for
facilitating change might focus on work design, customer-satisfaction criteria,
human resource and career systems, or ethics and values.

The change facilitator and the client should discuss their values, strategies, concepts, and working theory prior to establishing work plans and agreements, including project phases and shared accountability. This is a cooperative approach to reach predicted outcomes by clarifying expectations, resource
requirements and allocation, roles, milestones, and the use of data and feedback.

Helping a client to develop focus and direction is especially critical in the
consultation process. Change management facilitates more effective and realistic analysis and planning by emphasizing data-based change, which employs
action research and empowers people by involving them in the overall change

process. Consultation skills help organizations to improve the processes of planning, problem solving, and decision making in managing change. The following process skills can be transferred to the client system through consultation that helps individuals and groups to:

- Perceive the present situation more accurately
- Gain a sense of reality
- Facilitate information exchange and feedback
- Provide an assessment of assumptions
- Define goals more clearly
- Analyze problems
- Express and test alternatives
- Confront sensitive areas
- Reinforce commitments
- Develop new commitments
- Link and expand resources

These process skills help develop individual, group, and organizational resources to reach current and strategic performance objectives by facilitating effective change management .

Approaches to Change Consultation

Many discussions of change consultation approaches are centered around the difference between *imposed expert authority* to implement management initiatives and *collaborative process facilitation*, which transfers competencies and responsibility to the people in the client system. Schein (1987) suggests three models of consultation: the purchase of information or expertise, the doctor-patient model, and the process consultation model. According to Shein, in the *purchase* model, the client has already determined the problem; in the *doctor-patient* model, an outside expert diagnoses the problem; and in the *process* model, organization members take responsibility for diagnosing and solving their own problems through process facilitation.

The distinction between the expert model and the process model is important in our definition of change consultation. The expert approach depends on a technical resource or professional who comes into a particular organizational unit, determines the problem, and offers a specific solution or diagnosis. This internal or external resource is often present for only a limited period of time in that unit, offering counsel and or specialized training. For example, an organization may hire a recognized expert in organizational design and reengineering. The effect of this intervention may be powerful and immediate, but after the expert resource person leaves and the excitement fades, the system must be able to solve their own problems. This is true of both external and internal resources. In one organization, for example, a department became so dependent on an internal resource facilitator from human resources that they finally hired her as a full-time member of their group. The expert should train the organization members in a department or unit to be interdependent information gatherers and problem solvers who can work through the process of planned change and facilitate their own decisions. Experts can be a valuable resource but they have some responsibility to attempt to transfer essential skills and knowledge to the client system.

The best developmental approach to consultation is the team approach, which relies on group and organizational learning in reaching specific organizational goals. The team may include an expert resource as well as internal and external facilitators who can involve key people throughout the system. Teamwork in gathering information, analysis, and action planning is the foundation for influencing and managing a continuous change process.

The team approach is important for both internal and external change facilitators in increasing the credibility of the consultation process and generating ownership of the change within the client system. Clear agreements on expectations, roles, and goals should be established before the consultation begins. Encouraging collaborative inquiry in cooperative data collection, open information sharing, and team analysis and action planning can help reduce conflict and increase commitment to change on both a directed and nondirected level.

Six Phases of Consultation

Consultation technology provides a proven method of managing and integrating change through six major phases: (1) need and opportunity in change initiatives, (2) agreements: establishing working relationships, (3) data collection and analysis, (4) feedback, decisions, and action planning, (5) application and results measurment, and (6) continuity and renewal (see Figure 2.5). These phases are introduced below and described in more detail in later chapters.

Phase 1: Need and Opportunity In Change Initiatives

The first phase establishes the initial contact and entry for clarifying the work areas, roles, and outcomes of the consultation. As leaders of organizations explore more effective ways to deal with need and opportunity in global challenges, in continuous improvement, quality, and competitive resourcing, new

FIGURE 2.5 Consultation Technology.

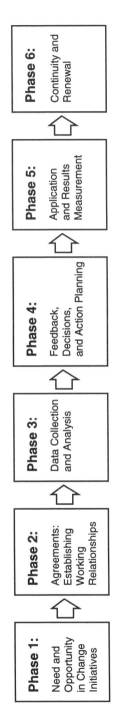

Phase 1:	Phase 2:	Phase 3:	Phase 4:	Phase 5:	Phase 6:
Need and Opportunity in Change Initiatives	Agreements: Establishing Working Relationships	Data Collection and Analysis	Feedback, Decisions, and Action Planning	Application and Results Measurement	Continuity and Renewal

An example of how the model might work in an organization

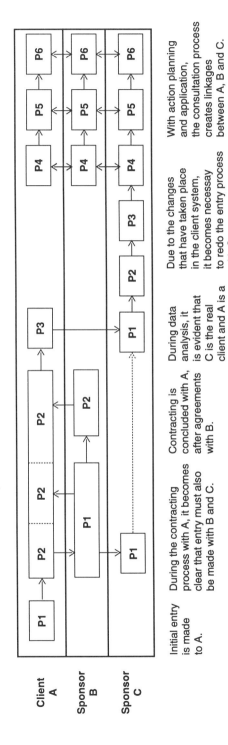

P1 = phase 1   P4 = phase 4
P2 = phase 2   P5 = phase 5
P3 = phase 3   P6 = phase 6

delivery systems are emerging within and outside the organization. These may include technical resource persons for self-directed work teams; application teams for working with line units; human resource, training, and education facilitators; social engineers who perform task analysis and work job redesign; career specialists who provide input for assessment, cross training, and career movement; and planning and measurement analysts. Some of these resource facilitators work in specific areas; others join together to manage a total system change.

A number of these resources may be brought in for a short interval from the outside such as preferred suppliers who are invited in to learn more about the organization and to provide specific competencies. Multi-disciplined and skill-based, these resource persons work in short-term fluid relationships performing action roles ranging from technical to process expertise. These services can include organization development, quality initiatives, system-wide facilitation of feedback data, executive-level interventions, and cross-continent facilitation of local training and education in the context of global markets. For example, based on a specific need or opportunity, a select team of inside and outside resources from various disciplines could be commissioned to work for a period of time with a line function or business unit to accomplish measureable results in quality and service improvement.

Consultation role definitions are part of this initiative phase. Other outcomes might focus on goal clarity; setting realistic expectations; establishing norms for openness and trust; finding out what current changes are going on in the organization; assessing overall readiness for change; exploring performance accountability; and anticipating the type of resources required to achieve the desired result. This phase should conclude in a concrete decision on whether the client and change facilitator will work together.

Several issues require attention during this phase. Sufficient time should be spent during the early part of this relationship to build trust and understanding. Often unclear goals, roles, and low trust levels are not openly discussed. There may also be a desire on the part of the change facilitator to please the client, who is the "customer," by promising too much too soon. Resource facilitators approaching the situation from their own vantage point instead of the client's perspective may find out later that they are pursing a different path than the client. They are starting at different places. The client and change facilitator may also agree on short-term solutions without a mutual investment in learning, experimentation and participation, and later find disappointment and limitations in achieving long-term results.

For effective startup of consultation, the change facilitator, client, and sponsors should have adequate time to inquire about the situation and to explore possible roles and outcomes. Once the client and change facilitator agree that they want to work together, they are ready to move to the contracting phase to establish mutual agreements.

Phase 2: Agreements for Establishing Working Relationships

Contract formulation provides the groundwork for how people will work together to achieve desired results. The focus of this phase is as much on the social and "psychological contract" (Levinson 1966) of the relationship as on some formal written agreement. This phase examines the five elements of contracting and getting agreement: need validation, roles, results, role relationship, and culture. As emphasized during the previous phase, there is either a termination of further interest on the part of one or both parties, or a movement toward some kind of agreement about the objectives, and conditions of an effective relationship for change management.

There are several ways to develop an agreement. This can be done on an informal, formal, or technical/legal agreement. On a personal level this may be informal. A formal level may include a letter of agreement or an action list from a meeting with agreed upon role responsibilities. A technical agreement is a legal document. The client and change facilitator can create a written contract so that expectations on goals, terms, and roles are spelled out for all parties concerned. Official contracts may be developed through the contracting department of the organization or formal letters of agreement can be sent by the change facilitator or the client. An informal letter, a telephone conversation, and other methods also are used to confirm the relationship. Key questions are discussed between client and the change facilitator to articulate desired outcomes; assess potential for change; define roles; share strategy and working theory; establish results measurement and accountability; define terms and investment; clarify role responsibilities; anticipate role competencies; and plan for application and continuity.

It is important to recognize the contracting phase of consultation as a continuous process throughout the relationship. Gaining understanding and agreement among all parties provides a balance for maintaining flexibility and accountability. Coordination and communication in progress reporting, for example, increases the quality of the feedback for planning new action. One can expect ongoing changes, and while things may appear static, there is considerable movement that occurs in the organization. Management priorities change. Careers and personnel change. Agreements must be adjusted for changing conditions. Commitment at the nondirected level should be linked to the strategic unity of directed organizational goals to integrate competitive resources across different units in managing change.

Training is critical to building a capacity for teaming and collaborative inquiry in change management. A potential pitfall during this contracting phase is the failure on the part of the change facilitator to make firm demands for appropriate training and education a part of involvement in change management. Another trap is to assume too easily that people who have been chosen to work together are ready and able to do so. A third pitfall would be not to involve key sponsors in setting performance criteria for measuring results.

Involving people increases acceptance of change at both task and social levels. As part of this phase, action roles for the consultation team include both process and technical competencies. For example, during data collection the change facilitator is both a technical specialist in advocating appropriate methods for data collection and a process specialist in determining how the data will flow back into the organization to gain ownership, interpretation, decisions, and actions.

Phase 3: Data Collection and Analysis

During the previous two phases, preliminary data was collected to diagnose and validate the need, to verify client system readiness for change, and to discuss perceived need. During this phase, more intensive diagnostic work is required.

The working theories that are influencing the collection and analysis of data should be known to provide a systematic approach to data collection. Effective consultation depends on clear validation of need and effective fact finding relative to change opportunities. Action Research Teaming (ART) is helpful in relating the data to the consultation phases. Increased client system involvement in collecting and analyzing data leads to greater ownership and commitment to change. Complex issues can be understood more creatively in a collaborative climate of data-based change.

Major methods of organizational data collection are observation, documentation, questionnaires, audits and surveys, instruments, and interviews. Specific data collecting and diagnosis activities might include interaction process analysis, benchmarking, human resource audit, Q methodology, delphi methods, focus groups, one-on-one and group interviews, facilitation of pilot programs, confrontation dialogue between units, and role negotiations among client, sponsor, and facilitator resources. Both formal and informal methods provide cross validation of the data and a more complete assessment for planning, implementing, and monitoring change.

Collecting and analyzing data for change management includes determining the macro and microunits of change and measurement, reviewing statement of need, validating the need, and choosing methods of responding to the need. The client system should be actively involved in all these phases of data collection and analysis.

Early decisions need to be made on confidentiality, design for feedback of the data, and how the data will be organized for the client system to understand and take action.

Phase 4: Feedback, Decisions, and Action Planning

Now that the data collection and analysis phases are completed, the feedback phase provides interpretation for action decisions. The consultation team presents the diagnostic findings; provides an opportunity for members to ask questions to gain interpretation of those areas viewed as most deserving of improvement; and helps people identify priorities, derive action alternatives, and plan first steps of action.

Feedback of collected results presents one set of data. Another set of data is generated through discussion and collaborative inquiry during the feedback session. The design for the feedback session should be based on climate setting, rationale, roles and expectations, and ways of responding to concerns. The facilitator maintains a nonjudgmental manner to encourage trust, participation, and ownership of the data. Feedback requires a high level of skill competence in process and content expertise. The facilitator should be perceptive to group dynamics and build trust with management and employees. The capacity to link both formal and informal communication networks is a key skill. Feedback of data-collection results requires a systems perspective to establish a context of relationships.

A number of action processes begin immediately. The facilitator may ask members to nominate candidates for temporary ad hoc committees or action teams. Action derivations include executive management conferences, team meetings, and retreat off-site sessions to review the findings. The consultation team continues to guide this process while shifting roles and supporting internal initiatives. People inside the unit know more about the kind of changes that need to be implemented, and are ideally the members who need to work on those changes.

Through the feedback sessions, employees' and managers' expectations become more focused. After this phase, the team enters the action planning and implementation phase. Collecting data about the organization is one thing; putting the information to effective use is another. This developmental process starts in the feedback phase, which legitimizes participation. It increases people's consciousness about what is possible and draws their attention to new agendas that prompt thinking, and facilitate conversations about things that haven't received much attention but are of great interest or concern. Feedback helps responsible change to happen.

Success factors for feedback and action planning include: involving the work force; dealing with ambivalence about change; establishing steps toward progress; supporting quality action; and maintaining the change momentum to achieve results. Each unit providing data is involved in the feedback and development of action recommendations.

Internal structural changes for feedback might focus on a temporary steering committee and action teams representing units throughout the organization. System-wide data generates distinct action that is more integrated than action based on small pieces of information. Systemic data provides clarity about what is happening, and a working knowledge to visualize or imagine what could be taking place given certain action. It is better to know about concerns and challenges to plan change rather than simply have it happen.

Multiple goals exist within the entire organization: short-term and long-term goals, goals coming from different people, goals from various levels and units of the organization, team goals, goals coming from past situations, and the change facilitator's own goals. Once identified, goals are selected and prioritized in terms of their value and importance. For each goal selected, the teams identify forces that restrain or hinder, and forces that support or help in achieving the goal desired. Alternative action plans are generated with feasibility testing. Checking the "what ifs?" is a vital part of the strategy analysis. Plans are also made to provide for ongoing feedback during the application phase. "The Image of Potentiality" goal-setting process provides a way to look at goals as they would exist at some future date.

Phase 5: Applications and Results Measurement

The objective of effective consultation is to have the clients successfully put their plans and intentions into action to achieve results. Getting new knowledge and insight is a good step, but unless insights and plans are converted into motivated and successful action, the efforts are of little value. Change facilitators are cautioned that once clients set new goals and expectations, they also require the support of sponsors and "champions" to achieve success in their risk-taking action. During this phase, it is important to focus on ways to help the client system internalize core competencies and to support skill development. Some ways to link goals, plans, and intentions to successful action are anticipatory practice, provisional trial run, defining accountability, eliciting feedback to guide and correct action, consequence assessment, and stepwise goal achievements with celebration. Role-playing with one or two colleagues can be useful to explore some of the preferred alternatives to check out consequences, and to add to the skill repertoire.

Conditions for taking effective action include role clarity, appropriate involvement, realistic analysis of the positive and negative forces operating in the system, balance of stability and change, coordination of who does what and when, use of appropriate measurements, trained personnel, and continuous review and reevaluation.

An important focus of this phase is the measurement of results. This requires determining and specifying how organization members will know when change is progressing toward the goal and if desired outcomes are being achieved. Issues concerning measurement are related to what progress indicators will be used; who is tracking these and at what frequency; and to whom the information is being provided. Measurement and feedback are vital for continuous improvement, and learning. Measurement validates individual and group work, helps to build confidence, and affirm their capability to risk innovation and integrate resources for managing change.

Often contradictions occur in the measurements and feedback received as well as in preferred strategies, priorities, goal unity, experience, and skill competencies. Anticipating differences in performance criteria and involving clients in measurement are important aspects of change management.

Phase 6: Continuity and Renewal

Inevitably, the process of consultation for a specific change effort has some termination point. Such termination may be an agreed upon date, completion of the goal, a withdrawal by either party, or a gradual diminishing of services. Whatever the circumstances, it is important to plan for contract completion to transfer competencies so that the client develops continuity and support for ongoing change management. This final phrase of the consultation process focuses on the goal of effective contract completion in the client system.

Key concerns are developing client system competence, creating support for the client, and establishing linkage systems and resources for change. This phase concentrates on goals for continued professional growth and the skills or competencies most essential to foster the change continuity.

Design for continuity and support ensures that the client system and facilitating sytem develop appropriate plans for diminishing services and for confronting continuity issues. A process of continuing renewal, dialogue, and collaborative inquiry gives continuity to the change by confronting old patterns and counter-reactions and dealing directly with the challenges related to continuous change.

COORDINATION

The third component in the change-management model is coordination. People within the organization must cooperate and work together with some shared understanding of roles, rules, procedures, and agreements on objectives and methods to accomplish results. Change happens through people. This includes executives, boards, managers, employees, suppliers, distributors, customers, and community members. Organizations are becoming more consultative and team-oriented. The coordination of various interrelated roles and responsibilities is essential to success in change management.

Coordinating Consultation Roles and Relationships

The key players in this process include the client system, the client, the sponsor evaluator, and the change facilitator. Consultation teams may be comprised of these people as well as other representative groups including managers, staff professionals, expert resources, and team leaders. The interests of customers, suppliers, industry groups, government agencies, and community leaders must also be coordinated to facilitate overall results in a context of continuing change.

Client System

The client system typically refers to the formal organization. This includes any person, business unit, or group directly involved or affected by the change-facilitation process. Schein (1987) identifies four categories of clients within this system: contact clients who approach the change facilitator or manager; intermediate clients who get involved in early meetings and planning; primary clients who own the problem; and ultimate clients who may or may not be involved but whose welfare and interests must be considered.

Client

This individual is the lead person with authority for decisions and the essential liaison with the client system which might include individual functions, committees, management, employees or customer groups. This person can make the Yes/No action decisions to facilitate desired outcomes. In most cases, the client contact should be an individual rather than a group. Within a group where several people are making decisions, one individual should be identified as the spokesperson or liaison for the group.

Clients may change depending on the timeframe and complexity of the effort as well as the continuity of personnel. There should be client-continuity planning because the client can leave the job or move to a new project or be transferred into other parts of the organization. This shift may involve a new client and require recontracting in terms of the change expectations. In some cases the initial client may become a sponsor, which helps to maintain some of the overall continuity.

Sponsor Evaluator

One of the most critical connections in the consultation process is the relationship between the client and the sponsor evaluator. This person can significantly influence the outcome of the change consultation and has a strong interest in the initiation, progress, and final outcome of the effort. In some instances the sponsor is the client's boss. Many times, particularly when working at the senior level of an organization, the sponsor is also the initial client. The role of the sponsor evaluator should be clearly understood.

There also might be more than one sponsor. The sponsors could be a group of people such as an advisory council, ad hoc committee, task force, or customer or supplier group. The CEO may be the sponsor for a senior management group whose members provide consultation to one another. An employee group could be a sponsor for a manager client who is initiating a change effort in a particular department. In this case the department becomes the sponsor. In another instance, key customers could be a sponsor group for a sales force working on a new product introduction in an international market.

However, these sponsors may not be known or involved at the initial stages of the change-consultation process. Often at the beginning of consultation, sponsors are hidden or unknown. They may become known at critical stages of the project and can create some problems if they are not kept informed and involved. The sponsor evaluator roles are essential to the success of the outcome and a key linkage in the political process.

Change Facilitator

A change facilitator can be a manager, staff professional, or technical resource person in any number of areas such as: planning, marketing, finance, information, human resources, communications, public relations, ethics, career and organization development, education and training, research and development, manufacturing, engineering, or legal services. People in any of these areas could be providing services and working with and through others using facilitation skills to achieve specific results within a change management process. Change facilitators can be either internal and external to the formal organization—or both. The following distinctions are useful in looking at these differences and how they complement each other in change management.

Intraunit Internal Change Facilitator: The intraunit internal change facilitator is an organization member of the client system being helped. This person is internal to the client system and the organization. For example, a manager can be a change facilitator to an employee-involvement group in her department. In another case, the council of a nonprofit organization that wants to look at its governance may request the services of an internal board member to facilitate planning and a review of the bylaws and constitution. However, the nature of the assignment could be highly political and the internal person might require some consultation assistance from outside the organization.

Some of the hurdles or concerns for the internal facilitator are perceived lack of objectivity, political pressures, and being part of the system that is being changed. Yet, internal resources have an advantage in their experience and knowledge of the system.

Interunit Internal Change Facilitator: An interunit internal change facilitator is a person from outside the receiving client system or business unit who is still a part of that organization. For example, a staff professional in organizational services provides consultation and facilitation to a manager in operations and his group on team building. A manager in one area might also serve as a change facilitator to another department or unit.

External Change Facilitator: The external facilitator is not organizationally, economically, or socially within the client system. This person has little or no organizational or political relationship with the client system. This is often someone with specific expertise or specialized skills that are not available within the organization. In larger systems the consultation relationship often involves internal and external customers and suppliers. This relationship might support consultative approaches to improving quality, total cycle management, or customer satisfaction.

An external change facilitator may also be useful when objectivity and creative new options and viewpoints are required. In many cases, an external resource can be more effective than an internal facilitator in diffusing conflict and bringing sensitive issues to the surface. This external facilitator might be a manager or resource from another organization, an expert professional, an academic specialist, an association executive, or a supplier.

Consultation Teams

Change facilitation roles involve specific individual contact persons within a team. Yet in complex systems we see more multidisciplined teams. This is complicated because of the need for accountability from the individual, the team, and the client system. Teaming is the highest level of consultation as members also serve in consultative roles to each other. Relationships, roles, and expectations among team members require contracting and establishing agreements as an essential part of the teaming process.

Teaming of Inside and Outside Change Facilitators: In some cases, internal and external teams work together with overall team accountability, and the internal and external change facilitators share responsibilities and coordinate their roles. As part of the client system, the internal change facilitator may be familiar with the politics, language, culture, structure, systems, style of management, human resource development needs and linkages among parts of the organization. The internal facilitator also knows what new technologies are anticipated, what changes are going on, who the internal champions are, and what informal resource networks are available for getting things accomplished. Yet, the internal resource person may already be overloaded with internal assignments and realize that temporary resource staffing from outside the organization is required to match a targeted delivery. The internal change facilitator can provide review follow-up, and reporting on progress check points for the client to insure continuity of results. Being an internal change facilitator does assume some element of risk, and may be perceived as being too close to the situation.

The external facilitator who is independent of the internal power structure provides objectivity, and can collect sensitive data especially at the senior levels when there is a conflict between department and business units. The external change facilitator is often helpful in initiating discussion for confronting and resolving concerns and issues.

Ideally, inside-outside teaming of two or more change facilitators or managers from various disciplines and functions will bring both technical and process skill competence in working to satisfy a "best resource staffing" need for specific projects. Assignments in which combined action teams are used might include work on instructional design for special projects; diagnostic expertise for needs validation; education and training events; quality measurement, benchmarking, organization mapping, total cycle management, and other technical projects; design and facilitation for data-based executive conferences; and administration of macrosurveys and audits with facilitation of feedback sessions for specific business units across the organization.

Client's Customer

The customer can be an individual or a internal or external group to the organization. They are usually an extension of the client system and users of the client's services or products. For example, a long-term customer or an experienced industry representative may provide valuable consultation to the organization. The client's customer also can be the ultimate evaluator or sponsor of the service in a sometimes hidden role. An internal customer may be the recipient of the client's service, such as training in total quality management. Another customer might be part of the work team that will receive feedback of the collected data from the client and the change facilitator.

Client's Suppliers

Suppliers might include a vendor, contractor, consultant, change facilitator, trainer, academic partner, or a sales or marketing account executive. Suppliers may be a permanent employee or a contractor to the extended organizational system.

Related External Roles

Other roles related to the change management process might focus on industry groups, competitors, other similar organizations, governmental agencies, and community leaders.

The complete set of coordinated roles indicates the multiple interdependent relationships in change management as well as the opportunities for team consultation throughout the total organizational system.

RESULTS

The final component or outcome of the change-management model is results. Results should be a central focus from the beginning because they establish a critical part of the context for change management. In a "get it done" culture, organization members may discuss change and plan, but to borrow a phrase from a pragmatic philosopher, the leaders in business systems are often most concerned with the "cash value of ideas" (James 1907). Managers and boards of directors want to know the meaning of change in terms of actual operations and economic advantage in a competitive market. Understanding and managing change in a complex and often fragmented world is a formidable task, which is often judged in terms of specific measurable outcomes and performance goals.

Changes that can be clearly defined and measured often have the greatest recognition and impact. Reduction in manufacturing costs, shorter product-development cycles, less inventory, and improved quality and reliability are more obvious markers than increased employee morale and commitment or greater responsiveness to multiple markets. Yet all results ultimately depend on improved coordination, communication, and shared responsibility for change management. Collaborative inquiry requires effective group interaction and problem solving. Results may also include an increased awareness of organizational practices and greater responsiveness, social responsibility, and self-determination for the organization and its members as part of a larger community.

Some results are extrinsic and objective based on a specific directed change and performance objectives that can be observed and quantified. For example, Aubrey and Felkins (1988) state that the extrinsic results of employee involvement can be measured in these specific areas: *quality* in reduced errors, defects, and complaints; *productivity* in reduced resource usage and costs; *service* in new, improved, or modified products and services; and *work environment* in changes to improve the quality of work life and safety. On a nondirected level results might also include increased understanding of organizational practices and policies, greater respect for colleagues and managers, reduced conflict, and improved collaboration in decision making. This performance is more difficult to measure.

Mink, Schultz, and Mink (1979) characterize results measurement in terms of unity, internal responsiveness, and external responsiveness in the development of individuals, groups, and the organizational system. *Unity* brings more stability and predictability to complex, changing systems by fostering shared values and goals and a clear unified vision that increases commitment and teamwork. *Internal responsiveness* is the organization's ability to effectively understand and develop individuals and groups within the organization through assessment, training, recognition, and empowerment with a sense of fairness and justice toward all employees. The results are more effective and competent employees possessing a greater commitment to the organization and to their jobs. *External responsiveness* deals with the ability of the organization to appropriately respond to problems and opportunities by gathering information from the relevant environment and utilizing that information to improve the organization and show social responsibility. The results are not only increased market share and profit, but also more cooperation, understanding, and goodwill from a variety of publics.

All results are influenced by perceptions and actions related to both directed and nondirected change. The integration of these two levels increases the benefits of change for individuals, groups, and the total system. All results should be tied to strategic organizational performance goals in a changing environment. Organizations cannot avoid change, so managers must learn change-consultation competencies to develop a healthy organization with a balance of stability and innovation in times of transition, growth, reorganization, and renewal. Some of the specific results of effective consultation for change management are:

- Sense of mission and direction at all levels
- Knowledge of the impact of cultural values, norms, and rules
- Actions based on core values
- Commitment to quality and service
- Teaming and partnering within and across units

- Recognition of employee knowledge and skill
- Respect for diversity and ambiguity
- Clear performance criteria and accountability
- Use of information to drive action
- Employees with commitment, energy, and enthusiasm
- Learning through experimentation, success, and failure
- Responsibility for individual and group actions
- Continuous feedback cycling to drive new action
- Total resource management
- Fluid organization structure and functions
- Confrontation of real problems
- Awareness of alternative views and applications
- Transfer of learning to new situations
- Responsiveness to a variety of publics

These results are based on the coordination of people throughout the system in integrating formal planned change with daily work practices and decisions.

MEETING THE CHALLENGES OF CHANGE

Our change management model is based on results, coordination, consultation technology, and context. Each of these areas encompasses some essential concepts and practices related to organizational change.

Change is a continuous, often contradictory process, which brings difficult challenges as well as opportunities. We have in some ways lost much of our wonder in relation to change and retained only the stress and anxiety it brings. The past century has brought so many amazing changes that we may tend to take change for granted as unpredictable and inevitable. Some organizations have accepted a more passive approach to change rather than attempting to confront issues and facilitate change in a positive and productive way.

Consultation skills can help managers and staff professionals to meet the challenges of continuous change and reduce the chaos and uncertainty it brings by fostering an understanding of the contradictions involved, facilitating the coordination of people and resources, and focusing efforts on the systematic, data-based management of change processes to reach organizational objectives.

This book challenges managers, leaders, and staff professionals to be more aware of change and to take a more active role in anticipating, planning, facilitating, and implementing organizational change through effective consultation skills and change management competencies. Managers, team leaders, and quality resources will be on the front line in facilitating change and creating the organization of the future. Competencies in managing change can help them to be more effective in moving the organization from the present toward the future.

3

Change Perspectives
and Pragmatics

Many metaphors and images have been used in attempts to understand and characterize the changing organization — from an impersonal machine to a living organism, from an information-processing brain to a psychic prison, from a sports arena to a battlefield, from an instrument of domination to a model citizen (Morgan 1986). These metaphors help in understanding organizational ideology, vision, and identity. Ultimately, the organization is created by people through their decisions, actions, and interpretations of reality. In order for change to occur, these interpretations must be shared and understood as a starting point for change management. Communication, dialogue, collaborative inquiry, and mutual influence should be prominent in any change management effort. Agreement on a working model or collective vision is critical to help coordinate and integrate directed and nondirected changes in the client system.

There may be conflicting approaches to change management based on different views of reality and alternative ways of thinking about change and the future of the organization. The guidelines for what constitutes an effective organization have shifted over time, from an orderly mechanistic view to a holistic, dynamic systems perspective, and a context of cultural interaction. An absolute objective reality and sense of controlled change have given way to a more flexible, creative, and interdependent sense of organizational change based on participation, dialogue, and teamwork to reach strategic objectives.

All organizational practices are built on some sort of working ideas or ways of thinking about change. These practices can also create and reinforce dominant ideologies and theories about how the organization works and what is "right" and "true."This conceptual base may be a formal theory, a collection of personal beliefs, or tried-and-true operating principles. These assumptions, generalizations, and perceptions establish a framework that provides structure, explains relationships between ideas and actions, and gives some measure of predictability or certainty about the world. Argyris and Schon (1974) refer to the ideas that directly affect our actions as "theories-in-use." These "mental models" (Senge 1990) may not always be accurate, but they are the foundation from which individuals and groups begin to make sense of the organization, create meaning, take action and decide what is important in a changing organization.

It is essential to spend some time thinking about how people think about organizational change. There are often conflicting "stories" and competing ideas and "truths" in interpretations of change. Thoughts and perceptions of organizational change are based on the ways in which we know about the world and collect information and the ways in which we process this information, make judgements, and decisions.

The concepts of C. G. Jung and analytical psychology provide a framework for understanding various perspectives toward change from different aspects of reality. Jung (1971) described four basic psychological functions: thinking, feeling, sensation, and intuition. These functions are discussed as two opposite and "mutually compensating" pairs: thinking and feeling, and sensation and intuition (See Figure 3.1). They are all part of a holistic perspective.

As Jung explains, we put order into our world through the way we perceive and judge our experience. His concepts have been applied to psycho-

FIGURE 3.1 Psychological Functions.

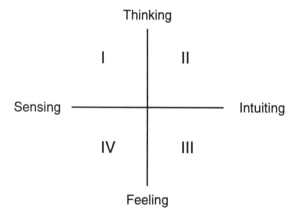

logical assessment, problem-solving approaches, management styles, decision making, and scientific inquiry (Mitroff and Kilmann 1978).

According to Jung, sensation and intuition come directly from our environment or our unconscious, rather than being derived from some judgment or analysis as thinking and feeling are. Sensation focuses on the conscious perception of external physical stimuli from all our senses. Intuition deals with unconscious perceptions that we are not always able to explain, such as hunches, "gut instincts," and creative concepts. Intuition may be subjective or objective depending on whether the stimuli are unconscious data from the self or subliminal perceptions of an object.

The sensation and intuition functions describe preferences for ways of knowing about the world and getting information and knowledge. For instance, one manager might depend primarily on experience in understanding change in work redesign and self-directed teams. This manager will visit plant sites, observe on the plant floor, talk directly to the people involved, and conduct extensive data collection and analysis. Other managers might also collect data but ultimately rely more on their intuition or insight based on past experiences and knowledge or a creative vision of the future. A number of organizational studies have shown the importance of intuition in managerial decision making (Rowan 1986; Agor 1984). Sensations and intuitions provide raw data from external and internal perceptions, which are processed through thinking and feeling.

The thinking and feeling functions involve processing, evaluating, and judging this information. Thinking brings scattered data and ideas into some conceptual connection. Directed thinking is based on rational laws and objectives such as those used in problem solving. Thinking may also be a more passive process when it is associated with intuition. Feeling imparts a value or judgment of acceptance or rejection, like or dislike. This is a subjective process that may be based on external stimuli or internal stimuli. Thoughts, as Bohm and Edwards (1991) explain, are often in the past tense, a "response to memory" that may not adapt to changing reality. Feeling types often create their own "rational" criteria for judgment and defend these with great certainty. According to Jung, thinking can at times be subordinated to feeling. For instance, supporting self-directed teams as a rational approach to improving customer satisfaction, and innovation may be clouded by some emotional perceptions of uncertainty and loss of control.

The thinking and feeling functions describe how we make judgments and evaluate data using logic or emotion. Often there is some preference in how we process data and make decisions, but these two functions are directly related. The "response to memory" may trigger an automatic thinking or emotional routine according to predetermined categories rather than a creative answer to new problems and challenges. Learning to be aware of our thought processes, to connect thought to current experience, and to differentiate and balance thinking and feeling functions is a part of the development process of individuals and groups in changing organizations.

Jung's ideas are useful in understanding perceptions and orientations to change because of his emphasis on maturation and development through finding and celebrating unity in opposites and contradictions, and realizing psychological equilibrium through mutually compensating functions. The organizational system, like the individuals who make up that organization, moves toward an integrated whole through shared awareness of these different perspectives and how they influence decisions and actions related to change.

This topology provides some basic understanding of how people in organizations might favor a particular function or perspective. Thus they interpret and deal with change from a specific mindset that determines the way they think and talk about change and often establishes expectations and boundaries in relation to change. An example of these different perspectives might be seen in a typical meeting. A group of managers are reviewing a report on operating performance and discussing specific changes to improve quality and productivity. While each thinks the others are coming from similar perspectives, they may in fact be looking at change from substantially different mindsets. Some focus more on problems; others on opportunities. Some want to work only with the numbers; others remind the group of the values and mission of the organization. A few are skeptical of any attempt to change. They also talk about facilitating and measuring change in different ways.

Each approach places some preconditions and limitations on the change process by imposing rules and expectations. Each perspective provides somewhat different answers to these basic questions about organizational change:

- How do we describe the change process?
- How much control do we have over the change process?
- How do we measure change processes?
- How are objective and subjective views of change related?
- What is the source of real knowledge about change?
- Is the primary focus of change on an individual, group, or organizational level?
- Whose interests does the change serve?
- What other interests are affected?
- What are the activities related to organizational change?
- What should be the results of organizational change?

Our change management model, described in chapter 2, groups these questions into four general categories as shown in Figure 3.2: Context, technology, coordination, and results. The context of different perspectives toward change establishes a foundation for all aspects of change management.

The answers to these key questions are determined in large part by particular approaches to change in the ideology, culture, and mission of the organization as well as in the perceptions and experience of individuals, and groups.

FIGURE 3.2 Change Management Model.

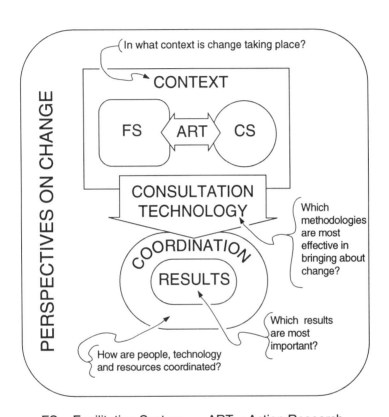

FS = Facilitating System   ART = Action Research
CS = Client System   Teaming

APPROACHES TO ORGANIZATIONAL CHANGE

Building on the work of Jung and the applications of Mitroff and others, we explore some dominant characteristics of each of four quadrants and apply them to specific perspectives or ways of thinking about organizational change (See Table 3.1). Each represents an "ideal type" and provides a particular structure for interpreting and managing change. All are interrelated.

TABLE 3.1 Perspectives on Change.

I. Rational/Behavioral

> Change is causal and predictable and can be rationally understood and controlled through: objective data; analysis of relationships between independent and dependent variables; and expert knowledge.

II. Systems

> Change is a holistic, homeostatic process that involves many interdependent components, cyclical patterns, and multiple conceptual relationships.

III. Cultural/Interpretive

> Change is socially constructed and interpreted through cultural practices, human interaction, and collaborative inquiry.

IV. Critical Humanism

> Change is action-oriented, dialectic, and based on economic and historical analysis; knowledge and awareness increase self-determination.

As shown in Figure 3.2, these quadrants are not rigidly divided, but instead fall into a continuum. The rational/behavioral approach to organizations, as represented by quadrant I, integrates experience and problem solving. The focus is on change as an external reality—a measurable, directed process with clear causal relationships that can be quantified and analyzed in a logical, objective way. The function most often is prediction, control, and improved efficiency within carefully defined limits and focus. Change comes through the manipulation of specific variables and conditions in order to achieve a verifiable effect or result. This change is most often focused on changing behavior or practice and reinforcing this change over time. The discussion of feelings is not encouraged, except when done in an objective manner as responses to a standardized instrument or in an experimental situation. There is a clear division between the researcher as a person versus the researcher as a professional.

FIGURE 3.3 Change Perspectives.

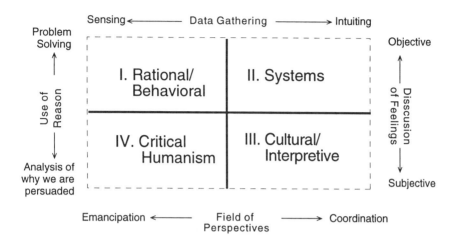

The systems approach in quadrant II combines thinking with the broader conceptual possibilities of intuition and abstraction. There is an emphasis on patterns, a gestalt of interdependent processes, and universal concepts, but with some ambiguity and speculation because of the complexity and extensiveness of the system. The natural function is in maintaining the system equilibrium and adjusting for disequilibrium in a way that balances opposites and contradictions and brings a slow evolutionary process. However, major change often requires complete transformation of the total system. Since there are many interconnected units, it is difficult or impossible to change one part without changing others to maintain the overall balance within the system. A high level of abstraction in this approach can make it both impersonal and objective, as well as exploratory and innovative, reflecting both scientific origins and intuitive imagination.

The cultural/interpretive approach in quadrant III represents a view of change as a product of social interaction and cultural values, norms, and thought. This approach recognizes the interpersonal and group interpretations of reality in collecting and analyzing information and making decisions. A cultural perspective is unique in its concern with the stories, myths, and everyday dramas that establish and maintain rules and practices as well as overall climate and cultural order. The meaning of change is created and established among people in an organizational system through their daily conversations and practices. Much of this is on the nondirected level. Change comes through a process of interaction and coordination as rules and norms are constantly being negotiated, created, and recreated by the people in an organizational context.

Quadrant IV, reflecting the critical humanism approach, is centered on experience and the judgments derived from feeling and analysis. This approach focuses on new ways of thinking that often question and challenge the everyday constructions of reality in the political, social, and cultural concepts of an organization. A critical perspective encourages individuals and groups to consider their thinking and the dominant ideologies that create their thought. Critical humanism is concerned with the effects of organizational structure and power on individuals and groups. Knowledge and understanding in this approach comes from individual experience and action. The goal is increased understanding and self-determination for individuals, groups, and organizations. In a critical approach, change comes through confrontation on issues that affect people, and the result is greater responsibility, awareness, and empowerment throughout the organization.

Quadrants I and II, rational/behavioral and general systems, are more objective approaches than quadrants III and IV, cultural/interpretive and critical humanism. All four approaches might recognize change as a continuous process, but I and II try to "bracket" and isolate change in a more specific time and space. Most directed change is influenced by these approaches. The rational/behavioral approach is most concerned with reducing contradictions and maintaining efficiency and unity in change management. A systems approach, in spite of contradictory elements, strives to maintain equilibrium and balance among all components.

The more subjective approaches in quadrants III and IV focus on people as learners, facilitators, and active participants in the change process. In these quadrants, many of the effects of an organization on people, and of people on an organization, are at the nondirected level. In the top quadrants (I and II) people are variables in a process, which may be more dependent on natural laws and scientific principles than the participants themselves. In the lower quadrants (III and IV) people are active agents of change, whether or not they recognize the consequences of their actions.

Members of the facilitating system, before entering or establishing a relationship with a client system, should evaluate their preconceptions, biases, and assumptions about change. They should explore and document what they think the client system will be like, what needs could exist, and what the future might look like. This analysis of individual subjective views can be invaluable in establishing a realistic foundation for change by starting where people are.

This analysis can be profitably repeated by the change consultation team at various points during the change management process.

The four-quadrant model can be used to assess individual, group and organizational concepts towards change. Such an assessment is essential. Otherwise the change facilitator and client can become captives of preexisting models of change that do not fit the client system's needs or changing contexts. The change facilitator sometimes accepts many of the client system's background assumptions about change and the resources available to produce change without questioning the working theories behind them. This model can be used as a tool to visualize the perspectives of managers, members of the consultation team, and key people in the client system.

In Figure 3.4, perspectives of the members in a hypothetical consultation relationship are plotted on the four quadrant model. Each dotted area shows the range of perspectives with which each person is comfortable. The client is a content expert and is most comfortable when discussing technical issues from a limited perspective. The sponsor has a broader perspective and sees more clearly that purely technical issues can have system-wide implications. Change facilitator A and the client share a common background in the client system, and are content experts. The change facilitator B is not a content expert. This facilitator will need to help members of the client system step back from their roles and look at both their feelings and the underlying reasons why they find certain approaches and options persuasive. Change facilitator A will have identification with the client but may also have questions. By reco-

FIGURE 3.4 An Example of Perspectives.

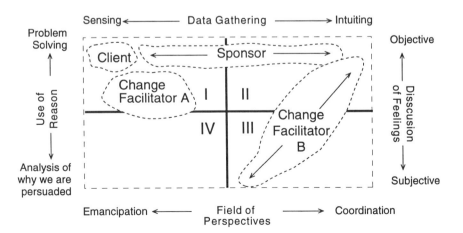

ognizing different and possibly conflicting approaches to change from the beginning of the consultation relationship, the team can broaden their understanding of the working theories and assumptions that affect change management.

The next four sections review in a more theoretical context some representative ideas for each of the four quadrants. When reading these sections, the reader should be aware, as illustrated by Figure 3.4, that most people actually span several quadrants. Practitioners who feel they have sufficient information about the model may want to move to the conclusions at the end of the chapter and use the following four sections as resource material.

Quadrant I – Rational/Behavioral Approaches to Change

The rational/behavioral approach is an attempt to understand and reduce complex change processes in the organization to explicit rules, procedures, and strategic actions to deal with all possible contingencies. With accurate formulas, prescriptions, and generalizations about human nature and action, proponents of this approach believe they can better control and manage the direction and impact of change according to the schedule and needs of their organization. This approach assumes that units of the organization can be isolated and analyzed in an objective manner based primarily on numbers and objective performance measurements such as productivity figures, control charts, attitude surveys, and ROI and market share.

From a behavioral perspective there is an operational definition of "supervisor," "manager," or "subordinate." Often in a clinical or experimental situation, "leader behavior" or "group behavior" is observed and all the relevant variables are identified, measured, and studied in relation to specific effects. The perspective is that of management and the goals are improving the effectiveness of management in developing people and thus improving the performance and productivity of the total organization.

Traditional rational and behavioral approaches to change might range from Fredrick Taylor's scientific management to computer-aided manufacturing and some aspects of total quality management. In each case, expert knowledge, training, and precise measurements are stressed. Often these methods attempt to refine complex processes to objective fundamental laws, rules, and processes for production and work design.

People are not always active, informed participants in this approach to change. For example, employees may be passive and uninvolved as management attempts to improve productivity with a particular leadership style or work redesign or technology. While this approach may have some immediate positive effects, the overall result may not be sustained if people are not involved in the change process in a meaningful way.

Change from a rational or behavioral perspective is often defined by the bounds of bureaucracy and hierarchical structures in organizational relationships and actions. Bureaucracy as a "rational" structure is defined by Weber (1947) as an organization with an emphasis on rules, hierarchy, specialized functions, and professional and impersonal management. The goal of most bureaucracy is to reduce ambiguity and overall inefficiency by making every action conform to some rule or rational structure through standardization and control of all processes and decisions. Accepting this seemingly closed bureaucratic model as the standard of efficiency can bring some resistance to change. Substantial change can be seen as a threat to this highly structured, secure order.

Taylor (1911) applied a bureaucratic model of order and efficiency to individual work practices and fundamentally changed the way we look at work. He was among the first to advocate something akin to "doing more with less." Time-and-motion studies, including precise observation and measurement of how individual workers did their job, led to new practices and behaviors based on extensive training, careful monitoring, and pay for performance. Taylor's influence is seen in many areas of organization, from industrial engineering and ergonomics to work simplification and quality control. Taylor realized, even in his obsession with measurement, that the organization must effectively manage both people and resources to accomplish organizational goals.

As an executive, Barnard (1938) tried to integrate the rational elements of organizational purpose and change with the human aspects of organization. In *The Functions of the Executive*, he first defines the elements of organization as communication, willingness to serve, and common purpose. In this classic management book, Barnard supports a rational, purposive organization but includes an emphasis on the variables of leadership, cooperation, and a network of mutual goals. As he explains, in order to influence change and development, the organization must be efficient in reaching specific goals and effective in motivating individual members.

However, many later behavioral approaches show an increasing emphasis on trust, openness, and participation in the change process. Maslow's (1954) model of a "self-actualized" human being focuses on a responsible, self-disciplined individual—not a "pawn" controlled by others. Many significant human resource innovations—from employee assessment and career development to quality circles and employee involvement—have grown directly from behavioral roots.

McGregor (1960) was concerned with "temporary and superficial methods" of attempting to change and improve human resources. He focused on management techniques as more effective ways to predict and control employee behavior and improve motivation and performance. His concern was in tapping the potential of human resources using social science techniques and knowledge to change the organization. McGregor summarizes much of accumulated management perspectives in two theoretical positions: Theory X, based on managerial direction and control, and Theory Y, focused on the integration of individual and organizational goals and employee responsibility. Each of these perspectives is determined by the manager's perceptions and ways of thinking about the employees.

These ways of thinking can encourage change and development or reinforce a routine and often disruptive pattern at the level of nondirected change. According to McGregor, with a *Theory X* perspective, the manager assumes that the average person is lazy and does not want to work. Therefore employees must be controlled and threatened. Thinking from this perspective, the manager also concludes that these workers prefer security and control to the risk and effort involved in taking responsibility. These beliefs and thoughts create conflict, a lack of trust and communication, and low employee motivation. Change in this model is imposed and often punitive.

A manager with a *Theory Y* attitude toward employees thinks in a different way and creates a positive environment for change and individual development. McGregor describes this manager as one who believes that work is as natural as play and that people will take responsibility and exercise self-direction if they are committed to the task and objectives and see an appropriate reward. This perspective nurtures the imagination, ingenuity and creativity in the workforce and builds on a positive change orientation that encourages learning and individual and group development.

However, McGregor's Theory Y assumes that the organization can create "conditions" to integrate individual and organizational goals by managing in a way that allows the individual to be responsible and creative. This behavioral approach to change places employees in a fairly passive position, although it does establish the potential for more creative contributions from individuals and groups in relation to change.

Likert (1967) also explores "science-based management" to improve the development of human resources and increase coordination and manage change in a highly functionalized organization. He integrates trust, cooperation, and communication into his approach, but leadership and management style are related most directly to quantitative performance characteristics in four distinct management approaches ranging from an exploitative authoritative model to an ideal participative group model emphasizing supportive relationships, participative decision making, and high-performance goals.

Likert attempts to show different ways of thinking and organizing from a rigid bureaucracy to a more humanistic, participative approach in four distinct systems: exploitative authoritative, benevolent authoritative, consultative, and participative group. Each of these presents a different motivational and behavioral context for change management.

In an *exploitative authoritative* model, managers have no confidence and trust in employees. They seldom ask for or get ideas and opinions from subordinates. All communication is downward and decisions are made by top executives. Threats and punishments are often used and rewards are seldom given. There is no sense of teamwork or loyalty to the organization. It is difficult to change this organization because of the fear, mistrust, and lack of open communication.

A *benevolent authoritative* system uses condescending trust and manipulations. There is some exchange of ideas and opinions but the communication is mostly downward. Policy decisions are made at the top of the organization and there is a prescribed framework for decisions at the lower level. Some rewards are given but employees may still be exploited. Change is imposed from the top of the organization with limited success.

A *consultative* system shows increased trust in employees as senior managers often actively seek ideas and opinions from employees and make constructive use of this information. There are rewards for involvement but employees are given limited authority in their own departments and units. There is upward and downward communication and moderate teamwork throughout the organization. However, broad policy decisions are still made at the top and some specific decisions are made at lower levels. There is within this system the framework for some effective directed change but nondirected elements are not always integrated.

In a *participative group* system, management shows complete confidence and trust in employees by involving them in collecting and analyzing information and making decisions. There are also economic rewards for group participation and involvement. Communication and feedback moves easily throughout the organization and there is substantial teamwork. Decision making is integrated through linkages and overlapping groups in all areas of the organization. This type of organization has greater competency to integrate directed and nondirected change.

Likert retains a rational definition of change in relation to internally consistent systems, but looks toward a broader systems view of change through transformation. "When change is desired, it should be a shift from one coordinated system to another." This means modifying all variables including leadership, decision making, communication, supervision, motivation, and compensation to form a consistent and predictable system. Communication and trust are stressed as well as appropriate recognition and involvement. Still, the overall perspective toward change is a behavioral one based on a clear cause-and-effect relationship within relatively closed systems.

Blake and Mouton were also working on the integration of task and people in change to develop a more productive and profitable organization. Their work centers on a behavioral science framework for increasing effectiveness known as the managerial grid (Blake and Mouton 1978). The horizontal axis shows "Concern for Production" and the vertical axis illustrates "Concern for People" concentrated on three "universal" factors in organizational development and change: purpose, people, and power. *Purpose* can be translated into production, bottom-line-results, and profits. *People* combines efforts of subordinates and colleagues as necessary to achieving purpose. *Power* involves directing the activities of others and using the hierarchy to achieve results through people. Training in skills such as teambuilding and conflict resolution is used to facilitate the process and move the organization toward an ideal balance in an organization with high concern for both people and production.

In most of the rational and behavioral models of change and development, consistency, conformity and order are emphasized more than innovation and creativity. There is a strong focus on efficiency and effectiveness in the internal organization, precise measurement of results, and coordinated stability and growth over time. Most often improvements and changes are maintained through training, control, measurement, and individual rewards.

In many cases, traditional approaches to change focus on variables outside the person, such as management style, working conditions, equipment, communication channels, or productivity levels. The assumption is often that change is neater and more controllable than it might be. If managers are more effective, then the organization will be more productive. All that is needed for change is to determine the right training program, technology, or the appropriate incentives for each situation. While this approach has been successful, its success is limited in some cases. Part of the challenge is in applying rational and behavioral principles to knowledge and service work where performance involves more than productivity.

Change from a rational/behavioral perspective often follows a familiar pattern using directed change to solve specific focused problems: managers decide change is needed, analyze available data to plan for the change, use expert advice as necessary, and decide on the direction and focus of the change. Staff professionals or outside resources train employees in required new skills, procedures, or attitudes; managers monitor activities and reinforce and reward appropriate behavior and results. Sometimes the aspects of change as a continuous, contradictory, people-oriented, cooperative effort are not as evident in traditional approaches. Change is more complicated than the formulas and prescriptions of a rational/behavioral approach might acknowledge.

Quadrant II – General Systems Approaches to Change

A general systems approach is a way of conceptualizing and thinking about change from a broad holistic perspective that attempts to integrate and align complex activities. Senge's (1990) analysis of the "learning organization" applies a systems perspective to management and organizational change and development. Like McGregor, Senge tries to show how managerial assumptions and mental models affect perceptions and organizational practices, but in a much broader systems context. He suggests that change comes from a "shift of mind" that recognizes interdependent connections within a complex, interrelated system. In this context, individuals, groups, and organizations learn to accept some responsibility for problems that they have helped to create. For example, individuals and groups begin to see how their practices might contribute to poor-quality products, and organizations recognize their responsibility for crises related to environmental pollution.

According to a systems approach, change processes within the organization are both complicated and simple. The key is seeing the overall relationships, taking a long-term view, and asking the right questions. What is the functional structure that integrates and maintains a complex organization? What are the dynamic relationships among different components? What are the feedback cycles and action patterns that regulate the system? How can all parts of the system communicate effectively with one another?

The semantics movement in philosophy and linguistics concentrated on language as reflecting the continuous and contradictory nature of systems change. Physicist Alfred Korzybski (1958) founded general semantics as the study of language and meaning from a systems perspective based on understanding meaning as a product of changing time and state, as well as complex levels of abstraction in language and thought. The familiar statements of the semanticists remind us of simple truths: "The word is not the thing" and "The map is not the territory." This is a challenge to rational objective approaches that try to precisely describe, measure, and control organizational change. The general semanticists suggest adding a mental "etcetera" to the end of statements to remind ourselves that we cannot say or know everything about anything, and that certainty is a rare commodity in a continuously changing system. The systems model is never complete, or stable; it is always becoming, creating new configurations among familiar interrelated components.

Natural scientists were among the first to articulate a formal systems perspective. Biologist Ludwig Bertalanffy (1968) defines "a general science of wholeness," an interdisciplinary theory that identifies universal principles and ordered interactions among components in seemingly different types of systems. At the same time, developments in other areas of science such as physics and engineering were also recognizing these shared principles of operation that included: a hierarchy of subsystems, interrelated components, homeostatic balance and equilibrium maintained by feedback and self regulation, and survival through adaptation and change in relation to the environment.

Systems principles of change must be understood and visualized through both logic and intuition. Complex systems concepts can be expressed in mathematical models and schemata or interpreted through elaborate social systems and networks of individuals and groups. However, as a dynamic, open system, the organization never really reaches true equilibrium as it is constantly changing and adjusting to new information and circumstances.

The social systems related to individuals, groups, and organizations are explored in the work of Kurt Lewin (1951) who moved psychology and social science into a systems perspective with "field theory," which stated that behavior is the function of a person in relation to his or her environment. Lewin described dynamic constructs based on "coexisting" facts and entities that were mutually interdependent, and introduced the concept of the "life space" to characterize this subjective psychological field.

Lewin associated change with learning and development. His concept of change based on field theory involves three distinct steps: 1) "unfreezing" of old habits and configurations in the life space; 2) movement to a new level or position; and 3) "freezing" or integrating this change into a stable pattern of behavior. This process also involves driving and restraining forces in a "force field" that reflect the dynamics of supporting and opposing elements related to organizational change. Reducing the weakest restraining forces and strengthening the strongest supporting forces offer alternative paths to a desired result. The force field is a useful tool in conceptualizing and understanding the diverse attitudes and practices that can impact directed and nondirected organizational change processes.

The dynamic forces of change within a system are moderated and adjusted through feedback. Consistent monitoring of results throughout the system and the application of that information supports the planning and facilitation of change. Feedback is a continuing process of mutual influence and coordination in a network of interrelated functional units. Senge (1990) discusses the cyclical application of supporting and opposing forces in reinforcing and balancing loops, which he terms "slowing action" and "growing action" in change processes.

In naturalistic systems, the principle of selection determines that systems that are unbalanced, do not use feedback effectively, or no longer fulfill their function cease to exist. Other more efficient systems replace them. In business systems, managers implement specific goals and objectives based on an overall mission, but ultimately each organization exists because it fulfills a necessary and useful function in society. It is a balanced functioning component of a larger community system.

Parsons (1960) identifies four functions of organizations within the larger social system: *economic production* involving goods and services; *political* functions related to the generation and allocation of power; *integration* in the adjustment of conflicts and direction of motivation toward institutional expectations and efficiency; and *pattern maintenance* in cultural, educational, and expressive forms. This functional systems perspective also identifies three levels in the hierarchical structure of the organization: the *technical system* responsible for production using physical, cultural, or human "materials"; the *managerial system* that controls and services the technical system by making decisions, administering resources, and mediating between the technical system and the community; and the community or *institutional system* that influences the managerial system through laws and regulations, public opinion, and public interest. Parson suggests specific "linkage points" for exchange of information and resources among these interrelated systems. These linkage points can provide the impetus for change and mutual development. Such linkage is evident in a statement by the CEO of a small, rapidly growing food-service organization: "As our company prospers, so should our employees and the community."

From a systems perspective, change can come in small shifts to maintain balance, or one tremendous upheaval or transformation that establishes an entirely new balance. The economic marketplace eventually eliminates the weaker, inefficient business organizations and forces others to make significant shifts and innovations. However, social service, political, and educational institutions may find themselves in a typical systems dilemma: effective systems change often requires a fundamental shift or transformation of all parts of the system. Some political systems, for example, spend the majority of their time in maintaining stability and control within the system rather than looking at innovation and change. Small changes in this bureaucratic network are often lost and quickly realigned to conform to the status quo.

The systems perspective reminds us that the organization is an interconnected network, which is maintained by cooperation and integration in managing people, technology, and processes within a dynamic whole undergoing continuous change. Yet within this apparently open system, the answers are not always clear. There are few direct, simple cause-and-effect relationships in the intricate and interdependent network of a large system.

Trying to change a system also brings out some of the inequalities and contradictions that might exist in the overall balance. For example, a duality of function is built into the bureaucratic structure of all organizations. Koestler (1967) defines this dichotomy in a systems hierarchy as the "Janus Effect," in which subwholes simultaneously have both the autonomous properties of the wholes and the dependent properties of the parts. Managers and staff professionals often deal with the Janus Effect in the contradictions of their roles, when, like the Roman god Janus, they have two faces—one independent face peering down to control the subordinate level and another, dependent face looking up at the higher levels as a subordinate. With empowerment, this contradictory contradictory dual function is extended to employees and team members.

While Janusian thinking brings some dilemmas, it is also a source of creativity. The axiom, "Think globally and act locally," allows us to consider opposite and contradictory concepts at the same time and determine that each is equally operative. As Rothenburg (1979) explains, this type of thinking has played a significant role in every major creative change and development in science and art. The principle of equifinality in an open system recognizes different ways of reaching the same results as well as different results from the same initial input.

The systems perspective of change is attractive in many ways because it combines some rational scientific perspectives with other more intuitive aspects that go beyond our direct experience. We cannot see all the interconnections or the outer realms of a complex system, but we can work with models and imagination to understand the impact of this functional structure. Systems approaches recognize new linkages, relationships, and options, but always within certain boundaries and structures that are not everywhere distinct. A general systems perspective gives us great flexibility in visualizing organizational relationships and operations through creative and complex mental models. These allow us to step back and take a more objective look at the big picture.

Mintzberg (1989) helps us to visualize the macrosystem with "configurations" that show us how the organization interrelates or synthesizes various attributes. He describes the basic components of the organization: the *operating core* that performs the work of producing a product or delivering a service;

the *strategic apex*, made up of one or more managers who oversee the whole system; the *middle line*, or the hierarchy of authority between the two sectors; the *technostructure* of analysts who form the organization as they plan and formally control the work of others outside the hierarchy of line authorities; the *support staff* that provides internal services including personnel, legal, and public relations functions; and the *ideology,* or culture, of the organization built on its own unique traditions, beliefs, and values.

Mintzberg suggests that the most effective organizational change does not come by adapting slowly over a period of time, but rather by taking "quantum leaps from one integrated configuration to another" in brief periods of "strategic revolution". The division of tasks and the coordination among various tasks produces specific configurations and changes. For example, if the key focus of the organization is the analysts in the technostructure, the configuration may be what Mintzberg calls the "machine" organization, with a standardization of work processes. Organizing around the operating core produces a "professional" configuration, with the standardization of skills. A "missionary" focus is produced by emphasizing ideology and the standardization of norms. Each configuration brings about a different balance and order within an integrated system.

Mintzberg uses a systems model to show the coalitions of "influencers" inside and outside the formal organization—the invisible power networks in and around the organization that affect change. The outside "influencers" such as owners, unions, suppliers, clients, competitors, government, and special-interest groups, may try to affect decisions and actions taken inside the organization. This external coalition may be passive, dominated by one strong group, or divided by contradictory demands. The internal coalition made up of the operating core, strategic apex, middle line, technostructure, and support staff is often unified by a shared ideology. Still, they may be competing in the distribution of internal power and limited organizational resources. Change is thus much more complicated from a systems perspective.

Ashby's (1956) cybernetic approach describes the shifts, jumps, and disconnections that may be present in systems change from "state to state" or from "transformation to transformation." Some changes might be characterized as a change in function or behavior; others bring a change in "the way of behaving." Watzlawick and his colleagues (1974) define these two types of change as first-order and second-order change. The first type of change occurs within a system, but the system itself is not significantly changed. The second type changes the system, creating "change of change." Second-order processes involve the change of rules, structures, and relationships that affect the total system rather than one person, group, or action. This may bring about a complete transformation of the system.

For example, teaching change management skills to a task force may improve a particular project, but it probably will not change the system or organization in which that team operates. Indeed, if there isn't broad system support for this process, it may be short-lived. A total quality management program integrates quality as part of process management and continuous improvement with shared objectives and measurement tools which involve people as active participants focused on customer requirements. This requires second-order change with a fundamental shift in the way the organization thinks about quality, service and teamwork as well as the change process itself.

Systems theory is a general view of the world and, at the same time, is a highly complex view because of the seemingly infinite number of interconnected and interdependent components and dichotomous relationships. The challenge is in "dynamic complexity" and the constant play of the components rather than "detail complexity" of precise measurement (Senge 1990). Systems research may provide some insight or understanding of networks and interrelationships, but overall systems views are not always useful in providing specific, detailed predictions and prescriptions for change. Yet they do establish a general framework for thinking about the synergy, equifinality, and the dynamic "connectedness" of change within the organization. A systems perspective increases our understanding of the balance of contradictions and opposite forces as a key element in change management.

Quadrant III – Cultural/Interpretive Approaches to Change

Both rational/behavioral and systems approaches assume a somewhat objective approach to reality, preferring to observe, measure, and intuit from a greater distance. They count communication as a way to "describe" reality. Cultural and interpretive approaches depart from this view by stating that through communication and interaction, reality is "created" in the subjective perceptions, experiences, thoughts, and actions of individuals and groups. There are no absolute laws, there are only the agreements and shared understandings in conversations and actions that support cultural norms and group objectives. Much of the change on this level occurs in the nondirected realm of social processes, language, and symbolic meanings.

From a cultural/interpretive perspective, reality is constructed and maintained by people talking together, telling stories, gathering and processing information, making decisions, and solving everyday organization problems. Interpretation is the process by which organization members make sense of the world and give meaning to change. Often people lack awareness of this created, taken-for-granted reality and its effect on their work and organizational relationships. This reality has been termed "commonsense knowledge" and "recipe knowledge" (Berger & Luckmann, 1966) because it allows individuals and groups to be competent in routine performances and also facilitates social interactions. Organization members often do not notice these automatic responses until they have a problem that cannot be answered or does not fit the mold, and then they must reconsider their knowledge and the value of the "rule" they have created and maintained. In some ways, the familiar statement from Walter Kelly's Pogo cartoon character seems to illustrate the dilemmas of this approach: "We have met the enemy, and they are us."

Cultural norms and ideology can exert hidden power and control. Organizational members may be logical and even mechanical in their thoughts and actions, but they can also be irrational, emotional, imaginative, and intuitive. There are unconscious factors at work. We can observe behavior, but not always that which is unspoken—the thought that is not put into action or the action that masks the thought. Ryle (1949) used the phrase "the ghost in the machine" to describe the objective and subjective aspects of mind and matter. The ghost of unconscious influences and feelings in the "rational" mind bring some contradiction and ambiguity to the most carefully planned change efforts.

The Hawthorne studies (Mayo 1933; Roethlisberger & Dickson 1939) were among the first to document a hidden social reality in organizations. Subjective elements of context and group norms haunted these scientific experiments designed to determine the most productive and efficient working conditions. The behavior of a group of employees could be carefully documented as their productivity increased, but the real meaning was not in the external conditions. Rather, it was in the group interaction and in the creation and interpretation of the situation by employees, managers, and researchers.

Information theory and systems perspectives have influenced some interpretive approaches. Communication within the organization often centers on information and objective data, but reality unfolds in the interpretive ways in which that data is processed and applied to organizational problems and contexts. Theorists such as Weick (1979) have linked these approaches and transformed the way in which we look at organizations and "organizing" by focusing on interactive processes such as communication, information processing, and decision making. Organizations, according to Weick, are not monolithic formal structures but "loosely coupled units" with small interlocked segments based on behavior, relationships, and processes.

Weick suggests that activities such as information gathering, decision making, and negotiating are continually creating the organization, making sense of its complexity and uncertainty, reinforcing organizational values, and facilitating or blocking change. The organization is always changing and continually needs "reaccomplishment." According to Weick, organizational change and stability are influenced by an interlocking set of behaviors and positive and negative feedback cycles in a sequence of three activities: enactment, selection, and retention.

Enactment occurs when organization members notice certain aspects of their environment and pay attention, thus creating by their awareness a specific environment or reality. From this attention they identify problems, opportunities, and circumstances that require some action or change. They also note the effects of change. Those objects or activities that organization members do not notice, in some sense, do not exist for them. Thus some problems are not solved and some difficult situations are not changed because no one pays attention to them and they haven't been "enacted" or validated as being real and important. This focus of attention may also be affected by ways of gathering information and knowing about the organization through the senses and or intuition. People "enact" change in different ways. Enactment can be an attitude and a state of mind that brings nondirected change to a higher level of awareness and integrates it with directed change.

The next step in Weick's model is *selection,* or the process of gathering and analyzing information, reducing the equivocality or ambiguity and complexity of the data, considering various options and rules, and deciding what to do. This is best accomplished as a group process, which increases resources, information, and skills directed toward solving the problem. This may also be influenced by dominant ways of processing data and making judgments through thinking or feeling.

Weick emphasizes the importance of past experiences and organizational rules and policies in the selection process. If the situation or problem is simple and straightforward, there may be rules and procedures that will answer all questions and save time and resources. Certainly bureaucracies try to have the rule or policy to fit every situation. Yet if the situation is complicated and information is ambiguous, these standardized responses don't work. This is when the group must use all of their resources to consider new answers and options. Organization members might change the rules to meet new circumstances, develop new solutions, or make new rules using past actions and experiences as a guide.

In the third stage, *retention,* the choices for action, the solutions, and new rules are stored in the collective knowledge of the organization to be used again. This storehouse may be filled with many rules, procedures, symbols, stories, lessons, and past solutions comprising the total organizational history. Since change is a continuous process and yesterday's rules may no longer apply, this storehouse needs to be cleaned up and reorganized on a regular basis as part of change management.

Retention is a hidden opportunity for managing and integrating nondirected organizational change. The decisions here can determine the overall fate of the organization in the rules, policies, and procedures that establish the day-to-day activities of the organization and often limit opportunities and choices for innovation and development. According to Weick's model, the least obvious areas of organizational activity—daily operating rules and routines—are often the most important in influencing change. This realization may help managers and staff professionals to ask some essential questions about organizational change and the way in which the organization processes and uses information.

Structuration is another way of looking at the process of producing and reproducing systems by creating new rules and reinforcing old ones. Introduced by sociologist Anthony Giddens and his colleagues, structuration focuses on rules, norms, roles, and communication networks that are created by individuals and groups and that affect their future actions in the interpretation of events, appropriate conduct, and power relationships. The duality of structuration is that "institutionalized routines" create and reproduce the ideology and structures of the organization and also provide in each reconstitution or repetition the opportunity for change. According to Giddens (1984), these structures are both the medium and the outcome. Contradictory structures may create dysfunction and conflict. This can be seen in a rapidly growing organization or in a merger where two distinctly different cultures are forced into a combined operating process or in conflicting subcultures or countercultures within a complex system.

Specific interpersonal applications are made in the "coordinated management of meaning" developed by Pearce and Cronen (1980). Rules organize hierarchies of meaning from literal to abstract and guide sequential actions and reciprocal patterns of behavior. The structure is dependent on the people in that situation and their individual interpretations of behavior in relation to mutually agreed upon rules for their interaction. Norms and rules can be changed through an informal process of negotiation and mutual interpretation that occurs in social interaction. An understanding of this model is useful in changing interpersonal relationships and reducing conflict related to directed and nondirected change. Modifying the language, changing conversations, and checking interpretations of organizational interaction and practice are essential in coordinating a larger organizational change process.

The key concept in many interpretive approaches is that organization members "construct" their reality in their conversations and interactions. As

Blumer (1969) explains, "It is the social process in group life that creates and upholds the rules, not the rules that create and uphold group life." Perhaps the greatest contradictions come when the dynamic processes of organizing and constructing are forced into a static model where the rules are institutionalized and become the unquestioned and unexamined "laws" of operation and cultural norms. Activities and relationships that were once flexible, responsive, and creative become mechanical and routinized with rigid scripts and roles in an ongoing organizational drama.

One dramatistic approach parodies the rigid bureaucracy and describes the organization as a "theatrocracy" (Lyman and Scott 1975) where meaning and structure are determined by the roles, language, and interaction of players in an organizational drama with plots and subplots and characters from heroes to villains, and strategic cameo roles. There are writers, producers, directors, and stage managers for the organizational drama. From the CEO to the receptionist, everyone plays a part, frontstage or backstage. Shakespeare described the world as a stage filled with players. Some cultural studies define "mankind as performer" (Turner 1986). In ways that are both creative and purposive, organization members invent and maintain their unique culture, motivated at some level by their engagement in an ongoing social drama.

Goffman (1974) also uses theatrical metaphors to describe "social actors" and "self-presentation" in everyday organizational scenes. His dramatistic approach identifies mental "frames" that may be taken for granted but that provide a primary guide for interpreting and understanding the meaning of specific actions and behaviors. According to Goffman, frames organize meaning and involvement as they determine organizational behavior and reinforce cultural norms and values. Frames, as a system of social rules or organizational policies, provide information and regulation in terms of appropriate behavior in the activity or scene.

Consider some typical organizational frames: a Monday morning departmental meeting; an employee-involvement group; lunch with friends in the cafeteria or performance appraisal with a supervisor. Each situation has its own rules and limits determined by an invisible frame that stipulates appropriate behavior. These unwritten and unspoken rules are always present in organizational performances and episodes. Often these cultural frames establish the routines and the boundaries of organizational activities and discourage and limit innovation and change.

Within most organizations, people follow specific rules of conduct or an assigned role that is confirmed when appropriate behavior is validated by others. According to Goffman (1974), "breaking frame" or going beyond an organized role in a particular frame of activity can be as uncomfortable and disruptive as an actor coming into the wrong scene. If an employee questions a decision of his supervisor in a public arena, everyone feels the tension of a broken frame. Change, such as the restructuring of a particular unit or experimenting with new procedures, may also break long-standing organizational frames.

In a broken frame with inappropriate or unmatched behavior, organization members are suddenly conscious of the habitual roles that they play in the overall organizational drama. Change demands a recognition of existing frames that are both relevant and legitimate for a particular organization as well as the creation of new frames that give permission for innovation and change. With this awareness, organization members can begin to write new scripts and scenarios that match a changed reality and to expand and modify old frames and mental models that no longer fit the new drama or organizational narrative.

Organizational culture constantly reinforces frames and dominant organizational scripts. Culture has been defined as a set of "control mechanisms" including rules, plans, and instructions for behavior (Geertz 1973). According to Geertz, these controls are not uniform across all cultures but are unique to each in providing order and understanding in specific contexts. However, organizational analysis of culture may also focus on universal cultural elements that are interpreted in unique ways. Deal and Kennedy (1982) identify these essential elements of organizational culture: values, heroes, rites and rituals, and cultural-communication networks. However, these elements as they are constructed and experienced within the organization create a culture that is unique to each organization and a context for interpreting and implementing change.

Values are the core beliefs of the organization. Some may be formally stated in the mission of the organization. Other values may be more informal, created in the daily interaction of members. The energy and direction provided by core values are at the heart of any successful change effort. Change based on teamwork, honesty and trust, respect for employees, excellence, and social responsibility has greater legitimacy. These values contain the justification and the direction for change and renewal. Values can also tie the organization to old ways and identities and thus block effective change. These traditional anchors cannot be easily changed.

Heroes are those people in the organization, past and present, who best represent and embody its core values. Heroes, or the memory of heroes, have often provided leadership and momentum in change efforts. Some Disney people still ask, "What would Walt have done?" The spirit of "Leo" and his "reach for the stars" philosophy of innovation and excellence are still at the heart of Leo Burnett's highly successful advertising agency. Yet, individuals and groups can be heroes just as much as a charismatic CEO or founder. Opinion leaders and committed employees at all levels of the organization can help facilitate and direct change.

Organizational *rites and rituals* reinforce and celebrate the values of the organization in specific practices and change efforts. These might include the president's annual recognition dinner, quality team logos and slogans, special management retreats, and new product introductions. Change efforts should recognize and integrate the rituals that are important to the identity of the organization in order to maintain stability in a process of continuing change. Rituals may also be created as a formal recognition of directed change, such as awards for innovation, creativity, and excellence.

Formal and informal *cultural communication networks* document and disseminate the stories, the history, and the core values of the company, using both realistic and idealistic narratives. Since facilitating any change process requires collaboration in collecting, sharing, and analyzing information, cultural communication networks are already existing information tools. Cultural communication networks include company publications, meetings, orientation, and training sessions, as well as the bulletin board and the grapevine. These channels reinforce values and cultural norms as well as communicate and integrate change.

Since culture is based on core values and shared rules of behavior, it is in many ways the major unifying and controlling element in the organization. Attempting to change a culture without the involvement of those who experience and create the culture may be viewed as an attempt to manipulate organization members. Culture can be a substantial resource in both directed and nondirected change processes; it can also be a major barrier to innovation.

The cultural/interpretive approach recognizes the influence of the informal, subjective elements of social interaction and the cultural symbols, stories, rituals, and rules that create unity and energize the organization. Change from this perspective is a collaborative effort based on core values, which involves people at all levels of the organization in planning, implementation, and evaluation. Change facilitators should respect people, alliances, and organizational cultures and subcultures as unique and essential resources in the change management process.

Quadrant IV–Critical Humanism Approaches to Change

A critical humanist approach may challenge traditional organization structure and the implications and use of power and control. While the cultural interpretive approach looks at the ways in which organization members construct reality, the critical approach focuses on "social reconstruction" (Mumby 1988) through a critique of power networks and dominant ideology within economic and social systems. This critical analysis attempts to bring greater reflection, self-determination, and responsibility for organization members. Ideally change from this perspective should be initiated from the inside-out based on increased knowledge and understanding, but in recent years, the media and special interest groups have played a pivotal role in bringing critical issues to the attention of a larger public and pushing change from the outside-in.

The impetus for change from a critical perspective can come from a variety of external special-interest groups, consumer movements, lobbyists, and government regulators. Calls for change may be the result of psychological, sociological, and historical analysis and critique of organizational power and structure. However, change initiatives may also emerge from internal forces including unions, whistle-blowers, and special-interest employee groups. For example, unions might encourage a critical analysis of the workplace, including safety on the job, benefits, and pension programs, employee privacy, and representation in decision making.

Values such as truth, freedom, and justice are cited to challenge the authority and "conscience" of the organization and demand a balance of moral and ethical obligations with economic and legal obligations. A specific objective of the critical approach is to examine the power structures of the organization and how and why inequality and hierarchy are accepted as legitimate by most organization members. A more general goal is to create alternative ways of thinking about organizational behavior and structure beginning with cultural analysis and critique.

Critical approaches are a reaction against mechanistic, objective, and positivistic views of culture and society. They are a response to what Barrett (1978) called the "Era of Technique," in which the machine itself becomes an "embodied decision procedure" and technology determines human destiny. The discourse is also a debate on the economic, social, and political implications of power, structure, and hierarchy. The critical approach is not only a critique of societal institutions and organizations, but also a commentary on the "postmodern" experience in a fragmented world with no real values and only elusive, transient relationships. As Lyotard (1984) states, while science once provided a "grand narrative" to make sense of the world, the postmodern condition is characterized by fragmentation with multiple voices and competing narratives and meanings. The self is also "saturated" (Gergen 1991) with multiple roles and conflicting demands on individual energy and resources.

Science still attempts to provide a "grand narrative" to make sense of the world, but this goal has been undermined from a number of directions: the application of a reductionist perspective to the study of the behavior of an individual scientist; the sociological study of the practice of science; the historical study of the development of science; and the rhetorical analysis of scientific discourse. None of this detracts from the practical value of scientific knowledge as such, but it does tend to diminish the assertion that science is marching ever closer to the Final Theory of Everything.

The rapid accretion of technological progress leads to many legal, moral, and ethical problems that will not be easily solved. Many of these touch on the most intimate areas of life and work. A critical perspective might ask whether we are busy creating a world that no one will want to live in. Kenneth Burke (1966) in his exercise to define humans, describes the interpretations and contradictions of symbols in constructing culture:

> *Man is the symbol-using (symbol-making, symbol-misusing) animal*
> *inventor of the negative form (or moralized by the negative)*
> *separated from his natural condition by instruments of his own making,*
> *goaded by the spirit of hierarchy (or moved by the sense of order)*
> *and rotten with perfection.*

In a critical perspective, the socially constructed realities can create alienation and leave people working on the "margins" of organizational power and rewards in the hierarchical structures of organizational life. This challenges the concept of the "Organization Man" (Whyte 1956) and the social ethic on which it is based. Traditional structure is questioned and characterized as manipulative. In critical humanism, change comes out of dialectical debate, discussion, and self-reflection, as well as coercive methods. Thus, change must be based on experience and real-world applications that come from direct confrontation of ideas and a historical analysis of practice. In a critical approach to change, self-awareness and responsibility are important goals in any action. Issues such as social responsibility and organizational accountability, power and hierarchy, business ethics, employee privacy, discrimination, safety, working conditions, and media images of organizations are the subject of critique discussion, and activism.

Someone working from this perspective might ask these questions: How can we make the organization a better place for everyone to work? How can the organization be more responsive to an increasingly diverse workforce, which includes more women, racial and ethnic minorities, and disabled employees? Broader critical debates might raise questions about the accountability and responsibility of organizations not only toward their employees, but also toward stakeholders, customers, and the community. What part does the organization play in protecting the environment and the health of people on this planet? What are the obligations of multinational organizations operating in foreign countries? What responsibility do organizations have in social issues such as education, crime, healthcare, and drug abuse?

Today, organizations are challenged on these ethical, legal, and economic fronts. The critical approach is a reaction to perceptions of a "mindless, uncaring bureaucracy" and the experience of people in a controlling structure. Weber (1958) described this tendency in bureaucracy: "the more the bureaucracy is 'dehumanized,' the more completely it succeeds in eliminating from official business love, hatred, and all purely personal, irrational, and emotional elements which escape calculation. This is the specific nature of bureaucracy and it is appraised as its special virtue." Morgan (1986) shares Weber's concern that we have consistently "overrationalized" our understanding of organizations by ignoring greed, fear, hate, desire, and other emotions. When emotions break out, they are immediately "banished" with apologies, rationalizations, and punishments that restore a "neutered" professional state.

According to a Freudian psychoanalytic view, the repression of natural instincts and emotions is the price people pay for being part of a "civilized" society (Freud 1961). In a professional organization, people protect themselves from the anxiety of real or imagined threats or dangers—from the boredom of routine work to the pressure of life-and-death decisions—by developing a variety of personal defense mechanisms.

This situation is mythologized in the character of Willy Loman, a tired salesman self-described at the end of his career as "an empty orange peel," the classic victim of an unfeeling organization and his own limitations. Willy represented a good salesman and a loyal company man, but he needed something more than "a smile and a shoeshine." Willy is just a shadow on some stage dying again and again for lost ideals, but critical writers continue to try to serve as the conscience of the corporation to bring the realities of working men and women to a broader public to create awareness and facilitate change with shared power and responsibility. Cultural elements are the subject of analysis and debate.

One revealing study is an oral history by Studs Terkel (1974) that documents ordinary people across America talking about their jobs. The following commentaries, one from the bottom and another from the top of the organizational hierarchy, illustrate a basic theme. In both cases, the individual describes emotions that have been repressed and even rationalized as each interprets his working experience in a dominating culture. As Terkel explains, this book is also about "violence" to the spirit.

Stock chaser: "This foreman, he walked around like a little guard. Shoot me in the back; I was doin' the best I could. I had never been on an assembly line in my life. This thing's moving, going. You gotta pick it up, baby. You gotta be fast on that. He was like a little shotgun. Go to the washroom, he's looking for you, and right back. ...You can do twenty years of right and one hour of wrong and they'd string you."

Ex-president of conglomerate: "Fear is always prevalent in the corporate structure. Even if you're a top man, even if you're hard, even if you do your job — by the slight flick of a finger, your boss can fire you. There's always the insecurity. You bungle a job. You're fearful of losing a big customer. You're fearful so many things will appear on your record, stand against you. You're always fearful of the big mistake. You've got to be careful when you go to corporation parties. Your wife, your children have to behave properly. You've got to fit in the mold. You've got to be on guard."

Organizations can also be trapped by the system and their own created cultural reality, which blocks needed changes and development and maintains negative patterns. As a group, people in organizations may develop their own "institutional defenses" such as rationalization, denial, projection and scapegoating to block and ignore change processes. These are accepted through mutual, often unconscious, agreement and preserved as part of the organizational social system (Kets de Vries and Miller 1984). Some organization members may spend substantial energy in merely dealing with the anxiety brought by complexity and change. As individuals and groups, they may deny the reality of an ineffective organization and create their own selective reality.

Such anxiety and stress can create distortions within the organizational psyche that limit change, integration, and development. Kets de Vries and Miller (1984) explore "neurotic" dysfunctions in the organizational behavior of executives and managers as well as superior and subordinate relationships, department and work-group relations, and the adaptive style of the organization as a whole. According to these researchers, each neurotic organization has its own "shared fantasy." Kets de Vries and Miller provide a review of five types of "neurotic" organizational styles: paranoid, compulsive, dramatic, depressive, and schizoid. "These represent long-standing, deeply ingrained ways of perceiving, interpreting, and behaving on the part of coalitions of very powerful members of the organization."

The *paranoid* organization is characterized by suspicion and distrust internally and externally and excessive control mechanisms. The *compulsive* organization is obsessed with control and perfectionism in every detail of organizational life. The *dramatic* organization strives to impress and to gain attention on a variety of stages with energetic and often impulsive actions. The *depressive* organization is characterized by low self-confidence, a sense of hopelessness, and fixed conservative actions. The *schizoid* organization is detached and aloof, with a lack of coordination and direction among isolated and conflicting goals.

These neurotic styles create "intrapsychic barriers" to change and distorted ways of relating to directed and nondirected change processes. Kets de Vries and Miller suggest that managers and other organization members can gain insight by confronting and clarifying internal events so that problems are recognized and understood and change can be facilitated. By working through the information and changing the "inner-representational world" of fantasies, assumptions, and faulty thinking, organization members can begin to reorganize and recreate their attitudes and beliefs to fit realistic situations.

Most critical perspectives are a critique of modern organizational life, with a sharp eye toward the distortion and oppression caused by the structures of bureaucracy, power, and domination. The central goal is emancipation from rigid structures and limited thinking to increased freedom, responsibility and understanding. Critical approaches seek to give voice to those who have not been heard and to expose corruption and manipulation caused by political and economic structures.

From a humanist perspective, the ability to understand and manage change comes through awareness of the shadow elements of organizational life—the unknown, unconscious, nondirected aspects that may both drain and energize the system. A critical approach to change begins with increased dialogue and moves toward shared confrontation and debate of critical issues. Critical agendas for change are both idealistic and revolutionary. The results for organization members might include a growing respect for people as thinking and feeling individuals, broader sharing of power, control, and responsibility and greater responsiveness to all stakeholders including managers, employees, suppliers, customers, stockholders, and community.

INTEGRATING PERSPECTIVES

An understanding of different conceptions of and approaches to change management is a logical and practical foundation for beginning any discussion of change consultation and organizational development. Because of the dynamic complexity of organizations, it is useful to explore organizational development and change from a variety of viewpoints. Together they present increased options for greater understanding, perceptive innovation and

TABLE 3.2 Different Perspectives on Change.

Approaches	Context	Technology	Coordination	Results
	In what context is this change taking place?	What methodologies are most effective in bringing about change?	How are people, technology, and resources coordinated?	What change results are most important?
I. Rational/Behavioral	Limited	Expert knowledge	Control	Understanding
	Regulative	Problem solving	Exclusivity	Knowledge
	Professional discipline	Objective measurement	Leadership	Improvement
	Management	Data collection	Information	Efficiency
	Industry standards	Instructional design		Prediction
	Market needs	Observation		Cost effectiveness
II. Systems	Macro and micro levels	Architecture	Interrelated groups	Relationships
	Environment	Organizational mapping	Hierarchy of learning	Unity
	Open and closed	Models	Communication	Alignment
	Holistic	Structure	Feedback loops	Resource utilization
	Input and output	Processes	Alliances	Discovery
	Global	Planning	Transfer competency	Transformation
	Competitive			

III. Cultural/Interpretive	Culture Community Episodes Group History Nation "Created reality"	Metaphor and symbol Narrative Language Dialogue Negotiation Facilitation Collaborative inquiry Futuring	Interaction Rules Conversations Roles Interpretation Core values Agreement Shared understanding	Consensus Coordination Responsiveness Commitment Cooperation Invention Innovation
IV. Critical Humanism	History Culture Politics Economics Society	Rhetoric Interest groups Linguistics Confrontation Dialectic thinking	Persuasion Power Structure Ideology	Awareness Emancipation Action Self-determination Autonomy Social responsibility

informed action. Table 3.2 illustrates the categories of questions related to to the elements of our change management model.

The four change perspectives—rational/behavioral, systems, cultural/interpretive, and critical humanism—establish a distinct foundation and context for conversations and inquiry about change. In a *rational/behavioral* perspective the primary vehicle for change is control through precise data collection and performance measurement. The change agent is most often a manager, staff professional, or external resource who remains somewhat objective and often takes on an expert authority role. The goal and the results of this approach are usually to make an operation, process, function, or person "better" than they currently are. From a rational and behavioral perspective, everything can be improved. With proper controls and directed change, the organization can improve in order to be more effective, efficient, productive, and profitable. The results of this approach are most evident in the application of new knowledge and technology to organizational problems and challenges.

The *systems* view is based on an inescapable concept of interdependence. The fact that everything is connected is both reassuring and limiting. Nothing can be realistically isolated in one big indivisible system. With this realization comes a clear dialectical approach to change. Change is either a basic adjustment that maintains overall balance with little deviation beyond the norm, or it is a complete transformation of the entire system. The system has its own internal laws in relation to change. The results of a systems perspective may be more effective alignment and unity, strategic alliances and more efficient resource utilization throughout the system.

A *cultural/interpretive* approach to change is based on communication, work practices, and cultural norms that affect overall results. The focus is interaction that allows for input, interpretation, and feedback as well as a sense of involvement and commitment. The result of change is increased coordination, which facilitates the smooth running of organizational operations and cooperation in organizational endeavors. Yet this should be a continuous, dynamic coordination that never hardens in an automatic-response mechanism. The need for agreements, interaction, and cooperation is evident in this view. Both formal and informal contracting and negotiation are a part of the everyday work practices of individuals and groups. Much of this occurs at the level of nondirected change and can affect any directed change process. Through this perspective, organization leaders and members can integrate directed and nondirected change and gain a more practical understanding of how perceptions and interpretations of events and policies on a nondirected level are related to motivation, commitment, and action in directed change.

Confrontation, from a *critical humanism* perspective, is a particular form of interaction that can be both enlightening and painful but is often essential for organizational change and renewal. Organizations are asked to look at the gaps between what they are and what they want to be. They are encouraged to consider the impact of organizational actions on people from line workers to community members. This critical focus is the starting place for discussion and debate of essential social and economic issues related to organizational change. The ideal result of a critical approach is emancipation from distorted views, rigid structures, and limited thinking. For individuals, groups, and the organization, this can bring increased freedom as well as greater responsibility. With the awareness of a critical perspective, opportunities for innovation and development are also more evident.

We recognize the influence of all these perspectives at various points in organizational history and development. Theoretical approaches to change cannot be based on rational laws alone; they must also recognize the organizational norms and rules that are continuously created through social interaction and work practices. As Weick (1979) explains, it is important that organizational leaders and change facilitators distinguish between the process of "organizing" and the more static concept of "organization." Organizing is a continuous dynamic process of creating meaning, making decisions, implementing, experimenting, and learning through the integration of directed and nondirected change processes in change management.

Each perspective helps us to understand the multiple voices related to change. Together these different interpretations and approaches provide organizational leaders, managers, staff professionals, and internal and external resources with a framework and set of application tools to facilitate change processes in both economic and human terms. Each approach places importance on different types of information and judges that information based on particular values and goals. No one perspective is complete or always appropriate. Each brings valuable information and applications for change management.

Organizations in the midst of continuous change are made up of diverse people and conflicting goals. Awareness and respect for different ways of thinking about change come from dialogue and collaborative inquiry. A shared understanding and knowledge of change perspectives brings greater cooperation and direction to facilitating and integrating directed and nondirected organizational change and establishes a solid foundation for implementation and results.

4

ART: Action Research Teaming
As a Strategy for Change

Action Research Teaming (ART) is at the heart of the relationship between the facilitating system and the client system. In change management, ART is both a process and a relationship. Action research teams help integrate the social and technical components of the organization and link work practices to overall performance. This is a common activity in many effective organizations even though people may not be aware that they are using the action research process. For example, a team designing a new computer system works with customers, suppliers and manufacturing to develop the best system. Teams involved in quality improvement also use action research as they collect and analyze data on performance standards.

One of the purposes of this chapter is to help organizations "rediscover" and focus the power of Action Research Teams. The components of action research—data collection, analysis, feedback, action planning, and evaluation—should not be fragmented as parts of an "accidental" process at the nondirected level. Data and analysis are too often the byproducts of other activities and are lost or disappear because they are not transferred to others or integrated with formal directed change efforts.

In order to plan for change management, team members must decide what action is needed and why. This can be determined by gathering information and sharing feedback with the people involved so that they not only have some common understanding but also set priorities and develop mutual objectives for implementation. In action research teaming, the people identifying problem situations are also involved in solving them. This collaborative process provides a higher-level capacity for follow-through and continuity, and ensures that plans for directed change will be effectively implemented and integrated with nondirected, routine work practices.

Action research grows out of the applied social psychology and the work of Kurt Lewin (1951), the founder of the Research Center for Group

Dynamics at Massachusetts Institute of Technology, and the sociotechnical systems concepts of E. L. Trist and his colleagues at the Tavistock Institute. Group dynamics, sociotechnical systems, and organizational development use the tools and techniques of action research to involve people in discovering ways to facilitate and manage change. Lewin's contributions include field theory in understanding the underlying context and interdependent relationships influencing change, especially the guiding principle that change should be data-based and involve those who will be affected by the change. His working theory was "No action without research and no research without action." Sociotechnical systems approaches grounded in the work of E. L. Trist and the Tavistock Institute, concentrate on the interface between people and the ways they work together using technology, tools, and techniques within the organization. Other recent interpretations and applications of action research include participatory action research (Whyte 1991), which allows participants to be partners in managing the process and generating results. Since the 1940s, action research has been a valuable form of inquiry. Now action research is being "reinvented" in innovative new contexts (Elden and Chisholm 1993).

In our approach, ART involves collecting data and facilitating team activities related to improvement in areas such as work design, performance and reward systems, communication, total quality management, customer service, career development, competitive benchmarking, cost reduction, strategic planning, innovation, and cultural change. ART projects can be used to help create and support high-performing teams that manage their work, gather data, measure results, and learn through cross-training and partnerships within and across work units. ART can facilitate data-based change and involve people in linking goals and performance within a responsive dynamic system.

DEFINING ACTION RESEARCH TEAMING (ART)

Action research is a process that can build unit and organizational capability. As an approach to relationships, ART focuses on the attitude and actions that support wider involvement and collaboration in facilitating data-based change. ART is a belief in opening communication channels, encouraging dialogue, transferring competencies, and sharing information to help build individual, group, and organizational competencies. As a process, ART consists of a systematic collection of data relative to a business challenge, need or opportunity; analyzing and feeding the data back into the organizational system; planning and taking action; and monitoring the results of actions by collecting more data (see Figure 4.1). Action research is a cyclical renewal process

Figure 4.1   Action Research Teaming Model (ART)

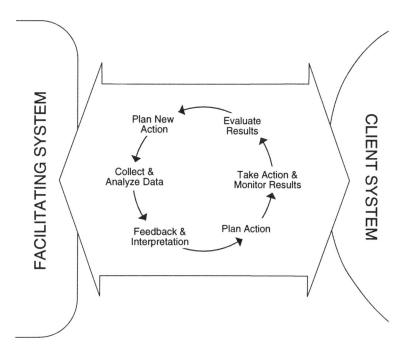

because the feedback from each action yields data for planning the next action.

Thus, ART is both an approach to participation and a collaborative process for anticipating, planning, facilitating, implementing, and monitoring change. It integrates the "local knowledge" of organization members with the broader perspective of overall directed change efforts. The team collaborates on all phases of the research and the planning for change strategies. Action research and teaming support voluntary change and the integration of directed and nondirected processes. The following concepts define action research teams:

- ART involves the planners with the doers.
- ART is data-based change.
- ART is an interpretive feedback process.
- ART develops individual, group, and organizational competencies.

ART Involves the Planners with the Doers

Planning and doing should be linked for effective change management. One creative multidisciplinary, multinational action research team suggested that all CEOs should become ARTLs (Action Research Team Leaders). They would in this way see all aspects of the organization, customer, and community and have more accurate information to form new decisions.

In complex organizational systems and hierarchical structures, those who plan change, CEOs, boards and senior managers, and resource professionals are often isolated from those who implement these plans. ART brings representatives of these groups together to facilitate more effective change management. This includes, for example, staff working with line, line colleagues working together across organizational units, boards working with their various constituents, and advisory groups, ad hoc task forces, committees, and resource facilitation teams collaborating to meet the challenges of change.

The process concentrates on joint efforts in identifying need, collecting and analyzing data, and providing feedback, decisions, and actions. Coordinated feedback increases discussion and informational exchange between those who plan and those who are responsible for implementing change. This dialogue helps leaders, managers, and organization members to acknowledge differences, collectively define new solutions, and plan for action to meet strategic objectives.

In the context of collaborative inquiry, action research encourages teaming, communication, and cooperation in establishing networks to support continual change management. Members of the client system work together to define the problems they want to address, define the methods used for data collection, identify the objectives, and evaluate and measure the consequences or results of action taken. Since action research involves the planners with the doers, the relationship between diagnosis, data collection, feedback, and planning for action is more relevant to group and organizational objectives. Each step in the action research process evolves from and develops the previous step. The client, the change consultation team, and the client system. are part of a cumulative and participative development cycle.

For instance, a training-and-development manager could apply ART methods to an advisory council project on planning for and implementing diversity in the workforce for the coming decade. The advisory council might include expert professionals and resource specialists as well as senior executives and employee representatives. They would facilitate collecting data on work diversity issues and training needs from various levels, functions, and business units. They could gather information through individual and group interviews, an audit or questionnaire, a discussion of skill and performance gaps as well as development areas, and observation at seminars and training sessions. Combining the resources of the advisory council and the change facilitator or manager, an analysis of the findings can then be prepared and shared with other parts of the system in feedback sessions. Interpretations and action derivations are made, decisions formed, priorities set, new action taken, and feedback recycled to monitor and modify actions as the organization develops current and strategic plans for meeting challenges and opportunities and facilitating human-resource development.

Action research teaming brings measurement to both planning and action. Action research teams establish a benchmark with criteria or standards for measuring progress. Learning from continuing data collection, organization members measure results, and this knowledge helps determine if their action is aimed in the right direction. Planning and action are integrated in a cyclical research process that helps managers to facilitate complex change processes on both a directed and nondirected level.

ART Encourages Data-Based Change

Action research teaming is based on a practical working theory of data-based change, which can facilitate learning throughout the organization. Implementing continuous quality improvement requires a data base produced by means of a systematic model for obtaining qualitative and quantitative data from multiple sources. Action research teaming is ideal for a long-term continuous improvement process aimed at collecting data about system-wide change initiatives such as total quality, leadership, productivity, customer satisfaction, morale, quality of work life, and coordination and communication across and within organization units. People in the organization help to collect and analyze data and feed it back into the organization, interpret and act upon the data, and evaluate and measure the results by collecting more data and beginning the process anew. This cycle continually clarifies values, renews purpose, reviews and modifies goal priorities, measures performance, and motivates change from within the organization.

ART can use a variety of data-collection methods: observation, audits, surveys and questionnaires, interviews, focus groups, content analysis, and documentation. The challenges in the data-collection process and various methods and instruments are examined in detail in Chapter 8. At this point it is sufficient to note that in a traditional expert approach to diagnosis, clients and other organization members may not be completely open and objective in the data-collection process. The client may withhold information or be overly biased or subjective in identifying issues and challenges. This can lead to distorted information. In the action research model, the relationships between diagnosis, data collection, feedback, and action planning are fully established as being client-centered and collaborative, so that the organization members can "own" the change process. This data-based, multiple-method participative approach increases understanding and effectiveness in managing change.

The characteristics of organization development and action research teaming are very similar. Both provide a type of active collaboration between a client system and a change facilitation team for the purpose of solving a client's problems, meeting challenges, encouraging innovation, and influencing change through research activity followed by actions and evaluation. Action research teaming methodology, however, ensures a quality intervention because it analyzes the same variables and issues through several cycles and identifies new challenges and opportunities in changing contexts. With the mutual monitoring process of action research, there is stronger probability for accurate and comprehensive data to guide future action.

For example, a Swedish multinational company headquartered in a small city worked with a consultation team with members from France, Norway, Sweden, and the United States (Chakiris 1981). The company leaders used ART to involve the union, managers, employees, and community to look at how the organization might attract, develop and keep its human resources by establishing a meaningful career process. They didn't want people going "over the mountain" to larger cities, and other jobs and organizations. This process included growing people within, developing them through international job assignments, and rotating them into leadership roles to develop organization capacity for the future. The consultation team used interviews and organizational maps to gather data. The feedback sessions were presented by organization members as dramas, followed by action planning and later implementation in new policies and options for employees. ART was an essential part of this data-based change process integrating diverse resources around a common goal.

ART Is an Interpretive Feedback Process

The change consultation team works with clients in the feedback and interpretation of the data and the planning for action to create a more effective organization. Change will be more accurately represented and more readily accepted and implemented when those who are most affected by the change have been involved in planning for it. Participation also presents the best options for resolving, identifying, and responding to needs and for taking advantage of opportunities. Feedback encourages this participation.

In ART, the organization's human resources are used in interesting, innovative, and challenging ways. Valuable skills are learned as team members practice group processes while working on real problems and opportunities. In this interactive process, individual, group, and organizational skills are strengthened and developed for change management.

Ideally, ART groups are voluntary, temporary in nature, and flexible in structure. The members benefit from training in ART consultation methods to build client relationships, and learn to work with and through others in an educational process based on dialogue, collective interpretation of issues and responsible and thoughtful action.

The discovery of the solution to complex strategic challenges may not necessarily emerge at the outset but can become known through the interpretive feedback process. Action research, as its name implies recognizes both continuing research and ongoing action. The outcome is not always certain in advance. Changes in the design may be necessary as the discovery process proceeds. Implications, solutions, and applications are a matter of joint exploration and responsible commitment to shared goals.

In the traditional consultation expert model, the faciliator provides the client with specific recommendations for action that the client reviews and then decides which to use. In ART each step in the process can be performed jointly (Fornaciari and Chakiris 1985) by the client, change facilitators, and action research teams. The collaborative steps are shown in Figure 4.2.

Figure 4.2. ART Collaborative Process

Need Suspected	Need Validation	Action Considered	Feasibility Determined	Implementation	Evaluation

Before beginning data collection it is essential to decide what information is needed and how it will be collected. Obviously, if the data is not pertinent to the needs deemed important by the client system, it will have only a marginal impact. On the other hand, if the process has been collaborative and the members of the client system have played a significant role in data collection and diagnosis there will be a greater chance for ownership. Together managers and team members interpret the data to explore the meanings and implications in their own system. Each of these steps gives life to the action planning phase. In the absence of this system ownership, planned action becomes less effective and may never be implemented or supported on an informal level.

Data belongs to those who give it. Therefore it is important to share data within the system for reflection, interpretation, application, and learning. Feedback sessions are crucial to successful action research. Information presented in feedback sessions must be relevant, understandable, descriptive, verifiable, limited, impactable, comparative, and unfinalized (Nadler 1977).

During the feedback session, the interpretation of the data and creation of action possibilities provides a second set of data, often the most meaningful information for gaining understanding and setting priorities and making action decisions. The feedback session needs to be designed with the members of the organization involved. These sessions often move at a high-energy level with both content and structured process as the context for gaining ownership, examining options, and establishing meaningful committed action.

Change management requires that people plan together and talk with one another about common organization issues, concerns, growth areas, and strategic goals. Most important, discrepancies are raised between the present situation and how people want the organization to look in the future. However, without planned feedback and collective analysis, individuals and groups are not given the opportunity to understand and influence organizational change and to work through old and new concerns. Without effective feedback and action links, the momentum and commitment that ART generates can be lost.

The ART change process bases action on the data collected, and new client discoveries are interpreted and acted upon through interactive developmental phases. Understanding, flexibility, insight, and continuous learning are the essential factors that drive the feedback process and the results.

ART Builds Individual, Group, and Organizational Competency

Action research teaming requires a high level of competence in data-based change and process consultation. Together these competencies—organizing and analyzing data, facilitating a diagnosis and prioritizing issues, planning and evaluating action—can provide the skill base, resources, commitment, and measurement needed for effective change management at the individual, group, and organizational levels.

Action research teams help to implement and integrate system-wide change at both a directed and nondirected level. These teams can progressively resolve chronic operational problems by understanding performance gaps and confronting and working through differences. They can identify emerging concerns and facilitate change by involving representatives from all organizational areas affected by the change. The action research process improves skill development in group dynamics and systematic problem solving while encouraging greater responsiveness and innovation in facilitating change at all levels.

ART takes time and training. The process requires that those who will be responsible for the action be involved in the data collection to assess needs and plan for action. This participation can be time consuming, but members develop competencies to build the capacity and flexibility of the organization in change management. The process encourages more effective solutions to current challenges and in new visions of the future because it is based on relevant, comprehensive data that is actively sought and thoughtfully applied. The action research process is enhanced and energized through teaming, which helps create a more cohesive organization, greater commitment to common goals, and increased capacity for cooperative learning and development.

ART Competencies in Change Management Roles

ART skills are interrelated and supportive of specific change management roles. Table 4.1 shows an integrated portfolio of competencies for these roles. Change facilitators, consultation teams, and managers must be flexible and responsive in a variety of roles and change contexts.

Table 4.1 ART Competencies in Action Roles.

Action Team Member
> Demonstrates "followership" and leadership capabilities
> Participates in both formal and informal leader roles
> Respects views and differences of others
> Listens in an active and understanding way
> Trusts others
> Informs others about feelings and concerns
> Exhibits flexibility and adaptability
> Supports teamwork

Facilitator
> Initiates and gives perceptive feedback
> Aligns goals with business strategies
> Designs meetings that bring about action with commitment
> Facilitates discussion
> Asks critical and thoughtful questions
> Clarifies roles and goal expectations
> Develops trust within groups
> Promotes individual involvement
> Uses media and learning resources

Data Collector
> Chooses appropriate data-collection techniques
> Designs and selects instrumentation
> Conducts interviews with individuals and groups
> Reviews documentation

Table 4.1 (continued)

Observes behavior
Involves and trains client system in data-collection methods

Feedback Specialist
Designs feedback sessions
Facilitates data interpretation
Generates action derivations
Identifies essential elements
Moves data from feedback, decisions and action, to results

Action Planner
Takes a systems perspective to action at macro and microlevels
Clarifies roles, goals, expectations and responsibilities
Analyzes change dynamics in forces that support and block change
Trains and links others to action taking

Applications Specialist
Matches appropriate resources to needs
Confronts collusive behavior
Mobilizes appropriate resources
Retains momentum of change support

Measurement Coordinator
Measures progress and results
Recycles data collection to redirect action
Uses measurement feedback to direct new action
Modifies action based on new direction and learning
Ties business results to individual and group performance goals
Anticipates and plans for continuous improvement and change

Action research allows the change facilitator, the client system, managers, and team members to practice many roles related to data collection and analysis. The research team monitors implementation of the action plan, collecting data to see how well the action is working. If the situation is not satisfactorily resolved, the data is used as the basis for another cycle of action research that results in a revised action plan. When the data indicates a new challenge, the team initiates another cycle of research. One distinct feature of the action research process is this provision for cycling and recycling data. Through this process the team strives to improve performance in everyday operations and integrate directed and nondirected change to reach shared goals.

TEAMING FOR ACTION RESEARCH

We are using the term ART to include teaming between a facilitating system and a client system to confront and resolve problems, to validate need, and to drive action related to change management. This teaming process embraces consultation technology, skills, and tools to respond to opportunities related to total quality, continuous improvement, customer satisfaction, competitive challenge, organization renewal, and change.

The action research team provides a temporary structure for weighing emerging concerns and opportunities in the organizational system. Members can explore alternatives, generate solutions to problems, and determine the best collective strategies for coping with change. The team is often focused around a specific task, project, application initiative, or change effort. The ideal action research team is composed of both internal and external resources to the client system receiving the consultation services. Action research teams may be constituted at many levels from a group in a specific unit of an organization to a community action team with broad representation.

ART purposively involves the appropriate constituents to legitimize and to insure buy-in and motivation for action. Action team members should be competent communicators and fact finders who show patience, competence, and tolerance of ambiguity. The team members also need to have facilitation and group-process skills. The following are some characteristics of effective ART members:

- Motivation, interest, and commitment
- Developed sense of self identity
- Communication and group skills
- Ability to elicit trust and maintain confidentiality
- Well-respected in the organization
- Representation of the population affected by the changes
- High level of involvement within the organization
- Recognition of a need for change
- Interest in mobilizing resources in new, challenging ways
- Skills in facilitating process questions in fact finding
- Capability to work with both internal and external people and resources
- Comfortable in challenging a diagnosis already made
- Effective group member with process observation skills

- Values continuing learning
- Future orientation
- Constituency-based representation
- Systematic data-collection capability
- Dialectical thinking open to the ideas of others
- Able to give and receive feedback
- Basic philosophy of collaboration and teamwork

In change management, ART frequently involves inside and outside resources. The inside resources are often staff professionals, managers, or specialists within a unit or organization. The outside resources might be managers and staff professionals from other areas within the organization, as well as consultation teams, suppliers, customers, community members, academicians, competitors, and experts from other organizations.

Action team membership should include representatives from those business units affected by the change. Sanctioned by top management, organization-wide change teams bring together appropriate senior executives, upper, and middle managers, staff resources, and employees. For change affecting a specific work unit, the team might involve representatives of line management, coworkers in the unit, and key people or groups who interface with the unit. In a small unit perhaps each person in the unit would be a team member. Different types of action research teams include:

- Interunit cross-functional team
- Intraunit team
- Internal-external team
- Project team
- Matrix team
- Benchmarking team
- Management team
- Business team
- Customer team
- Supplier team
- Community team

Ideally, ART would draw from a cross-section of organization members committed to the principles of collaboration and willing to review their own function and work together on a regular basis. These teams should not hesitate to use external resources, which bring expertise, facilitation and consultation competencies, and some objectivity. Learning and cooperative relationships are highly valued and support a commitment to valid data collection. Action should not be based on hearsay or a simple diagnosis, but rather on relevant data from directed and nondirected levels.

The personnel of functional units and line managers can collaborate to develop competencies, establish benchmarks of preferred outcomes, build and transfer new practices, establish capacity for change, and develop leadership at all levels. ART adapts effectively to a network of relationships including temporary units, ad hoc task groups, advisory councils, project teams, business coalitions, alliances within various networks, and other key liaisons of the enterprise. An effective team is open to modification of its own operations as members share in specific roles and develop reciprocal roles, negotiate new agreements, and complete tasks that support change management.

FACILITATING CHANGE THROUGH ACTION RESEARCH TEAMS

Action research teams are designed to increase feedback, improve problem solving, and facilitate data-based change in the organization. These groups also become a structure for self-initiated change. The teams assist in resolving conflicts and taking advantage of opportunities in the whole organization as well as those in specific business units or combinations of units. Organization members themselves become change agents through diagnosis, data collection research, planning, implementation, and evaluation.

No matter what the goals of ART, the consultation process for change management must start where the client system is. This means gathering data to assess a culture from the perspective of organization members throughout the system. The data generated by action research helps to validate need, confirm intuitive assumptions, challenge real or false perceptions, and illuminate emergent issues or blindspots. Teams must work within a specific organizational power structure that possesses its own business objectives, hidden agendas, and cultural biases.

When action research teams are established by senior management, they have a link to formal power and a declaration for directed change based on business objectives. When groups are self-initiated at lower levels, they often have no formal power from management. This makes it more difficult to acquire resources of time, get commitment to action, and access to structures and information within the organization. Some linkage to the executive level is an essential element in facilitating change through participation.

Action research teaming can empower organization members and bring about the democratization of the workplace through thoughtful action, collective participation and codetermination, with increased individual and group responsibility for change management. ART supports the psychological core of democracy with quality interventions intended to move beyond perceived hierarchical control to responsible participation and involvement by all employees. Some of these characteristics of organizational democracy as defined by White and Lippitt (1960) include:

- Open-mindedness, which means freedom of speech, listening receptively to the point of view of the other person, sharing in the other person's goals and ideas, and teaching by example.

- Self-acceptance and self-confidence based on achievement, with both pride and humility.

- Realism and respect for the facts with a continuous reorientation to the present and to the possible reality of the future.

- Freedom from status-mindedness; with a spirit of equality without loss of dignity or authority.

Participation may not always be "democratic." ART units can become a power in themselves, an elite group that can be disconnected from the real goals of ART. The teams should strive to represent the interests of people throughout the system and share data through feedback and collective analysis. This supports a more democratic approach to change.

THREE APPROACHES TO ART

There are three basic approaches to action research teams emphasizing developmental stages of the facilitating system and the client system: 1) research model; 2) action model; and 3) action research teaming model. Each represents a level of development in relation to client readiness, openness, client control, change facilitator competencies, available resources, and investment in training and development. The three approaches are also characterized by different degrees of client involvement. The method used depends on the situation, the timing, the growth stage of the organization, the skill competence, the relationship with the client, the strategic goals, and the client's style, and the organizational context or culture.

Approach #1—The Research Model

In the research approach, the facilitating system collects data, analyzes, and prepares an action-recommendation report for review by the client system.

Only the initial stages of the total action research process are completed. The collaboration is also limited as the change facilitator is put into an expert reporting role. The need or problem is already defined and the focus is predetermined by the client.

Activities

Diagnostic data-collection is conducted regarding some aspect of an ongoing program, process, system or activity such as total quality, customer satisfaction, productivity, performance system, employee morale, compensation, career development, or succession planning. A written report and action recommendations go to the client, who is usually a senior executive or manager. Only a few other copies of the results are available and these are carefully controlled by management and not shared with others. The level of openness and information exchange is low.

Results

This research is often focused on data collection to help solve a problem or respond to a need or opportunity. The long-term results of this approach are usually disappointing and may even discourage further research as the initial process will seem to have few benefits. Voluminous reports with many tables and impressive charts are created. However, these may be ignored, not explained, or integrated with real needs and current work practices and policies. The client may read the report with serious concern but be unable to use the findings in any meaningful way to introduce significant change. A lack of action research teaming competencies prevent the study from moving into action. There is research, but narrow action. The information has minimum ownership and meaning, when not applied with interpretive participation of the client system.

Client System Involvement

The client is a passive participant and depends on the research expert or team to gather and analyze the data and come up with the recommended action to solve the problem or respond to the need. There is no intentional feedback of the findings to employees or others in the system for interpretation or action planning.

Approach #2 — Action Model

In the action model, the consultation team collects data and facilitates selective feedback with client involvement in determining action interventions. This can be a quick fix model. The action research cycle is more developed than in the research model, but still incomplete. The concern is more with immediate results and outcomes rather than interpretive analysis of data and collective decisions.

Activities

Data may be collected from participants of some unit or the total organization. Feedback of the findings is provided as an intervention to influence or facilitate the ongoing action process of the group or system on a macro or microchange level. The process is controlled by the client to meet specific short term objectives.

Results

An action approach is a deliberate planned intervention to influence directed change through feedback of information and data collected. The results are more desirable than in the research approach alone. Participation in feedback and action planning diminishes resistance to change. The more resistant the group is the more important it is to provide active rather than passive feedback. If the group is open, change can be affected by active interpretation and analysis of the data collected. Some action may be taken based on the data, but it is an isolated directed change, often reflecting the dominant management agenda.

Client System Involvement

The client and client system may be moderately involved in this approach, and ready to take some action. There is selected feedback of findings as trained discussion leaders help facilitate interpretation, action derivations, and action decisions based on the findings. There is little or no attempt to create networks or involve people in other parts of the system. Action is still largely controlled by management with little employee input or influence on decisions and actions.

Approach #3—Action Research Teaming Model

The action research team model is based on a complete cycle of significant collaboration between the change facilitation team or consultation team and the client system. Members of the client system are partners in collaborative inquiry based on their own definitions and approach to change. Client system involvement is evident in all phases of data-collection, data analysis, interpretation, feedback, decisions and action planning. This model includes the most comprehensive use of action research teams in change management. There is a sense of exploration and discovery through data-based change.

Activities

Participants in a unit or the total organization are involved in the data-collection process related to their work. Organizational members identify issues, concerns, and gaps in their own area. They use the data they have generated to review attitudes, practices, and procedures in order to take some developmental action and make changes. They gather additional data to monitor the results of this action and discover other options and opportunities for change. A network of action teams operate throughout the system and collaborate in sharing data and exchanging practices.

Results

There are a number of advantages with this approach. Individuals who are involved in the planning and collecting of the data acquire greater ownership and acceptance of action decisions and implementation. Data collected by voluntary, trained internal subunits including task forces, project teams, clusters, and multidisciplinary teams are more economical and provide a broader perspective on change. Data is of higher quality and more comprehensive. Directed and nondirected levels are integrated for more effective change management.

Client System Involvement

This approach has the highest degree of client and client-system involvement. The client system is actively involved in data collection, feedback, decisions and action. This model is most sophisticated and participative in ensuring effective linkage between fact finding, decisions, and action. However, this does require some developmental activities for the client system including training and role practice using data-collection methods, trial or test projects, skills in organizing and coding data, and additional specialized training in teamwork and communications. Facilitators and action research team leaders also need training in feedback, facilitation, and change management competencies. Learning and the transfer of competencies is an essential part of this ongoing cyclical process.

BENEFITS AND CHALLENGES OF ART

ART helps form strategic partnerships throughout the system and involves more people in change management. This collaboration develops influence trust, and leadership and reinforces a basic philosophy of consultation in integrating directed and nondirected change. ART also clarifies values, renews purpose and increases acceptance of change. This improves implementation of system-wide change and increases motivation and understanding.

A survey of executives, boards, managers, and human resource professionals who have been trained in action research teaming competencies documents the benefits and challenges of ART. They have practiced this process in a variety of business organizations, manufacturing facilities, social service agencies, and educational institutions. Samples of their statements (Chakiris 1991) about the practical benefits of ART are included in Table 4.2.

TABLE 4.2 Benefits of ART.

Builds Organization Capacity for Change Management

Helps an organization learn how to solve its own problems.

Transfers new skills and concepts to the client system.

Uses available "mind power" in the organization.

Models an ongoing consultation process.

Clarifies organizational values.

Renews a sense of purpose.

Empowers people to take responsible action.

Can be readily taught to line management.

Teaches teaming process while engaged in a real situation.

Transfers a reusable process to new situations.

Develops and uses new skills.

Recognizes the importance of diversity.

Designs Quality Action

Bases change on data.

Increases the likelihood that change will be accepted.

Nurtures ownership through action research.

Allows those affected to participate in planning for change.

Draws out new skills and encourages creativity.

Ensures quality action by linking planners and doers.

Increases commitment and ownership of data and resulting action.

Supports planned interventions.

Provides a framework for data collection to gauge success.

Recognizes directed and nondirected change efforts in evaluation.

Uses proven organizational developmental concepts.

Leads to client and resource facilitator discovery.

Confronts people with data they can use.

Involves client as an active participant in action planning.

Uses proven research methodologies.

Helps organization members become agents of change.

TABLE 4.2 (continued)

Creates Ownership With Accountability

Involves those affected by change in the planning.
Increases client understanding to act on changes.
Identifies pressing problems.
Works through options of action.
Is data-based with proven methodology.
Leads to client discovery.
Ensures quality interventions.
People confronted by useful data tend to utilize the findings.
Actively involves the client in deriving action implications.
Avoids a quick-fix syndrome.
Gives data greater creditability.
Develops commitment and ownership of data and resulting actions.
Develops responsibility to deal with change.
Encourages ownership of the data.
Helps client to understand data.

Involves People in Change Management

Coordinates the expertise of the organization to solve its own problems.
Provides for mutual influence among team members.
Supports a philosophy of collaboration and participation.
Involves representative and diverse levels of the organization.
Builds collaboration.
Encourages teaming with people working together effectively.
Involves people in the change process.
Builds greater participation within the client system.

Utilizes Teaming As a Resource

Creates greater economy in collecting data.
Oriented in an action outcome.
Uses available mind power of group.
Allows progressive resolution of chronic operational problems.
Builds effective action research teaming into the process.
Accepts learning relationships as important.
Examines team functioning in getting work done.
Encourages learning from different perspectives.
Builds group-process skills while working on real problems.
Involves client in analysis of data and planning of action.

The statements in Table 4.3 are a sample of the responses of managers and other professionals assessing the challenges of ART (Chakiris 1991).

TABLE 4.3 Challenges of ART.

Possible Misuse of Data

No single interpretation of unified approach.
Lack of confidentiality.
Danger of leaks before the feedback session.
Misinterpretation of data.
Perception of overwhelming "problems."
Data perceived as negative rather than developmental.
Client unwilling to expose or share negative data.

Lack of Skills

Underdeveloped action research and consultation skills.
Perceived as too novel for the organization.
Difficulty acquiring resources of time and space.
Necessity of training fact finders.
Lack of process in sharing decision-making power.
Requires influence skills.
Feedback becomes "gripe" session if not effectively facilitated.
Collusive past practices discourage innovativeness.
Lack of skills in opening up communication and feedback channels.

Resistance

Data collection perceived as a threat to the present order.
Client unwilling to expose negative data.
Concern about unwelcome expectations within the workforce.
Underdeveloped facilitation skills for feedback sessions.
May reinforce employee gripes.
Necessity of obtaining the support of people in the operation.
Fear and uncertainty related to change.

Structural Conflict

Viewed as erosion of management and the loss of formal authority.
Has no formal power or authority without management support.
Sensitivity to management suspicion.
Viewed as management tool when imposed by head of organization.
Employees suspicious and hostile when faced with imposed change.
Low commitment to the task of data collection and feedback.
Dysfunctional teams lack training and feedback skills.
Appropriate levels and diversity may not be represented.

Concern About Subjectivity of Data

Difficulty in obtaining unbiased data.
Subjectivity from direct involvement.

TABLE 4.3 (continued)

No external resources for objective view.
Political agendas affecting data collection and analysis.

Resource Requirements
Dependent on a high investment of energy and trust.
Takes people away from their primary job.
Can be disruptive and time consuming.

Those who have used ART have found that the benefits are substantial and long-term in building organizational capacity and competency for planning, facilitating, and implementing change. Consultation competencies can help to meet the challenges and reduce conflict and barriers to change. Working through integrated goals and mutual agreements, ART can increase commitment and involvement in a productive and responsive process of organizational discovery and renewal. Action research teaming supports reciprocal, cooperative relationships that encourage continuous learning and integrated change management.

The following case studies illustrate the successful application of action research teaming in two different organizations.

Case Study: Action Learning—Executive Conference

This case involves a large bulk power supply cooperative and a system-wide change effort that took place over five years (Lippitt and Chakiris 1980). This regional organization had the primary purpose to plan, design, construct and operate the necessary power plants and associated transmission facilities to provide its customers with a dependable supply of surplus electricity at the lowest possible cost. As a consumer-owned regional cooperative, this organization provided wholesale power for approximately 120 rural-electric systems and more than one million consumers in the upper-Midwest with a service area of 400,000 square miles including North Dakota, South Dakota, Wyoming, Iowa, Minnesota, Colorado, Montana, and Nebraska.

The cooperative was experiencing a rapid rate of growth in power demands from its customers. Yet the management group knew that the substantial growth in construction of new power generation and transmission capacity would level off, and that rapid growth in employment would also decrease, which it did. This movement from a construction to an operating mode meant that this organization would need to take time to assess its operations and consider the type of organization it should become in the future.

The decision was made to work with an outside resource group to conduct a series of action learning conferences on organization renewal involving the general manager of the cooperative and his nine senior staff members. The management conferences were conducted over a period of three years and involved the manager and his senior staff, the board of directors, and managers from the largest member systems in the cooperative. The conferences were facilitated through the combined efforts of both internal and external resources, with conference agendas agreed upon by all participating parties.

These biannual executive conferences included specific follow-through action completed by internal resources, which involved the general manager, senior staff, and internal professionals with expertise in human resources, finance, law, environmental issues, and operations.

The preconference data collection was conducted with the internal senior consultant administrator, the CEO and his senior staff, and the board. Data-collection methods included one-on-one interviews, survey questionnaires, consensus-type agenda formation with attendees, and an organizational effectiveness survey for all employees.

Prior to the conference, the data collected was analyzed, general issues identified, a feedback report prepared, and the design for the conference submitted to the internal executive administrator who performed this role working with external resources for approval and changes.

The conference design included feedback of the data, interpretation of the data, discussion and validation of the issues, and problem-solving work sessions to confront the data and form new action decisions. This design supported both content and process activities related to strategic planning for change, team development, quality of work life, environment and natural resources of the region, relations with member cooperatives, leadership style, succession planning, employee participation, and productivity.

The purpose of the executive conferences was summarized in four basic objectives:

1. Jointly explore and discuss matters of concern in the data collected prior to the conference. Some of these concerns and issues were generated in one-on-one interviews with the external resources regarding the organization's operations and its future.

2. Learn more about each person's concern and vision for the organization's future.

3. Share ideas and work in cooperation with primary customer members and the board to shape the future of this energy organization and its members.

4. Develop action plans to deal with the general manager's succession and to move forward as an organization with new leadership.

Over a period of three years the organization, through the efforts of the senior group, board, and staff, proactively planned its future direction in the areas of energy, regional resources, and international energy planning. As a result of these efforts and the renewal process taking place, this group decided to move the process down into the organization and involve more people. The decision was made to collect data from all employees and to involve them in feedback, decisions, and action planning.

A survey was used to collect organizational diagnostic data from all employees. Other action-learning instruments were developed to validate the need for "renewal" in board meetings to become more responsive to the needs of the board and senior management as well as members. The results of the audit showed many strengths that employees saw in their organization as well as their desire to produce a quality product and provide quality services to their customers. Areas for development were also expressed through the audit.

Feedback sessions were held with all employees to share the audit results, to facilitate employee interpretation and understanding, and to give employees the opportunity to prioritize those areas requiring future attention. After the feedback session, trained internal facilitators worked with units of the organization to initiate an action-planning process to address the organization-wide concerns identified in the audit. The issues that were identified were communicated to the appropriate level in the organization for resolution.

At the organizational level, nominations were made for the formation of an action research team as an ad hoc task force with broad constituency representation. At the executive level a steering committee of senior staff members addressed the issues identified and the action recommendations provided by the intraunit and interunit task force. The task force consisted of those individuals who had been designated as the contact people for the Human Resource Audit in each of the nine units. The process of implementing the recommendations and monitoring their effectiveness for this effort was facilitated by an appointed internal organization development coordinator.

This organization showed that it had the vision to carry out an ongoing renewal process that addressed both the immediate change occuring in the construction-to-operations shift and the ongoing effect of changes in the environment in which it operated. The renewal process formally started with the senior management group beginning to work together to identify the future of the organization and also to share their perceptions with and to invite ideas from the board of directors and the managers.

The Metrex Human Resource Audit involved all employees in the ongoing renewal process. The emphasis was on helping to prepare the organization to be continually responsive to the changing needs of its customers, constituents, and employees in a rapidly changing environment. Perhaps the most important aspect of the audit was the extent to which the methods of ART involved individuals and temporary resource groups within units and across organizational lines in sharing ideas and working together to initiate the needed change.

Voluntary, trained ad hoc task forces researched the issues and facilitated feedback, decisions, and action both within and between units. At the same time, the ART process built a capacity for employee-involvement processes into the future. ART processes were internalized within this organization with continued use of the methods at the senior level, in working with member organizations, customers, and the board.

Case Study: Action Research Teaming Interventions

The need for organizational change in this case grew largely out of the transition of enforcement authority at a government agency (Lippitt and Chakiris 1981). Every effort was made to ensure a smooth and orderly transition but top management found that even under the best of circumstances, planning and phased transition efforts anticipate the effects of extensive changes on employees.

In this case, change meant the elimination of two large programs, and the shifting of case inventories, backlogs, and files. This also required a myriad of planned personnel transfers and changes inside and outside of the various divisions. Management observed evidence of the traumatic impact on employees.

The shift in work-load priorities and quantities as well as the creation or evolution of new job positions clearly revealed the need for an organizational assessment. The following objectives were established for the action research study:

- Improve the ability of employees to effectively communicate their ideas and influence actions;
- Involve management with employees down through the organizational structure;
- Extend mutual support among coworkers;
- Encourage employee initiative;
- Assess perceptions of organization image;
- Determine the appropriateness of rewards and recognition.

The diversity of functions, administrative structures, and enforcement requirements supported the consultation team's belief that a carefully planned feedback cycling process was critical for achieving a sense of movement and accomplishment based on data from an action research study. They were also aware of a variety of pending changes in regulations that could affect the work priorities and work loads of some of the employees. The changing enforcement climate strongly suggested a need to identify how the organizational climate could be improved to cope with these enforcement changes. The proposed study team brought together professionals with an extremely high level of experience and competence in organizational development, culture, and change facilitation including internal and external change facilitators. This team emphasized four key points related to action research in their discussions with management:

1. There is little value in collecting data unless it is followed up with feedback and action.

2. Data is valuable to management. Clients are unanimous in stating that an accurate picture of employee thinking at a particular time is helpful. Significant information must be gathered for problem solving and future planning.

3. Follow-up is not easy. While planning and administration of a study is relatively easy, planning and follow-up after a study calls for imagination, competence, and dedication.

4. There is no one right way to follow through after a study. There are a number of procedures that work well in government agency settings, but for the most part, each follow-through item needs to be tailored to each office and to specific findings in the study. There is general agreement that a good follow-up pays big dividends in long-term productivity and motivation.

5. Action is what counts. Research and data collection should lead to action. In summary:

To LOOK is one thing,

To SEE what we look at is another,

To UNDERSTAND what we see is a third,

To LEARN from what we understand is still something else,

But to ACT on what we learn is what really pays off.

Management Concerns About Organizational Assessment

There are at least six concerns that usually surface in the administration and interpretation of an assessment or survey. The managers in this organization asked similar questions about the process. The consultation team's comments follow each question.

1. Is this the right time for an organization assessment?

   COMMENT: It is always possible in any organization to find reason for not making a survey "at just this time." The "right" time never arrives, so the assessment is never made.

2. Would our employees show interest in an organizational assessment and take it seriously? Would they reveal their true feelings?

   COMMENT: Experience suggests an unequivocal "yes" to each question. Employees welcome an opportunity to express their ideas and concerns. They generally want to be more involved and informed.

3. Do organizational surveys or audits nurture negative thinking among employees and increase griping?

   COMMENT: Some unfavorable attitudes and some unfavorable conditions may be revealed, of course. This may simply mean that these feelings are situations were present when the survey was made, not that the survey caused them to develop.

4. Will the survey findings upset management personnel?

   COMMENT: Some individuals may be concerned when they learn how their management style is perceived and how their units are viewed by their employees. However, this situation is simply revealed, not caused, by the audit. The supervisor should not be bypassed in planning an organizational assessment. Management should explain the function and purpose of a study or assessment to supervisors in advance of the process.

5. Will we have "a bear by the tail" and find ourselves in an embarrassing situation if, after doing the survey, we are presented with a large number of problems or issues that need attention that we can't give at this time?

   COMMENT: It probably would be better in most instances not to conduct a study than to conduct one and then do nothing about the findings. Do not ask your employees for their ideas unless you are prepared to act on them or to explain why such action cannot be taken.

6. Do audits, assessments, and surveys give an accurate, valid picture of employee attitudes?

   COMMENT: If this question cannot be answered in the affirmative, little value or importance can be attached to any phase of this organizational study. Although surveys contain many questions about other matters, no one pretends that employees are in possession of all the facts. However, the organization needs to learn more about employees' ideas and attitudes. No one else can supply this information, and it is important to the organization since the employee's attitudes can affect work practices and support of change.

ART Intervention Steps

The challenge of this study was to both assess the effectiveness of the organization and to utilize the findings for facilitating improvement efforts based on the survey results and interpretations. The total team operated in the tradition of Lewin's action-research model, as illustrated by the following step-by-step description.

Step 1: Review of documents defining the mission, roles, and responsibilities of people involved, and staff memos providing background on the need for the study.

Step 2: Getting nominations of where to conduct diagnostic group interviews with two or three small groups to "probe" objectives and to collect the concrete data needed to construct a relevant study for the unique needs of this organization. This step resulted in construction of a set of questions in organizational readiness and climate for change. The research team recommended the initial need validation include these areas:

- Readiness for change.
- Assumptions about the consequences of attempts to influence upwards.
- Prevalence of "mandating" versus "persuasion" versus "involvement."
- Values, attitudes, and techniques of influencing downward.
- Norms supporting and restraining peers from asking for and giving one another help and support.
- General attitudes and assumptions about the feasibility of initiating change.
- Other factors critical to knowing not only "how things are in this organization," but also the readiness to be involved in or initiate efforts for continuous improvement, and to team with others in change efforts.

Step 3: In tailoring the study, the team used their insights from the exploratory group interviews in Step 2, knowledge of the effective strategies of involving employees in such an activity, a basic orientation to collecting change-oriented data, and experience with precoding and computer analysis to guarantee efficient and quick turnover of responses. The first draft of the instrument was pretested with a small sample, including a special consultation review by those employees who had collaborated in the group interviews.

Step 4. The administration of the audit was carefully designed to involve the appropriate personnel at each site with face-to-face interpretation of the purposes of the survey and orientation on the ways confidentiality would be protected, the way the data would be summarized, and the opportunity employees would have to participate in the feedback process, interpretation of the data, and the action decisions for the application activities for the continuous-improvement effort.

The consultation team worked with the client to establish an open interactive process for data collection. To get a candid picture of employees' ideas and opinions, some organizations spring questionnaires, audits, and surveys on their employees with no advance notice. They argue that to give notification is to invite collaboration and politicizing among the employees. While recognizing that such things may occur, the advantages of informing the employees of the data-collection activities far outweigh the hazards. Employees tend to get together to discuss job matters whether or not data-collection is planned. The point might even be made that it is helpful for the employees to discuss office matters prior to a survey so that the answers they give are not simply spur-of-the-moment reactions but thoughtful responses. Most organizations give advance notice. One company with a creative internal organization development professional provided short video commercials in the lunchroom several days prior to the administration of the data-collection activity. This created a favorable impression among employees and a high voluntary response rate.

Step 5. The computerized data was converted into small visual modules of results that illustrated different clusters of meaningful findings.

One of the great shortcomings of feedback preparation is to overquantify the results and overload the participants with detailed data charts. Extensive graphs and numbers in typical reports simply do not have the dramatic impact needed to communicate credibility and get involvement in thinking about the data. Data packages were developed to present information in an accurate and complete manner that would be easily understood.

Step 6. Feedback sessions were facilitated for managers to share findings, develop strategies for involvement of subordinates, and generate high-level support to help create a climate of acceptance and ownership. The research team encouraged an interlocking discussion group plan.

Step 7. This step included a sample of probe and prediction interviews. As soon as the main themes of the audit inquiry were clear. The team constructed a probe interview schedule to explore in depth the tentative generalizations and hunches about motivation, readiness for change effort, and other issues that were indicated. A 10 percent proportional sample was utilized on an individual, and group-interview basis. These prediction interviews were useful in preparing managers for the total report feedback process.

Step 8. The appropriate groups and designs for feedback sessions were developed to facilitate movement toward nondefensive openness to the implications of desired change and create motivation to participate in change efforts.

The external team's research on motivation indicated that presenting data with polished interpretations of the meaning and implications of the data is a serious trap. The employees in feedback sessions, regardless of level, must be involved in interpreting the finding, and in brainstorming the implications for possible actions to improve their situations and productivity. The design and leadership of these sessions is one of the most crucial factors in determining whether the organization and its employees will get a payoff from the investment of time and financial resources.

Step 9. After the involvement of employees in an analysis of the implications for improvement and indications of readiness to change, the next step was to review the results of their feedback-sessions with top management. This provided an opportunity to clarify strategies for using these results to quickly and appropriately support, authorize, and delegate the improvement efforts with new procedures, modified rules and regulations, or communication initiatives. Close teamwork with top management was designed as part of each step. Working as an outside resource, the resource group knew it was important to team with the appropriate internal staff persons so that competencies could be transferred to the client system to ensure follow-through momentum. Clients used change management tools to assist in challenge definition, role, and goal clarification for action planning.

Step 10. The final report was then delivered to designated officials. This report included a capsule summary and a detailed summary of the findings, analysis, interpretation, feedback comments and recommendations, and follow-up suggestions. The outside resources working with the internal team are responsible for submitting the report. Continuity is also discussed with emphasis on the sustained involvement of a cross-section of the employees and managers who will facilitate follow-up and motivation for action.

This 10-step process ensures that the objectives of the action research in an organizational study are met as comprehensively and as professionally as possible based upon the needs of the client to conduct the survey, interpret the results, report and feedback these results, and take action.

CHALLENGES FOR ACTION RESEARCH TEAMING

Experience with many ART projects has helped us to be sensitive to several potential challenges that can reduce the effectiveness of collaborative inquiry, feedback, and action-taking projects. The following recommendations can help to create more effective action research teaming processes:

1. Involve top administration in the rationale, plans, and reviews of procedures.

2. Initiate a grassroots discussion with select respondents from all levels of the organization to collect the "scouting data" needed to adequately prepare the survey and feedback procedures.

3. Combine the conceptual value and results of previous action research projects with the comparative properties of data collected from many subunits.

4. Facilitate agreement on communications from management to sanction and support the survey, before administration, and a statement of commitment to use the findings.

5. Clarify the policies on confidentiality and feedback to each participant at the time of the audit or assessment.

6. Determine management's willingness to understand, and to respond positively and nondefensively to the feedback results.

7. Provide how-to support to develop clear action steps from the findings.

ART provides a context for quality consultation in which the change management teams intentionally form strategic and interdependent relationships with constituents throughout the client system. If teams want to be successful, they must have a recognized need for change, a systematic data-collection process to diagnose needs, challenges, and opportunities, set goals, and develop action plans to achieve those goals. ART activities give people the capability to form strong relationships that produce a high level of performance results within the organization. These partnerships work most effectively when reciprocal influence rather than weighted authority determines the relationship.

ART is a strategic process, and a cooperative relationship to help the facilitating system and the client system work together to build the organization's capacity for managing change and achieving results. As a process it consists of a systematic collection of data relative to a challenge, need, or opportunity, and feeding that data back into the system, taking action, and measuring the results of these actions by collecting more data. The measuring and monitoring of each action yields data for planning the next action. There is a high degree of continuous learning that benefits the individual, group, and organization and other stakeholders in dealing with complex and continuing change that affects their collective future.

PART II

A Context
for
Integrated Change

5

Need and Opportunity in Change Initiatives

Change can be initiated by executives, managers, team leaders, advisory group members, or resource professionals who come together in various contexts to discuss specific needs and opportunities. The situation may be ambiguous because roles are not defined, goals are unclear, expectations are too high, resources are limited, and change perspectives are conflicting. These are the challenges for the startup of change management as people join together to accomplish what they cannot do alone.

The need for change may not be as dramatic as the "near-death" experience of Xerox, which moved from over 90 percent of market share to less than 15 percent. However, as the change facilitators at Xerox attest, pain and crisis are often a necessary part of large system change (Kearns and Nadler 1992). At Xerox, much of the need and change initiative came out of organizational difficulties created by past decisions and actions. At General Electric, change began with the vision and power of a CEO who called for a "revolution" against an inefficient bureaucracy (Tichy and Sherman 1993). Change initiatives also come from the "demand system" (Beckhard and Harris 1987) in the consumer market and the economic and social environment outside the organization. For some experts, the forces that bring change can be reduced to the "Big Three": the relationship between the organization and its environment; organic growth through the organizational lifecycle; and the political struggle for power within the organization (Kanter, Stein, and Jick 1992).

Change is affected by the traditions, values, and rules inside the system as well as external events over a period of time. Change encompasses past, present, and future. Part of the change initiative lies in recognizing and acknowledging problems and opportunities in the present and linking them to the past events, and applying that experience and learning to the future. The difficulties and stress in moving from the present to the future may not be fully realized in the initial stage of the change initiative. The challenge is in getting from here to there. Beckhard and Harris (1987) describe three stages in the change process: the present state, the future state, and the transition state in moving from one to the other. In identifying needs and opportunities for change, it is important to think and plan in relation to all three perspectives. Leaders, managers, and organization members should consider these questions: What do we want our future to be? How much choice and influence will we have in creating our collective future in the present? Where are the gaps in our performance and knowledge? What will happen in the transition period to move us from the present toward the future?

Planning for and managing change requires a variety of consultation competencies to build on the change initiative. The major skills for managers and consultation teams at the change-initiative phase are:

- Free-flow open communication
- Shared facilitation and leadership
- Clear purpose and self-identity
- Starting where people are
- Capacity to understand change resistance and acceptance
- Recognition of the impact of ongoing directed and nondirected change processes
- Strategy, theory, and experience base
- Diagnostic competence in validating need
- Business skills
- Technical knowledge

This chapter will review the basic activities and decisions in Phase 1 of the six-phase change-consultation process. The initiative process can be summarized in four general areas: 1) recognizing the need, 2) developing relationships, 3) gathering initial data, and 4) making entry.

RECOGNIZING THE NEED

The first step in initiating change is recognizing the need for change. Part of change initiative involves "enactment" (Weick 1979) in paying attention to the current organizational situation, seeing what might not have been noticed before, or interpreting organizational practices and structures in new ways. This awareness can be the beginning of effective change management. For example, people at the front lines of customer service or production have valuable knowledge and understanding of the day-to-day workings of the system. They see needs and opportunities that senior management may ignore or overlook. Much of this knowledge and insight is at the nondirected level and not integrated with formal directed-change efforts.

This story illustrates the gap between formal and informal organizational intelligence: After a 1980 shareholders meeting at which the president of Xerox made a report on major problems with a new copier and the resulting recall, a factory worker walked up to the president and said, "Why didn't you ask us what we thought about it? We could have told you it was a piece of junk" (Kearns and Nadler 1992). This was the beginning of many insights for Xerox management as they "reinvented" their organization through benchmarking, total quality management, and teamwork. Entrepreneurship and change management can be fostered among employees. The discovery of the resources and knowledge of employees, customers, and suppliers can fuel a change initiative with new information, insight, and energy.

Since change is a continuous and often contradictory process within complex systems, the beginning of change might be a rumble in the collective thinking of the organization, resonating from the nondirected level. Because so many aspects of the organization are based in institutionalized routines and habitual responses, opportunities to anticipate, plan, influence, and implement change are sometimes missed or ignored. Pain and acute symptoms often are necessary to bring attention to these problems and opportunities and encourage a change initiative.

This initiative could be focused at the directed level in a desire to solve a problem, to identify specific challenges, and to respond to new opportunities for change. Yet organizations don't always learn from past experiences or transfer knowledge and skills to other parts of the system. All change involves some significant learning in understanding the contradictions and complexity in an ongoing strategic development process. In change management, the client system learns to identify needs and opportunities, plan for and manage change, and transfer these competencies to new situations. Through effective consultation, the client, managers, and the consultation team learn together, beginning with the identification and understanding of change initiatives and how these relate to the past, present, and future of the organization.

The learning process starts when people in the unit or the organization acknowledge that they have a need to facilitate change or renewal. Whether they focus on evidence of homeostatic imbalance in the system or the feeling of an uncomfortable dissonance in the individual or group mind, this disequilibrium or perceived incongruity on the part of the individual, the group, or the organization often creates a change initiative. In a sense, there needs to be some constructive dissatisfaction and an acknowledged need for improvement.

Out of this situation comes the momentum to get data to find out what is causing poor quality, reduced productivity, or lack of responsiveness to community and market needs. The most important motivation is often the future and the survival of the organization (G. Lippitt 1982). This realization and data collection help to focus the task forces and action research teams as they start working on crucial issues and needs that affect the total system.

Systems Approaches to Change Initiatives

Successful change management recognizes the organization as an entire system. When directed change is introduced into one unit, the whole system may be affected on both a formal and a nondirected level. The consultation team, client, and the managers involved should be aware of the potential impact of change in relation to the architecture and culture of the entire organization. Teamwork is also essential in a systems approach to change initiatives. Asking others to help facilitate change should be perceived as a strength and not a weakness. "Putting the right heads together" (Lippitt 1979) invites the formation of ad hoc groups or loosely federated units that integrate experience, interests, and skill competence in multiunit, multidiscipline, and multinational connections to facilitate change throughout the system.

Mink, Schultz, and Mink (1979) describe the system in its "healthiest" state as a unified, responsive "open organization." Initiatives toward this model may focus on second-order change in a fundamental reorientation that builds on organizational strengths and core values. Second-order change management often requires the resources of outside change facilitators with a different, more objective perspective to work with internal groups.

An inside and outside consultation team is most effective when bringing about a systems change as each member brings unique skills and perspectives to the relationship. External resources contribute a specific expertise, competence, or technology to the client system while internal resources bring an understanding of the needs, culture, and relationships within the organization, community, or country. The depth of an internal view blended with the broader external view creates the best leverage for diagnosis and planned change initiatives.

Organizational problems do not stand alone but exist in a larger interactive context in a process of continuing change. This approach to change management avoids a superficial response to change that deals only with reducing symptoms and handling the crisis of the moment. All actions and parts of the system are seen in context of interdependent political, cultural, and economic relationships that make up the organization. From this perspective, organization leaders, managers, and consultation teams can anticipate the effect of any action on the whole system. They can be more sensitive to the support and resistance that may be present in the organization relative to any project or directed change and avoid blind spots or nearsightedness in change initiatives and planning.

Client Perspectives on Need

The initiative to explore change management projects and identify needs often involves a discussion between the client and consultation team, which may include managers and staff professionals to identify needs. Client change initiatives often target one or more of the following objectives:

- Improve customer service
- Increase employee satisfaction and commitment
- Achieve total quality
- Maintain continuous improvement
- Develop service strategy
- Respond to competitive challenge
- Improve return on shareholder equity
- Assess and improve community image
- Increase market share
- Encourage innovation and creativity
- Develop technology and manufacturing strategy
- Improve new product-development cycle
- Improve marketing and sales strategies
- Develop leadership skills throughout the system
- Increase teamwork and coordination across units
- Improve communication and feedback channels
- Implement career-development programs

Content and Process Focus

It is also important to assess the change initiative along a continuum from content focus to process focus. This perspective helps to identify specific factors within the organizational culture, which can affect the decisions, roles, and relationships at the directed and nondirected level. Change management requires both content competencies and process skills for managers, change facilitators, and consultation teams.

FIGURE 5.1 Dimensions of Change Initiative.

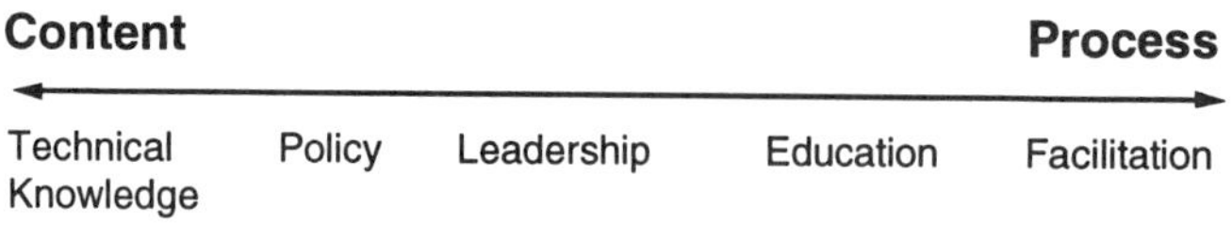

Content   **Process**

Technical   Policy   Leadership   Education   Facilitation
Knowledge

Content competencies may include areas such as manufacturing technology, policies related to obsolescence, and continuing training and education. Process skills build competence in areas of facilitation, relationship, influence, innovation, and feedback. The initiative depends on client need, organizational context and culture, the competencies of the consultation team, and other resources. The continuum in Figure 5.1 illustrates the dimensions of the change initiative from technical content to process facilitation. These include technical knowledge, policy, leadership, education, and facilitation.

Technical knowledge involves the underlying structure of the organization in relation to products and services, procedures, environmental data, budgets, and specialized knowledge. This establishes the critical information base of the organization and provides material and intellectual resources for change.

Policy supports the ethical and legal concerns related to formal and informal agreements that affect how change initiatives are made based on organizational data and knowledge. The overall values, philosophy, and beliefs of the organization also impact actions and decisions related to change. Issues of justice and fairness must be considered as well as compliance with rules and regulations. International and global alliances and joint ventures also bring additional information, responsibility, and obligation at the policy level.

Leadership by management, boards, staff professionals, and consultation teams is the point of decision and balance between content and process in change initiatives. Relationships are determined by the way authority, hierarchy, and accountability are interpreted and applied. There are opportunities for involvement, delegation, and self-directed efforts in the change initiative. Coordination is also a factor in integrating and practicing leadership skills at many levels.

Education through continuous collective learning transfers competencies to the client system. This process involves knowledge, understanding, skills, and experience acquired through stages of development and growth. Education and training help to increase total resource utilization through teamwork and collaborative inquiry, which helps integrate content and process in change management.

In *facilitation,* the emphasis is on building relationships and helping people to initiate change and learn together with trust and acceptance. Change facilitators use influence rather than control. Effective facilitation can increase the acceptance of change and involve people throughout the system in continuous improvement with individual, group, and organizational learning.

DEVELOPING RELATIONSHIPS

The start of the consultation relationship begins with needs or perceived opportunities. Either the client, sponsor, or a third-party resource facilitator can initiate the process. The awareness of need or opportunity for change often encourages the client to seek help from resources within or outside the unit or the organization.

The initiative phase may include a myriad of events, activities, and processes all taking place at a current point in time or perhaps extended into the long and sometimes painful transition period in moving toward the future. The initial phase of change consultation and start-up relationships are usually fraught with concerns that things are moving too fast or too slow. Many managers and organization members are not comfortable with the ambiguity of what is going to happen. This can create unrealistic expectations that cannot be accomplished. The consultation team or action-research teams may not be adequately legitimized by the client or sponsor. Individuals and groups throughout the system may be concerned about their roles. Some may feel anxiety because they don't know how the change initiative will affect their job and security.

Making the initial decision to begin the process of change management may be difficult for leaders, boards, and senior management. This decision means that the organization must make a commitment to change and that leaders must examine their own ideas about structure, power relationships, objectives, authority, and teamwork. Often organizations seek outside help in complex systems change and this too requires a new kind of teamwork. The following paragraphs illustrate these concerns in an internal dialogue by a senior vice president of a diversified manufacturing and service organization as she prepares to meet with an outside consultation team to discuss major directed change initiatives.

> *I'm doing my job well. After all, doesn't my working on everything myself continue to strengthen my image that I can lead this company into its future? I'm headed for a top position in a few years. And isn't it true that when you work with another person it may imply*

weakness? Asking for help may make it look like I don't have my act together?

How will others view the risk and budgeting investment of paying for these outside change facilitators? Besides losing control, professional resources don't come free. There's the cost of consultation fees, materials, and travel. Then there is the loss of my time and energy in working with outside people, sitting in meetings, getting prepared for their visits, reviewing data, having them move too fast for our executive group, and involving our employees, customers, and suppliers. Am I really ready for all of this with my current work schedule and responsibilities?

Am I really certain that this consultation group is the one to do the job? It's true they come highly recommended and I basically liked what I heard at the last executive committee meeting when they presented a possible two-to-five-year plan for our organization. But have we sufficiently explored other resource people? Are we certain that the whole project can't be done by an internal resource group or by staff?

Wait a moment—what am I thinking? This change consultation could produce some significant results for us! This team has had impressive successes in helping other organizations with similar challenges and issues. And I liked their approach of transferring competencies, involving our people, and training them in the research techniques and methods for change and not creating dependency. Besides, I'm convinced some of the data to be collected will be too sensitive for our internal staff to coordinate. In fact my preference would be to have an objective outside perspective from the beginning.

We should not limit our growth and development in change management. Maybe I need to put aside my negative thinking and consider the importance of this opportunity. The need at this time in our organization is to increase our local and global marketing. It seems that our purposes are clear and there are sufficient reasons for me to explore a working relationship with this change-consultation group. Their firm comes highly recommended by our key supplier and the two partners have technical competency, background, and experience to match the needs we expressed at our last strategic planning session to facilitate our company into the position of industry leader by the year 2000 and build markets for the next decade. I think this change consultation may help us reach our goals.

Whether the change management team is composed of internal or external resources, the dilemmas are similar. There are often issues related to power and authority. Hostility, anxiety, and readiness for change must be carefully assessed. Appropriate timing for change efforts should also be considered. Open access to data and the opportunities to gather information without creating defensiveness depend on the amount of trust and cooperation in the relationship. This foundation is established during the initiative phase.

Change facilitators must establish credibility without accepting the role of "expert" that many client systems want to impose. This role requires legitimization by the client and key sponsors and involvement of people throughout the system. However, the client system must feel it is alright and not a sign of weakness to ask for help and use external resources or managers outside their unit or area. These role relationships are affected by the client's experience, both positive and negative, of working with outside resources and the degree of openness and trust. Aspects of counterdependency or dependency versus interdependency should also be resolved. The client system and change facilitators must perceive that they can work together effectively. In this phase, the facilitating group begins to establish rapport with the unit, department, or organization that is the client system. The competencies of establishing roles and relationships in a change initiative include:

- Establishing rapport and credibility
- Developing trust and openness
- Identifying stakeholders
- Involving key players
- Creating clear expectations
- Reducing unrealistic dependency

A major part of entry is the getting-to-know-you stage. The focus is toward greater comfort with the client, consultation team, and the situation. The client has the authority to make the decision. The consultation team must work with and through others using influence rather than authority. A challenge for the consultation team may be to use dual and multiple entry to avoid being trapped into a "special relationship" with only one subgroup, which could make it difficult to work with other subgroups.

The consultation team and client should share values, strategies, and conceptual frameworks to develop a working theory upfront prior to the project plans being established. This information can include both the perspective of the client and the consultation resources about: learning design, approach to intervention, methods of data collection, use of action learning, application techniques and procedures, as well as overall change-consultation approaches. More specific discussion might focus on preferred work style, success criteria, personal motivation and career interests, and values related to forming a cooperative task relationship for action research.

The initial work plan documents role responsibility, method or approach to achieve predicted outcomes, expectations, required resources, progress milestones, and periodic feedback between client, consultation team, and sponsor for continuous development of the collaborative relationship throughout the change management process.

GATHERING INITIAL DATA

Data-based change and action research teaming (ART) help organization members to understand the change initiative as they define the problem, see the need for change, and identify initial directions. This data also provides a basis for measuring and benchmarking results and showing progress over time. Part of the commitment of the client toward change is in setting specific goals and outcomes that must be defined at the beginning of the consultation process so that there is a basis for continuing measurement and performance evaluation.

Intelligence gathering and a preliminary diagnosis of the system helps a change management team to learn about the organization. This data helps explain structure, history, mission, markets, culture, and leadership, as well as current programs and challenges. Information gathering leads to a more results-oriented process focused on specific performance measures and outcomes.

Diagnostic Skills

A high level of competence in diagnostic skills is required for the change-initiative phase to verify the readiness of both the client system and facilitating system to validate the need. This diagnosis also helps to determine the actual client, assess different levels of readiness, and consider the micro and macroperspectives toward change. The change management team must also determine appropriate methods for data gathering to provide useful information and decide how to give and receive feedback relating to the relationship and the objectives of the directed effort.

In order to identify issues and goals and to clarify the need for change, the consultation team facilitates inquiry to uncover and validate issues and to match need with the appropriate resources. Use of initial data-collection methods, such as interviews to explore issues with management and employees can help isolate and broaden perspectives of need and target concerns and opportunities.

The initial task for the change initiative is to collect sufficient data to determine whether the client, client system, and sponsor-role relationship will work effectively to benefit all parties and coordinate specific results for the organization.

Helping to identify and clarify the need for change requires some exploration of the culture, norms and practices of the client system. Sometimes surveys are used to obtain data. Other approaches may include individual or group interviews. It is important that the consultation team be experienced in listening, probing, and providing feedback at this phase. Inside change facilitators have the advantage in this situation with their insight and experience with the system, although outside resources can be more objective and may bring broader experience and knowledge.

The personalities of the people involved as well as their professionalism, ultimate goals, and values all contribute to the success of consultation relationships. The facilitating system and the client system may "test" each other to speculate on the mutual gains and losses of working together. Change management resources are often invited in to bring about a directed change, solve a problem, or take advantage of an opportunity. Part of the initial task is to make sure that the situation is clearly defined. This is a crucial test for all parties in achieving overall success in change management.

Scouting Activities

Prior to initiating contact and entry, the change facilitators should do some "scouting" (Lippitt, Hooyman, Sashkin, Kaplan, 1978). This means gathering information about the client system in order to make an informed decision about matching resources to need, learning about values, judging whether sufficient resources are available, and determining whether consultation services would be appropriate. During the scouting phase of consultation both the client and the change facilitators are deciding whether they want to work together. Information collected on the organization during the scouting phase will be validated later during the diagnostic phase of consultation.

Our view is that change consultation requires an investment of time prior to contracting. A compromise can be to initiate a trial period when both parties agree to work together to determine whether they will make a continuing commitment. Some caution should be exercised when using this approach since the learning and impact of change management occurs over a longer period. Thus the shorter time may not be perceived as effective even though the milestones in an extended timeframe would be recognized as significant accomplishments toward the desired results.

Ideally, both client system and facilitating system have a history of working together and have learned realistic patterns of effectiveness in accomplishing results. However, organizations today are caught in accelerated change in both career and role relationships, providing a continuing challenge for new clients, resources, and sponsors. "Checking out" all parties, both those who accept the change and those who may resist or reject the change, is essential during this scouting phase. To be effective, the consultation team and the client should identify roles, functions, and power relationships in the formal and informal structure, and the important linkage or entry points to assess change readiness and to gain appropriate ownership. The information needs and sources for the change initiative are summarized in Table 5.1.

TABLE 5.1 Scouting Inventory.

Information Needs

Client needs and desired outcome

Business dynamics related to decision makers, current issues

Relationship with suppliers, competitors, customers, community

Competitive resourcing for budget decisions

Current programs, services, systems

Historical data regarding change implementation

Past success criteria when change was accepted or rejected

Power structure and career movement of both client and sponsor

Critical challenges of the organization or business unit

Organization measurement and reward system in use

Resources that will be available during consultation

Intraunit and interunit effectiveness

Quality strategy and client motivation for continuous improvement

Information Sources

Dialogue about entry, approaches, and individual thinking

Discussions with client, sponsor, employees, and colleagues

Documents on plans for the unit and organization

Measurement from the perspective of financial, quality, customer, human
    resources, and suppliers

Performance criteria for organization, unit, and individual

Structure of formal and informal role relationship, power, and authority

Publications: annual report, newsletter, catalogs, and training brochures

Studies of training need validation, benchmarking, and productivity

---

Once the initial scouting and information gathering has been completed and the data has been studied, the change consultation group is ready to make a formal entry into the client system.

MAKING ENTRY

Entry is defined as the situation faced by a change facilitator or consultation team and a client when they first try to enter into a consultation relationship. The goal is to move toward optimal entry with clarity and congruency about need and role perception (Glidewell, 1959). Table 5.2 illustrates the basic types of entry into a client system based on Glidewell's hierarchy.

TABLE 5.2 Entry Hierarchy.
congruent need and role perception
congruent need perception (agreement on need)
trial entry observation phase (let's see how we do)
entry in the dark (reasons, roles, needs not clear)
entry in conflict (moving into a conflict situation between two parties)

Change facilitators may be human-resource professionals entering a unit, a manager in one department working with managers in other departments, or external resources participating as part of an internal-external change management team. Entry into a "conflict" situation between individuals, groups, or units can be difficult and ultimately fail because of the underlying political agendas related to change. Entry "in the dark" requires data collection and information to illuminate the context, needs, and expectations. The "trial entry" may be useful in some situations, but should not be the norm. It is not enough to agree on need; both needs and roles should be clear in an optimal entry.

Types of Entry

It is essential to assess organizational entry dynamics and determine the level of commitment for both the client system and the facilitating system to explore the readiness for change, to determine level of resources needed, including time, energy, technology, human resources, structural, and financial resources for change management.

There are three ways in which the consultation team might come into the client system: 1) self-initiated entry, 2) invited in by the client, and 3) imposed by another person. In some cases the potential client may seek out a facilitator or resource to help the client system move toward a desired future. In another instance, staff professionals and change facilitators may approach a potential client to market consultation services related to a particular skill or competence. A third party such as a manager or a former client also may connect the client and the resource group. When imposed as a third party, the consultation need is usually mandated by a sponsor, often a senior executive, who perceives the problem or opportunity and brings in a change facilitator or consultation resources to work with a specific client.

Whether the consultation team consists of inside or outside people or a combination of both can affect the contact and entry. Inside change facilitators may have difficulties marketing their services internally. An outside resource may have some objective advantage and expert credibility, although entering into the situation can be more difficult for an external facilitator. Open honest communication is critical. Both the client and the consultation teams have to explore their potential relationship and see if they want to work together.

From the perspective of the change facilitator, some of the decisions about this working relationship can be clarified through these questions:

- Are we a good match?
- Can we work with this client and this unit or organization?
- Can we build rapport?
- What are the stated needs? Other hidden needs?
- Is the client and client system ready for change?
- What is the level of commitment and motivation for change?
- What are the goals? Are these goals clear?
- What commitment is evident from senior management?
- Who will make the action decisions?
- Are there other influencers?
- Are expectations for change realistic?
- Are there shared values about change?

Each party tests the potential for working together and discusses issues related to openness, trust, role and goal clarity, values, realistic expectations, dependency, and interdependency. It is important for the internal resources to maintain some separation between their internal position and their role as a change facilitator. Establishing a balance of objectivity between the client and the facilitation team is essential for effective change consultation. The facilitation team openly discusses values with the client, but remains independent and neither party imposes its values on the other (Argyris 1970).

Consultation Teaming in Change Initiatives

Teaming with mutual and recipient influence between the facilitating system and the client system is the most effective way to approach change management. People report that they are more receptive to change when they feel strong; trust in the influencing person, group, and system; are in a collaborative, rather than a competitive climate; are encouraged to confront rather than avoid issues; and are rewarded for goal-oriented thinking and behavior. Team learning in a responsive interdependent system can give a sense of achievement and strengthen individual and group capability for managing change.

When bringing about a systems change, an internal and external consultation team can be the strongest combination because internal resources will bring firsthand knowledge of the culture of the organization as well as information about the informal communication, relationship channels, and power networks. Internal facilitators provide inside coordination to the consultation effort. This can facilitate the transfer of the technology, skills, and processes for future use by the organization. External resources bring objectivity and a detached focus, which can place perspective on the experiences and information of the client system. By working together, the internal-external team can more effectively build capacity and continuity for change. However, all parties should be concerned when the client or sponsors have high expectations that may verge on unrealistic goals or inappropriate dependency.

Together an inside-outside team can collaborate to bring about understanding, insight, new approaches and energy not possible for either group alone. The dynamics of an internal-external consultation team develops the capacity to manage change on both a directed and nondirected level. The external facilitator is not bound by the group norms and conceptual biases of the client organization, and can help the client system to discover solutions that transcend "home-bound" thinking. The inside resources also provide the vital continuity and consistent effort to sustain and extend change management competencies. The use of an integrated consultation team is a strategic force for effective change management.

The facilitating team must also be aware of the "customer" for the change initiative. The customer may be an individual or a group which may include the client or sponsor evaluator. Internal or external to the organization, customers are usually an extension of the client system and users of the client's services or products. Inside change facilitators serving an internal customer have distinct advantages such as knowing the "cast of characters" and the operative values of the organization, the jargon and language of different units, as well as the cultural background, norms, and political realities better than someone from the outside. Internal facilitators know more about potential linkage with other parts of the organization. However, these managers and professionals may lack a power base and not be seen as a potential resource in their own organization. They may also be perceived as being available to devote more time to a program because of accessibility, location, and cost.

Sometimes the internal facilitator as well as the client may be part of the problem with vested interests, political obligations, long-term relationships, and career implications that are difficult to ignore. Internal resources are usually connected with the system's needs, pains, and aspirations. Thus, they may lack perspective and not want to take risks because they have to live with the results. Internal facilitators may lack the specific skills competence, knowledge, or objectivity required and need additional support and outside resources, for system-wide change management.

The external change facilitator who may be external to the organization or external to the specific unit receiving the consultation services, is usually perceived as having more initial influence with the client system. Clients tend to be more open with this person about concerns and issues. External facilitators have more varied experiences and resources, and provide a broader perspective with objectivity because they are independent of the power structure. Pay and continued use of their consultation is usually tied to results. They can leave the situation when the consultation is complete, and choose not to work on a particular consulting assignment. While internal resources may turn down questionable assignments, they run some risk unless they can convince the client that the timing is off or the resources are not adequate. They may also try to reframe the project in a more realistic way.

It is evident that in a system-wide change project, an inside-outside consultation team offers a number of advantages. The internal person knows the language of the client system and the political realities better, but external resources often are more respected as a content or technical expert who can help link resources. Together, the internal and external team compensate for each other's strengths and weaknesses. In order to keep the change effort on the beam even after the consultation teams' official role ends, it is imperative to have an internal team that can maintain the new structures, roles, or processes and generally take over the functions of the external resource. This helps to integrate directed and nondirected change as part of a continuing process of learning and development.

Internal Consultation Teams Among Business Units

To initiate change in identifying challenges and concerns and take advantage of opportunities, the internal change facilitation team of managers and staff professionals establishes a voluntary role relationship with leaders or staff professionals in the unit or organization needing services. In this relationship, the consultation team acts as a collaborative resource to the client system in a temporary relationship related to a project or issue.

A psychological "outsider" posture is essential to those who practice consultation activities and processes within their own organization, including personnel from human resources, organizational development, marketing, quality control, manufacturing, finance, customer relations, and information services. They must maintain some objectivity and not be caught in the politics and personal agendas. Like the external change facilitator, managers and internal professionals need a high level of consultation competence to work effectively with business unit leaders to achieve results.

Ultimately, the goal is to build client capacity for change management. Consultation roles to support this process include roles as advocate, technical expert, trainer/educator and mentor, collaborative problem solver, action research teaming (ART) facilitator, collaborative inquirer, and process specialist. At entry, clients often expect the consultation team to perform the role of expert, advocate, and teacher in telling them what to do and controlling the relationship and the process. This can create an unequal dependent relationship. The team should move to a more interdependent capacity taking the roles of facilitator and process observer to build competency in the client system for change management.

Entry Activities

In designing entry activities the consultation team conducts interviews with the client, sponsor, and other resources. They can gather information at all levels and across the organization. Phone discussions, conference calls, computers, fax, mail, and courier exchanges also facilitate data collection. On-site visits to the business location of the resource group may be helpful. The external consultation team also could design an event such as a showcase or pilot to make a trial entry and market their services.

It is important to prepare for an entry meeting by proposing and agreeing on an agenda. The consultation group should know the people who will be attending by their proper names and functional titles. They might match the list of names with individual perspectives toward change and expectations of outcome. The facilitator should also check the physical location and facility layout to insure that it is comfortable, quiet, and properly equipped for presentation and discussion with members of the client system.

TABLE 5.3 Targets of Entry.

Goals

Ambiguity, unclear goals for working together					Clear goals and consensus
	1	2	3	4	5

Roles

Unclear mix of roles to be performed	1	2	3	4	5	Clear roles

Trust

Low trust	1	2	3	4	5	High trust

Expectations

Very high or low expectations of help	1	2	3	4	5	Realistic expectations of help

Dependence

Dependence or counterdependence	1	2	3	4	5	Interdependence

Sponsorship

Unclear or low sponsor linkage	1	2	3	4	5	Multilevel sponsor linkage

Adapted from *Consulting Process in Action Skills Development Kit*. By Gordon L. Lippitt, Ronald Lippitt, B. J. Chakiris and Robert W. Pirsein. 1978. B. J. Chakiris Corporation.

Targets of Entry

The targets of entry shown in Table 5.3 can help both internal and external change facilitators to assess the success of consultation activities in understanding change initiative and exploring a working relationship with a client. Ultimately the goal of entry would be to progress from the left to the right on the scales—to move from ambiguity to clear goals, from low trust to high trust, and from inappropriate expectations to realistic expectations.

Entry activities for the consultation team include the following outcomes:

- Analyze need and readiness for change;
- Assess diagnostic interest and available data;
- Determine how the consultation team is perceived;
- Familiarize client and sponsor with consultation resources;
- Develop an early concept of who should be involved;
- Establish rapport, trust, and openness;
- Develop role and goal clarity, and sponsor linkage;
- Anticipate next steps of action, including making an agreement.

Diagnostic Questionnaire for Entry

The questions appearing in Table 5.4 represent the types of information needed to prepare for an entry inquiry discussion between the client and the change consultation team.

TABLE 5.4 Diagnostic Questionnaire for Entry.

Need-Entry Dynamics

What type of entry is this: Invited? Imposed? Self-initiated?

How will the initial contact occur: Phone call? Letter? Personal contact? Third party?

What objectives and agenda are required for the initial meeting?

How does the client indicate the need for change?

Is the potential client clear about need?

Will data be collected to validate this need?

Are specific services, programs, or processes appropriate for discussion?

Does client know about significant directed organization changes in the past? Present? Future?

In what ways will consultation contribute to the goals of the client system?

What change theories are operating? Rational behavioral? Systems? Cultural interpretive? Critical humanism? Is there a dominant perspective?

Are there organizational studies or reports to review related to current or past directed change?

Is high-level design required? Is design time billable?

Are client resources available?

(continued)

TABLE 5.4 (continued)

What need is articulated and by whom?

When did the need became known? How can the need be validated?

Roles

Who is the initial client? Eventual client? Sponsor?

Who is the potential sponsor who will need to sign off on the contract?

How will the consultation team establish trust, confidence, and legitimize themselves as a viable resource?

What is the client's positive and negative experience working with consultation?

What perception exists regarding consultation? By the client? Sponsor? Client system?

What selection criteria will be used to choose resources?

Will this be done by the client? By the consultation team?

Do all parties perceive benefits from the relationship?

What are the desired roles for effective change management?

How comfortable and open are the parties with each other?

Are there any hidden agendas?

Results

Based on the annual report, what specific strategy, values, and performance measurements can be identified?

What are the critical challenges for change identified for this client and client system?

How will the change management be positioned as a strategic business investment?

What are the boundaries for change given the goals and resources available?

What unit of organization would most benefit ? Why?

Has the client discussed success criteria for change outcomes?

What strategic advantage will change consultation provide the client and organization?

Are financial resources available?

What client budget and time will be needed for this proposed change initiative?

What are the client requirements for achieving results?

Does the project outcome contradict some other goal?

How will directed and nondirected change be integrated?

Are there differences in expectations for results? How can these be clarified?

(continued)

TABLE 5.4 (continued)

Role Relationship

How can the level of commitment to change be tested? From the client?
   Sponsor? Other key players?

How will the client and sponsor be involved in the process?

Who beyond the client will be needed for buy-in, approval, and
   commitment?

Are client and sponsor expectations realistic given the time perspective?

How accessible is the essential data?

Who needs to be involved in data collection?

What motivation exists for the client? Consultation team? Sponsor?

How does the client view roles? For client? For consultation resources?

How appropriate are these roles? Should the consultation group redefine the
   roles?

Are there some initial concerns about the relationship?

Does the relationship reflect shared values?

What are the client's career goals?

What linkage is required with the internal consultation team? Sponsor?
   Client system?

What are the client's requirements?

What contract procedure exists? Competitive or single sourcing?

How might internal and external resources be involved?

What is the proposal format?

What selection criteria will be used by the client? By the consultation team?

Will the client's performance goals become known during the entry
   discussion?

Culture

How can both parties identify reward expectations?

What other directed changes are going on at this time in the client system?

Is entry timing appropriate?

What is the readiness for change?

Are there any client concerns related to power, control, or structure?

How will shared power be facilitated?

What are the forces that favor or impede successful outcomes?

What participation will be required for effective change management?

In what areas is action research teaming appropriate?

What is the current level of participation in the system?

Dialogue around these questions helps the consultation team to understand the major elements in change initiative dynamics. Consultation has the

capacity to coordinate a high-level relationship that is temporary, voluntary, and interdependent, providing value to those parties who agree to work together to manage change. A number of areas should be considered: entry and legitimization, openness and trust, need and expectation, dependency and interdependency, and power and authority. The change facilitator or consultation team must establish credibility and show competence during the initial entry. Yet they must avoid the traps and authority position that could create dependency and conflict in the client system.

Many of the most important questions center around commitment and readiness for change. These involve some self-analysis and reflection on the part of the consultation group and the client as they explore processes and relationships that will be most acceptable and appropriate as they work together to build capacity for change management. The performance goals for both the client and the consultation team are significant in relation to their own career goals and professional development. Through cooperative inquiry and team learning, the individual, group, and organization can generate clear, integrated change initiatives to meet strategic goals.

6

Agreements: Establishing Working Relationships

Your client is talking about some unexpected responses to the new quality initiative in the organization. His words illustrate a familiar scenario.

> *I received a call yesterday from the vice president of human resources who asked about the data-collection interviews next week. Her questions were the result of comments made at a staff meeting. One of the managers had received a call from the vice president of finance who was concerned about how the data would be used. Another manager reported that he had talked with some employees from information systems and learned that many people in that department did not see the value of any additional data collection. They pointed out that the last time people filled out questionnaires nothing happened and they never got any feedback on the results. Employees wonder what will be different this time.*

Your client seems a little tense as he tells you about these doubts and questions. You wonder why he refused your request to meet with each department to provide a clear explanation of why data was being collected and how it would be used as a benchmark for the new total quality initiative. Why didn't he buy into the idea about the importance of involving people prior to the data collection? Now it appears managers and employees are confused and concerned about possible changes. All this could have been avoided with some discussion and clear agreements at the contracting stage. Perhaps you can tighten up these early gaps in understanding and expectations, learn from them, and change the course of this change management project. Certainly, your client understands some of the dilemmas better now.

This client and change facilitator are learning about the importance of upfront agreements and clear objectives and expectations during the process of change. Agreements are important not only between the client and facilitation team, but also among different parts of the client system. The client and change facilitators or managers need to bring out and clarify key organization members' perceptions and understanding of the change process. Informing people, inviting their input, legitimizing their concerns, and responding to their questions are essential to gaining ownership, establishing trust and openness, and agreeing on both the process and outcomes of change management. This is Phase 2 of the change-consultation process.

DEFINING AGREEMENTS

The unique characteristics of the consultation relationship are that it is voluntary and not imposed, temporary, and interdependent. The relationship is based on agreements defined upfront in a contracting process. Positive value should be perceived by the persons involved in change management through shared agreements regarding goals, roles, and responsibilities. Contracting is the process of getting this agreement.

Agreements can be defined in three categories: informal, formal, and technical. *Informal* agreements are based on a high level of trust in personal relationships and shared context. They may be based on a handshake or a group consensus. *Formal* agreements can be in the form a letter stating the desired outcomes, roles, responsibilities and methods to be used in a directed change process. *Technical* agreements are legal documents prepared or reviewed by an attorney or legal resource counsel.

Contracting is ultimately a continuous process that should be open for discussion and review as part of continuing change management applications. This negotiation can reflect changing circumstances and roles. An agreement does imply commitment and responsibility. It confirms a shared understanding of how people will work together and how they will mutually set expectations for results and rewards.

During the initiative phase, the client, sponsor, and change facilitators or managers explore the potential of working together. Contracting for reaching agreement is not just a one-time event; it is an ongoing process of coordinating goals, roles, and results. This provides both content for defining agreement areas and a process for legitimizing collaborative inquiry in the relationship with regular feedback, interpretation, and action planning by the facilitating and client systems.

Contracting requires both content and process expertise. Content skills may include knowledge of business, technology, science, engineering, quality, cycle time, total customer satisfaction, diagnosis, human resource systems, sales, and marketing, ethics, and strategic planning. Process skills focus on the facilitation of change outcomes; coordination of resources; timing and appropriate pacing of collaborative inquiry questions; feedback processing for decisions, and action priorities; and strategic intervention designs to achieve results in technical areas such as quality, cycle time, total customer satisfaction, and global marketing.

Contracting facilitates informal, formal, or technical agreements ranging from a complex document to a verbal understanding (see Figure 6.1). Informal verbal declarations can include statements made in a meeting, a recap of phone conversations, or comments from a discussion at breakfast or a luncheon. Verbal statements can be committed to written documents and concise briefs. The written word provides content for verifying understanding, analysis for the specifics of responsibility, and terms of accountability. A high percentage of promises and requests are still being made in an informal communication between high-level clients including chairpersons, chief executive officers, and human resource and chief administration vice presidents. Many individuals work on a day-to-day basis with integrity and achieve significant results with only a handshake or a brief memo.

During change management it is often necessary to revise agreements

FIGURE 6.1 Dimensions of Agreement.

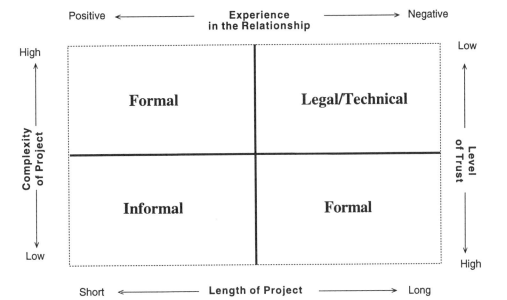

when the client establishes new priorities, competitive resources are reduced, or roles and goals change in the client organization. Contracting establishes progress checkpoints where client and facilitation team can determine go/no-go decisions about a change in program, activity, or process continuation. Trial and preplanning periods provide the client and facilitators with a better sense of how they might work together. This may include work with specific team members and leaders on special projects. Relationships can be temporary or longer in duration depending on the project scope and the involvement of both the client system and the facilitating system.

All parties enter the agreement freely and of their own choosing. Adaptability is built in for renegotiation of terms when needed by either party. Consultation decisions include how to involve appropriate client system members without alienating others; how to retain flexibility while defining tasks and responsibilities; how to advocate for legitimate time extensions when client priorities and resources change; and how to maintain confidence in the consultation team while being honest about limitations or developmental needs.

ELEMENTS OF CONTRACTING FOR AGREEMENT

After the client determines that a change initiative would be beneficial, an explicit agreement can be negotiated to clarify the desired outcomes. Decisions involved include the who, what, when, how, and where of the change consultation; the time perspective, results, and performance criteria; choosing and developing competence in both technical and process action roles; legitimizing continuous feedback for improving quality and productivity in the relationship and results areas; agreeing on project schedule, and identifying the dedicated resources and the participants' obligations to the change management process.

The five elements of contracting—need validation, roles, results, relationships, and culture—provide the architecture for seeking mutual understanding and agreement for collaborative change management. Questions related to these areas form the agenda of meetings, written documents of the contract, or discussions between client, sponsor, and change facilitators.

Elements of contracting should encourage collaborative inquiry among clients, sponsors, and other stakeholders. Change facilitators must anticipate the need for building client system capacity for support during the change effort, and the need to cycle feedback, measure results, and complete the agreement. Discussion among the consultation team should focus on how to transfer the change technology to members of the client system.

A key dilemma in consultation is deciding when to let go of the supporting relationship. This should be openly discussed during the early part of the contracting phase. The client system can regularly assess progress and determine what ongoing resources are needed. At the same time, the team should explore ways to develop the internal competence of the client system.

Deciding which contract elements are most important and need agreements and client accountability to achieve results is part of the contracting process. The future agenda items for the client and sponsors also are important in establishing new agendas of agreement between the client, consultation team, and sponsor.

Each of the five elements of contracting represents a range of questions for participation and understanding to clarify roles and goals and to define agreements related to expectations and results in change management (see Table 6.1). These can be measured using the consultation audit (Chakiris 1992).

TABLE 6.1 Elements of Working Agreements.

---

1. Needs validation

    Perceived need, challenge or opportunity in the present or the future

    Articulating desired outcomes and objectives of change

    Assessing potential for change

2. Roles

    Client

    Sponsor evaluator

    Change facilitators

    Consultation teams

    Client's customers

    Client's suppliers

    Other stakeholders

3. Results

    Sharing strategy for change management as competitive advantage

    Strategic business goal unity

    Integrated directed and nondirected change

    Performance measurement and accountability

    Investment and terms

TABLE 6.1 (continued)

---

4. Relationship
 Openness pact
 Role relationships
 Shared tasks
 Commitment test

5. Culture
 Facilitating change applications
 Client organization and constituents
 Core competencies
 Ethics and professional development
 Continuity and renewal

Contracting strengthens complex relationships, but each element requires open dialogue and discussion to reach agreement. Some aspects are routine if the client and change facilitators are familiar with each other's philosophy, style, and work patterns. Other elements are more complex because they have not been previously discussed. There can be substantial unknowns in organizational relations and people may not be certain what will work effectively. Contracting gives everyone an opportunity to explore mutual objectives and resources, and to set up guidelines, and agreements for a specific collaborative relationship for change management.

Needs Validation

The first element of contracting is needs validation including identifying challenges and opportunities, determining outcomes and objectives, and assessing the potential for change. The questions appearing in Table 6.2 help the consultation team to evaluate and understand this important area within a specific organizational context.

TABLE 6.2 Needs Validation.

Perceived need, challenge, or opportunity
 What is the perceived need, challenge or opportunity in the present and in
  the future?
 Why is change management needed?
 Who identified the need?
 Is this an imposed or voluntary change?

TABLE 6.2 (continued)

What diagnostic data collection methods can be used to identify and validate
    need?
How will data be interpreted and applied?

Articulating desired outcomes and objectives
What future industrial, economic, technological, and global trends might be
    anticipated?
What future condition is desired by sponsor, client, facilitators, and other
    key players?
What change perspectives exist and how can differences be recognized and
    coordinated?
What are the objectives of the change management process?

Assessing potential for change
What is the current growth stage of the organization, function, and unit?
How are jobs described (level of autonomy, challenge, variety, work load,
    role clarity, satisfaction)?
How effective is communication, cooperation, problem solving, self-
    directed teams, work facilitation, and feedback in work relationships?
How do organization members perceive the structure, rewards, policy, rules,
    regulations, decision making, and authority of the system?
How effective is organizational performance in building capacity for
    change, management of conflict, quality of products and services,
    training and development, safety and environment, and community
    image?
What are the motivators for productivity and the quality of work life?
What are the organizational priorities and readiness for change?
What are the potential resisting and supporting forces operating within the
    organization that might affect change?
What is the degree of senior-level openness and desire to learn and explore
    new approaches?
How will the client use feedback to search, learn, and transfer experience to
    new situations?
Is this planned change intervention appropriate for the growth stage of the
    business unit?
Is the timing appropriate for this directed intervention?

One of the complaints heard from both the client system and the facilitating system is that they moved too quickly into contracting without exploring
overall needs and whether the relationship would work effectively. The entry
phase provides a safe period for this exploration and can be used to test and

explore mutual values and desired outcomes as well as how some possible goals and roles might look. During this phase the client and change facilitators should identify what time perspectives are important, what support systems are available for change continuity, and the sponsor's agenda for strategic priorities and needs related to change management.

These initial discussions are pertinent to contracting and can be explored in some depth through sensitizing interviews with individuals and specific sponsors or with groups at the senior level of the organization. Group meetings also can be conducted with project teams such as action teams and marketing, customer, supplier, and technical groups. Matching expected change outcomes or results with appropriate resources should be a priority. This match based on the need or opportunity initiative should be assessed before moving toward a more formal working relationship in a contract.

A short-term contract may be used for front-end analysis and feedback projects. This approach can validate needs before a formal implementation contract is developed. Then one-on-one or one-to-team communication and coordination with the client can help clarify need, commitment, working format, and outcomes in a more formal sense before committing to longer-term phases and more extensive research designs. A challenge of consultation after this basic awareness and exploratory period is to match competencies and legitimize the need for change management. The client should determine the value of an outside objective analysis and extended internal resource teaming to integrate directed and nondirected change.

Over the long run there is a need to sustain and renew the change, to develop internal capacity for the change, to assign resources internal to the system, and to adapt the ideas to fit the specific units and diversity of the organization. Futuring or imagining the change two to five years out helps people to view success in real terms and to understand motivation and satisfaction related to change. They can choose the future and role they prefer, choose how their work life will have become more effective, what personal development activities they will have participated in, and how the organization will look in the future.

Bringing these future images into the here and now provides a better understanding of needs and resources required to support integrated change. Part of the potential is also in the key players, managers and team members, and their motivation and accountabilities for planning and implementing change. Effectively facilitating change applications requires some validation of the commitment of the organization in working with others to collect information and to plan collaborative action. Complex data-collection studies are often required to validate the perceived need. Involving the client system in the action research teaming (ART) process is essential. The client and sponsor should take an active role versus a passive role. Involved client and sponsor roles, as well as participation by employees, managers, boards, suppliers, and customers, helps define ownership and performance accountability for achieving effective organizational performance. Identifying competitive resources based on desired outcomes and needs links the appropriate resources to accomplish these goals. All of this must be considered in initial agreements related to change management.

Clarifying Change Facilitation Roles

The second element of contracting is clarifying and getting agreement on roles and responsibilities. This includes the roles of the client, sponsor/evaluator, resource facilitators, consultation team, and other stakeholders (See Table 6.3).

TABLE 6.3 Roles and Responsibilities.

Client

Who is the client?

Could there be more than one client?

Could the client change as the project continues?

What future client may be needed at what level of the organization?

What experience, both positive and negative, has the client had in working
with change facilitators?

Is the desired outcome part of client performance accountability?

Is the project important to career development or succession plan for client?

Sponsor/Evaluator

What experience has the sponsor had with change facilitators?

Who are the persons or group who comprise the sponsors?

What will the sponsor evaluate and how will this evaluation be done?

Are there any hidden sponsors with hidden agendas?

Is the project sufficiently linked to the power structure?

Are stakeholders and constituents represented?

What other intermediaries need to be considered?

Will the sponsor be involved in data collection, feedback, and action
decisions related to change?

Resource Facilitator

What type of consultation team is appropriate?

How will internal and external resources be used?

How do change facilitators feel about the project?

TABLE 6.3 (continued)

What priority does this consultation have in relation to other projects and
   programs?
Are the resource facilitators willing to devote time and energy to this
   project?
What rewards can the facilitators expect?
Is this part of performance accountability?

Consultation Team — (client and change facilitator)
Who is the spokesperson for the resource team?
Who are the potential internal and external team resources?
Have all the team members been oriented to the project?
What training is needed for the team to work together?

Customer of the Client
Who is the customer or "end-user" of the services or change ?
What procedures are required for customer ownership of the change?
Does the project outcome respond to customer need and satisfaction?
What data collection, feedback, and action planning will be done with the
   customer in relation to the change?

Supplier of the Client
How does the supplier relationship affect desired outcomes? Should
   client/supplier teaming be considered?
What supplier involvement is desired during data collection?
Is the supplier involved in feedback and action planning for change?

Government, Community, or Other Stakeholders
What alliances are needed for gaining more competitive resources?
What government rules and regulations should be considered?
What community relations should be used on a local, national, international
   level?
What about competition? What data should be shared or not shared?
Are there other stakeholders — political, economic, social, environmental,
   industry associations, community, non-profit sector, university–that
   should be considered?

Competent change facilitators choose appropriate roles and involve the
client in expanding knowledge and skills that allow learning throughout the
system, and the transfer of competencies to employees, suppliers, and
customers. The consultation team should use feedback sessions with client
system interpretation of data and actions. Both the facilitating system and

client system are involved in learning and development to improve their skills. Internal managers and staff professionals can also benefit from an exchange of practices. This might include rehearsals of contract formulation dialogue using observation, feedback, and critique of case application and contract language. It is important to facilitate a plan with the client system to transfer the consultation technology inside the organization at each phase in the process.

Roles should be clear in the contracting. Written agreements on roles and responsibilities prevent later misunderstanding. The change facilitators may be involved in a variety of consultation role relationships with the client, sponsor, team leaders, team members, client, and customer contacts. Often the role of clients changes with new clients appearing and disappearing at different stages. The agreements made with clients need to be sufficiently open and flexible to adapt to new charters, unexpected proclamations, emerging needs or opportunities, and shifting resources and roles. Because of changing contexts and conflicting needs, resistance can be expected from some participants during change consultation. This resistance comes from imposed change and concerns about performance effectiveness. The consultation team can increase acceptance through role clarification and the ongoing involvement of client, facilitator, and sponsor around concerns and changing needs.

Inside and outside facilitators working together strengthen consultation roles and provide additional resources for the client. The outside facilitator offers objectivity in determining the strengths and opportunity areas for improvement and the readiness for change. The inside manager or staff professional is more attuned to reaction, resistance, and acceptance, and can help to identify the informal cultural factors that will contribute most to the success of any directed change effort. Emphasis on teamwork and shared competencies should be a part of the role expectations and responsibilities in contracting.

Results

The third element in contracting is agreement on results, which help the consultation team to focus on business goals, performance measurement, accountability, and investment as they develop contract agreements for managing change. The questions in Table 6.4 should be considered as part of the discussion.

TABLE 6.4 Results.

Sharing strategy—change management as competitive advantage

What is the high-level design of the directed change?

What shared values, concepts, and working principles are evident?

What are the perceived challenges of the organization related to change management?

Is change management viewed as a strategic investment and competitive advantage?

What disconnections exist that could affect results?

What improvements are essential for linkage and integration?

How can change facilitators advocate an ART approach?

What concerns should be known and shared at the sponsor level?

What contradictions exist related to change?

What are the unknowns that might affect this project?

Strategic business goal unity

In what way does change management contribute to these business performance measurements?

Are business goals sufficiently visible?

Do individual, business unit, and organization change management goals align?

What are the key performance measurements for positive change?

   Be a preferred supplier?

   Become a preferred employer?

   Have a strong image in community?

   Aim for increased market share

   Achieve quality in Six Sigma, Deming, or Baldridge criteria?

   Become more market driven?

   Have a strong relationship with key customers?

   Have insight to meet and anticipate customer needs?

   Improve business performance?

   Create capable, experienced management?

   Have a strong spirit of teamwork with dedicated employees?

   Achieve demanding performance requirements?

   Seek new initiatives to produce tangible results?

   Become efficient in overall business operations?

TABLE 6.4 (continued)

Target financial measurements to improve ROI and profits, reduce working
    capital, redirect capital toward high return use, deploy financial assets,
    restructure pension plan, innovative financial strategies, increase value
    for stockholders, repay debt, identify new investment opportunities,
    generate strong cash flow, enhance stockholders' value?
Seek technical leadership?
Have a high R&D investment?
Create strategic alliances and ventures with companies, governments,
    nations?
Achieve a worldwide presence in expanded multinational markets?

Results measurements and accountability

What measurement is required for midterm and end results ?
What current end results exist now and what end results are desired? What
    are the gaps between these two results?
What performance criteria are relevant?
What performance deviation is anticipated and how can that be overcome?
How will feedback occur throughout the relationship?
Will documentation and evaluation roles require client support?
What will success look like in both quantitative and qualitative terms?
What method will be used to communicate and make visible progress
    milestones?
How, when, and by whom will progress be measured and monitored?
Who will prepare, analyze, and record reports?
How will feedback progress reports be given to the sponsor, client,
    consultation team, and client system?
Who will provide these reports and how often?
How will measurement information be used?

Investment and terms

What resources are needed?
How will dollars, time, people, information, technology, and other
    resources be allocated?
Is change management viewed as a strategic investment rather than a cost of
    the business?
What investment is required of senior level sponsor?
What are the client's internal requirements and supports?
What are the consultation resource requirements and supports (type of resource;
    decision of calculating billable time by unit, hour, or day; manner of payment
    or resource allocation; and frequency of resource usage in financial, staffing,
    and other areas)?

Assessing client system readiness, resources, and outcomes for change management is essential before committing to the outcomes and before the work plan begins. A simple formula is not to promise results in areas in which the client does not have control. The team should also be aware of areas in which the role responsibility is unclear. This could lead to problems in accomplishing the outcome. Blurred areas of control and role responsibility may be a sign to include another level of sponsor involvement, so that questions of feasibility and commitment to the desired outcome can be articulated with greater authority. Overall results measurement should position change management within the strategy and structure of the organization. The desired outcome for each unit involved should clearly align the goals of the unit, individual, and the organization on both a directed and nondirected level.

The contract can supply a written agreement of responsibilities and expected outcomes or results. Written contracts provide insight about what is most important to the relationship, determine target goals in order to measure progress, and provide information about who should be involved. The contracting discussion tests commitment to the process and the results, and legitimizes strategic questions of why, what, who, when, where, and how. With a clear agreement, goals can be assessed regularly to see if everything is on track toward desired outcomes.

Results are facilitated by both experience and skills in multi-disciplined areas of research, engineering, quality, manufacturing, cycle time, marketing, and human resources. However, technical skills must be complemented by process competencies for the proper balance in teaming with other people and using the collective knowledge and experience for change management. For example, data-collection activities require some knowledge and expertise in areas such as benchmarking, organization mapping, organizational-effectiveness audits, customer surveys, and the technical components of quality improvement.

Competency in process methods and design is required for translating data into meaningful action to achieve results. Facilitation and high-level feedback design help gain client ownership and commitment for action accountability. For instance, when collecting sensitive data that can expose both strengths and areas that require improvement, the consultation team has the challenge of establishing trust and openness while providing accurate information and moving the group toward their action objectives. Results are related to competencies in both technical and process skills.

Relationship

The fourth element of contracting is relationship. This includes openness, role relationships, responsibility, and commitment. These are essential to the overall success of the change consultation process (See Table 6.5).

TABLE 6.5 Relationship.

Openness pact and relationship norms

Is there openness, trust, acceptance, legitimization, and confidentiality?

Will the team have access to data?

How can all parties reduce or eliminate surprises and embarrassments?

Does the client plan any significant changes?

Are there any concerns about structure and power hierarchy?

Are all parties skilled in confronting sensitive issues?

What concerns exist and what action will be required to deal with change ambivalence?

How will personnel changes in key roles be managed to lessen project disruption?

Role relationships

What responsibility and authority exists and with whom?

What information sharing will occur regarding politics and change readiness?

Is the contract sufficiently collaborative, with the client owning the change?

Who will communicate what with whom?

Who has the responsibility to inform the client about the project and at what intervals?

What is the role relationship between the change facilitators and the client?

What is the role relationship between the client and the sponsors?

What is the role relationship between the change facilitators and the sponsors?

As the project develops are future clients assessed for effective entry contracting?

Shared tasks

Who is responsible to do what?

What tasks are to be completed by the sponsor? Client? Change facilitators? Action research team? Others?

Are action-planning steps appropriately sequenced?

Are there any steps that are too big or too long?

Who will ensure that sufficient milestone celebrations do occur?

TABLE 6.5 (continued)

Commitment test

Where is the directed change project in the priorities of the sponsor and the other stakeholders? Priorities of the organization? Client's priorities?

Will the client devote timely attention to the change?

Will the client provide the facilitator with accurate and timely information?

Will the client involve the team resources in appropriate planning meetings?

How can the client involve employees in the project?

Are resources within the organization being fully utilized?

What resources are required and committed by the client?

Is there a need for internal external teaming resources?

Is there a commitment to inside-outside teaming for managing change?

We often assume that people chosen to work together are ready and able to do so. Often, this is not so. A process for learning how to work together is required. Guidelines and criteria for making decisions, identifying outcomes, and measuring results are essential for determining if the consultation team is on track. Use of open feedback and negotiation in the relationship provides data for confronting real challenges and conflicts related to change.

Contracting is the process used for relationships to help people work together to facilitate change management. Open-ended in concept, this process seeks to establish understanding and gain voluntary, rather than imposed, participation from the client, facilitator, client organization, sponsor, team members, leaders, champions, customers, suppliers, and other constituents. Contract agreements should provide for the participation of the members of the client system in the decisions and direction of change management as it affects them. This includes who will be involved, the time commitment, the rationale and purpose of the action being recommended, and the benefits for the organization, individual, and the group. Having an open contract with voluntary relationships is a basic value in the consultation process to integrate directed and nondirected change.

Given changing structures involving cluster groups and virtual organizations, relationships are not established permanently on specific work assignments. Facilitating systems and client systems are wise to consider the beginning, checkpoints, and completion of the project or assignment as well as necessary changes in roles and responsibilities. Rotation among various clients in different sub-units should be anticipated as well as changes in team composition. The original client may also shift and become a sponsor of the change consultation, requiring contracting activities with the new clients and sponsors to establish appropriate relationships.

People want to be involved in matters that affect them and their input is essential in integrating directed and nondirected activities for effective change management. While the contract is an intentional effort to provide more structure to the relationship, the agreement needs to remain flexible, adaptive, and open. The consultation group should consider possible teaming roles among the change facilitators, the client, the sponsor, managers, and employees of the client system in various departments, divisions, functions, and strategic-business units, as well as customers, suppliers, and other constituencies. Coordinating these groups requires the development of effective working relationships and the facilitation of involvement through formal and informal agreements that bring alignment and value to all parties.

A higher level of understanding and involvement in change helps define the working-relationship agreement. This includes agreeing on the time perspective, choosing appropriate action roles related to both technical and process needs, coordinating performance-criteria measurement, legitimizing ongoing feedback to assess progress, and measuring goal achievement.

At the beginning of the relationship, participants must gain ownership and commitment so that the contract is focused on achieving shared objectives. "Fast starts" without adequate contract discussion skip important relationship elements and create "hills" of tension and conflict later in the process. This is seen in excessive stops to clarify misunderstanding around coordination, purpose, meaning, and motivation for change. Effective work-relationship agreements in the contracting phase improve this success ratio.

Culture

The fifth element of contracting is culture, which establishes the context or environment for agreements about change. This includes directed and nondirected change in factors such as norms, decision patterns, organizational intelligence, competencies, teamwork, ethics, structure, rewards, power, and communication channels (See Table 6.6).

TABLE 6.6 Culture.

Facilitate the change application

How will these agreements facilitate change application?

What will the success look like?

What norms are established to discuss contract renegotiation at any time?

What cultural norms might affect this agreement?

What are the nondirected implications of this process?

How can people identify go or no-go decision points between phases?

TABLE 6.6 (continued)

Client organization and constituents

Who (client, change facilitator, project team, ad hoc groups, action research teams, advisory committee, councils, sponsor, customers, suppliers, constituents) should be involved and when should they be involved?

What ongoing assessment will be made of unit and organizational cultural dynamics?

What ongoing line accountability is required to support change?

Are plans being implemented to develop the internal resources and competencies of the client system?

Is effective work teaming now occurring within and across units?

Will additional resources be required during the implementation phase?

Core competencies

Is there a need to develop client and sponsor skills?

Is the consultation team skilled in technical and process roles?

Is the team competent in confronting sensitive issues?

Is the client skilled at confronting sensitive issues with the sponsor?

What ART skills are required for facilitation of data collection, feedback and interpretation, action decisions?

What fundamental business skills are required?

What human resource skills are required?

What career development planning is needed at the individual unit level?

What skills, techniques, knowledge, and behaviors are required to support change?

Does the client adequately understand the need to build sufficient resources to manage change over time?

Ethics and professional development

What are the shared values and beliefs about change?

What are the shared performance guidelines or criteria?

How are critical decisions being addressed to avoid dilemmas and pitfalls?

What will determine and ensure quality client-owned interventions?

What development is planned for organization members?

Are exchange-of-practice sessions scheduled for sharing and learning from the experience?

Continuity and renewal

How can the consultation team determine interface and develop communication?

Retain momentum as a safeguard from possible entropy?

Provide feedback to modify plans?

TABLE 6.6 (continued)

Assess the ongoing situation?

Integrate directed and nondirected change?

Create procedures for progress review and performance feedback?

Provide ample time for trial effort and revisions?

Assess feedback, evaluation, reexamine goals, and revise action?

Develop action strategies as part of the overall project?

Provide early warning signals?

Practice proactive versus reactive posture toward changing goals?

Schedule celebrations and rewards?

Is there mutual support for quality interventions in data based, feedback, decisions and action planning, rehearsals, and pilot projects?

Have time and resources been calculated at the time of contract formulation?

Have participants legitimized "revisiting" elements of understanding throughout the relationship?

Will sufficient time to be spent on learning and mutual exploration and inquiry throughout the client system?

The impact of specific aspects of organizational culture should not be underestimated in the contracting discussion. The formal and informal "rules" for behavior, the underlying power base in relationship structures, the storehouse of organizational knowledge and procedures for decisions and actions in work practices can affect how people within the organizational system approach change and how they respond as individuals and groups to opportunities for collaborative inquiry, participation, and innovation.

The different perspectives of change discussed in Chapter 3 must be considered as part of this culture. Conflicting perspectives can create misunderstanding and resistance. Taking time to assess "local theories" about change can increase understanding and agreement about shared approaches to change management. During the contracting phase the client system can provide input and ideas based on past experiences, readiness for change, and doubts that some people might have. It is important to hear the stories about what works and does not work in a particular system.

Trust and openness continue to be a core value during the contracting process. The client system should be willing to share data, confront issues and concerns, and work as a team to develop agreements to which they are all committed. The facilitating system must be sensitive to the timing of contracting questions to determine with the client and sponsor when to collect the data, what confidentiality pacts should or do exist, how data will be used, what views are important during feedback, and what preferred roles and goals the client and sponsor want in the data interpretation and action planning process. Contracting provides mutual direction, confidence in relationships, and commitment to collective goals.

The consultation team should explore discussion about strategic challenges of the business; cultural dynamics related to structure, systems, and organizational effectiveness; job and work group relationships; long-term strategy; the performance of each operating unit; organization priorities; and global intentions in various markets. It is essential to know how decisions are made and how decision-making patterns will impact predictability for achieving outcomes in the desired time cycle. All of these factors are related to core values and norms in the culture of the organization.

Dilemmas related to an imbalance in power and participation are not uncommon in change management. Conflicts are often triggered by perceived inequity in reward systems, lack of meaningful and shared performance criteria, unrealistic time and expectation perspectives, and lack of involvement and commitment by some organization members. An organization with a rigid hierarchical structure and substantial differences in power and status can pose major consultation challenges and create barriers to change management. that can affect relationships and results. These cultural norms and rules should be discussed when formulating contracts and agreements.

DILEMMAS OF CONTRACTING—WHY THINGS GO WRONG

The following section reflects the experience of internal and external facilitators, managers, consultants, and human resource professionals who were asked to identify some of the factors that cause consultation to fail. Many of these dilemmas can be avoided through effective contracting based on realistic roles, relationships, and results.

Lack of Adequate Data

During the initial start-up of the relationship, the desired outcomes are not articulated or validated by the client system or sponsor. Initial data collection is insufficient, resulting in inaccurate diagnosis for designing an appropriate intervention. Readiness for change is not identified and discussed, especially during the early phases.

Resistance

Resistance to change is unduly created by not asking people about their concerns and giving employees opportunities to express their fear of the consequences, such as the politics of the change or anticipated job rotations due to structural modifications. This anxiety and resistance should be recognized from the beginning.

Shift in Client

During the initial entry phase the change facilitator starts out with one client but is quickly moved to another person without working through the appropriate new start-up procedures, such as finding who would be authorized to make decisions and the level of readiness on the part of this new client for change. Facilitators should not assume that contracting or mutual agreements established with the initial client will automatically be accepted by the second client. This can create confusion and dissatisfaction until a new contracting phase is established. Personnel changes and transfer of critical functions must be anticipated during the change consultation process.

Sponsor Conflicts

Sponsor roles make or break successful outcomes. Credible leadership involvement and commitment require some diagnosis of the agendas and priorities of key sponsors in the initial stages of change consultation. Often internal clients are not attuned to these agendas and find that a sponsor's hidden agenda may interfere with a change project just as things are going well. Sponsors are usually in the senior executive group, but not to be overlooked are the key sponsor roles of customers, employee group such as action teams, and other stakeholders who need to provide input and gain ownership of the goals of change. The role of all of these sponsors should be considered in the contracting.

Over-Advocating

The change facilitator can overemphasize the advocacy role in telling people what to do. This results in lopsided responsibility, which does not allow the client to build an internal capacity for change and creates client dependence on expert resources. The advocacy role, while important during the early phase, is not in the best long-term interests of the client. Appropriate action roles established in the contracting stage reduce dependency. For example, at the beginning of the relationship, the change facilitator as a technical expert may be asked by the client "What is the appropriate action?" However, as the relationship continues, the client should be acquiring this technical expertise and become knowledgeable about what determines an effective decision. The transfer of competencies to the client system should be one of the goals established in the contracting phase.

Lack of Teaming and Linkage

Change facilitators often overlook adequate linkage to other resources and professionals who are working within the same client organization. Lack of teaming creates disconnections. For example, in one situation a facilitator provides benchmarking assistance while another technical resource supports strategic planning and a third staff professional is assigned to team development. Integrated teams can provide better services to the client system. Yet many organizations overlook the possibilities for agreements that align these resources and increase overall effectiveness of change efforts.

The client and the sponsor may be kept out of the loop when facilitation services are being delivered. The case in point is the client who calls in the resource facilitator to develop the work unit team but is not involved in the data collection, feedback, interpretation of the data, and the team's action planning activities. Lack of client involvement keeps these key players from demonstrating leadership and prevents the appropriate linkage and continuity required for long-term organizational benefits.

There are many pertinent questions for professionals trying to create linkage: "Are we on the right path?" "Who might help us look at this?" "What are the perceptions of this change?" Choosing the appropriate action is also an ethical consideration for facilitators and client. The contract is the first step in establishing this ethical base.

Effective change management should result in a higher level of service and customer satisfaction. Whether it is quality, total cycle time, organizational effectiveness, strategic marketing, or new product design, the contract states this outcome or benefit. Customers or end users should be part of the process. The insight that customer input provides should not be an area of compromise—customers must be involved in change management.

Supplier participation should not be overlooked. Challenges related to quality, technology, work practices, and productivity can be better understood through input from suppliers and other stakeholders, including employee action teams, shareholders, directors, consumer and community panels, international organizations, educational institutions, governments, and associations.

No Shared Theory or Strategy

Theory or strategy is often not shared to create an appropriate frame of reference during the early phases of change management. Change consultation requires a broad, integrated perspective. Without grounding the process in some theory or defined strategy, approaches can appear fragmented instead of systematic. The consequences of not assessing the theoretical and functional development stage of the organization can result in expecting too much too soon. For example, an organization that has a highly skilled, well-trained employee base is not the same as an organization in which little training is provided. Each organization has a different "starting place." Even though the desired outcome for two organizations may appear the same, the design for achieving those results is unique based on the distinct needs and culture of each organization.

No Linkage to Business Goals

Business goals should be considered an essential part of the contract discussions about performance and results. Ideally change management is linked to the strategic business goals. An assessment of strategic goal unity should uncover whether the goals align with the strategic direction of the organization. For instance, the client who wants to change the direction of marketing, sales, and distribution may find this goal in conflict with a recently announced new strategy, which contradicts the findings of a research study about how marketing and sales functions must change in the next decade. Facilitation teams should not overlook the value of consultation activities in strengthening the strategic position of the organization. This value is translated into financial and market-share returns.

Lack of Feedback and Measurement

Facilitating systems and client systems working on change management may find that the lack of specific performance criteria and feedback measurements prevents them from uncovering concerns and issues for correcting action, setting a new direction, and measuring the consequences of action. Criteria for performance must be established during contracting and continually monitored in relation to stated outcomes.

The need to identify early warning signals, maintain momentum, and reduce possible entropy are identified as key skill areas for clients and change facilitators. Not creating procedures for trial efforts and revisions can prevent realistic and necessary adjustments and modifications.

Steps that are too big or too long and not properly sequential with stop sessions for review, diagnosis, feedback, and results measurement can have serious negative consequences. For example, progress midpoints are often overlooked and consequently momentum disappears and morale and motivation issues begin to surface. When results are examined objectively based on a performance criteria established at the contracting phase, participants can see and document progress. They can also recognize and celebrate their success in achieving organizational and group objectives for change management.

Underestimating Resource Needs

Miscalculation of time and underestimation of the cost of the project based on projected days versus documentation of actual hours are practical concerns. Internal professionals and technical resources find that their clients sometimes assume that internal assistance does not entail cost or that they underestimate the cost. However, with limited resource time, the allocation to one project or another is a decision of priority. Projects are often priced too low with a minimum concern for realistic time allocations based on cost.

Another danger is underestimating the need for specific resources and overestimating what can be done in a limited amount of time. While cycle-time experts seek to reduce time and cost without loss of quality, experience and learning caution consultation teams to gain experience with time factors. Reducing resources can affect change continuity with high or low returns for the overall change effort. Assessment tools should be used to monitor project costs with a structured process for feedback and adjustment. Many teams learn that they need to improve contracting to insure realistic resources estimates and increase ownership and accountability for achieving and sustaining longer term results.

Resource commitment by the client system is a foundation to sustain effective change. During the change consultation process needs should be reviewed periodically to identify resource gaps. Inadequate use of organizational resources includes not sufficiently involving the work force in the change and consequently building barriers that later have to be brought down, not connecting with external support as needed, and scheduling insufficient time for feedback and progress discussion at each phase.

Lack of Openness

Unless ambivalence and conflict regarding change are confronted at the beginning through open communication and trust, resistance to the change and the collaborative relationship can be expected. An "openness pact" early in the relationship can address personality conflicts, trust, and interdependence, and legitimize sharing complete, timely information. This allows the parties to expose and confront real issues that could cause problems later.

When value is placed on the "protection" of information, autonomy, and competition rather than on teaming across the organization, there can be substantial obstacles to change management. Facilitators, managers, team leaders, and staff professionals should work together in exchanging practices and experiences that will help others to confront and deal with these obstacles and increase overall openness and cooperation in change management.

Dependency

Planning for continuity and ongoing change after the project is completed is a common concern of clients and facilitators. This should be addressed as a part of the initial agreement. There can be a tendency by the change facilitators or staff resources not to let go of the support relationship. Yet the completion and transfer of competencies should be part of the process, with periodic follow-up support provided as needed. Facilitators and clients should plan for completion in the early phase of consultation, during contracting, with discussion of what the "completion" will look like.

Most of these dilemmas can be avoided with effective initial contracting and continued monitoring and negotiation to check agreements, review progress toward goals, confirm commitments, and make necessary adjustments. Honest and open communication between the client system and the facilitating system is essential to a successful working relationship (Swartz 1985). To help establish this relationship, the consultation team may develop a policy statement on practices so that the client can gain a better understanding of how they conduct business and consultation activities. This agreement should include an openness pact. The statements in Table 6.7 illustrate some of the components that might appear in this openness pact.

TABLE 6.7 Openness Pact Agreements on Relationship.

Expectations from the change facilitator's perspective

Work with and through client.

Avoid the creation of client dependence.

Endeavor to increase the internal resource capabilities of the client system.

Reject techniques and methodologies that could embarrass or degrade individuals, groups, or units of the client organization.

Adhere to the principle of "no surprises" for client.

Work closely with an internal person designated as a consultation partner.

Take only those assignments for which competence has been established.

TABLE 6.7 (continued)

Expectations from the client's perspective

Keep facilitator informed of any developments that could affect the outcome of the assignment.

Develop indicators of progress against which the contribution of the mutual change effort can be measured.

Encourage and welcome objective feedback between client and facilitator at any time during the assignment.

Place a realistic priority on the mutual project so that time, effort, and dollars can be allocated accordingly.

PRACTICING CONTRACTING SKILLS

Contract elements are often presented in the form of questions to discuss with clients and the consultation team. As we have shown, each of the elements—needs validation, action roles, results, relationship, and culture—has inquiry areas for the assessment of understanding, agreements, and satisfaction among the client, facilitators, and sponsors.

Skill practice in contracting is highly recommended for managers, staff professionals, and other resources working with change management. Simulated role playing on getting agreements can be practiced with a group, colleague, or coworker. Observation feedback and self critique are useful in developing content and process skills. Competence includes both process, in how contracting is done, and content, in what is asked. Contracting is a continuing sequence of articulating and documenting effective working agreements throughout the consultation relationship. Contract formulation requires skillful facilitation of exploratory questions with win-win language; credibility, trust, and openness in contract discussions; and the ability to create documents of understanding. Process skills are essential in collecting data, providing feedback, group dynamics, checking understanding, timing and pacing of questions, and recognizing a sensitive balance between getting results and not imposing too much too soon.

Activities such as role playing and rehearsal can help develop contracting competencies. For example, in an exchange of practices or a training session, team members may select a real case situation to rehearse with other colleagues. They identify the contract element that they want to rehearse and discuss this with the group. This includes a briefing on the situation and the type of outcome desired in the contracting discussion. Then participants prepare for the discussion by having one of the team members play the role of the client. The other members can observe the rehearsal. The facilitator may stop the action for discussion with feedback from each person. Then they role-play again using the corrected action. After receiving feedback the group turns to another case situation.

The purpose of observation and feedback is to provide descriptions of the specific behavior of the persons simulating the role of change facilitators. A guide sheet can help to organize perceptions of the skill rehearsal or practice that is observed (see Table 6.8).

TABLE 6.8 Observer Guide Sheet.

CONTENT (What?)	PROCESS (How?)
Choice of words	Orientation
Asks vs. recommends	Focusing attention
Seeks to understand vs. interprets	Summarizing and linking
Listens for meaning	Recognizing progress
Starts where client is	Getting agreement
Facilitates clarifying questions	Pacing
Links resources to outcomes	Closing

The communication model (Felkins and Chakiris 1981) is useful for managers and consultation teams in facilitating the contract discussion and making sure that points are understood and agreements are clear (See Figure 6.1). The model illustrates the core activities related to the process of getting agreements.

The basic components of the the communication management model are: orientation, focusing attention, summarizing and linking, recognizing progress, getting agreement, pacing, and closing. *Orientation* opens the meeting and provides the parties with pertinent information to help to orient them, bring them up-to-date, and prepare them for the meeting. *Focusing attention* keeps the participants on track and limits the discussion to the necessary agenda. In *summarizing and linking* the facilitator rephrases, clarifies and checks the accuracy of information, consolidates major ideas, and establishes dialogue transitions. In *recognizing progress* the facilitator cites movement toward agreement, recognizes accomplishments and achievements in reaching the contracting goals, acknowledges understanding, and gives an indication of "where we are now." *Getting agreement* makes sure that all parties have consensus on a specific point before moving on to the next one, establishes

FIGURE 6.2 Communication Model.

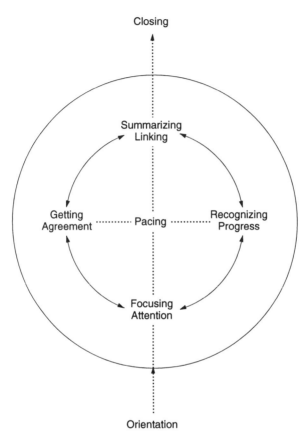

common ground, and provides support for a cooperative effort. *Pacing* is central for the facilitator in recognizing the amount of time available, not spending too much time in one area, and accomplishing mutual objectives in an efficient time span. In *closing* the parties establish mutual agreement on commitment to roles, responsibility, action, and follow-up.

Following are some of the key questions change facilitators might ask themselves about discussions related to agreements and contracts:

- What are our major objectives for this session?
- What are the key issues for the change facilitators? For the client?
- What support materials or data are needed?
- What can we anticipate are the needs of the client?
- What past communication have we had with the client system?

- How can we establish rapport early in this conversation?
- How will we establish clarity about roles?
- Do other people need to be involved?
- Are there specific corporate guidelines we must follow?
- Do we understand and agree on the basic procedures?
- What are the most likely points of agreement and disagreement?
- What decisions may need more negotiation?
- What are the short-and long-term considerations?
- How can we summarize major ideas throughout the discussion?
- How can we gain mutual agreement and commitment to action in this conversation?
- What language should be used to summarize agreed-upon action and responsibility?
- How can we test the client's agreement and commitment?
- What items require follow-up and additional discussion or negotiation?
- What type of contracting is most appropriate?

FORMAL AND TECHNICAL CONTRACT GUIDELINES

Change initiatives involving complex coordination of multiple resources including people, technology, finances, time and schedules, restrictions, and specific outcomes require a formal or technical agreement (Swartz 1985) between the client system and the facilitating system. Often these agreements are approved and co-signed by an individual client, sponsor, and a change facililtator or external resource professional.

Project Estimates

All project estimates are based on the client's delineation of the assignment, initial analysis of project size and complexity, the facilitator's past experience with similar assignments, and, when applicable, the assigned resource fee schedule. Often it is difficult for the consultation team to predict the scope, complexity, and length of a project. For this reason, a multi-phased approach is suggested in contracting for organization-wide projects. This allows the client and facilitator to make go and no-go decisions between phases.

Types of Contracts

Contracts can be formal or technical depending on the client's specific needs and to best match the type of project. The basic contract types are: 1) Daily fees plus expenses, 2) fixed fee plus actual cost contract by phase or project, 3) total project price, or 4) retainer on a monthly, quarterly, or annual basis. Legal contracts may be used with outside resources. Many internal contracts are formal letters of agreement. Internal clients may also use transfer pricing in internal billing to different accounting systems. Budget allotments are increased as funds are generated. In some cases internal consultation resources operate as a separate business with both internal and external clients.

Daily fees plus expenses

Billings for this type of contract are based on the actual time worked at the established rate for the assigned resource person. Work may be performed at the client's location, the consultation group's offices, or at other locations appropriate for the assignment. A minimum of four hours is generally billed for work performed at an alternative location.

A client's location may require that the change facilitator or team travel a half day or more. Fees may be billed for this time if the resource group is performing work for the client's project. This special understanding should always be negotiated between the client and the consultation group at the beginning of the relationship.

Fixed fee plus actual cost

The fixed fee plus actual cost contract is negotiated by phase or for an entire project. This is most appropriate for well-defined, long-term projects.

Total project price

This type of contract includes a total project price including fees, expenses, materials, and other items. This contract is most appropriate for specific short-term directed change projects.

Retainer

A monthly, quarterly, or annual retainer arrangement may be most mutually beneficial to the client and the resource group. This is appropriate for longer-term follow-up work. It also makes professional resources available in case they are needed and ensures come continuity.

Expenses

For fees plus expenses contracts, expenses incurred on behalf of the client are billed at cost. They may include:

- Clerical and reproduction services
- Materials
- Telephone calls
- Ground travel at prevailing rates per mile
- Air, train, and bus travel at coach-fare rates unless first class is approved
- Meals
- Lodging
- Gratuities for necessary services
- Expenses from pilot projects
- Other out-of-pocket approved expenses

On lengthy assignments at the client location, the client generally provides round-trip transportation to the change facilitator's place of lodging or home at agreed upon intervals and pays expenses for layover weekends, if necessary.

Cancellations

Occasionally, it is necessary for a client to cancel a consultation date. In the event this occurs, the consultation team may reschedule that event at no penalty to the client. However, in order to protect the facilitator date and to hold dates open for other clients it may sometimes be necessary for external resources and internal facilitators to charge a cancellation fee based on cancellation guidelines provided to and agreed upon with the client.

Billing and Terms of Payment

Statements are generally rendered at the close of each calendar month for fees and expenses incurred during the month. Other billing arrangements can be negotiated to meet the client's needs.

Normally, the client payment is anticipated within 30 days after receipt of the billing statement. Resource professionals should maintain a close working relationship with the client and discuss all aspects of the contract in an open and complete manner to insure that expectations are clear and the client is satisfied with services.

Nonprofit and Government Bids

Structured requests for proposals (RFPs) and other proposal formats require written documentation or letters of written understanding. These documents usually provide the background history of requirements. Fax communication can also be used to send faster responses to requests.

When bidding on government or nonprofit assignments, general guidelines may be used and adjusted to meet specific needs (Miller 1989). As a starting point, informal rules are used for discussion with the client prior to the preparation of proposals. Guidelines for public bidding and project contracts are available for public review. Table 6.8 is a sample section of a bid.

TABLE 6.8 Sample Non-Profit or Government Bid.

Direct Professional Labor
17 training days @ _____/day $ _____
2 days for instructor overlap @ _____/day   _____
3 days travel status @ _____/day   _____
3 day coordination and customization of the program
    @ _____per day   _____

Overhead
The current overhead rate for all contracts negotiated
    during_(year)
    is 100% of Direct Professional Labor
        _____ x 1.00 $ _____

Materials
Preparation and delivery of one camera-ready copy (provide
    range or establish number off published price sheet)
                            $ _____
Learning instruments, surveys, audits
                            $ _____

Suggested Margins
a. On Direct Professional Labor @10% =
    .10 x _____   _____
b. On Overhead @7% =
    .07 x _____   _____
c. On Materials @4% =
    .04 x _____   _____
        TOTAL $ _____
Transportation and per diem to be paid by client.

CONTRACTING AGREEMENTS

Table 6.10 illustrates a sample contract brief for use when preparing a written document of agreement for a consultation project related to change management. This sample agreement can be used as a starting point to review the elements that might go into a working document. Additional information can be provided in a letter format, a proposal, or a draft outline for discussion with the client group prior to providing a written contract.

TABLE 6.10 Sample Contract.

Client Information
Client _____
Change Facilitator/Resource _____
Sponsor _____

Duration from_____ to _____

Agreement Areas
Reasons services are requested:
Goals or outcomes desired:
Client expectations: (Please note if sponsor has different
    expectations)

Time frame: (Provide milestones for short and long horizon)
Description of services: (estimated number of days)
Phases with checkpoints for Go/No-Go Decisions:
Client and client system involvement:
Methodologies that will be used: (data collection, analysis,
    feedback cycling, and applications)
Evaluation and feedback methods:
Investment costs:
Deliverables:

Contract distribution and signatures:
Client_____ Date: _____
Sponsor(s)_____ Date: _____
Change Facilitator/Resource _____ Date: _____

Getting agreements and identifying elements of understanding are essential to successful change consultation. If this is not done well, the entire project can jeopardized. Contracting discussions are the point at which needs validation, roles, results, relationships, and cultural impact are initially determined. Contracts and agreements should never be set in concrete but remain a continuous process that acknowledges the dynamic and sometimes unexpected aspects of change management. Change consultation practices require continuing informal, formal and technical agreements, from group agreement to extend a meeting time to deciding on team responsibilities for data collection and feedback to developing a legal contract with an outside resource group. These agreements build the foundation for everything else that happens as people make a commitment to work together to manage change.

7

Teamwork as a Structure for Change

Action research teams provide a structure for facilitating collaborative, data-based change management. Teamwork is about how people can work more effectively together within a variety of group contexts to facilitate change. Management teams, task forces, clusters, project teams, employee involvement groups, self-directed teams, business groups, cooperative research alliances, federations, and multinational joint ventures—all are indications that teamwork is a significant vehicle for organizational change and development on both a local and a global level. In a changing social and economic environment with shifting structures and roles, the future of the organization depends on teamwork among managers, employees, suppliers, distributors, customers, government agencies, community leaders, and widely dispersed stakeholders.

New organizational configurations make teamwork essential for effective performance. Organizations are becoming more fluid with flexible structures and an increasing need for coordination among loosely aligned components. For example, in one multinational organization human resource professionals and project managers at headquarters may team with local nationals in company locations around the world to produce coordinated training materials. In another organization self-directed teams in a manufacturing facility may meet with suppliers and customers to find ways to improve delivery and service. As organizational structures are transformed, teams can increase competency and coordination amid the conflict and contradictions of ongoing change.

The term "adhocracy" has been used to describe a structure of temporary alliances that challenge traditional bureaucratic forms with teams that come together to gather and process information, solve problems related to a specific project, and then return to their units or other groups. With little previous interaction, teams must join together in a timely and efficient manner with skill, creativity, and energy to meet new challenges and facilitate change processes. Adaptive "temporary" organizational structures are characterized by task forces made up of "relative strangers" with a variety of relevant professional skills and expertise (Bennis and Slater 1968). Action research teams also fall into this temporary category. Mills (1991) suggests a more unified system of semi-permanent "clusters" with people from different disciplines working together in teams to respond directly to customers or clients. There may be a similar cluster for action research teams with rotating membership from different disciplines as needed.

Action research teams can be a short-term commitment to facilitate data collection and planning. However, action research as a process can be used by employee involvement groups and self-directed teams that have a continuing team structure as part of a participative culture. The "high-involvement" organization spreads information, knowledge, power, and rewards throughout the system (Lawler 1992). This allows more people to participate in organizational change and to influence their collective future. Managers and team leaders must have effective consultation skills to facilitate this group development and integrate data collection, action planning, and analysis in both directed and nondirected change contexts.

Teamwork is also affected by changing organizational structures that do not always allow for the regular interaction, loyalty, and sense of community characteristic of more traditional organizations. Handy (1989) visualizes the changing organization in a "shamrock" configuration with three distinct clusters: 1) permanent professional core, 2) contractors and subcontractors, and 3) part-time and temporary workers. Each of these groups has different expectations and relationships with the organization, yet their information and output must be integrated to meet structural objectives. Handy also describes other organizational forms such as a "confederation" that combines autonomy with cooperation. In this decentralized system the core coordinates, advises, and influences independent units in a consultative model. These configurations are evident in an increasing number of organizations.

Mintzberg (1993) defines the organic decentralized, customized structure of the future as an adhocracy and differentiates two types: operating adhocracy and administrative adhocracy. An *operating adhocracy* of multidisciplinary teams innovates and solves problems under contract with different clients. Administrative and operating work are blended. The *administrative adhocracy* of line managers and staff experts work together to complete projects that serve the administration of the organization. The operating core is contracted but separate. Both of these forms can be ambiguous, politicized, competitive, and demand greater communication, negotiation, and coordination among teams and units.

The types of team projects, the level of group involvement and influence, and the participants may vary according to organizational structure and needs. In an age of "technoservice" (Maccoby 1988), systematic knowledge and information technology are used to more effectively serve customers and clients. Alignment through teamwork, collaborative inquiry, data sharing, and strategic alliance is crucial to competitive success. Ishikawa (1985) emphasizes this in total quality control, with its customer orientation, "management by fact," and cross-functional management that stresses cooperation and respect in breaking down the barriers of sectionalism.

Teamwork is also important in transferring information and resources within a global organization. A "borderless" economic world (Ohmae 1990) places an increasing emphasis on multinational strategic alliances, international joint ventures, partnerships in shared research and development, and groups that link business, government, and financial organizations in a network of mutual support and cooperation. In both Japan and Germany this network of cooperative teams includes workers, managers, suppliers, customers, the government, and other businesses (Thurow 1992).

Effective change management encourages teamwork as a way of linking resources, integrating goals, and involving people in learning together and exchanging competencies. This means developing authentic relationships with trust, openness, mutual respect, and reciprocity. Teamwork not only includes groups inside the formal organizational structure, but also relationships with suppliers, distributors, customers, and community leaders within an expanded and interrelated system.

Change management competencies related to teamwork help the organization to accomplish the following objectives:

- Clarify roles, goals and expectations;
- Integrate directed and nondirected change;
- Increase overall organizational competency;
- Create a synergistic competitive advantage;
- Increase coordination and alignment of resources;
- Develop greater responsiveness to customers;
- Reduce cycle time;
- Improve communication and cooperation;
- Collect and analyze data to develop new action;
- Link planning and implementation;
- Achieve world class quality

- Encourage feedback; and
- Connect the organization to its environment.

Teamwork in information gathering, feedback, and analysis is a continuing process that integrates change and aligns resources to accomplish organizational performance objectives.

TEAMWORK AS A CULTURAL VALUE

Teamwork is evoked in business meetings and discussions to support organizational spirit, strategy, and mission. Managers receive training in developing high-performance teams. Action research teams are formed to define needs and collect data. Yet the reality of teams is in the way in which they are interpreted by managers and employees in their daily work practices. Experts stress the importance of "team learning" in changing organizational systems (Senge 1990). Managers and employees can learn together through collaborative inquiry in sharing information and making decisions as a cooperative team. Action research teams are based on this interpretive feedback process.

Yet within an "informated" organization, a "learning relationship" can pose some threat for middle managers who are supposed to be the people who "already know" (Zuboff 1988). In traditional systems, managers are the people who have control of information and decisions. Action research teams give more people an opportunity to collect and analyze data. Employee involvement and participative programs can be perceived as a challenge to the authority and position of managers. Some companies have simply said to managers that they must learn to be more facilitative and "fold into the team" or seek other job opportunities. However, managers and teams must be trained and supported in new consultative roles, that help them to deal with transformed organizational structures and roles that give more influence and information to organization members.

Just as there are different perspectives on change, there are also varied concepts of teamwork. Some who take a behavioral view might see teams as a tool or technique to improve quality, productivity, and service and more effectively meet organizational goals. Others may interpret teams as employee empowerment and an opportunity for people throughout the organization to influence decisions and actions related to change.

While the organization is formally structured in terms of groups, departments, units, and divisions, teams are in many cases an interpretation and extension of that formal structure. There are many types of teams in the modern organization. Indeed, one management guru suggests that self-managing teams should be the basic building blocks (Peters, 1987). While self-directed teams are a highly developed form of employee involvement characterized by a gradual transfer of management authority to teams, there are many steps in between. Some professionals describe an evolutionary process in team development in organizations: 1) setting the stage for involvement; 2) developing parallel structures such as quality teams, with focus on one specific problem or issue; 3) creating natural work teams from existing groups without structural change; and 4) redesigning work structure for maximum employee involvement in self-directed teams (Schultz 1992).

Many quality teams are based on a participative model that integrates with a more conventional organizational structure and begins a broad developmental process for individuals, groups, and organizations. Involvement teams are defined as small groups of people who do similar work, voluntarily meet on a regular basis to identify and analyze causes of problems, recommend their solutions to management, and, where possible, implement the solutions (Aubrey and Felkins 1988). These teams are often part of a continuous process of improvement and learning through collaborative inquiry and group problem solving. Through data collection and analysis, team members begin to appreciate the complexity and interrelationships within the organization and develop more effective work practices to support quality, productivity, and service in changing systems. The facilitation and consultation skills of leaders, managers, boards, and team members are crucial in helping individual and groups to be part of a collaborative change-management process.

Action research teams bring some of the routine, nondirected aspects of change into the awareness of people within the facilitating and client systems, and helps to integrate nondirected and directed change. Organization members become more responsive to internal and external customers as they begin to see how the system works and how the units and components of the system are interrelated in terms of functions, goals, and responsibilities. Systems perspectives reinforce team orientation as members join together to create their organization with a shared vision and the knowledge that they are interdependent and must work together for successful performance.

Even though teamwork may be a stated organizational value, people seldom take time to assess the perceptions, values, expectations, and unwritten cultural norms that influence teamwork in daily work practices. As one employee said, "We don't have time for teamwork; we are too busy getting the job done." Teaming is an operational definition used to refer to particular processes, goals, and relationships. In some respects it is an example of our "created" organizational reality. The reality of teamwork may be in hallway discussions or in the unwritten rules for behavior, the private codes of communication within a particular unit or team, the hidden agendas and individual motivations, or the flourishing grapevine. Effective organizations recognize that procedures and project assignments may dictate team membership, but the informal cultural aspects of the organization energize that group and ultimately make them a cohesive or a disjointed unit. Understanding the informal culture of the organization and the impact of nondirected change helps to develop an adaptive team structure able to meet the requirements of a continually changing environment and shifting organizational priorities and needs.

Managers and employees might consider the possibility that "team" is in some ways an artificial, manufactured cultural concept created out of some basic need to find connections within a rapidly changing, technologically complex, and often impersonal organizational context. Perhaps it is based on a longing for the feeling of fellowship, belonging, and unified action in stressful and fragmented lives. As Drucker (1992) explains, people still need a sense of community and companionship at work. For organizational leaders, cultural values may dictate that it is better to be a team than just an ordinary work group. The word "team" seems to imply greater coordination, commitment, and effectiveness.

However, relationships in teamwork also assume some equality and opportunity for influence. The "myth of team" (Kanter 1983) implies that real differences do not exist and that everyone has an equal chance to participate. Like representative government, this concept is accepted more on faith and a view of how we want things to be rather than how they are. Inequality, politics, and power are facts of life in the organization, and they affect the interpretation and implementation of teamwork in change management.

Teams often operate in a contradictory, often paradoxical context within bureaucratic organizations. They are task-oriented and "empowered" yet integrated in a way that is consistent with controlled procedures and structures that provide efficient use of specialized resources and knowledge. In principle, all organization members have a chance to participate and many are members of productive teams. Yet participative teams may not always be democratic or support codetermination (Elden and Levin 1991). Employees don't believe they are given real opportunities for participation. Managers don't believe they are being given options around teaming and participation. Some employees don't always want to take the additional responsibility of involvement, and some managers are initially uncomfortable with empowerment and self-directed teams. People who have spent a good portion of their careers in bureaucratic, hierarchical systems may have to adjust personal style and skills to increase their overall effectiveness in a participative teaming culture. Today's managers are being required to be effective in parallel structures of both traditional and nontraditional forms within the same system. This creates contradictions and potential conflict for managers and employees that must be addressed in change management.

Part of this disconnection and conflict is due to the lack of process consultation technology for change management. Consultation skills create greater equity in management-employee relationships and encourage ongoing collaborative inquiry and problem solving in all units of the organization. Teamwork is the integrating element in allowing organization members to influence and manage change through an interactive, cooperative network. However, this is often an ideal. ART can create an elite group caught up in data collection and analysis that is not always linked to action or strategy of the organization. Self managed teams can sometimes lose their perspective and become an isolated and defensive unit. Teamwork requires specific competencies that must be learned and reinforced in relationships that support integrated and cooperative action that achieves mutual goals.

DEVELOPING TEAMING COMPETENCIES

Continuing training and developmental programs are critical in transferring and practicing the competencies for effective action research teaming and change management. It is especially important to train boards, managers, supervisors, and team leaders in teaming skills. The checklist in Table 7.1 is useful in assessing developmental and technical aspects of teamwork in integrating directed change with nondirected change in everyday work practices. These competencies provide a way to evaluate and support teamwork on an individual, group, and organizational level.

TABLE 7.1 Teamwork Competencies.

Systems perspective
- Balance micro and macroview of the organization
- Recognize interrelated components
- Establish linkage
- Consider the flow of information and activity
- Build connections among departments and units
- Determine areas of influence and control

TABLE 7.1 (continued)

Cultural orientation
 Work from organizational values
 Identify heroes and informal leaders
 Recognize cultural stories and narratives
 Develop organizational pride
 Create a sense of belonging and identification
 Integrate cultural norms
 Use cultural-communication networks

Communication
 Participate in organizational conversations and discussion
 Use multiple communication and feedback channels
 Clarify different "interpretations" of messages
 Express ideas clearly and directly
 Share information in an open, consistent way
 Be an active listener
 Confront issues and differences in a positive manner

Participation
 Involve people in planning and implementation
 Encourage voluntary participation
 Use the resources and skills of organization members
 Reward cooperation
 Build commitment
 Develop individual and group resources for change

Motivation
 Recognize contributions and commitment
 Reward on a team level
 Celebrate success
 Recognize individual needs within the team
 Set realistic change goals

Cooperation and coordination
 Make group goals clear
 Involve people in planning for change
 Share information
 Understand divergent views
 Recognize common ground
 Respect others
 Establish trust
 Maintain feedback channels

TABLE 7.1 (continued)

Innovation

Encourage appropriate risk taking

Consider alternative options

Recognize the positive aspects of change

Look for opportunities in change

Seek new linkages within the organization

Support openness

Task focus

Make agreements

Gather data

Analyze information

Summarize data

Link new knowledge to existing data

Make decisions

Take action based on data

Evaluate results

INVOLVING PEOPLE IN CHANGE MANAGEMENT

Beckhard and Harris (1987) refer to the "critical mass" of people who must actively participate in order to provide the initial energy for change. A few powerful people can initiate a directed change process, but the majority of people within the organization must support this directed change or it will fail. Participation and collaborative inquiry can reduce resistance to change and increase commitment on an informal level.

From an organizational perspective, there are many practical reasons for involving people in change processes. As team members, people can be more effective in their work and more committed to change. They will have more of the information and resources they need to do their job and greater appreciation of team contributions to overall organizational goals. Teaming in data collection, action planning, and implementation also increases support for directed change management.

Table 7.2 illustrates some of the ways in which leaders, managers, and consultation teams can facilitate support for change or, perhaps unknowingly, create barriers to successful change management.

TABLE 7.2 Supports and Barriers.

Facilitating supports

 Provide rationale for change

 Create team orientation

 Develop forum for dialogue

 Legitimize concerns

 Involve all levels of the organization

 Be open to creative options

 Use feedback to interpret information

 Be sensitive to context and timing

 Establish inclusiveness

Creating barriers

 Top-down approach to control

 Keep helpful information secret

 Do not empower people

 Impose change

 Disregard career concerns

 Ignore work patterns and norms

 Overlook perceived risk of failure

 Implement change without feedback

 Underutilize diversity as a resource

These supports and barriers to change point to the clear advantages of involving people who will implement change in the change-management process. Without this team effort, the change is not likely to be positive or appropriately integrated into the organizational system at both the directed and nondirected level. People ultimately determine the success of any change effort in how they interpret that change in their actions and work practices. This includes everyone from employees to distributors and customers.

Within the complex dynamics of organizational systems, a collaborative approach provides information and a coordinated effort to improve productivity, quality, and service by facilitating a more flexible, adaptive approach to data-based change management. The teaming process also develops people and reinforces commitment through greater knowledge of how the organization works and how individuals and groups can contribute to managing continuous change. Moving a culture from competition and hierarchy to teamwork and cooperation is a slow, facilitative process that requires commitment from all parts of the organization. Knowing how to facilitate collaborative inquiry and cooperative action through teamwork can be a valuable asset in reducing the ambiguity, contradiction, and conflict in transforming and restructuring organizations to improve performance.

FACILITATING TEAMWORK

Facilitating group learning and teamwork in change management demands an understanding of some basic concepts: diversity and commonality, communication and coordination, and confirmation and renewal. The dynamic relationships among these are shown in Figure 7.1.

FIGURE 7.1 Team Dynamics.

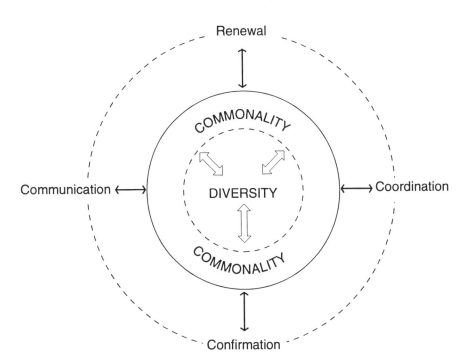

Multidisciplinary teams and temporary alliances are common in changing organizational structures. Project teams and clusters are brought together because of their diverse knowledge and specialized skills related to product development or service issues. Applying the energy and resources of diversity toward common goals is the essence of effective teamwork. This is central in managing the continuous and often contradictory aspects of change.

Team development begins with recognition and appreciation of diversity as a part of establishing commonality. *Commonality* assumes some shared values, norms, and objectives in working together. Too often teams start by imposing commonality in task orientation rather than acknowledging individual difference, competencies, and values in creating shared objectives. This initial orientation period in group development is important in establishing trust and respect for continuing team performance. *Diversity* broadens the team's perspective, helps them to be more innovative, and integrates each person's unique talents into a more dynamic group synergy.

Successful teams are supported by effective communication and coordination that integrates directed and nondirected change in collective actions and daily work practices. *Communication* helps the team coordinate the task and social dimensions of their work and form links with other teams throughout the system. *Coordination* is built on collaborative inquiry, negotiation, feedback and agreement for reaching shared goals.

Together confirmation and renewal sustain the team over time and validate the team as part of a larger network or system. *Confirmation* comes from both the team members themselves and from the organization system in recognizing and affirming the values of the team and their contribution to organization performance. *Renewal* demand that the team regularly assess their work together, meet new challenges, confront difficult issues, and exchange resources with other teams to create partnerships or form new teams.

The interactive "eye" of this teamwork model is diversity which gives energy and new possibilities to the teaming process. However this eye can be constricted or closed by bureaucracy, groupthink, and rigid structures. The following sections discuss the challenges related to diversity and commonality, communication and coordination, and confirmation and renewal in team structures for change management.

Diversity and Commonality

Teamwork requires cooperation and agreement, as well as conformity to mutually agreed norms and rules, and commitment to collective evaluation. Diversity and commonality provide a healthy tension between the "I" or expression of self authenticity and individuation, and the "me" or group expression of self (Mead 1962). Diversity, in how team members view and honor their differences together, and commonality in the ways teams form goal unity are essential components to effective teamwork. A major challenge for managers, group leaders, and and module advisors of self-directed teams is to provide a balance of both diversity and commonality, to satisfy individual needs for some unique identity and recognition, and the equally important need to belong and be part of a larger group. Mills (1991) suggests that the "cluster organization" provides more options for combining individual initiative and teamwork because teamwork in clusters enhances the individual and provides support for greater achievement. This balance is still a major challenge for supporting team structures in changing organizations.

Most definitions of group include common goals and regular interaction over a period of time. Yet the most crucial characteristic of groups is that people have some perception of themselves as members of a common team. While membership in organizational teams may not always be voluntary, there is a voluntary choice in how the individual interprets and establishes a relationship with the group. An effective group is defined in terms of mutual influence (Shaw 1981). In a team this influence is based on reciprocal trust and respect for people and alternative ideas, with equity among leaders and team members.

Leaders and followers are both part of the same dialectic. The leader's effect on organizational success may be only 10 or 20 percent, while followership is the factor that determines the other 80 to 90 percent of success (Kelley 1992). According to Kelley, this followership is not passive but active and "exemplary" when people choose to work with others rather than compete—to support what is right and to get the job done.

While action research teams and employee involvement groups have a strong task orientation, members must also recognize the socio-emotional aspects of teamwork if they want to be successful. People learn and develop in relationships as they define themselves in relation to others with some investment of competence, risk, and purpose (Hampden-Turner 1970). The result is a synergistic relationship in which individuals and groups can increase their competence and understanding of themselves and others.

This balance of individual and group needs is illustrated by the "Healthy Cell Group" (George 1991), a self-renewing team concept developed for use with congregational groups. This structure is based on interdependent roles including a *facilitator* and *apprentice facilitator*, a *host* or *hostess* who handles administrative matters, a *seeker* who wants to explore and learn about the group, a *growing person* committed to the group goals and personal development, and an "*extra grace required person*" who may need more support from the group. This cell group is also unique in that it always has an *empty chair* for a friend or an outside resource. A *coach* is also available for the facilitators if needed. In one congregation more than half of the membership is involved in these cell groups. They make agreements for learning, feedback, goals, action, and individual and group development. Membership rotates every 12 to 18 months and new groups are formed.

Managers and team leaders with change management competencies can help teams develop higher synergy and unity in reaching goals by facilitating individual and team learning while creating and maintaining the value and dignity of the individual and team.

There are advantages and disadvantages to group work. Most people agree that groups can be more creative and effective than individuals in many task-oriented contexts. The "synergy" or the combined energy or output of the group is a valuable resource. Groups maximize overall knowledge, skill, and experience, and increase the number of options and approaches to problem solving. Participation in groups also increases the acceptance of change and helps organization members to better understand and implement changes. However, group synergy can be reduced by group conflicts and disagreements, hidden agendas, dominant individual roles, and pressure for conformity or groupthink. Facilitation and communication skills may mean the difference between a united team and a collection of dissatisfied and disorganized individuals. Managers and team leaders must negotiate conflicting interests, coordinate resources and time requirements, support innovation and risk taking, and encourage consensus, compromise, and cooperation in an environment of continuing change. In this process the team should recognize the needs of the individual, the group, and the organization as interdependent.

Team spirit and group performance can be enhanced through training, support, and recognition of both the group and the individuals who comprise the group. Aubrey and Felkins (1988) suggest that goals of the team should include the development of its individual members as part of achieving broader organizational objectives. Through teaming, individual employees have an opportunity to develop self-knowledge, interpersonal skills, leadership, and increased understanding of the job and how the organizational system works. In the change management process the individual applies these skills to becoming more effective as team member and as a person.

While groups provide certain individual interpersonal needs such as inclusion, affection, and control (Schutz 1966), these needs are also dependent on others in the group. Current analysis of group motivations indicate more complex individual development needs with a new generation of "self-developer" employees who see work as an opportunity for learning and personal growth in increasing their competence and independence (Maccoby 1988). In defining motivation for work, Maccoby identifies value drives or needs such as survival, relatedness, pleasure, information, mastery, play, dignity, and meaning. Work helps develop integration and purpose for individuals and groups in a changing world.

Employee demographics and attitudes are more complex with a diverse workforce. Management can no longer assume commonality or conformity in the organizational system. Employees and stakeholders represent a variety of different perceptions, attitudes, and experiences. Since organization members may have divergent and conflicting goals and values, it is essential that teamwork in change management include some agreement on common goals, expectations, and roles. Unity can be found in the diversity if all participants are committed to developing a genuine collaborative relationship to meet mutual goals that serve both individual and group needs and build on diversity.

Just because an organization works toward some common goals does not predispose it to unity. From ethnic groups and demographic differences to functional departments, from part-time workers to senior executives, recognition of diversity challenges the creation of teams based on core values, knowledge, and experience. Teams must have a flexible core. In global organizations as well as local, regionally, or domestic based organizations there is increased ethnic, gender, age, and racial diversity as well as differences in knowledge and skills. Traditional distinctions in status and authority may also be confused by new roles and structures. Diversity is a great resource, but it must be coordinated with some agreements on shared goals, vision, and rewards to support teamwork in change management.

Cultural values and norms are not easily put aside when people walk into the workplace. Teamwork becomes an increasing challenge within multinational corporations where language and cultural norms may be more prominent and conflicting in everyday work practices. This can also affect teamwork in a task force or action research team. For example, in a large global construction firm, some engineers had a difficult time working on a project with a team leader who, in their home culture, would be perceived as a member of a social level below theirs. While Japan is often cited as the prime example of the power of group and national unity, westerners can misunderstand the Japanese interpretations of conformity and diversity. In Japan the individual is seen as a member of a group, institution, or society and, as a member, must occupy an appropriate place and meet all of the related social obligations and duties. This shared experience is both a personal and cultural orientation, which creates a commonality that is not easily interpreted or transferred to other cultures.

The challenge of teaming is often in striking a balance between commonality and diversity. Just because a group of people are together in the workplace or assigned as members of a project group does not mean that they are a team. With an increasingly diverse workforce, teamwork is a matter of choice and commitment as well as of knowledge and experience. Team members can work more effectively as a group if they discuss the following questions and come to some agreements on their differences and their unique values, goals, and ways of working together:

- What are our shared work values? Social values?
- What are our common goals for change management?
- What are the rewards for individuals? For the team?
- What responsibility do we have to other team members?
- What responsibility do we have to the organization?
- What formal procedures affect our group functions?
- What unwritten rules or norms do we follow?
- How do we make agreements?
- How do we collect and analyze data?
- How do we respect differences?
- How do we handle conflict?
- How do we maintain diversity?
- How much influence does our team have?
- How do we plan for action?
- How do we evaluate project results? Team relationships?
- How do we monitor and change rules or procedures?
- How do we celebrate our success?

One challenge for change facilitators is maintaining diversity and innovation in an organizational environment that often fosters conformity and commonality to increase control and coordination in times of rapid change. This rigid emphasis on being a "team player" can create groupthink, which is characterized by self-censorship and the "illusion of unanimity" with a lack of reality testing and judgment because of in-group pressures toward order and conformity (Janis 1982). In this situation, groups are so confident of their own knowledge that they do not consider alternatives or pitfalls, use available data, or seek outside opinions or expert resources to help manage change. They may even ignore the reality of change and the challenges it brings.

Groupthink protects some "undiscussables" (Argyris 1985) and covers up organizational conflicts and needs with the veneer of common goals and values. Managers are sometimes caught up in this collusive behavior. Indeed, Ryan and Oestreich (1991) list "management practice" as the number one undiscussable. According to their research, other undiscussable issues include coworker performance, compensation and benefits, equal opportunity practices, change, personnel systems, individual feelings, bad news, conflicts, and personal problems. These undiscussables are often at the nondirected level and not brought into formal organizational conversation. They can scuttle even the best directed change efforts by creating gaps and "holes" in the organizational team at the informal level in everyday work practices.

The lack of open discussion and analysis blocks creativity and confrontation of essential organizational problems that point to the need for change. Teams and organizations have many "defensive routines" that protect their cherished ideas and thoughts from attack and explanation (Argyris 1985). These defenses often support groupthink and resist directed change.

Groupthink can be avoided when members are critical evaluators of the team output. They can seek outside information and opinions in collaborative inquiry and add diverse new members and resources to the team. Action research also helps to push teams out of the groupthink rut. While individual members may share a common vision, teams should also have permission to explore and experiment with new ways of looking at continuing change and the challenges it brings. Confrontation also prevents groupthink and is part of the effective facilitation of change. Consultation skills in the confrontation of unspoken assumptions and the use of reflective feedback are useful in breaking through collective defenses to help individuals and groups discover the opportunities and learning that change can bring.

Most organization members will accept the "team" concept only when they are satisfied that their own goals, integrity, and interests will be fulfilled within the context of teaming. For managers, change facilitators, and team members, an understanding of teaming means an exploration of working relationship built on common goals that recognize the value of diversity as well as a shared vision in encouraging innovation and energy for change management.

Communication and Coordination

Once the initial agreements are made and some sense of unity and teamwork is established, teams must recognize a continuous process of communication and coordination to maintain their effectiveness throughout the system. Control and predictability are often the goals for management in directed change. However, organizations are not naturally orderly systems, especially if we recognize that they are in a process of continuous change, both directed and nondirected. In accelerated change, role relationships are in flux with a high degree of ambiguity. This demands effective communication and coordination.

The organizational team is not just composed of internal groups, but may include suppliers, distributors, customers, community, and other constituencies and stakeholders. Among these groups there are many "disconnects" that must be bridged through effective communication and alignment to create a successful team and to meet the challenges of rapid change. Coordinating these diverse teams and resources is often one of the major challenges in change management because change creates additional conflicts, and demands on the energy and resources of individuals and teams.

Organizational groups in specific functions and departments have been described as "tribes" that are often in conflict because of differences in language, values, experiences, and thinking patterns (Neuhauser 1988). For example, the "accounting tribe" may not understand or work effectively with the "sales tribe" or the "research and development tribe." In a healthcare system, the nursing group and the doctors may experience some "tribal conflict." These cultural differences are crucial in understanding teamwork and improving communication and coordination. Each tribe has its own hidden agendas as members seek power and resources within the system. Much of management's time may be spent in resolving tribal conflict and communication problems related to ongoing change.

Tribal conflict, real or perceived, can create disjunctions of communication. One of the typical disconnects in organizations is that between management and employees. To be effective, teamwork must have the open support of management at all levels. Managers should also model teamwork in their own practices. The attitudes and actions of management are critical in facilitating a team perspective for managing change with an atmosphere of trust, openness, and group learning. The challenge for change facilitators, team leaders, and managers is to foster cooperation and a problem-solving orientation in the minds of group members by encouraging open communication and collaborative inquiry in change management. When people discover that they really do need one another in order to be effective they develop an "operational trust" (Senge 1990) in their awareness of the position of other members and the belief that team actions will be cooperative and complementary in changing contexts.

One challenge for team coordination in a diverse workplace is posed by the flexible shifting structures of project teams, action research teams, and other groups that must work effectively from their first day together with little time allotted for group development. As Kanter (1983) explains, teams in rapidly changing organizations never have the continuity or stability they want and thus require constant negotiation in order to accomplish their tasks. Groups need some time to learn to be a team.

Tuckman (1965) summarized group development in four phases: forming, storming, norming, and performing. In the beginning, group members have to get to know one another and to define their task and identity as a team. This process may result in conflict on both an emotional and a task level. The questions are difficult: *How* do we do this? *Why* are we doing this? There are many people competing for leadership and control. After a time, this conflict is resolved and the team develops cohesion and direction with shared goals and mutually compensating needs. Members feel comfortable expressing ideas and listening to the ideas of others. Now the group is ready to perform effectively in making decisions, solving problems, and working as a cohesive team to help manage organizational change.

The stages of maturity for self-directed teams may also follow this general pattern: start-up, state of confusion, leader-centered teams, tightly-formed teams, and self-directed teams (Orsburn, Moran, Musselwhite and Zenger 1990). Teams must first find some leadership within their ranks and deal with their own autonomous identity before they can integrate their team as a productive and responsive part of a total system.

Team development is an evolutionary process that begins with initial agreements about how the group will work together. Communication skills in contracting and clarifying roles, goals, and expectations can prevent misunderstandings later in the process. Contracting for agreement, whether it is an informal consensus or a formal group document, helps to establish the rules for teamwork. However, these rules must be flexible and open to renegotiation within a changing organization.

Groups create the rules and expectations that affect their behavior as part of a cultural or social group. As Giddens (1984) explains, there is pressure toward conformity in maintaining these rules but each decision to support or reinforce the rules is also an opportunity to change the rules. Much of our experience tells us that when a group gets together to talk about a particular topic, they create their own reality in relation to that topic. They make their own standards and judgments and may reject opposing views. Teams develop distinct patterns of communication and private codes. Through their interaction, they determine rules and procedures that may or may not fit the specific norms and objectives of the organization. The challenge for managers and change facilitators is to help the team recognize its responsibility in creating the collective future of the organization, as well as the need to coordinate rules and practices to meet new challenges and opportunities.

Communication in teamwork requires some shared thought and coordination. The "collective phenomenon" of thought is based on dialogue and learning to suspend judgment in order to listen and understand the ideas of others (Bohm and Edwards 1991). Bohm distinguishes dialogue from discussion. *Discussion* is more like a ping-pong game or back-and-forth debate that each person wants to win. In *dialogue* people listen to each other, suspending judgement and competitive needs in order to truly understand and learn from the ideas and experience of others. In a team, collective thinking and dialogue are the essence of learning, as participants become more aware of their own thought processes and their sometimes faulty assumptions. Teams can learn to be a team through dialogue and communication. Managers, supervisors, and employees may have regular interaction, but this does not mean that they are a "team." Being a team is a conscious choice made as a result of dialogue, agreements, and shared experience within a specific context.

Through communication and coordination, members become more effective in cooperating as a team to meet challenges related to change. They gather data, analyze that data to implement action plans, and continue to gather additional data to monitor results. The problem-solving process has been described by some group researchers as a successive spiral in stages of diverging and converging as members seek new information, integrate that data, and then collect more data and explore options in a cumulative development of consensus (Schiedel and Crowell 1979). In this way the group is constantly creating itself, changing and making agreements through communication and coordination.

According to Ketchum and Trist (1992), the team coordination process includes three basic steps: action, pause for learning, and planning for action in the next cycle. The pause for learning allows the team to assess their work together and then transfer their learning and experience into planning and implementation in new situations. This sociotechnical approach attempts to integrate task objectives and technology with the way people work together.

Traditional management may focus on task and social aspects of group communication as distinct elements, yet their clear priority is on task orientation. On the task level of directed change, work-related goals and communication are centered around getting information, analyzing information, making decisions, and taking action. On the more informal, nondirected social level, the team is concerned with maintaining cohesiveness and meeting the individual needs of members. The integration of these levels supports coordination for successful change management.

Since project teams may be regularly shifting, it is important to get an overall sense of the task and the interpersonal elements of teamwork in the interaction of the total organization. This requires a critical look at communication networks and patterns in specific units as well as throughout the system. The consultative manager can support teamwork in his or her unit by helping others to understand the way they work together.

A "stop session" in a team meeting allows members to talk about how they are communicating with each other in accomplishing their task as a team. Some facilitative questions for this team dialogue are:

- How do we communicate with one another?
- Who gets information? Who needs information?
- How well do we listen to one another?
- How do we acknowledge understanding and agreement?
- How do we handle disagreement and conflict?
- How do we communicate with other teams?
- What private codes do we use that might exclude people?
- What types of formal and informal language do we use?
- What are the themes in our conversations?
- How does our language correspond to our behavior?

One overlooked source of data in facilitating and managing change is the content of organization conversations about change. How does the team interpret change? What is their response to change as individuals and as a group? The way in which the team resolves the contradictions associated with change can be crucial in effectively planning and implementing change in their work practices.

Sometimes teams in business organizations are placed in direct competition with one another. This discourages open dialogue and makes discussion difficult. The teams are not linked as part of the total system, and the coordination that is required for effective change management is diminished. The challenge of teaming is in developing linkages and alliances across the organizational system. This means breaking down traditional barriers, territorial imperatives, and competitive battles.

Gibb's (1961) classic model of supportive and defensive climates is helpful in working toward effective communication and coordination of teams for change management. A supportive climate encourages collaborative inquiry in *description* and *problem orientation.* There is *equality* and *empathy* in cooperative relationships that show trust and respect for individuals and groups and equity in team relationships. *Spontaneity* and *provisionalism* encourage innovation and creative options in planning and implementing change.

However, a defensive climate, as Gibb describes, works with *evaluation, control,* and *strategy* in a centralized structure that relies on authority and expert decisions. An impersonal sense of *neutrality* and lack of concern for individuals and groups allows leaders to show *superiority* over others by controlling information and making decisions that affect others. This creates a one-down relationship. Innovation is reduced by the *certainty* that there is only one right decision or action, most often the accepted bureaucratic policy. For example, teams can create a defensive climate when they decide to have "secret" meetings and do not share their knowledge and experience.

Change management endeavors to create a supportive cooperative climate among organization members. Change facilitators should encourage teamwork and collaborative inquiry within a reciprocal relationship that meets the challenges of change. Yet organizational culture can also nurture defensive and supportive climates that affect the way the organization communicates with other organizations and with people inside and outside the system.

Pearce (1989) describes four approaches to communication interaction: monocultural, ethnocentric, modernistic, and cosmopolitan. Each of these can represent a group perspective toward communication and coordination with others.

In *monocultural* communication, everyone is treated as a member of the same group, sharing a common culture. Bureaucracies are often monocultural in their rigid, closed communication patterns that encourage groupthink and conformity. Change is difficult in this cultural context because there is only one group and diversity is not tolerated or recognized.

Ethnocentric communication distinguishes clearly between "us" and "them." In this communication style, "our story" is held as the superior and right way of knowing and doing. This is a common form of communication in complex systems with multiple economic and social distinctions among different groups. Misunderstanding and conflict are often the result of ethnocentric communication. Within the organizational system, ethnocentric communication may create artificial, but real, barriers between units, distort information and decision-making, and prevent effective teaming in change management. On a broader level, ethnocentric communication prevents organizations from being effective in a multinational and global market.

Modernistic communication establishes boundaries between those who are in the know with the latest technology and theoretical perspective and those who are not. It is unstable, and information and resources are constantly at risk in the quest for something "newer" and "better." Modernistic communication is change-oriented and focused on the future, but it can be unbalanced and one-sided in the quest for "progress" and development. A sense of collaborative inquiry and coordination is often lost in competition and a feverish push toward accelerated change often controlled by a small group of experts. Specialized action research teams and project teams may isolate themselves with this elite attitude.

Cosmopolitan communication is a perspective and a practice that meets the challenges of complexity and diversity in organizational change. This type of communication accepts the risks of understanding and acknowledging dissimilar ideas and worldviews. Cosmopolitan communication stresses coordination among dissimilar groups and "social eloquence" (Pearce 1989), or skill in recognizing and seeking the potential for understanding in human interaction and diversity.

Differences in values, perceptions, and needs do exist among organizational teams in changing systems. The goal is to coordinate and understand these differences as part of an intriguing mosaic, rather than trying to force coherence in which everyone must conform to a predetermined script. Coordination should also encourage innovation, respect diversity, and integrate the contradictions associated with change. This moves the organization toward genuine growth and development as part of a larger social, economic, and political environment. Coordination encourages team learning and development rather than the building of barriers. Communication is a taken-for-granted reality in most organizations. Developing awareness of communication barriers and breakdowns can help coordinate teamwork and increase organizational effectiveness in integrated change management.

Confirmation and Renewal

Rather than always focusing on problems, and trying to fix and improve organizations, managers and team members must also recognize positive aspects and what is good and right with the organizations. Suresh and Cooperrider (1990) suggest the need for more "appreciation" and affirmation in organizational dialogue. This nourishes self-generative possibilities for new knowledge and action. According to Cooperrider, "affirmative competence" is essential to the collective process of creating a positive future based on the human potential of the organization.

Confirmation is a sometimes overlooked element in change management that proclaims the value and contribution of the team and the process. Confirmation includes both intrinsic and extrinsic recognition of teamwork by management, team members, and the larger organizational system. Renewal is not only confirming the worth of people and practices but also confronting areas that need development and change. Renewal is a continuing process of learning and growth. Confirmation recognizes that development.

The Hawthorne studies first helped managers and researchers to focus on the effect of confirmation. These classic and somewhat infamous studies of work groups were based on experiments from 1927 to 1932 at the Western Electric Hawthorne plant in Chicago. In their rational/behavioral approach to change, these studies focused on specific working conditions and their effect on productivity. The primary results are reported by Mayo (1933) and by Roethlisberger and Dickson (1939). Despite changes that logically would seem to reduce productivity, productivity increased. Traditional theories did not fully explain these results and the researchers were forced to acknowledge the impact of increased group interaction in communication and decision making as well as the social norms and sense of teamwork created by such group interaction. Workers were more satisfied because they were receiving more attention and confirmation from supervisors. They were included in team decision making and directly rewarded for their work. The Hawthorne "experiments" showed the importance of teamwork and the impact of the informal organization that exists in daily interactions and work practices beyond the formal rules, roles, and procedures that supposedly structure the organization. Participation is tested at the nondirected level.

In most cases, people do want more participation in the organization. These individuals are more motivated and satisfied with their work when they are part of a team with the information and the responsibility they need to do their job and influence change. As part of participation team members need some recognition and confirmation that they are a part of the organization's ultimate success. This need for confirmation also includes management. Structural changes and self-directed teams can eliminate one or more layers of management or supervision as the traditional position of the supervisor "disappears" (Orsburn, Moran, Musselwhite and Zenger 1990; Lawler 1992). Managers and supervisors who survive are thrust into different ways of working that require new competencies and team applications for change management.

Teamwork can be interpreted in many ways. One of the most important elements is the recognition and belief by individual members that they are part of a "team" both as a distinct project team or workgroup and a larger organizational team in a holistic interdependent system. A recognition of team members as colleagues and friends is the foundation of group cohesiveness. Cohesiveness has been defined as the level to which group members are attracted and personally committed to the team (Fisher 1980). This feeling of loyalty, pride, or satisfaction with the group is a confirmation that comes from each individual group member. A team name, slogan, or logo as well as team stories and celebrations are visible expressions of this unity and cohesiveness.

Confirmation of teamwork is a core value in successful organizations. Sam Walton, the late founder of Wal-Mart, created a hard-working "family" atmosphere in which every employee was part of "Sam's team." He made informal visits to his stores and invited employees to picnics at his home. An observer chronicled one of these social gatherings: "The traditional employees' picnic in the Walton's front yard in Bentonville, Arkansas, attracted 2,500. They were handed box lunches, and the head man, in a blue-and-white Wal-Mart baseball cap and shirtsleeves, wandered around listening intently to ideas and suggestions, greeting old friends, and posing for pictures" (Trimble 1990). This was an active confirmation of the collective Wal-Mart team. This team has helped to change retailing.

Another part of confirmation is the way in which team members talk about the group, communicate with one another, and make decisions together. One classic measure of the statements of group members is Bales' (1950) interaction process analysis based on positive statements (shows solidarity, shows tension release, agrees) and negative statements (shows antagonism, shows tension, disagrees) in social-emotional areas of group interaction and task-oriented questions (asks for orientation, asks for opinion, asks for suggestion) and attempted answers (gives orientation, gives opinion, gives suggestion) in task areas. These individual statements help to confirm and challenge the group process on both a task and social level. Other research focuses on interactive group communication related to group development, problem solving, and decision making. Fisher (1980) explores different patterns of interaction and suggests four phases in the process of group decision making: orientation, conflict, emergence, and reinforcement. This process parallels the overall development and maturity of teams as they learn to create their own confirmation of teamwork through their dialogue and action.

Even if a team is temporary, the people in a team need to make a periodic confirmation check and assess their teamwork. The questions in this checklist offer some guidelines for peer and team evaluation:

- How do we determine the members of this team?
- How do we work together to solve problems?
- How do we confirm our team in our conversations?
- How would we describe ourselves to others?
- What have we learned from our major successes? Our failures?
- What are some of the stories in our group history?
- How do others in the organization perceive us?
- How do we celebrate our success together?
- How do we learn together to improve our team?
- How do we make decisions as a team?
- How we facilitate feedback to each member? To the team?

- What are the most important rewards for our team?
- How is our team recognized by the organization?

Confirmation of teamwork at the corporate level should also be a part of integrated change management. This involves recognition including public actions, rewards, and celebration. Since the reality of the team is created by its members' interaction, it is important that the actions of the team reinforce that team identity. The organization must also recognize and reward the performance of the team as a group. The team should never be reified as a thing-in-itself. Results cannot be counted solely in the number of self-directed teams, the dollar savings, or the total quality projects completed. The team is a dynamic collection of skilled, committed people, influencing organizational actions, facilitating change, and helping to create a collective future. Teamwork is a process and an attitude that must be recognized, understood, nurtured, and rewarded.

There is considerable debate as to the appropriate rewards for teamwork. Much of the discussion relates to bonuses based on profitability, employee ownership, and gain sharing, which establishes a baseline and rewards gains in performance as a percentage of salary. Some experts believe that in high-involvement organizations, part of the pay should be dependent on organizational performance (Lawler 1992). There are conflicting views on the value and application of financial rewards for the team and individual members.

Rewards are an explicit sign of value and recognition. Teams have their own personal rewards including new knowledge and skills, increased understanding of organizational processes, and evidence of their influence on the system. Often, the greatest intrinsic reward and confirmation is knowing that their team made a difference and had some specific impact on managing organizational change. Teams often have their greatest influence in integrating directed and nondirected change processes. Members should recognize small milestones and major accomplishments, and celebrate their success as a team.

The larger organizational system also has public ways of rewarding and recognizing team efforts in change management through formal ceremonies, trophies, plaques, awards, and tokens. This recognition can include coverage in organizational publications such as newsletters and magazines. Annual reports might also recognize teamwork and action research in facilitating change throughout the system. A visible confirmation of teamwork by top executives and senior managers is essential in maintaining motivation and effectiveness in change management. Celebration in public ceremonies and social activities is another aspect of group confirmation. All of these rewards confirm the value and contribution of teamwork in planning, facilitating, and implementing organizational change.

Renewal is at the core of confirmation and teamwork in an integration of directed and nondirected change. Lippitt (1982) defined renewal as the process by which an organization confronts situations and searches for solutions, as well as the process of "coping" with facts and circumstances in implementing solutions. Renewal requires a constant emphasis on learning, development, and change, which helps the organization maintain what they value and identify what they want to change. A recognition of the gap between "where we are now" and "where we want to be" is often the beginning of the renewal process for teams and organizations. Renewal develops human resources to facilitate change and to create the collective organizational future through improved problem solving and increased commitment, greater creativity, and significant learning from successes and failures. In change management, renewal integrates the human, technical, and financial resources of the organization to facilitate data-based change throughout a responsive, productive, socially responsible organization.

From a team perspective, renewal means confronting challenges and opportunities, seeking creative options and taking risks, and assuming responsibility for team development and for group actions. This may include renewing individual and group commitments to the values and goals of the team. Team members may also recognize that they need more diversity and should include others in their group. They may decide that they need additional training, experience, or knowledge in order to continue to work effectively in change management. A part of renewal is also looking at the continuing viability of the team. Both recognition and renewal are important reality checks for the group in determining the future of their team in a changing organizational structure.

Integrating Teamwork

Diversity and commonality, communication and coordination, and confirmation and renewal must be integrated in successful teamwork. The effective performance of a continually changing organizational system is based on teamwork in units, clusters, task forces, self-managed teams, action research teams, and strategic alliances with suppliers, customers, and the community. Change management emphasizes group learning and cooperative inquiry in meeting the challenges for innovation, renewal, and learning in a competitive, dynamic marketplace. Teamwork maximizes the effectiveness of organizational resources and enriches the organization in the process.

Change from a systems perspective often requires a transformation of organizational culture and everyday ways of doing business. Organization members should be active, responsible agents in the change-management process, as organizations are restructured, reinvented, and reengineered. However, these people must believe that their teams are authentic and able to influence the organization and not just an empty archetype or the latest management fad to improve quality, productivity, and service.

Teamwork is a recognition of the holistic nature of organizational systems and the need for people to think and learn together. Change-management skills can facilitate group learning and link organizational resources to meet strategic objectives. The organization may be divided into departments, units, and divisions, but the partial elements are incomplete and inefficient if they are not integrated into a coordinated organizational team.

As one consultation group acknowledges, in managing change there are three types of people—those who make it happen, those who help it happen, and those who let it happen and get in the way (Kearns and Nadler 1992). Teamwork can make it happen. The marketing slogan of a highly successful electronics firm acknowledges a shifting context with new rules in a simple statement: "The game has changed." Organizational structures, roles, and work practices are being transformed, and teams are at the core of this process.

Many organizations are now in a transition period in changing from an old bureaucratic paradigm to a new participative paradigm. During this transition phase, employee involvement and teamwork can help people to do what needs to be done. Competent and informed team members are committed to making the organization more responsive and productive. The change management competencies of leaders, managers, staff professionals, boards, and teams will help to create the future of organizations.

PART III

A Data-Based
Change Process

8

Data Collection and Analysis

Data collection is the beginning of a collective process of discovery and learning, not an end in itself. It is a part of every phase of the change management process. Effective managers know the value of data in strategic planning, coordination, implementation, and evaluation of change. This chapter provides information that managers, staff professionals, team members, and change facilitators can use to improve their skills in collecting and analyzing data for change management.

While we have assigned data collection to Phase 3, it is an activity that is used during all of the six phases. For example, in scouting and entry as well as reaching agreements change facilitators will be collecting data, analyzing it and getting feedback from the client system through a variety of methods. Phase 3 represents data collection as a visible and explicit component in a change management process. This phase of consultation uses action research and collaborative inquiry to move data toward shared understanding and action.

In Phase 3 of the change management process, managers, change facilitators, consultation teams, and action research teams may be transformed into explorers, detectives, archeologists, and scientists as they collect and analyze data related to the past, present, and future of the organization. The facilitating system and the client system work together to establish the foundation for data-based change. The type of data collected and the way in which that data is interpreted depends on specific assumptions about data collection and analysis as a part of change management. It also depends upon and is affected by a number of factors within the client system.

Dimensions that Affect Data Collection and Analysis

Data collection is affected by the following factors in the client system:

- Information needs
- Unit of change (individual, group, intergroup, organization, or society/global)
- Visibility of feedback within the client system
- Timeframe
- Client system involvement

All of these are influenced by client system readiness for change, which determines the amount of overall structure needed in data collection and analysis. The interactions of these dimensions are shown in Figure 8.1.

FIGURE 8.1 Factors Affecting Data Collection.

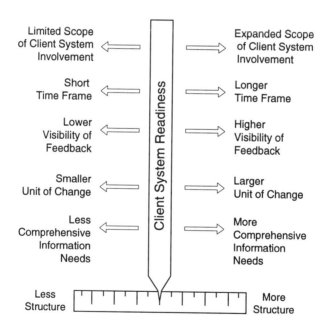

If information needs and time are limited, the data collection will be less structured. If the project is more complex with extensive involvement of the client system and comprehensive information needs, data collection will be more structured and formal. Data collection for a small unit of change such as a group in one unit of an organization will be less structured than a directed change for the entire system. The visibility of feedback is also a significant factor. If the feedback will be conducted throughout the organization and the CEO will be involved in analysis and implementation, the process will be more structured.

For instance, data collection for entry in Phase 1 is often more informal and less structured. As the client system becomes more involved and assumes more ownership and readiness for change, data collection becomes more structured and integrated. This is a development aspect of transferring competencies for change management. Organization members learn to collect and analyze data in both formal and informal ways to help manage change in their work practices.

Approaches to Data Collection and Analysis

This chapter provides a design resource for managers, staff professionals, and data team leaders who need to collect and analyze performance in a systematic and relevant way. Research methods provide a structured approach to data collection and analysis based on working theories and accepted procedures for knowing and measuring "where we are now." Action research, as described in chapter 4, is applied research that helps people to manage change more effectively. This chapter deals with research activities and options.

Miller (1991) describes three patterns of research: basic, applied, and evaluative. *Basic* or pure research seeks new knowledge and is most often associated with traditional scientific investigation. *Applied* research attempts to provide "useful knowledge" that can be used in direct action implementation and problem solving. *Evaluative* research provides an assessment or appraisal of ongoing programs and processes.

Organizations often find applied and evaluative research most useful for continuing improvement of quality and service, as well as individual, group, and organizational development. The process of collecting and analyzing data within these frameworks helps integrate directed and nondirected change. For example, action research challenges limited causal thinking and increases the responsibility of the client and organization members to meet challenges and recognize the consequences of specific actions and decision in daily work practices. Evaluative research helps to benchmark, monitor, adjust, and improve performance based on relevant criteria and changing needs.

Rational/behavioral approaches to data collection, such as scientific methods or experimental research, gather data and use inferential statistics in order to predict and control specific phenomenon. Researchers develop a hypothesis about relationships among or between variables and test that hypothesis through experimentation and measurement. Key terms must be defined in an operational or testable way. Statistics, charts, and numbers are valuable tools for planning and evaluation, but in some ways this data is limited by the ways in which it often fails to represent the dynamic reality of the organization and the people who create that reality in their decisions and actions. Quality goes beyond control charts and inspection.

Numbers and computer models can measure only a part of organizational performance and effectiveness. As an analogy, quantum physics has caused many scientists to rethink the very definition of "reality" and the way it is measured. Heisenberg (1958) describes a twofold world: one consisting of potentials and possibilities, and another of facts and actualities. Using this metaphor, we can conceptualize that between the possibility and the reality of time and space, and the present and the future, there is uncertainty in any attempt at precise measurement of organizational systems and culture. The act of measurement creates changes. Data collection and analysis may help us to reduce some uncertainty, but with every fact or observation there are other possibilities that we might not consider and variables whose relationships we cannot adequately measure. Data can provide insight through historical analysis of past actions and consequences, performance measurement in the present, and speculation and prediction on the potential of the future. Yet no amount of data collection and analysis can eliminate all of the uncertainty in a world of calculated risks and an exploding knowledge base where change is equated with rapid progress in developing the "better" and "more efficient."

In some areas, scientific approaches, with their emphasis on a division between the measurer and the measured, may not be adequate for understanding the cultural and systems interactions in the informal creation of the organization in daily conversations, attitudes, and practices. A critical postmodern perspective suggests the loss of an overarching unified meaning in many social institutions and organizations. Handy (1989) describes the current period as the "Age of Unreason," a time of confusing and disturbing discontinuous change that breaks our grand rational and traditional patterns of meaning and order. According to Handy, this age requires not only the reflection and testing of ideas but also a fundamental reframing of the way we think and solve problems. He calls this approach a kind of "upside-down" thinking that allows multiple perspectives and characterizes problems as opportunities for learning and development within flexible, changing organizational structures.

While a classical approach to data collection and analysis may assume exact operational definitions of product and process, the reality of organizations is not always so orderly or easily predicted by inferential statistics or reliability measures alone. Action research teaming encourages shared collaboration in data collection and analysis based on innovation and learning in multiple approaches to data collection and analysis. Action research reframes problem solving in an interactive organizational context where "problems" become "opportunities" for collective learning to benefit individuals, groups, and organizations. In action research, both objective and subjective information is included in a continuing, proactive process of data collection, feedback, and analysis to recognize ambiguity and complexity, reduce uncertainty, and integrate directed and nondirected organizational change.

Data collection and analysis in applied research help people in organizations to see problems and contexts in different ways. Evaluative research allows assessment of how well the system is working and a comparison of what is happening and what should happen in a process. A competitive, global environment demands a higher level of awareness and a continuous spirit of discovery, improvement, and innovation in structure, operation, and service. In all areas of organization there is an increasing need for people to take responsibility for information and collaborate in understanding and applying data to change management.

Any approach to collecting and analyzing data should follow some systematic plan based on information needs, resources, and organizational objectives. We encourage the use of several integrated approaches and methods and the direct involvement of the client system in all aspects of data collection and analysis for managing change. The data collection and analysis process can be summarized in several interactive steps:

1. Diagnose and analyze needs.

2. Determine units of change and measurement.

3. Mobilize action research methods and design.

4. Identify sources and gain access.

5. Give feedback, monitor, and assess results.

Many of these steps affect and in turn are affected by previous and continuing phases in the consultation process. The change management model (Figure 8.2) focuses some of the key decisions relating to data collection and analysis. Note the key question related to each of the basic components. The reader may also want to refer back to Table 3.1 in Chapter 3, which explores additional questions related to context, consultation technology, coordination and results.

FIGURE 8.2 Change Management Model.

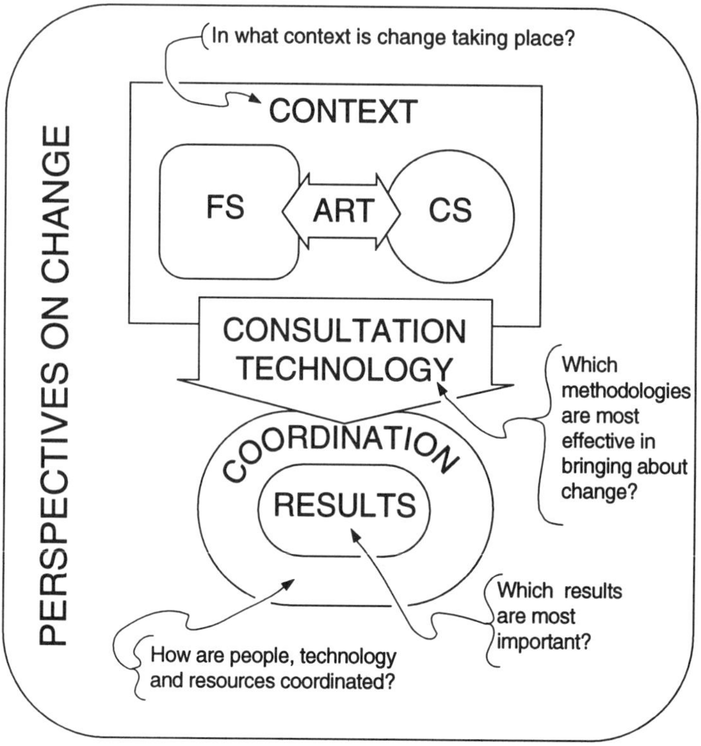

FS = Facilitating System   ART = Action Research
CS = Client System   Teaming

The context in which the change is taking place affects the needs identified as well as the units of change at the individual, group, intergroup, or organizational level. Status and power relationships may also be influential in this context. Consultation technology may help determine the use of multiple methodologies, identify sources, establish focus, and match needs with resources for data collection and analysis. Coordination supports collaborative inquiry and action research teaming which involves people throughout the system. The expectations for results and the direct application for data-based change focus data collection and analysis on specific outcomes.

TABLE 8.1. The Context of Data Collection

Diagnosing and analyzing needs:

Select appropriate sources and data-collection methods to fit situation, type of client, and anticipated intervention design.

Establish performance criteria for monitoring and evaluating action and providing feedback cycling for planning new action.

Determining macro and microunits of change and measurement:

Involve client in data-based change, diagnosis, interpretation, and planning for action.

Develop a systematic approach to overall data collection and analysis.

Identify the forces that impede or facilitate movement toward the desired outcomes.

Mobilizing action research teams:

Use an action research teaming (ART) approach with the client to establish involvement, commitment, and accountability.

Identify appropriate readiness activities to prepare the client for involvement and feedback activities.

Design ART interventions.

Establish support for change effort through high-level sponsors and action research team leaders and members.

Facilitate training in methods of data collection, analysis, feedback, and action-planning events.

Use group development methods for teamwork effectiveness.

DIAGNOSIS AND NEEDS ANALYSIS

The first step in data collection is often diagnosis and needs analysis. Table 8.1 details the initial data collection process. This provides a clear focus and helps to establish the gaps in performance and the areas of greatest concern and opportunity for change management. Performance objectives are most valuable in assessing current organizational practices in relation to current and future goals. Table 8.2 shows some typical performance objectives that can be used for organizational diagnosis and needs analysis.

TABLE 8.2 Performance Objectives.

Become a preferred supplier
Become a preferred employer
Develop a strong image in the community
Increase market share
Become more market-driven
Develop a strong relationship with key customers
Meet and anticipate customer needs
Improve the spirit of teamwork among employees
Develop total quality management
Operate a more efficient business
Maintain continuous improvement
Conserve limited resources
Improve return on investment (ROI)
Redirect capital toward high-return use
Identify new investment opportunities
Generate strong cash flow
Enhance value for stockholders
Invest in research and development (R&D)
Increase social responsibility
Make strategic alliances and ventures
Establish a worldwide presence in multinational markets

In a needs analysis, managers and change consultation teams should consider how data collection and analysis contributes to specific organizational performance objectives. This ensures that business goals are clearly visible and aligned through appropriate units within the organization. A needs analysis also assesses what measurement is required and how that measurement can be made. Data collection might occur in relation to specific indicators such as market share, profitability, quality, work design, productivity improvement, competitive advantage, or cost reduction. Needs analysis includes data collection, feedback, interpretation, and planning for action implementation. Needs analysis also helps in selecting the appropriate sources and data-collection methods for additional action research cycles. The steps of a needs analysis are:

- Statement of a need
- Validation of the need
- Methods of meeting the need

Needs assessment often begins with a statement or identification of a need. For example, this might be a definition of standards for optimal levels of proficiency for a task or job position. Current levels of proficiency are measured and the differences or gaps between optimal and current needs are determined. The next step is validating that need through documentation, interviews, questionnaires, and various benchmarking activities.

The questions included in Table 8.3 help the action research team to conduct a needs analysis based on data collection. The list contains some of the concepts that were discussed in Chapter 6 on the contracting phase. Contracting is a continuing process that may occur at all phases of change management. In data collection, a needs analysis provides a coordinated direction, establishes measurement criteria, and focuses energy and resources on productive and relevant activities to meet the need. Once needs have been assessed, and agreed upon the next step is determining the unit of change at the individual, group, intergroup or organizational level.

TABLE 8.3 Needs Analysis.

Performance Measurements

What performance measurements exist now?

Where are the gaps in measurement?

Where are the gaps in "where we are" and "where we want to be?"

What performance criteria are required?

What documentation is available?

What previous survey data exists?

Are there any field studies related to the performance indicators?

What kind of longitudinal data is available for these indicators?

Process

What data is required for priority measurements?

What parts of the organization will be involved?

How will feedback on these performance areas occur?

How and to whom will the data be reported?

How does the action research team gain access to data?

How will members communicate during this process?

Roles and Relationships

Who is the client? Sponsor?

What are the priority performance indicators for the client? Sponsor?

What is the incentive for the client? Sponsor?

What are the perceived incentives for participation?

Will the client system accept the data?

TABLE 8.3 (continued)

Resources

What financial investment is needed?

What internal and external resources are available for data collection and processing?

Will documentation and evaluation require support?

How much time will be needed?

Will training be required for data collection and analysis?

Results

How will success be measured?

What will be the output or "product" of data collection?

How will progress be measured and monitored?

How will measurement data be used?

DETERMINING MEASUREMENT AREAS AND UNITS OF CHANGE

Planning for data collection and analysis requires an understanding of the context for measurement and evaluation. While a needs analysis helps in developing a pragmatic focus, the consultation team must fit these needs into a systematic plan of data collection and analysis for effective change management. This means that they must consider the information needs in relation to continuous change processes within a complex system. Preparing a design for collecting and analyzing data from multiple perspectives, helps to focus on interrelated units of change. The questions below encourage more systems thinking in relation to performance measurement areas in the change process.

- What are the inputs and outputs related to each performance objective?
- How are inputs changed or modified within the system?
- What factors have the greatest impact on the overall process or product design?
- How are positive and negative feedback loops used?
- What factors can lead to entropy and chaos in the system?
- What factors contribute to synergy and cooperation?
- How are specific components related and aligned?
- What are our target values for variation of a design or process?

- How do communication channels affect performance objectives?
- What environmental factors affect performance objectives?
- Are there other options for measurement?

The answers to these questions can help the team to focus data collection on key performance areas and the interdependent context in which measurements are made.

Change management, unless guided by a systematic diagnostic framework in data collection and analysis, is like a ship without a rudder. The diagnostic process involves data collection, data organization, and data analysis. Because of limited time, lack of adequate resources, and personal and professional biases, change consultation groups and action research teams often make choices that limit the kind of information gathered, the organization and presentation of that information, and the analysis of this information. A clear understanding of measurement objectives and units of change encourages more cost-effective, focused data collection and analysis.

The basic questions that should be considered in relation to measurement criteria and units of change are:

- Which performance objectives and measurements are most important to the client? Sponsor?
- How are these different measurements related?
- What type of microlevel data is needed? Macrolevel data?
- How will individual performance areas be measured? Group performance? Intergroup? Organization?
- Is there a priority unit of change?
- How will this data on various units of change be integrated for analysis?

In measuring performance, data collection serves descriptive, evaluative, and predictive goals. *Descriptive* data allows organization members to better understand the interactions and processes within the organization. This type of data often answers the questions: Where are we now? How are we working together? Descriptive data may include organizational mapping and process flowcharts. This information helps in assessing current need as well as in planning and developing future programs. Descriptive data also can establish a benchmark for performance measurement. Benchmark data based on a specific model of performance with quantitative and qualitative standards can provide a continuing picture of change and development in quality, product and process design, and service.

Evaluative data requires judgment and is more quantitative in measuring processes and progress toward performance goals. For example, cycle time, or the clock time for one unit to go through the plant, should be no more than twice direct labor time (Bhote 1991). Statistical analysis may be used to provide a direct measurement of effects and results based on precise guidelines as well as patterns, probabilities and specifications within the system. In an audit this measure may be made against specific performance criteria. *Predictive* data is based on inferential statistical measurements that allow generalizations to a larger population or context. This requires a representative random sample of respondents. Together these quantitative and qualitative measures can provide more reliable data for all units of change including individual, group, intergroup, organizational, societal, and global. Table 8.4 lists these units of change and some specific performance indicators for each.

TABLE 8.4 Units of Change and Performance Areas.

Individual measurements
   Work satisfaction
   Productivity
   Quality
   Job knowledge
   Organizational knowledge
   Participation
   Medical expense

Intragroup
   Productivity
   Quality
   Teamwork
   Commitment
   Communication

Intergroup
   Information exchange
   Coordination
   Alignment
   Cooperation
   Teamwork

Organization
   Profitability
   Quality
   Productivity
   Return on investment (ROI)
   Shareholder equity
   Profit and loss
   Customer satisfaction

TABLE 8.4 (continued)

Societal and global
  Social responsibility
  Ethics
  Environmental concern
  Conservation of resources

For example, quality measurements can be made at all levels of the organization. However, differentiating and aligning quality objectives at different units of change can help in understanding and facilitating total quality management throughout the organizational system.

One way to collect initial data from a systems view is to develop a force-field analysis of the supporting and resisting forces in the system in relation to a specific directed change. The model shown in Figure 8.3 might be used as a guide in looking at units of change—individual, group, intergroup, organizational, and societal and global—in context.

FIGURE 8.3 Dynamics of Change.

Driving Forces   Restraining Forces

individual
group
inter-group
organizational
societal and global

All of this positive and negative energy exists in a larger macrocosm of social, cultural, and economic influences within a complex and continually changing system. Understanding data collection from a systems perspective encourages action research teams to focus on strategic areas in gathering information and to analyze that information in relation to a larger interrelated network rather than a single unit a division.

This perspective immediately makes data collection and analysis more equivocal and challenging. Components are interrelated and interdependent and continuously affect each other in subtle and dynamic ways. A systems approach to data collection reminds us that we are taking a particular data collection at a specific time and at discreet points within a continuous system. Thus, information must be collected and interpreted in view of limitations on human and technological ability to precisely measure "reality." Multiple confirmation through a variety of quantitative and qualitative measures is necessary in a complicated system. Data is a resource and a tool that is fully understood only in a collaborative and interactive context that reflects diversity and complexity of the data and the system.

The focus on units of change may also influence the type of information required. Data may be *primary*, *summary*, or *secondary*. *Primary* data comes from a direct interaction and is most often completed at an individual or group unit of change. *Summary* data combines and organizes primary data in an overview or outline of major results. This focus is more often on change in the organizational, intergroup, or departmental unit. Individual data may be summarized in attitude surveys or opinion polls, but this data is usually at least one-step removed from direct observation or personal interaction. It can be unwieldy to present all primary data in feedback sessions. Often summaries and combined results are more efficient and allow people to see trends and patterns most clearly. However, some data is left out in this process. *Secondary* data is even further removed from primary sources. This data is the result of surveys, interviews, and documentation completed in the past by someone who may or may not be part of the organizational system. This data may be found in specialized libraries as well as in the files of the organization. For example, national opinion polls or industry surveys may provide general information on issues and trends and reflect on organizational, societal, and global units of change.

An understanding of performance objectives and units of change helps in planning for data collection and analysis. In a dynamic organization, data collected 18 months ago may be more historical than descriptive of the current state of the system. Yet in a rigid bureaucracy, data collected three years ago still may reflect the current organizational culture. Realistic data collection demands interaction with primary sources and documentation of directed and nondirected change through both quantitative and qualitative measurements. The individual unit of change is the most basic, but this data should be aligned with group, intergroup, organizational, societal, and global perspectives for effective change management.

MOBILIZING ACTION RESEARCH TEAMS

Getting Involvement

When people are involved in gathering and analyzing data, they tend to support the results of that cooperative work and subsequent data-based change. In ad hoc committees, task forces, advisory committees, councils, and panels, it is direct involvement and participation that creates organizational commitment and support for change management.

The client system should participate in data collection activities and not be a passive receiver of data. Efforts should be made to establish client system involvement, commitment, and accountability in data collection and analysis throughout this process. Progress reports and summary data can be shared in feedback sessions, memos, and publications as appropriate.

In all cases, top management support is essential. Management must communicate a willingness to believe in and act on the data collected and participate in planning and action based on the data. The commitment to collaborative inquiry and data-based change throughout the organizational system should be evident in the actions of management, the client, and the change management team.

Data collection is not just a task for the consultation team. Data collection and analysis should become a natural and useful part of everyday work in integrating directed and nondirected change. A concerted effort at data collection involves those who have specific data and those who need data in a mutual quest for shared understanding and cooperation. In a realistic sense, not everyone is directly involved in a specific data collection and analysis process. However, representative members of all the groups affected by the change can be included in some manner. Special efforts should be made to involve those who have information on current day-to-day customer, supplier, and market contacts as well as those responsible for internal operations.

After discovering sources of data, the data collection process involves members of the organization as active participants. Below are some critical questions in mobilizing and facilitating these action research teams for data collection and analysis:

- Who should be part of the data collection team? What specific contributions and resources does each person bring to the task? How does each member relate to the total system?

- How can the consultation team get the client and the client system to accept the need for objective fact finding to supplement their own change assumptions?

- How can the team involve the client system in the diagnostic data-collection process so that they feel ownership of the data and accept its validity?

- How can the change facilitator help people to understand the commitment of time and energy that will be required in ongoing data collection and analysis?

- How can the appropriate parts of the client system review the data and draw implications for action?

- How do the action teams ensure that all relevant groups are receiving data feedback?

- What feedback facilitation is needed to move the client system from data feedback to decisions and effective actions?
- How will members of the team be involved in action planning and implementation?
- How will action research teams monitor results during and after implementation of a directed change?
- When will the responsibilities of the ART be completed?
- What orientation or training will be needed for the teams?

Training for Collaborative Data Collection and Analysis

No one should expect that action research teams will automatically have all of the skills and experience that they need to be effective in data collection and analysis related to change. While they may have substantial individual talents and knowledge, the challenge is to create a synergistic and targeted application of that energy. One of the first things members must learn is how to make informal agreements with other team members to support coordinated activities. In order to do this they need specific skills in communication, group process, and research methods. The change facilitator plays a significant role in helping to transfer and nurture these competencies.

One of the roles of the consultation team is training to transfer competencies in data collection and analysis to the client system. This training may occur through informal methods such as coaching, modeling, and mentoring, as well as in more formal, specialized group sessions. The areas of training to develop both technical and process capacity for change management are listed in Table 8.5.

TABLE 8.5 Training for Data Collection and Analysis.

Technical Skills
    Data collection
    Data analysis
    Presentation of data
    Action planning

Process Skills
    Facilitation
    Teamwork
    Communication
    Group dynamics
    Implementation
    Monitoring

Specialized training might focus on methods of data collection such as surveys, questionnaires, interviews, and observation. Teams may also need some training in how to organize information in charts, graphs, and reports and how to analyze data according to specific visual and performance objectives. Practice in presentation skills and the use of visual aids including flip charts, overhead projectors, and large computer screens are useful for data-feedback sessions. Action research team leaders and managers require some advanced training in facilitation process techniques.

Through practice, members of action research teams gain valuable competencies and a greater understanding of the total organizational system. They also learn to integrate the collaborative inquiry process into their everyday work.

Team facilitators, managers, and staff professionals may perform a variety of roles in action research teaming interventions:

- *Advocate* to protect confidentiality, assess organizational dynamics for overall design of subjective and objective measures;
- *Technical expert* to provide skills, knowledge, and experience in specific methodologies of data collection and analysis;
- *Trainer/educator or mentor* to develop the skills of others to collect and analyze data;
- *Fact finder* to faciliate data collection and analysis;
- *Process facilitator* to design interpretive inquiry feedback process to link data into action;
- *Reflective observer* to give ongoing feedback to facilitating and client system, for interpretation, insight, and new action.

The specific interventions related to data collection and analysis begin with formal or informal agreements on roles and objectives and continue with specific decisions and actions related to methodology, sources, data access, feedback, monitoring, and assessment of results.

Deciding on Appropriate Methods and Design

The selection of methodology depends on specific factors such as the focus of organizational performance measurements, the level of data required, the unit of change, the objectives of the data in description, evaluation, or prediction, and the available resources for data collection. The research design may ultimately be a subjective choice made by the client, the manager, or the action research team. For example, the design might include descriptive surveys of a total population of employees or sample surveys of a representative group of people from across the organization. Field studies of an organization, community, or industry could be used to evaluate and benchmark specific processes, methods, or organizational values. Case studies based on interviews and observation can contribute to an understanding of individual or group activities and attitudes related to change.

The selection of methods design should be based on overall objectives, resources, and information needs. Yet this selection is often influenced by the specific interests and expertise of the members of the consultation team or action research group. This might be called the "law of the instrument" (Kaplan 1964). Kaplan explains this law with a story about a small boy who is given a hammer and suddenly discovers that everything needs hammering. Many professionals do have a favored methodology and an area of expertise such as survey research or focus groups. They may tend to use this method for everything rather than exploring other methodologies that may be more effective or appropriate for different situation.

The questions in Table 8.6 can help the team in choosing data collection and analysis methods.

TABLE 8.6 Checklist for Data Collection.

What data-collection methods have been used most frequently?
What formal methods (e.g., surveys, audits) have been used?
What informal methods (e.g., interviews, focus groups) have been used?
Which methods have been more effective? Why?
Which methods have not worked effectively? Why?
Why has the data collected sometimes not been used?
What are some of the challenges for data collection in this organization?
What are the expectations of data collection in this organization?
How has data been analyzed in the past ?
What approaches to analysis have been most successful? Least successful?
How can primary data be gathered?
How can summary data be used? Secondary data?
Where is there access to data?
How many people will be required for the sample?
Is a random, stratified, or purposive sample needed?
How complex is the data required? Are there multiple variables?
What surveys, audits, and instruments are available?
What equipment or resources can be used for processing data?
How much time is available for data collection and analysis?
Will a test study be required? Pretest on materials?

The type of data collected depends on the the the methodology used. The two basic perspectives to collecting and analyzing data are quantitative methods and qualitative methods. *Quantitative* methods yield numerical data related to performance that can be analyzed through statistical measures. This could include surveys, questionnaires, audits, content analysis, and numerical documentation. *Qualitative* methods produce descriptive data that helps in understanding the "why" of different attitudes and the underlying structures of values and perceptions affecting change. Qualitative methods may include group and individual interviews, focus groups, observation, trend analysis, and issues monitoring.

Effective change management requires that action research teams determine the kinds of data needed to meet specific change objectives. This means that both quantitative and qualitative approaches to data must be considered. Together they provide a more holistic and accurate understanding of what is going on in the organization.

The quantitative approach assumes cause and effect in an orderly universe where there is directed change and a precise relationship among variables that can be objectively observed, precisely measured, and controlled. The concept continues to influence data collection and analysis in many organizations. This logic often attempts to reduce data to numerical forms, charts, and statistical models. The observable reality and directed change efforts that can be documented and measured are considered the most valid data for planning and decision making. The approach to data collection reflects some of the values of Quadrant I, rational/behavioral perspectives, as discussed in Chapter 3.

However, the exclusive use of this approach has been criticized because in many cases it creates an artificial split between objective and subjective ways of knowing about the organization. Quantitative methods assume an objective position for the person gathering the data. This break between objective and subjective data has been compared to a man walking outside his house and looking in the window to see if he is home. (Barrett 1986). Even researchers who seek objectivity are influenced by their own selectivity and attitudes in developing hypotheses choosing data collection methods and interpreting data. A holistic interpretive perspective focuses on the integration of emotion and reason in a world in which people do not merely observe but create their reality. This interactive approach is characteristic of Quadrant 3, a cultural/interpretive perspective toward change.

A qualitative approach seeks understanding of the changing organization from a variety of subjective cultural perspectives including participant observation, description, intuition, narrative, and experience. Qualitative research is an attempt to document and understand attitudes, values, perceptions, and actions from an informal perspective that focuses on individuals and groups in conversations and activities in the everyday organizational world in which they live. Change is a complex, continuous, often contradictory process that is interpreted and facilitated by people. Many decisions, such as eliminating services or downsizing, are more complicated than the numbers show. The most effective data collection and analysis uses both quantitative and qualitative data to ensure a more complete picture of the "reality" of change. Each approach picks up different kinds of data and analyzes that data from different perspectives. Together they create an integrated picture of the organization and provide valuable data for change management at both directed and nondirected levels.

Quantitative data is most often gathered through formal methods. Informal methods provide more qualitative data about attitudes and responses to change. Formal methods employ statistical measures and results that are both descriptive and evaluative. Informal methods can be systematic and highly structured but the data is mainly descriptive rather than statistical or inferential.

TABLE 8.7 Methods of Data Collection and Analysis.

More Formal Methods	More Informal Methods
Survey research	Observation
Questionnaires	Freeflow interviews
Audits	Futuring activities
Structured interviews	Focus groups
Experiments	Environmental monitoring
Learning instruments	Secondary analysis
Content analysis	Feedback sessions
Assessment	Delphi
Q sorts	Panel
Performance checks	Forum
Advisory boards	Action learning conferences
Career instruments	Storytelling
Case study	Simulations
Field work	Film/video interpretations

The list of formal and informal methods of data collection in Table 8.7 is meant to be a suggestion of alternative approaches to data rather than a rigid classification. Many of the methods listed, depending on how they are implemented, can be viewed as either "formal" or "informal."

Formal and informal methods provide different types of data about change. For example, managers have a substantial amount of data in their experience and knowledge of the organization. Gathering and applying the combined organizational intelligence of managers, staff professionals, employees, suppliers, and customers is one of the challenges of change management. An organizational survey may yield valuable, formal data. Yet it may not take advantage of the informal knowledge and insight managers and other resources possess.

An action learning conference model of data collection and analysis based on study group research might be an alternative method to understand ideas, perspectives, and attitudes of individuals and groups in a more free flow flexible, creative format. In this approach the agenda is designed with both content and process based on the data collection and analysis of the issue or challenges identified. The emphasis is on collaborative inquiry and shared understandings of the feedback. With skilled change facilitators helping to integrate information gathering, feedback, and action planning within a team process. The data provides insight and helps focus teamwork around shared knowledge and integrated values, which are created and legitimized by data. The group learns to manage change in an interactive, data-based context.

Later in this chapter a detailed summary is provided for some of the major methods of data collection and analysis. This reference is designed for managers, action research teams, and client system groups that want to learn more about their organization to manage change more effectively.

IDENTIFYING SOURCES AND GAINING ACCESS

Like explorers searching for treasure or detectives looking for clues, action research teams must develop some sort of map or plan for thinking about the location of data and possible sources. Even though data can be everywhere in the organizational system, the team cannot examine everything. They must decide on the most representative and revealing areas to search for information about directed and nondirected change.

Sampling of sources or respondents is usually random, stratified, or purposive. A *random* sample is one in which every member of the population has an equal chance of being chosen. One convenient alternative to this is systematic sampling, which takes every "*nth*" item beginning at a random place in a list of all the members of a given population. A *stratified* sample attempts to identify a representative group of respondents or subjects by dividing the population according to some specific characteristics and drawing a sample that represents the approximate proportion of people in the total population with each of those characteristics. This might be geographic location, number of years with the organization, or level in the organization. A *purposive* sample is based on the judgment of the researchers and specific data needs. A sample such as top executives or long-term suppliers is chosen as a representative subgroup because they have certain characteristics or experience that are the focus of the study. This sample should be chosen carefully because there can be a greater chance of bias in the results.

Many of the choices of sample are purposive. Therefore, it is important to consider a variety of sources throughout the organizational system. The questions in Table 8.8 are useful to teams in discovering and using data sources.

TABLE 8.8 Identifying Data Sources.

Are we asking the appropriate questions in developing our research design? To what sources do these questions lead us?

Who are the people within the organization who have information and experience in this area?

Will we have access to all data? How do we get access?

Where are the documents and records related to this performance indicator?

What data might be most valuable? Not valuable?

Are there hidden sources that we have not considered?

What external sources or third-party sources might help us?

Which sources do we consider most "reliable"?

Which sources have been used most often in the past?

Which sources might give different perspectives on change?

What are some undiscovered sources or alternative sources that may not have been considered?

Which sources provide the most relevant information?

Which sources provide the most timely information?

How do we maintain the privacy of sources?

What responsibility do we have to give feedback to the sources who provided the data?

Taking the easiest or most convenient sources is similar to the parable of the "drunkard's search" (Kaplan 1964) in which a drunkard searches for his keys in the light under a street lamp even though he has dropped his keys some distance away. When asked why he didn't look for the keys where he had lost them, he said, "It's lighter here." This logic sometimes affects those who collect and analyze data. Some action research teams may search only in the most obvious, traditional, and available ways without recognizing new methods or alternative sources of information. Organization members also might choose to ignore or hide the shadow side of the organization. Often the troublesome "undiscussables" and subjective elements related to power and relationships are not confronted directly. Even with a systematic and logical plan, data collection is based on some subjective choices. All these factors may prevent appropriate assessment of the nondirected aspects of change in attitudes and daily work practices.

Much of organizational research concentrates on employees, but in a more diversified workforce "employees" no longer fit into standard traditional categories. Their ethnic, national, racial, and demographic diversity may be reflected in different experiences, values, and attitudes. Increasingly flexible organizational structures may contract more employees and depend on part-time workers. Data-collection techniques should be sensitive to the perspectives and experiences of these diverse sources. There are many potential resources within an extensive organizational system including executives, managers, suppliers, distributors, and customers. Third-party sources could involve community leaders, government agencies, financial analysts, industry associations, competitors, legal advisors, educational institutions, and customer groups. Gathering data from these sources may concentrate on formal research methods such as surveys, questionnaires and audits, or informal methods that include individual and group interviews or panels. A variety of viewpoints can also be valuable in analyzing and applying data from rational/behavioral, systems, cultural/interpretive, or critical/humanism perspectives or described in Chapter 3.

There are many unobtrusive sources and methods such as documentation and secondary-data analysis that do not involve direct observation or interaction with the client system. Internal publications, marketing materials, annual reports, and executive speeches can be useful in assessing how the organization communicates with a variety of critical publics as well as how the changing organization chooses to present itself through these controlled media. Internal documentation such as quality reports, control graphs, organizational mapping, documents, productivity levels, absenteeism, succession planning charts, and turnover rates provide vital information on organizational change, fitness, and operation. Documentation allows an opportunity for secondary research that "reanalyzes" data from different perspectives and makes comparisons. Much of the analysis of this printed data may be informal research in spotting trends and patterns for change. A more formal content analysis can provide specific numerical comparisons as well as valuable insight into the language and "conversations" related to change in the organization. Content analysis of printed and taped materials is also unobtrusive since the questions are asked of the data and the printed text.

Through internal interviews with representative individuals and groups and content analysis of organizational communication, some of the taken-for-granted reality of nondirected change emerges. Weick (1979) describes a kind of "storehouse" of organizational intelligence that is retained in the routine of the rules, policies, and standards of everyday behavior and decision making. While some of this information is unwritten, many of the formal rules and policies of the organization are included in the documentation, operations, and orientation materials. Going into this storehouse and examining the current rules and policies to see how they affect the organization provides revealing data for change management.

Business and trade publications offer a forum for monitoring economic, social, and political changes on current and strategic issues that might affect the organization and the industry. Specialized libraries also can be useful for examining technical data and research summaries. Reviewing industry surveys, polls, and research reports can provide valuable data for secondary research. A government agency, industry group, or national polling firm may have already done a survey related to a specific directed change. Teams can save time and resources by looking first at existing data. Computer data bases are essential sources, and specialized computer networks and the special-interest groups that are part of these networks provide an opportunity for collaboration and information exchange.

Searching for data to help in change management is a process of learning, but it must be based on some systematic plan. A working theory or model provides a structure or architecture upon which to collect, analyze, and feedback the data. Otherwise the amount of data may be too wide or too narrow and the quality of the data lower than expected. Those who collect data would do well to use a variety of sources, but maintain a clear focus on overall information needs, priorities, and objectives related to change management.

ANALYSIS AND ASSESSMENT OF RESULTS

Change management is a cyclical process of feedback, monitoring, and assessment of results. The action research teaming process encourages shared learning as organization members gather, interpret, and apply data. People expand organizational intelligence and improve performance through shared knowledge and integrated objectives that help the organization to deal with complex, ongoing change. Involving a variety of people in data collection and analysis helps to insure the effectiveness of the process as well as the accuracy and reliability of the data and the decisions based on that data. Weick (1979) suggests the principle of "requisite variety," which encourages organizations to match the effort in gathering and analyzing data to the complexity or equivocality of that data. Organizational development and change is a complex process that can involve a network of action research teams throughout the system.

Data collection and analysis is the fuel for continuous improvement and integrated change on individual, group, intergroup, and organizational levels. The questions in Table 8.9 help to assess the effectiveness of data collection and analysis methods from a variety of perspectives.

TABLE 8.9 Assessing Data.

Does the data have utility? Is it useful to the organization?

Does the data collected help to answer our specific questions about performance?

Does the analysis of this data increase our understanding of change?

Is the data analyzed with some historical perspective?

Is past data available for comparison?

Is the data clear or ambiguous?

Are the sources reliable? Knowledgeable? Honest?

Is the sample representative of the population?

Is this data timely? Does it include the latest informational or figures?

Are we measuring what we think we are measuring? Are some unknown factors affecting the validity of our results?

Is the data reliable?

How complete is the data collected?

What is the response rate? Is this response adequate?

Will the results be the same next month? Next year? What might change?

Could another group collect and analyze this data and come to some of the same conclusions?

Do we have multiple confirmation of results by using different methodologies?

How cost-effective are different methods of data collection?

What is the value of the data collected for change management?

Utility, or the value of the data in answering specific questions and helping to meet organizational objectives, is one essential test of the effectiveness of data collection and analysis. The GIGO (garbage in, garbage out) principle also applies here. Substantial time and resources can be spent on collecting irrelevant and inaccurate data. The clearest measure of utility is the usefulness of the data for change management and effective performance.

Validity and reliability are also important concerns in data collection and analysis. *Validity* deals with certainty in measuring what you intend to measure. What areas does the data support? For example, does this survey accurately measure employee attitudes toward quality initiatives, or are other "contaminating" variables affecting the results? *Reliability* involves consistency in results. Could someone else use this employee survey with this group and get the same results? Would a similar survey measuring the same group at the same time yield the equivalent overall results? To insure reliability and validity, those administrating the survey should have some training to maintain consistent presentation and format, and the survey should be pretested with a similar group to verify that it is direct and unambiguous in eliciting the required information. There must also be clear, shared criteria for analyzing results. Multiple confirmation of results through both quantitative and qualitative methods also increases the validity and reliability of data. In assessing the validity and reliability of data, some researchers refer to systematic error and precision error. *Systematic error* is caused by a flaw in the methodology or bias in the instrument. *Precision error* is often a logistical problem or a mistake in calculation.

In a practical sense, there are many factors that might affect the validity and reliability of data collection and analysis in organizational systems:

- Lack of resources for data collection
- Failure to acknowledge differences in perceptions
- Lack of confidentiality and privacy
- Lack of privacy
- Lack of interest or commitment to data collection
- Disguised or wrong answers
- Lack of trust
- Bias in preparation of instrument or in analysis
- Hidden agenda for use of the data
- Tunnel vision and failure to see other options
- Lack of experience and training in data collection
- Respondents try to give the "right" answer
- Inappropriate methodology
- Failure to collect both qualitative and quantitative data
- Uninformed or biased sources
- Nonrepresentative sample of respondents

All data collection and analysis requires some agreement related to open communication and feedback. One of the major foundations in gathering data is to establish trust in individual and group interviews and in the administration of surveys and audits. Participants do have a right to know the objectives of data collection and how the data will be reported and used. In one organization, for example, a management audit was presented as a way to improve overall quality and assess employee attitudes. In reality the survey was used to identity top-performance and low-performance managers as a basis for making rightsizing decisions within the organization. This approach to data collection raises not only questions of validity and reliability, but also of ethics.

Gathering valid, representative data related to directed and nondirected change is a challenge. Yet the quality and integrity of that data can be diminished and distorted through inappropriate or biased interpretation and analysis. These are some of the ways in which data can be misused:

- Selective use of data
- Defensiveness about sensitive data
- Subjective analysis
- Overanalysis of data
- Wrong statistics for type of data
- Misinterpretation
- Lack of multiple confirmation of results
- Reliance on specialized jargon with no common "language" for analysis
- No clear criteria for analysis
- No integration of results across the organization
- Lack of alignment of results with organizational goals
- Censorship of critical data
- Limited number of people involved in interpretation and analysis

Data analysis for directed change efforts should be balanced and involve representatives from all areas of the organizational system affected by the change. In analyzing data, the experience and knowledge of action research teams can improve interpretation and check judgment, since people may not initially see the relationships between diverse and even contradictory data. Qualitative data can help in understanding quantitative results. In action research, people are encouraged to see other options and explore the dilemmas and opportunities of change through data collection and analysis.

APPLYING MAJOR METHODS OF DATA COLLECTION AND ANALYSIS

This section will briefly describe some of the major methods of collecting data within an organizational system. Each method has specific applications for action research and data-based change management. These methods include:

- Observation
- Documentation and secondary research
- Content analysis
- Environmental monitoring
- Questionnaires
- Audits and surveys
- Assessments
- Charts and visual models
- Individual and group interviews
- Q-Methodolgy
- Learning instruments
- Simulations

Observation

One of the best ways to find out about people and processes in organizations is through regular observation. This is a way to focus on some of the nondirected aspects of change. These methods involve direct observation, nonparticipant observation, or participant observation. *Direct observation* may be participant or nonparticipant observation and may integrate some objective observation with interaction and interviews. *Nonparticipant observation* does not engage the observer in any interaction with those being observed. This is an objective assessment often made according to some chart, checklist, or standard for measurement. The event that is observed can range from a videotaped meeting to a live ongoing work process. The observers must be trained in what to observe and how to record their observations.

Participant observation can be used to gather qualitative data on the current mood and state of the organization and the overall flow of organizational processes and activities. Even though organizational diagnosis needs to be measurement-based as much as possible, the best place to start may not be with numbers and statistical measures. Management by walking around,

(MBWA) does have some distinct advantages. However, Deming (1986) does not agree that walking around provides the manager with useful data unless the manager also knows and understands the work of the employee. The simple act of moving through a plant or an office, observing the activities and taking time to talk with employees, may provide valuable data on directed and nondirected change activities. However, if this is an infrequent occurrence, the results of the observation may be distorted as employees try to look busy and say what the manager or data collection team wants to hear. The best observational data is gathered in an unobtrusive way. The natural observation of people in meetings, on the job, interacting with customers, packing materials, or assembling products can be a valuable source of data. Managers have natural observation opportunities while visiting meetings and observing group dynamics or by simply walking around and noticing the activities related to a specific change process.

Like other methods, observation can be open-ended and relatively unstructured or it can be directed toward specific questions or standards. For example, employees may be asked to keep a journal or a checklist based on their observations and work experiences in order to increase quality awareness, customer response time, reduce frequency and types of complaints, and stimulate ideas for improvement. Groups can also designate a member of their team to step out of the participant's role and into the observer role.

If the observation is formal and must be done according to a specific set of guidelines or formats, there may be interpretation and coding problems and the observers will need to be trained in what and how to observe. A panel of observers can help reduce bias and cross-validate observations. Rehearsal and practice improves observation skills, and increases competence in recognizing "unobtrusive measures" and "traces" that provide data on the nondirected level (Webb, Campbell, Schwartz and Sechrest 1966). For example, the number of quality initiative forms still on the table in the cafeteria may say something about the process and the response to this particular directed change.

Observation has advantages in that it is flexible because the observer can detect additional factors that might be important and include them. The disadvantages are the subjective qualities of observation and the bias and selectivity that may distort information. People who are observed directly also may feel uncomfortable and even alter their behavior as a result of being observed.

Observation is a subjective measure that requires some time and effort and is not always practical or accurate. One executive diagnosed his system daily by taking a morning walk around the plant, observing, inquiring, and intuiting. He believed that he could "read" his organization accurately, and made each day's decisions confident that he was acting on good knowledge of what was going on in the social and technical sides of his enterprise. However, when his company expanded to three, then five, and then later seven plants, this technique no longer served him well. In complex systems, periodic "sensitizing" interviews with key people may be needed to keep in touch with some of these more subjective nondirected aspects of the informal organization. Observation is useful but it must be combined with other methods of data collection, analysis, and feedback to create a realistic picture of the changing organization.

Documentation and Secondary Research

Every organization has a vast warehouse of data in files, computer, and management information systems. This documentation can provide a valuable history of the changing organization, past and present. Turnover reports, accident reports, budgets, sales reports, competitive analysis, client lists, contracts, customer inquires, complaints, supplier contracts, letters of correspondence, and termination records are all sources of data. Documentation can help answer basic operational questions: How responsive are we to customer inquiries? How are our quality indicators compared to our increased quality emphasis in employee training and orientation? The answers may encourage change initiatives based on strategic performance objectives.

The results of previous audits, surveys, and questionnaires can also provide some perspective and a benchmark for current surveys and audits, especially if a similar method and focus is maintained over a period of time. Too often these studies are left to gather dust on a shelf and the information is not integrated into the bank of organizational intelligence. If the survey was someone's pet project and the data was not shared, it may be difficult to find copies of the results.

While the official records and files are useful, organizational documentation also includes company publications such as stockholders reports, the annual report to employees, newsletters, magazines, sales brochures, product sheets, and bulletins. These organizational narratives may also be subjected to content analysis to determine specific language and themes.

Other documentation may include internal video news programs, orientation and training videos, and documentary footage. Articles, publications, speeches, and presentations by the top executives and professional staff of the organization provide data on the vision and strategic position of the organization. Records of media coverage on television, and radio, and in newspapers, magazines, and trade publications might also be helpful in assessing the interpretations of change.

Library and archival resources may provide valuable data for secondary analysis. Results of government and industry surveys are often available in specialized reports and journals and this data can be reanalyzed with a different focus. External documentation may include a computer search for bibliographic references to issues facing the industry and how other similar organizations have managed change.

There are several advantages to this method of collecting data. This approach does not interfere with ongoing work or raise expectations or concerns about data collection. It is anonymous and low-cost. Most documents are easy to quantify or code. Disadvantages can include problems with the retrieval or availability of such data. There may not be permission for access to some confidential material. This documentation can also be overwhelming in its sheer volume and require systematic and selective focus in data collection and analysis.

Content Analysis

Content analysis concentrates most often on the "manifest" content of an actual printed page, a lecture, a discussion group, a video image, or an audio recording. This analysis may also deal with latent content in deeper levels of meaning associated with context, intention, and underlying values. Content analysis takes the communication of a particular person, group, or organization and tries to understand the meaning and intent of that message based on the specific words and images and the way those words and images are organized and presented. This may include both the intrinsic data in words and images as well as the extrinsic analysis related to the specific context or environment in which the communication is presented.

Content analysis can also answer basic questions about the effects of the communication relative to a specific directed change. What are the words and symbols used to describe the change? How is this message organized and presented? To what audience is this presented? What is the intent of the speaker or writer? What might be the effect of this message on organizational members? What is the tone of the coverage about an organizational change in newspapers and trade publications?

Content analysis also may answer some questions related to nondirected change processes in daily work practices throughout the system: How do we talk to our customers when they call in with complaints? What are the themes and words we stress most in our communication with employees?

Management may think that they are communicating total quality to all of their employees, but is their message strong, clear, and consistent? What is the content and tone of executive speeches, employee orientations, newsletters, bulletin boards, and memos? Content analysis in this sense may test specific assumptions. A content analysis of the president's recent speech to employees or this month's issue of the company newsletter might be useful in checking the quality focus. The newsletter also can be a valuable tool in helping employees to understand and participate in the change process.

Content analysis requires some systematic sampling of manifest content. Both probability and purposive sampling can be used. However, purposive samples cannot always be generalized to the total population. Obviously the researcher cannot include every word or image produced by the organization over a period of time. The first step is to define the population. This might include all issues of the company publications over the past five years or all customer complaints received over the last year. Depending on the amount of time and resources available, some sample must be chosen from this data base. A stratified random sample might draw a certain number of publications based on specific characteristics such as month of publication or unit focus. A systematic interval sample can be drawn by choosing every nth item on a list for detailed analysis. The sampling interval depends on the total number of items and the desired sample size. For publications, sampling units might include only titles or the first three lines of each story, or random 100-word blocks of copy.

The sample content can be analyzed according to specific categories. For example, media coverage of the organization may be classified as positive, negative, or neutral. Specialized content and subject areas can also be recorded. For analyzing publications and printed content, computer analysis can provide frequency and type/token ratios for all words sampled. A dictionary program can pinpoint the use of a particular word or a cluster of related words. Themes can be analyzed by looking for specific referent words. Consistency and contradiction in spoken language can also be measured. In analyzing the content of telephone conversations with customers, the specific language, tone, and information content can be assessed as well as the length of the conversation.

Content analysis is one of the oldest and most traditional tools for communication analysis. This method of data analysis can help organization members to understand the construction, presentation, and impact of specific messages and narratives as part of a total change management process.

Environmental Monitoring

Environmental monitoring is most often a part of the issues management, public affairs, marketing and public relations functions within the organization. However, it is also an important tool for managers in understanding change and change processes in relation to the larger social, political, and economic environment. Trends and issues affecting the organization and the industry are evident in the content of the mass media as well as the specialized trade media. Environmental or media monitoring might begin with the regular reading of a variety of newspapers and magazines, both general interest and industry specific. Editors at these publications and producers of television and cable programs are selective in their presentation of information. They have only a limited amount of space and time, so they choose those items that they believe best communicate what their readers and listeners want to know. Major issues affecting organizations are usually reflected in specialized business publications and news broadcasts of daily business reports and interviews with expert professionals.

Environmental monitoring involves two basic processes: scanning and tracking (Brody and Stone 1989). *Scanning* is a continuing examination of current events and media coverage of the organization and the industry to spot activities or "trigger events" that may point to significant changes and trends. Data collection is generally accomplished through regular monitoring of the print and broadcast media, with emphasis on industry and special-interest media. *Tracking* monitors and assesses these trends to determine possible threats and opportunities for the organization. What does this emerging issue mean for our organization? What is the potential impact of this change on our industry and the way we do business?

In order to be proactive in responding to continuous and sometimes erratic change, the organization should have some form of environmental monitoring. The systematic examination of media content over a period of time might be done by an individual, a group, or contracted to a specialized firm. In this method of data collection, publications are monitored and selected materials with references to the organization or the industry are clipped or documented. This information can be regularly distributed to managers and analyzed to help understand major issues. Once identified, issues can be followed more carefully. Some current issues may already be in a legislative stage where new regulations or laws are being debated. If strategic issues are identified early, the organization has more options. Dealing with change on the organizational, societal, and global levels requires environmental monitoring and awareness through continuous data collection and analysis.

Questionnaires

Questionnaires are often developed by an organization to gather specific information on a topic or issue related to change management. A questionnaire is essentially a self-administered interview instrument that uses a printed format. Questionnaires can contain open-ended questions or closed questions that list several response options. Attitudes, opinions, experiences, practices, and perceptions could be documented in a questionnaire. The responses and answers can be written or inputted directly into a computer. Questionnaires are self-directed or administered through the mail, over the phone, or in group or individual meetings.

In developing a questionnaire, the objectives and data needs should be clear. Questionnaires can provide descriptive and explanatory data. The important point is to decide what data is needed and to make sure that the questions get to that data. Questionnaires are often misused and poorly designed. If the action research team does not have some experience in questionnaire development, they can use specialized resources.

The questionnaire should be organized and pretested with a similar group of respondents to check on clarity, understanding, time required for completion, and quality of information for each question. Some questions may not be clearly understood. Others questions may not provide the kind of data that is needed.

The following guidelines are helpful in developing questions and designing a questionnaire:

1. Use questions that are short, simple, and direct. Avoid long, elaborate questions.

2. Make sure that the language is appropriate to the respondents and is at their level of understanding and experience.

3. Ask only one idea in each question. If you have two ideas in the question, you will not know whether the respondent is reacting to one or both of the concepts. For example, a statement such as "Quality and productivity are important in our organization" may not provide valid data.

4. Avoid vague words and phrases such as "most" or "several." These words can be interpreted in different ways.

5. Do not use ambiguous terms, slang, jargon, or abbreviations.

6. Avoid biased or leading questions and emotional language.

7. List open-ended questions or stop-boxes for comment at the end of a section or the end of the questionnaire.

8. For closed questions consider the advantages or disadvantages of adding "other" or "don't know" to the list of responses.

9. Begin the questionnaire with easy, nonthreatening items. These initial questions should also arouse interest.

10. Use white space. Don't crowd questions together. This makes the questionnaire easier to read.

11. Group questions with a similar format together. For example, all of the questions that have a similar response format, such as Likert scales from "Strongly agree" to "Strongly disagree," should be put in the same section.

12. Questions on a related topic should be grouped together. These may also be listed under a subject heading.

13. The overall questionnaire structure should follow a logical sequence of development and thought. For example, questions might move from more general to specific aspects of the topic.

14. Make sure all of the instructions are clear. This can be checked during the pretest.

15. Prepare a personalized cover letter if you are mailing the questionnaire.

A questionnaire is flexible and allows for a variety of practical and creative uses to explore issues and plan for change. The *Delphi* technique uses written questionnaires to collect information from a select group of people through several rounds of questions. Participants are often a specialized group of experts who have a direct commitment and established interest in the topic. Their responses are pooled, analyzed, and distributed again for further analysis and feedback. The information is summarized and sent out to the same people until a consensus is reached.

This process also can be used to take advantage of the knowledge and experience within a dispersed, multinational organizational system. In the initial stage, diagnostic data on a specific topic or issue is gathered from representative members of the organization in focused and/or sensing interviews. This data is analyzed and a preliminary report is sent out with new questions to probe specific key areas identified in the first step. When the data has been collected and reviewed, a list of suggested options is sent out for dealing with the issues identified as needing attention. Each participant is requested to send feedback on these options and make additional proposals.

Questionnaires offer adaptability and cost-effectiveness for action research teams in data collection. However, questionnaires must be carefully developed and pretested to ensure validity and reliability. Direct administration of questionnaires is most effective. People in different organizational locations may respond to a questionnaire via electronic mail or fax. If questionnaires are given in a formal group setting in the workplace, the return is high. If the questionnaires are left in the cafeteria or lounge for the employees to pick up and return, the response rate may be much lower. Unless people have a compelling reason or some incentive for completing the questionnaire, few may respond. Mail questionnaires such as those sent to customers may have the lowest return rate and often require extensive follow-up efforts. Even if the forms are returned, the research team cannot be sure who actually fills out the questionnaire.

In general, questionnaires allow the team to gather information from a large number of people at a relatively low cost. The data is easy to quantify and fixed-response questionnaires can be summarized and analyzed quickly. Questionnaires, however, have some disadvantages. They can be misinterpreted or over interpreted. Respondents may have different expectations and interpretations of the data. They can also manipulate the data and give false responses.

Audits and Surveys

While questionnaires can be more qualitative and situation-specific, audits and surveys provide a consistent quantitative measure over time in a variety of organizations and contexts. Audits and surveys are more theory-based and focused on a benchmark or structure for descriptive and evaluative performance measurement. Results may be reported in graphs and charts as well in anecdotal data.

Many professionals make a distinction between audits and surveys. Attitudinal *surveys* are commonly used for organizational diagnosis, to discover how people feel about the organization. Surveys may be administered in person or over the phone. The attitude survey can cover a variety of topics and issues. The *audit* is a more formal evaluation made against a set of established standards. The audit asks respondents at various levels of the organization to measure their organization in terms of these standards.

In both audits and surveys the total population, or a representative proportional sample, is selected. These people complete the survey or audit, which is then processed, collated, and interpreted through a process of feedback and analysis, which helps to translate data into a summary report and respondent action recommendations. This process can be used on a periodic basis to provide a picture of the whole organization or specific units.

Most organization members will give reasonably valid and reliable information when they see the data-collection process as a first step to influence change in their organization. Audit information will also be more useful if people are given a contributing role in interpreting the data and giving their input as action recommendations. The survey or audit should be part of an ongoing process of collaborative inquiry and teaming in data collection, analysis, feedback, and action decisions.

A variety of surveys and audits are available for organizational development. Some measure specialized areas such as quality, productivity, and teamwork. For example, the quality-control (QC) audit (Ishikawa 1985) is an examination of the way in which quality is built into a product. This may involve the control of subcontracting, implementing quality assurance at each step of planning, development, and production, as well as handling customer complaints. The QC audit might also include an audit of the supplier by the purchaser. The emphasis is on clear responsibilities, cooperation between divisions, and education and consciousness about quality and quality control. Data is collected, analyzed, and used to improve the overall quality system.

Audits for specialized groups such as suppliers, customers, dealers, and employees as well as focused surveys can provide essential data for change management. The Environment Survey for Quality and Productivity Improvement (Chakiris 1992) provides a perspective on continuous improvement from the employees' point of view. The survey domains, which focus on Deming's (1986) concepts, are shown in Table 8.10.

TABLE 8.10 Quality and Productivity Domains.

Constancy of purpose
Adopt the new philosophy
Cease dependence on inspection
Stop buying on price tag
Improve constantly forever
Institute on-the-job training
Institute supervisory leadership
Drive out fear
Break down barriers
Eliminate slogans
Eliminate work standards
Remove barriers to pride
Institute vigorous education
Everybody participates

Other surveys and audits focus on the structures and systems of the organization from the perspective of human resources. Audits, can stimulate change and help the organization identify strengths as well as areas for development and improvement. The audit process encourages open communication and feedback between management and employees. Audits can establish benchmark measurements and help the organization plan for integration of directed and nondirected change. However, an audit increases expectations for change and participation. The organization should not conduct an audit unless management is prepared to take appropriate and timely action as a result of the feedback.

The Human Resource Audit (Chakiris 1992), based on the principles of effective organizational performance, has been validated and refined through implementation in hundreds of organizations. The audit is built on a theoretical model that views organizations as responsive systems that can be audited at individual, work group, and organizational levels. Some of the domains of this audit are shown in Table 8.11.

TABLE 8.11 Human Resource Audit.

Productivity and motivation factors
Quality of work life
Organizational priorities
Degree of openness
Styles of management
Work facilitation and teamwork
Organizational performance and effectiveness
Quality in products and/or services
Communication and coordination
Organizational structures and systems

The Audit covers individual job domains such as autonomy, challenge, work load, role clarity, and satisfaction. Work relationships are assessed in relation to supervision, work-group, and intergroup levels. This includes work facilitation, performance feedback, participation, cooperation, problem solving, and communication. Organizational systems and structures are evaluated in attitudes toward the fairness and appropriateness of rewards, rules, and policies, participative decision making, and authority. Organizational effectiveness and performance are measured in quality of products and services, productivity, safety, environment, resources, conflict management, training and development, diversity, and impact on community.

The feedback provided by the Audit also focuses on intraorganizational comparisons among business units, departments, divisions, plants or offices, units, management, and employees or other subunits or specified groups. Such comparisons identify those subsystems most in need of support and development. Subgroups can also be defined in other terms such as location, job level, or selected functions. The Metrex® Human Resource Audit contains 112 to 115 statements and incorporates closed questions with response options, open questions, and checklists. Special items, can be added to the audit to tap additional areas that might be of particular interest to the client system.

The instrument is generally administered to groups by a trained facilitator working with a leader. Most people take from 30 to 40 minutes to complete the audit. All materials are processed by an outside research firm. The audit can be used in a variety of organizational systems including service and manufacturing. The Audit is best used as part of an action-research teaming model that focuses on an integrative, cooperative process of data collection and analysis. This requires initial planning meetings involving top management and the audit committee or action research teams. The team may also coordinate basic activities including audit administration, feedback sessions with management and employees, participative action planning, implementation, and evaluation. In most organizations the basic audit process takes from four to six months. The initial audit establishes a benchmark for future audit measurements that can provide valuable longitudinal data to monitor organizational effectiveness in change management.

Assessments

Assessments are designed as a purposive systematic approach to data collection and analysis related to a specific area such as leadership development or performance appraisal. The goal is most often individual and group learning related to targeted competencies and objectives. Assessments may point to specific needs for training to integrate directed and nondirected change.

For example, an assessment form designed to gather data on performance planning and appraisal might include standards as well as a process or form for appraisal. The standards indicate the expected level of performance and should be specific, attainable, measurable, and challenging. Standards are determined by organizational objectives as well as by the supervisor and employee involved. The performance appraisal gathers data on how well a performance criteria is being met. Performance planning integrates key responsibilities related to a specific position with the business goals for a planning period. Target dates and specific end products should be included in the contracting process. The actual results are documented and formally assessed every 6 or 12 months depending on the organization. The assessment criteria might also include relationships with others, teamwork, communication, and process and technical knowledge. Performance objectives should also include personal and professional growth related to change management.

Assessments are a valuable method of data collection and analysis for both managers and employees. Assessment should be a regular part of change management for the development of individual, group, and organizational resources. Informal, ongoing data collection and assessment related to performance measures is essential for managers, facilitators, and team leaders in coaching, training, and developing individuals and groups in the process of change management and continuous improvement. This is an area in which managers and change facilitators can use consultation techniques with employees and groups as clients.

Individual and Group Interviews

This section will concentrate on data collection and analysis in face-to-face interviews with individuals and groups. This includes personal interviews, depth-interviews, group interviews, panels, and focus-group interviews. These are used extensively to gather specialized data and also to interpret and evaluate data. Interviews may be informal and spontaneous, moving from one topic to another, or highly structured with an agenda and a series of predetermined questions. In all formats, some structure is required in order to make an overall comparison and analysis of data.

Interviews are appropriate in many phases of the change management process. For example, sensing data is often gathered during contact and entry in Phase 1 and prior to making agreements in Phase 2. Sensitizing interviews are appropriate with key managers and specific individuals who represent a broad perspective of the organization. One method for identifying key organizational members is to use the "reputational" approach and have each leader identify additional people who might be interviewed. Sensitizing interviews help in understanding the culture and practices of the organization as well as fundamental perspectives toward change. In beginning any directed change process, interviews are important in getting a feel for the level of commitment, openness, and trust in relationships. The time spent at the start of the project can provide many benefits including reduced costs, improved cycle time, stronger action continuity, and increased ownership of the change.

Personal depth interviews are best in working with senior executives and sensitive issues when there is a need to clarify differences in a one-on-one discussion, or when there is a need to elicit confidential data that would not be appropriate in a group setting. An outside data collection facilitator may be used to create a nonthreatening environment for both personal and group interviews.

Group interviews present different challenges and provide valuable information from a team perspective. They may also increase individual and group motivation for change and also reduce resistance by facilitating openness, and recognition of different perspectives toward change. Respondents can build on the ideas of others and begin to develop some shared understanding for effective change management. Group interviews encourage cross-unit communication among different areas of the organization. However, confidentiality must be assured. Trust and openness are critical to the validity of this data.

The environment for the interview is important in creating a comfortable, informal mood. The location should be in an area where the interview will not be interrupted. A round table might work best to create a sense of equality. Make sure that the group is not so large that individual input is discouraged. Allow plenty of time for discussion and consider a break and refreshments as part of extended group sessions.

The group interview should have some structure and a logical sequence of questions. An agenda of general categories for discussion might be given out before the day of the interview. Some established policy on general confidentiality should be discussed at the beginning of the session. The interviewer or facilitator opens the session by stating the purpose of the interview and answering any questions participants might have. Members should agree not to have interruptions, except in an emergency. There might be an explanation of the methods of documentation such as a flipchart or recorder. The facilitator gets agreement with the participants about the amount of time the interview will take. All members should have an understanding of what will be done with the data. In some cases, the consultation team might use a pilot group to test out the questions, setting, and facilitation style. Interviewers should be trained to facilitate lively discussion and to elicit feedback during and after the session.

Focus groups and panels may be conducted with internal or external groups. The overall objectives and level of involvement may be different with external groups. *Panels* are used to gather strategic data in areas such as quality, customer reaction, marketing, product development, and issues management. A panel may consist of a group of experts who are interviewed as individuals or as a group at various points over an extended period of time. A customer or a supplier panel may also be used to collect and analyze data related to organizational indicators and performance in change management.

Focus groups usually consist of 6 to 10 individuals who have experience or knowledge in a specific area. They may be systematically chosen or randomly selected from a target group such as employees, suppliers, or customers. Screening interviews can also be conducted before the focus groups. However, because of the small number of individuals and the often purposive samples, there can be some bias. This does not mean that the data is not valid in providing understanding about attitudes and perceptions related to change. It simply requires that the bias be recognized in analyzing data and that the data not be overinterpreted.

Focus groups are most effective when coordinated with other more quantitative methods. These collective interviews can be used at the beginning of the data-collection process to develop an understanding of issues and concerns before developing a questionnaire or choosing or validating a particular survey or audit. Focus groups can also be employed after a major audit or survey to explore the "why" of more quantitative statistical results. Focus groups may also be used to assess perceptions and actions related to products, services, and work procedures. Prediction interviews can be conducted with senior executives and teams prior to feedback to develop a readiness for the client system to receive the data.

Depending on the complexity of the issue, the number of focus groups required to gather adequate data may range from three to eight groups (Morgan 1988). When the data becomes predictable and repetitive, this is an indication that the data collection from the groups is complete. Focus groups require a skilled facilitator to move through a logical progression of questions and involve all participants in a structured discussion. This facilitator may be an outside resource or an internal professional who understands group dynamics and the overall information goals.

Interviews have many advantages. They can uncover more data than observation. An interview is flexible since questions can be modified and other changes can be made to adapt to the situation and the individual or group being interviewed. Interviews also build rapport and show respect and recognition through empathic listening and the opportunity to participate in and contribute to organizational change and development. A sensitive facilitator can adjust to the participants and gather valuable information that might otherwise be overlooked or hidden.

Interviews have some disadvantages in organizing, coding, and interpretation of data. Validity may be affected if information is distorted by the interviewee. Care must also be taken in conducting and analyzing interviews to ensure that the interviewer's bias does not alter or distort the information collected. Personal interviews may be too costly and time-consuming if significant numbers of people are involved. Cost-effectiveness should be balanced with the need for involvement and specific data requirements.

In preparing for feedback reporting, the change facilitator and action research team should think about what they owe the individuals and groups from whom they collect data. Internal participants develop some expectations that must be considered and answered. In internal data collection and collaborative inquiry there is an implied responsibility to informants for data feedback and individual group interpretation prior to action planning.

Q-Methodology

Many of the quantitative approaches to data gathering concentrate on objective, rational measures. Q-methodology provides a systematic, quantitative method for exploring and understanding subjectivity in different approaches to change. Q-methodology is based on the work of William Stephenson (1953, 1967). According to Stephenson, subjectivity is an individual's point of view on a particular subject and is communicated from a position of "self-reference." This methodology can be used to help understand change as it is interpreted by executives, managers, employees, suppliers, and customers.

The process of Q-methodology involves developing a sample, which consists of representative statements related to a specific topic. Samples of statements may be naturalistic or theoretical. A *naturalistic* or ecological sample is taken from the respondents' oral or written statements such as those made in personal interviews, letters, organizational publications, or speeches. A *theoretical* sample is developed from outside, secondary sources such as the mass media, books, or surveys. Pictures and cartoons have also been used. The Q-sample, or concourse, provides a collection of representative statements about a particular topic or issue. Each of these statements is placed on a card with a reference number at the bottom. These cards form a Q-deck that is sorted by each respondent. Q-sorting consists of rank ordering these statements along a quasi-normal distribution in a continuum from + 5 to - 5. This distribution might range from "strongly agree" to "strongly disagree," from "like" to "dislike," or "most like my view" to "least like my view."

Q-methodology is designed for a small number of respondents in the number of person-samples, or P-sample. The number can range from one individual in an intensive sample to as many as 50 to 60 people in an extensive sample. Stephenson often focused on understanding the subjectivity of an individual in a single case study. Q-methodology can provide data on employee attitudes, management interpretations of corporate mission and visions of the future, or community perceptions of the organization's image.

For example, a Q-sample of statements about the organizational mission and values might be taken from interviews with top executives and or organizational speeches and publications. Each of these statements is put on a card and these cards are sorted by senior managers in the organization. Each individual first sorts the deck into three piles: one pile contains those statements that the individual sees as similar to his or her views; one pile has statements that do not represent his or her views; and a third pile contains statements toward which the individual has no particular feeling. These piles are then further rank ordered into columns on a distribution from + 5 (most like my view) to - 5 (least like my view). Neutral statements are put in the middle of the continuum. The individual is then asked to comment on the choices made in the + 5 and - 5 columns. For example, they are asked, "Why is this statement most representative of your current view of the organization's mission and values?"

With an intensive sample of four to six executives, each respondent might be asked to sort the same Q-sample from several conditions of instruction over more than one session. Some of these hypothetical perspectives might include the following:

- How do you think the CEO would sort these cards?
- How do you think a manager would sort these cards?
- How do you think a customer would sort these cards?
- How would you sort these cards from a total quality perspective?
- How would you sort these cards to represent the organization five years from now?

By using a small group of respondents and multiple conditions of instruction, shared values as well as conflicting perceptions can be discovered in patterns of subjectivity among the respondents.

Q-methodology has been used to gain understanding of organizational communication and image, assess management attitudes toward organizational development and change, uncover areas of differences, support teamwork, and develop strategic planning. The results help managers to discover and understand their perspective toward change as well as the perspective of other key players in the organization as they are reflected in the factors.

The data is coordinated through Q-factor analysis designed for small-sample behavioral research. People associated with a particular factor have some common perspectives on the topic and individual loadings on the factor indicate the degree of association with the factor array or representative Q-sort for that factor. However, the interpretation of factors requires some experience and understanding of the psychological, theoretical, and statistical base of Q-methodology (Brown 1986; Goldman 1990).

An increased interest in Q-methodology has been fostered by the International Society for the Scientific Study of Subjectivity founded at the University of Missouri at Columbia in 1989, which concentrates on the development and application of Stephenson's concepts. Q-methodology is an approach to data collection and analysis that focuses on the discovery and understanding of subjectivity. It can be used to probe individual perspectives within the organizational mind in a profound and creative way to gather previously unaccessible or hidden data related to change.

Learning Instruments

Learning instruments include a variety of work sheets and creative tools for helping change facilitators and consultation teams to collect and analyze data. Many of these instruments are designed to be completed as part of a workshop, training session, or meeting and processed immediately by respondents. Most learning instruments are qualitative and gather descriptive data with quick feedback. They provide insight and understanding in an interactive learning context and are especially useful for initial data collection, and interpretive discussions.

A *critical-incident* analysis can be used as a learning instrument to gather data on specific individual experiences related to a variety of topics from leadership styles to conflict resolution and change orientation. Each incident is described in detail including the location, time, people involved, language, actions, and responses as recalled by the individual. For example, participants might be asked to complete a work sheet in which they give an example of a situation in their organization where response to change was positive. They are then asked to describe an example of a situation in which a change was not effective. Analysis and discussion of some of the differences in these two incidents can be especially important in helping the individual and the group process data based on their own perceptions and responses to organizational change. By collecting and analyzing their personal experiences related to change, individuals and groups learn some valuable lessons about organizational change management. Instruments can be especially helpful in exploring the impact of nondirected change in everyday work practices and attitudes.

The *force-field analysis* (Figure 8.3) also serves as a learning instrument in understanding change efforts through identification and analysis of supporting and resisting forces in a particular change effort. A simple work sheet with space for supporting forces on one side and resisting forces on the other side can provide a visual model of the potential conflicts and challenges in a change process such as reengineering and work redesign. The group can list items individually on the work sheet or brainstorm together using a flipchart. To ensure participation from all members, it may be most useful to have individuals do some brainstorming on their own, then share their ideas in a round-robin sequence for group discussion and analysis.

Every workshop or planning session offers the possibility for collecting and analyzing data quickly through some type of learning instrument in the form of a work sheet, checklist, or outline. Learning instruments can provide personal data for each individual or group data for collective analysis and understanding. The main advantage is that these instruments create a systematic method of informal data collection and analysis related to directed and nondirected change processes as they are interpreted by organizational members.

Charts and Theoretical Models

Charts and theoretical models provide a more detailed and extensive method for data collection and analysis. Formats such as a network analysis, flow diagram, a cause-and-effect diagram, and organizational mapping help to structure information, highlight relationships and processes, and establish priorities and focus in change efforts.

Charts and models may range from a simple diagram to a complex theoretical map. Many employees in quality improvement teams have been trained in elementary statistical process control (SPC) and have used these tools to collect and analyze data related to simple quality problems. The tools include graphs, charts, checksheets, frequency distribution charts, Pareto charts, cause-and-effect diagrams, and control charts.

For example, on a basic level a *cause-and-effect diagram* can be useful as a model for systematic brainstorming on the causes of a specific problem. A variation of this format, CEDAC or cause-and effect diagram with the addition of cards, allows employees to use cards to update changes and document causes as they see them during the work process. In this process the team uses their own experience and knowledge to explore the possible causes of a specific effect, such as loss of productivity, quality, defects, or poor service. By dividing the possible causes into four major categories (people, methods, materials, and machinery), the group is able to organize information, recognize relationships, and focus change efforts on the areas most likely to bring improvement.

Flowcharting illustrates in a visual format a sequence of specified operations including inputs and outputs as well as transformations, movements, and distinct steps in the process. Decision points are also indicated on the chart. These are especially important in offering an opportunity for change. Each primary function in the process is described as a specific action verb and charted. Flowcharts can be useful for planning changes in work design, work simplification, and resource allocation.

An employee-involvement team may use a flowchart to gather and analyze information related to improving quality, service and communication in their unit. Aubrey and Felkins (1988) list some of the questions that might be considered in analyzing the information on a flowchart as one of the steps in the *work-simplification* process.

- What is this step? Why do we do it? Is it necessary?
- Where are we doing it? Why there? Can we do it some other place?
- When do we do it? Why at that time? Can we do it another time?
- Who does it? Why? Can someone else do it?
- How are we doing it? Why? Is there some other way to do it?

This data collection and analysis may point to specific ways to improve the work process by eliminating repetitive or unnecessary tasks, combining similar or related tasks, changing the place or sequence, or improving the method of doing the job. This is the level at which nondirected change can be integrated with productivity improvement and other directed change programs.

The flowchart concept is more sophisticated in *organizational mapping*, which can be used to redesign existing processes and to develop new processes for the systematic, continuous improvement of performance. This moves from a vertical concept of organization to a horizontal systems view which focuses on the customer, the product or service, and the flow of work. Senior managers initiate and facilitate the process. Rummler and Bache (1991) suggest the following steps for process improvement:

1. Identify a critical business issue based on a problem or opportunity that affects overall strategy.

2. Identify the cross-functional processes that could resolve this issue.

3. Select representatives from these functions as process team leaders.

4. Train the team members.

5. Develop a process and relationship map that describes the current state of the organization, an "is" map.

6. Identify the disconnects in the process that could affect results.

7. Assign individuals or subteams to identify the causes of these disconnects.

8. Develop a "should" map that shows the streamlined activities in the process that delivers a quality product or service for the end-of-line customer.

9. Establish process and subprocess measures and goals.

10. Plan changes and develop recommendations.

11. Implement changes.

The entire eleven-step process typically is completed over two or three months in team meetings.

Theoretical models such as Motorola's Six Sigma help to focus data gathering and analysis on quality improvement principles that serve as a benchmark and a guide for action and values. At Motorola quality is a principal element of corporate strategy and a superordinate value. According to Keki Bhote (1991), the expert who has helped Motorola implement a world-class system, quality must be redefined as "systematic identification, analysis, reduction and eventual elimination of all variation around a target value, in order to maximize customer satisfaction, reduce cost, and enhance competitiveness in the marketplace." Bhote's approach to change focuses on the statistical design of experiments, total cycle time reduction, benchmarking, and supply management.

The four quadrants representing different perspectives on change as discussed in Chapter 3 of this book also provide a theory-based model for data collection and analysis. This model can establish a stimulus for discussion of the differences and similarities in change orientation within an organizational system. A work sheet could be created for a development session on change orientations. Respondents might be asked to describe the characteristics of the language and actions associated with each perspective within their own organization: rational/behavioral, systems, cultural/interpretive, and critical humanism. They can then recognize the dominant perspectives in their work environment. Respondents can also identify their own approach to change and compare it to their colleagues and to the overall organizational vision. Particular departments or units may represent a distinct perspective toward change. Data collection based on this model might be implemented through interviews, an individual work sheet, a questionnaire, or a Q-sort. Data collection related to individual approaches to change in the initial phases of change management can reduce later conflict and misunderstanding, and help clarify and focus collective change objectives for improving overall performance.

Figure 8.4 illustrates different data collection methods most associated with specific quadrants. This is merely a suggestion of how an approach to change can affect the choice of data collection methods. Some methods may be placed into more than one quadrant. The four-quadrant theoretical model is valuable in understanding many aspects of change management.

FIGURE 8.4 Preferred Methods of Data Collection.

Rational/Behavioral	Systems
Surveys	Enviromental Monitoring
Questionnaires	Feedback Sessions
Experiments	Action Learning Conference
Audits	Organization Mapping
Content Analysis	Simulations
Structured Interviews	Models
Learning Instrument	Flow Charts

Critical Humanism	Cultural/Interpretive
Critique	Freeflow Interviews
Historical Analysis	Focus Groups
Dialectics	Futuring
Ideological Analysis	Storytelling
Political Economy	Simulations
	Case Study
	Q Sorts
	Field Work
	Feedback Interpretations

Simulations

A simulation is designed to allow managers to practice change and explore options in a compressed, risk-free "microworld" in which they can test their model of how organizations work by creating and managing a company, establishing the roles, making the rules, and seeing the results. The simulation is diagnostic and provides opportunities for collecting data on individual and team performance in a nonthreatening yet realistic interactive context. In order to be effective, simulations must have a skilled facilitator, immediate feedback, and an opportunity for debriefing, discussion, and analysis of key learning points. The knowledge and insight from this experience can then be integrated into organizational practices for change management. By "sitting in the CEO's chair" participants expand their own horizons in thinking about the future and making decisions in the present. Groups may manage a company for three to five "years." Simulations often use computers to provide data and feedback, as participants learn how an interrelated organizational system works and the challenges of managing change.

In the organizational simulation OrgSim™ (Blanchard and Murrell 1982), a tailored training simulation runs from six to eight hours including briefing and preparation time. In this phase the participants create, operate, and develop an organization according to how they think it should be done. Teams are free to determine the structures and systems for what they consider an ideal organization. They can also experiment with their own behavior in various roles and situations. Rival organizations can be formed and marketing competition may be intensive. Team must learn to work together in a creative and efficient manner to meet customer needs.

Following this simulation phase, a debriefing and processing session is conducted. This may begin on the first afternoon and continue the next day. In the debriefing sessions the participants are facilitated in reflecting on both their shared experiences in creating the organization and in their experience of participating in a work community of their own making.

Through this simulation process, participants experience common communication problems in organizations. They understand more about motivational dynamics in relation to self, group, and organizational issues. They learn to manage the natural conflicts within the organization. Managers recognize how they can create positive work norms and reduce dysfunctional norms. They practice greater freedom and responsibility and experience the difference between organizational control and empowerment. Individuals learn how to work with uncertainty and ambiguity, and handle stress. Finally, the participants discover their own leadership potential and how they can facilitate change and motivate people toward individual and group achievement. Simulations build technical and process competency and provide a creative format for data collection and analysis. Other simulations focus on strategies, competitive analysis, and globalization (Murrell and Chakiris 1992). Simulations have also been used to explore ethical issues related to work and family issues (Blanchard 1993). There are a broad range of applications for simulations in developing competency for change management.

CASE STUDY: THE IMAGE OF AN EDUCATIONAL INSTITUTION

A university-wide task force was interested in assessing the image or perceptions that various publics had of the university in order to develop a comprehensive communication strategy for internal and external publics and plan for change (Felkins and Chakiris 1985). The task force worked with an internal-external consultation team to develop a plan to collect and analyze data. The consultation team encouraged the use of multiple research methodologies and worked within the limited budget, time, and resources of the project.

The overall goal of this consultation process was to help the university to plan and implement effective communication programs to support the overall mission and goals of the institution. Some specific objectives of the task force included an assessment of the effectiveness of current recruiting, public relations, and community programs, and the creation of a marketing plan to take advantage of opportunities in emerging issues and trends related to higher education. The data collection was designed to explore the criteria by which specific publics evaluate and select colleges and universities, and to identify areas in which the university could work more closely with businesses the community and other constituencies.

The major publics identified by the committee and university administrators were businesses, donors, the administration, faculty, staff, prospective students, high school counselors, current students, parents of students, alumni, religious groups, minorities, community residents, and the media.

The project phases for this change management project were:

1. Planning and goal setting.
2. Preparation of research instrumentation.
3. Coordination and training of internal resources.
4. Data collection.
5. Computer input and organization of data.
6. Analysis of data.
7. Preparation of feedback report.
8. Feedback and action planning.
9. Strategy implementation.
10. Monitoring and follow-up.

Data Collection Methods

In choosing each methodology, the consultation team and client system sought to answer specific questions from the perspectives of the target publics. Both quantitative and qualitative methods were used to ensure that the data was balanced and accurate. A variety of methods also provided greater reliability through the multiple confirmation of results and helped to answer a variety of important questions. These methods included questionnaires, Q-sorts, group and focus interviews, executive interviews, and content analysis.

Questionnaires

A survey questionnaire was designed to answer the following questions:

- How do target publics get information about colleges and universities?

- What characteristics are most often associated with an outstanding university?

- How does the university rank in relation to other area universities?

- How important are various aspects of college life and study (teachers, curriculum, location, reputation)?

- How are perceptions related to demographic characteristics?

The key publics were determined through executive interviews and the task force recommendations. A stratified random sample of 1,000 people were mailed questionnaires presented as a "study of attitudes toward higher education." There was no direct reference to a client or the university. Follow-up phone calls were made as necessary. Approximately 35 percent of the respondents returned the questionnaires providing a good representation of the target publics. The results were analyzed with cross tabulation on key variables.

Q-Sorts

Q-methodology helped to probe these specific questions related to perceptions of the university:

- What pictures, statements, or symbols best represent this university in the minds of target publics?

- What pictures or statements least represent the university in the minds of target publics?

- Which target publics have similar perceptions of the university?

- What characteristics of the university are accepted by all groups?

- How do the printed statements about the university correspond to the visual representation of the university?

- What do target publics view as the most important aspects of the university? Least important?

The consultation team developed two Q-card decks, one containing pictures and another with statements about the university experience and educational philosophy. Forty-eight people, including representatives from each of the target publics, were selected to sort the cards. Each participant completed a Q-statement sort and a Q-picture sort and also participated in an interview to discuss their perceptions of the Q-pictures and statements. A factor analysis of the data revealed five statement-factor types and five picture-factor types.

Group and Focus Interviews

Focus groups were structured to explore some questions about the attitudes and perceptions of target audiences:

- How do selected business leaders view the educational priorities for universities?
- How can universities work more effectively with business?
- What are the major strengths and weaknesses of area schools?
- What are the trends for the future of education?
- How do faculty and staff view the university's image with different publics?
- How do students view the university's image with specific publics?

Selected focus groups of 6 to 12 participants representing the key publics (business, donors, students, faculty, staff) were conducted. Focus groups were held on all campus locations with a structured sequence of questions. Focus groups were also held off-campus with business leaders to discuss "attitudes and perceptions of higher education." All sessions were recorded and the statements were content analyzed with an emphasis on topics, themes, comparisons, and perceptions related to the university.

Executive Interviews

Twelve in-depth interviews were conducted with top university officials including the president, vice presidents, and deans. They were asked about their perceptions of the university and how they thought others might view it. Executives interviews provided insight into the current mission, values and objectives of the university as well as strategic future goals.

- How do administrators see the goal and mission of the university in relation to its image?
- What opportunities might the university take advantage of in relation to its image?
- How will the university's present and future image change?
- Where are the strengths in communicating with key publics? Where are the weaknesses?

Content Analysis

A content analysis of university publications sought to answer the following questions about the message and communication style:

- What words does the university use to describe itself in publications and printed materials?
- Is there a consistency in the overall appearance and "look" of university publications and printed materials?
- What themes are most evident in the publications?
- What is the frequency and number of certain key words used in university publications?
- How are the university logo and other identifying elements used?

The research team collected representative samples of publications from all departments and programs at all campuses of the university. A random stratified sample of 60 publications was chosen with representation for all areas of the university. A random sample of 100 words of text was taken from each of these 60 publications and inputted into a computer to analyze frequencies, dictionary themes, and comparison of publications in terms of language, format, and campus location.

Results

One of the major findings of this study was evident in all the data collected. The current university marketing slogan was perceived negatively by all key publics. Within months after the results were reported and analyzed by the task force, the slogan was dropped.

Another conclusion from the study was the strong concern of the publics for a "traditional" education and a "traditional look" for the university. Most respondents saw this university as having its greatest strength in a tradition of education, caring, and values.

The study also revealed some marketing concerns for the university. Several publics felt that it needed to clarify its somewhat "blurred" image in relation to similar institutions in the area. The university needed to identify its uniqueness in relation to the competition.

The management focus groups revealed a perception among business leaders that what most universities taught was sometimes a mismatch with what was needed in business. These participants expressed a willingness, even an eagerness, to get more involved in cooperative programs with universities in the area.

Some of the changes implemented at the university did not come immediately, and some are still in progress. Approximately three years after this initial study, the university hired an outside consultation firm to research the university image as part of a large fund-raising campaign. While some of the areas of focus were different and the multiple methodologies were not as comprehensive, this later study confirmed many of the results of the initial study. While the university was changing in response to market demands the core values remained the same.

9

Feedback, Decisions, and Action Planning

Feedback is illuminating. Sometimes it reinforces current practices; at other times it starkly outlines issues and concerns that have been pushed into the shadows and corners of organizational life. These hidden forces often exist at the level of nondirected change. Feedback, decisions and action planning are the point at which formal and formal data is gathered into relevant action. Organizations need accurate information and cooperative decision making in order to survive. Without relevant feedback and collaborative inquiry in decisions and action planning, leaders, managers, boards, and team members may stumble in managing change.

Consider a hypothetical feedback session. The scene takes place in a room used for presentations. There are several flipcharts and an overhead projector. A change consultation team is scheduled to conduct a feedback session to brief managers about recent survey findings. Two managers arrive early and read the message written on the flipchart:

> *Welcome. Take a seat anywhere and find a partner to interview using the printed interview schedule. You and your partner are asked to discuss what you predict the survey report will say about these items:*
>
> - *What motivates employees in this organization?*
>
> - *Given 100 percent of work-related time, at what percentage did our employees rate their productivity?*
>
> - *How did our employees rate Quality of Work Life in this organization?*
>
> - *What did employees perceive as our organizational priorities? How did they reorder these priorities, with their preferences?*

The two managers get some coffee and find a place to sit. They see the activity materials, manila folder, felt-tip pens, and the interview sheets on each table. One of them takes some of the materials and prepares to begin the discussion using the interview schedule provided by the facilitator. The manager introduces himself to the other person and explains his expectations for the feedback.

I'm not sure we've met. My background is in the area of mathematics, computer science, finance, and human resources I'm the manager of information systems with 12 staff people in my group, mostly individual contributors, who are assigned to projects in human resource management systems. We're working on team compensation , succession planning, and other human resource measurements. Recently, I was asked to serve on an advisory council of the corporate senior vice president. His top-priority assignment comes from our new CEO who wants to benchmark outside companies for innovative ideas on how to develop new measurements to keep senior management informed about customers, suppliers, and employees. The CEO talks about becoming a preferred employer, preferred supplier, and good citizen of the world community. I'm not sure how all of this fits together with my work but I'm interested in looking at how we gather data for new actions.

I'm especially interested in the feedback we're getting today, particularly from my technical people with their high level of competence in new technology, both in the software development side of the business and the hardware capabilities. I wonder what their views were on this human resource audit? My hunch is they rated their productivity high, probably at 90 to 100 percent. I suspect that what motivates them is the challenge of their work. How open were they? I would hope very open. About organizational priorities I predict that they will say that our top priority is profit; however, their preferences are probably around developing people. This should be a higher priority for us. It seems the cuts we recently made in the budget took away some of the opportunities for their development activities. Several of our people were scheduled for professional conferences around the country and had to postpone these events for the balance of the year. I don't think they were pleased with these changes. As a manager I'm always concerned about losing my good people. They're scarce resources and we have a great team.

I sure hope this recent HR Audit will receive the attention and commitment of our senior executives and encourage them to put a high priority on the training and development that people need for their job. This is a good organization but we need to constantly improve if we're going to remain the best. I'm looking forward to hearing the results of this audit. This feedback is important for all of us.

The facilitation team for this session has essential responsibility related to the change management process. In general, the challenge for a change facilitator is making the feedback session an opportunity for participation in the interpretation of data within a supportive environment that allows for the exploration of concerns, needs, expectations, and hidden agendas. This requires the preparation of data packages for understanding, client ownership, and action. The change facilitators must also ask critical and thoughtful questions that promote individual and group involvement in change management.

The change consultation team cannot come like an "elf out of the woods" with data that will bring magical, painless answers to complex organizational problems. The data may reveal some difficult challenges and concerns for the organization. Facing the reality of the situation can be uncomfortable, especially for senior management. For example, how do you talk to a somewhat bureaucratic executive about audit results that show 75 percent of the people in the organization are asking for more involvement in decision making? The consultation team has an ethical responsibility to provide realistic and honest feedback to the CEO and other organization leaders and participants. An action research team should keep people informed and involved. The responsibility for providing feedback also extends to every employee who supplies data and participates in an interview or audit. Organization members need to know the results of data collection.

Sometimes managers and resource professionals are not trained to facilitate feedback sessions and get involvement, decisions, and actions based on data. Many organization leaders tend to focus more on the hard numbers related to directed change, and not integrate cultural interpretive aspects in the concerns and perceptions of people in their informal nondirected response to change. The feedback session should bring hard and soft data together to provide a more realistic picture of change in the organization. The data feedback is part of a macroview that also has to be interpreted and applied by other action teams throughout the organization.

Feedback should provide accurate, timely information. People in the organization need and value information that they can use to make decisions and to plan action. In the absence of clear information, rumors and speculation create distortion and anxiety. A skilled manager with change management competencies works as a team with employees to collect and analyze data about what is going on in the organization, and provides employees with the necessary information to do their jobs and understand how their work fits into the changing organization structures, roles, and goals.

The dynamics of data feedback and the decisions and actions based on that data work together to facilitate continuous improvement and organizational renewal. This phase, Phase 4 in the consultation process, provides both focus and direction for change applications, and results. The basic competencies for feedback, decisions, and action planning are:

- Contract how the data will be used, by whom, when, and with what outcomes;

- Design group feedback and interpretation of the diagnostic findings;

- Create a supportive culture for participative feedback activities including dialogue sessions, team-building, and planning meetings;

- Prepare data packages that create understanding, gain ownership, and mobilize action;

- Plan action derivations and ownership through facilitation of interpretive inquiry to identify specific trends, issues, or patterns as seen in the data;

- Facilitate action derivations from the data and involve the client system in the design of interventions and planned action;

- Define effective feedback interventions to involve the client, to design action, and to provide resources for interventions such as futuring, understanding where goals come from, and exploring ethical dilemmas related to feedback and action; and

- Develop a working schedule including roles, goals, performance criteria, measurement, next steps of action, people who need to be involved, and allocation of competitive resources.

Feedback, decisions, and action planning are crucial for continuous improvement in organizational effectiveness, quality, service to the customer, relationship with suppliers, alliances and networks with global partners, cross-cultural learning activities, program and product design, and training and development. Effective change management, using action research teaming, comes from confrontation of issues, feedback of findings, and collaborative inquiry and *interface* (Lippitt 1982). According to Lippitt, *interface* is a combination of *dialogue, confrontation, search*, and *coping. Dialogue* is built on the confrontation of "being and truth" in authentic communication. While feedback is the human capacity to receive, process, understand, and act, reciprocity in dialogue is a more equitable exchange with a mutual attempt to solve, know, empathize, and understand. *Confrontation* involves honoring others and self while trying to reach a higher level of understanding in relation to real issues. Part of the *search* for understanding is reaching out to the other person and establishing some linkage. *Coping* is perhaps one of the most

FIGURE 9.1 Action Research Teaming Model.

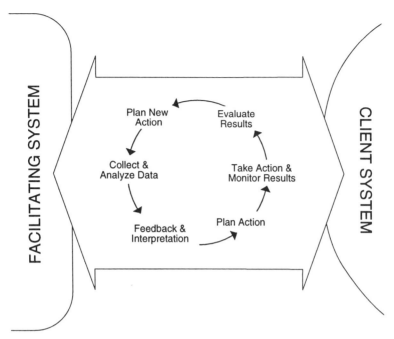

important aspects of the action research teaming model (see Figure 9.1) because it involves the transfer of learning from one situation to another and helps the individual and organization deal more effectively with rapid change. The action research cycle supports "coping" behavior as people learn more about managing change.

Feedback sessions should be an opportunity to bring ideas into the open, out from the minds and emotions and into a collective space or arena in which situations and responses can help determine appropriate action. In this approach, healthy confrontation can strengthen and renew the individual, group, and organization. The targets of feedback appearing in Table 9.1 illustrate the twelve dimensions of effective feedback. The consultation team can use this as a checklist for designing and evaluating feedback sessions.

Dialogue, confrontation, search, and coping in these dimensions develop more open, collaborative inquiry and learning for effective change management. Teamwork is strengthened through trust, understanding, recipient influence, and shared goals. Suspended judgment and learning readiness encourage dialogue.

Effective feedback can link the directed and nondirected aspects of change into a coordinated effort that supports individual, group, and organizational goals.

Table 9.1 Targets of Feedback.

More Effective					Less Effective

1. Trust

More Effective					Less Effective
There is confidence, commitment and belief in a future yet unseen	1	2	3	4	There a disbelief and lack of commitment that positive change will take place

2. Understanding

There is a readiness to listen and start where the client system is	1	2	3	4	There is a lack of knowledge and insight about the system

3. Diversity Sensitivity

People are encouraged to tell their story through their own language and culture	1	2	3	4	Self expression and differences are not recognized or supported

4. Collaborative Inquiry

Questions reflect a commitment to searching for creative solutions together	1	2	3	4	People are holding back not wanting to ask difficult questions or share information

5. Interpretative Sharing

Openness exists to interpret and take mutual responsibility for data	1	2	3	4	There is no collective search for creative options for complex issues

6. Recipient Influence

A synergy emerges and people share ideas to work together	1	2	3	4	There is a tendency not to listen or validate the view of other parties

7. Voluntary Resourcing

There is a capacity for effective teaming and resourcing	1	2	3	4	People feel imposed upon with limited choice

Table 9.1 (continued)

8. Learning Readiness

| People are reflective and ready to learn from the data and the interpretation of others | 1 | 2 | 3 | 4 | People appear impatient and closed to new opinions and ideas |

9. Ambiguity Tolerance

| There is a high degree of spontaneity in developing mutual action and exploring options | 1 | 2 | 3 | 4 | People want quick answers and direct action recommendations |

10. Confrontation Comfort

| The feedback is reality based with people taking ownership and confronting issues | 1 | 2 | 3 | 4 | There is evidence of distancing from the tough issues and not taking ownership |

11. Suspended Judgment

| Statements are neutral, descriptive, and information is provided in an objective manner | 1 | 2 | 3 | 4 | There is evaluation, fault finding, and blaming of others |

12. Shared Goal Priorities

| Clear goals emerge and action plans are shared with goals and role defined | 1 | 2 | 3 | 4 | There is a lack of collective goal priorities and action accountability |

FEEDBACK

The managers, team leaders, or staff professionals serving as feedback facilitators must create a climate (Chakiris 1987) of acceptance, ownership, and involvement to gain support for action implementation. Feedback is a continuing process that integrates directed and nondirected change and brings people into an active, data-based change management process.

Role Relations in Feedback

One of the most important components of successful action in continuous improvement and change is to gain senior-leadership involvement for input, critique, acceptance, approval, and commitment. This can be done on a one-to-one basis or with representatives or the total management group, board, or team participating in feedback sessions. However, change facilitators cannot be seduced by senior management's agenda. They must maintain the message of the data and balance it with the truth from various management perspectives. This requires integrity and ethics around data collection, feedback, and interpretation.

Close teamwork with management, including the CEO, chairperson, and in some cases, the board, should to be designed into each step to gain support, authorization, and delegation for the directed change. Individuals participating in feedback sessions, regardless of their level, should be involved in interpreting the feedback data results and in brainstorming possible action steps. Throughout the process, action implementation teams must work with appropriate individuals and groups to transfer competencies and knowledge and to ensure follow-through momentum. They should also consider the possibility that some key roles may shift during the change consultation. For example, from the start-up phase during the change initiative to the action-implementation phase, client roles, and feedback requirements may change.

There are a variety of role relationships and role responsibilities in the feedback process: ART teams, ad hoc groups or clusters, councils, or free-form groups; team leaders; internal and/or external facilitators; participating employees; relevant functions; project unit or team; customers or suppliers; and sponsor or sponsor group. The consultation team should also consider how these roles can be clarified and coordinated.

Some of the questions about role relationships in the feedback process might focus in the following areas:

- Who needs to be informed?
- Who must be or should be involved?
- Who must approve decisions?
- What are the relationships at the intraunit and interunit level?
- How effective are these intraunit and interunit relationships?
- What are the critical challenges anticipated for the feedback and action-taking sessions?
- How can these issues be verified and supported?
- What are the expectations of individuals, groups, and units?

- How can these expectations become known?
- How might these expectations change?

The need for clear roles and responsibilities is essential to the feedback process. This includes the roles of the CEO, senior executives, unions, project directors, business unit managers, department or division directors, managers, supervisors, individual workers, and internal and external resources. Where appropriate, other sponsors or stakeholders, customers, suppliers, competitors, and relevant groups such as the community or family members should be represented. There must be collaboration regarding the concrete use of the data including interpretation, implication, and explicit planning of action as a consequence of the data-based findings. Feedback can also be used to monitor the ongoing direction and impact of change management.

Design Elements for Feedback Sessions

The design and leadership of each feedback session provides an opportunity to balance both content, in what the information is saying, and process, in how the information is communicated and used. Understanding roles and goals, confronting sensitive areas, establishing priorities, and facilitating meaning and action derivations are crucial elements in the design.

Managers and team leaders performing facilitative roles in feedback sessions must be able to apply these basic skills:

- Coordinate a meeting that brings about action planning;
- Contract with the group regarding agreements about roles, schedule, time, involvement, and outcomes;
- Develop trust within the groups, with honor and respect;
- Promote voluntary individual involvement;
- Initiate and give perceptive feedback;
- Design a process for team action planning and action priorities;
- Facilitate open discussion using questions to clarify and confront;
- Use appropriate timing to move toward closure and action;
- Clarify and reach agreement on roles and goal expectations;
- Generate evaluation information to learn ways to improve future sessions;
- Prioritize action outcomes based on criteria including resources, timing, and schedules;
- Use media such as computer graphs, charts, easel, overhead, simulation, or video.

The discussion in this section assumes that trained facilitators are designing and conducting the feedback sessions. These facilitators often work as a team, especially with a large conference model, and create a shared learning context. Effective feedback sessions take place in a highly supportive environment in which people can suspend judgments in order to listen and understand other points of view. The facilitators must protect the integrity of the data as the "voice of the people" and provide a nondefensive climate in which openness, acceptance, and support is given.

The decision as to who should be involved in the feedback session is made by the client, the sponsor, and the change consultation team. It is important for the facilitators to know who will be involved in the sessions, and to anticipate their goals and expectations as well as the kinds of questions that might be asked. Specific feedback designs can be developed for each group. In situations where defensive behavior is anticipated from individuals or groups, it may be helpful to meet with them before the session on a one-on-one basis to promote understanding and improve participation and communication. The client and sponsors should be briefed ahead of time so that they can understand and interpret the data. Senior managers can also show their commitment and gain ownership by being directly involved in the session, perhaps making some opening remarks, reviewing overall organizational objectives in relation to the project, or providing a summary of the findings.

Feedback data from surveys, audits, and customers, as well as supplier information, can provide a picture of the organization. However, this picture must be interpreted through open feedback and dialogue throughout the client system. Information should be stated in a way that ties the data into the desired goals of the organization. For example, the information can be clustered together based on questionnaire, interviews, and other relevant information. A variety of media can help to organize this material and make it more interesting and comprehensible to the participants.

It is important to convert data into creative small units of information or results. This is sometimes overlooked by those who design and facilitate the feedback session. A frequent concern expressed during feedback is that too much data is presented and people feel an overload of information with relevant context but unnecessary detail. To ensure proper balance and integrity, all feedback information can be tested with representative members of the client system. In selecting information from the findings—results from focus groups, surveys and audits, questionnaires, interviews, quality statistics, or customer observations—the facilitation team should give feedback on both strengths and developmental areas or gaps (Chakiris 1987). Using a variety of media and formats such as computer printouts, graphs, overheads, electronic visuals, video, key word charts, and newsprint for feedback helps organize and address different perspectives in the findings.

Feedback sessions also need to be designed to provide a participative process for collaboration in mutual problem solving and planning for change. Part of the session may be a report on the data, followed by interactive discussion. Then the participants may form action-planning subgroups and with assistance from facilitators, individuals and groups will have an opportunity to give their feedback interpretation and move into action planning.

Developing an Agenda

The design of the interactive session, the selection of the resource leadership, and the type of process used to plan for action are important for an effective feedback process. The content in the data provided must be closely balanced with the process of how the data is communicated and acted upon. Fairness and justice in organizational activities require an ethical context for feedback with an egalitarian approach based on open discussion and voluntary action.

The agenda provides an organized schedule for thinking about the data and facilitating discussion using process questions. This requires some agreements with the client and the sponsor before the session to clarify understanding, expectations, commitment, and responsibility. The introduction and purpose stated at the beginning of the session provide an opportunity for informal "contracting" with the participants around these same elements.

Table 9.2 is a sample agenda (Chakiris 1987) for a feedback session on the results of a company-wide human resource audit. The agenda was developed in discussion between the client and the consultation team. This agenda is focused on developing ownership and involvement within the client system for data-based change.

Table 9.2 Sample Agenda.

I. Introduction and Purpose
   Feedback rationale
   Climate setting
   Roles, expectations, and responsibilities
   Emphasis on involvement and commitment

II. Expectations of Feedback Sessions
   Seek understanding.
   Gain initial interpretations.
   Identify priorities.

TABLE 9.2 (continued)

III. Summary of the Data
Data clusters
Graphs
Macro and micro relationships
Anecdotal data and summary of comments

IV. Initial Interpretation of Data
What do you see that looks familiar to you?
What does this data suggest to us?
What are some of the reasons that people might respond this way?
Are there any surprises in this data?
How do you interpret this specific data?

V. Action Derivations
If you were making the decision and could act on three items, what would
  you choose to act on?
Individual: What action can you take on your own?
Intraunit: What action can be done by teaming within your workgroup?
Interunit: What action can be done by teaming across work units?
Organization: What action is required by the total organization?

VI. Nomination of Action Team Members
Criteria for selecting action team facilitators
Nominations for unit or organization-wide task forces

VII. Future Action
How can we keep people informed and involved?
When should we recycle audit or make additional data collection?
Evaluation of feedback session

Evaluating the Session

The design for the feedback session should include an opportunity to test,
modify, and redesign prior to rollout across the organization. It is also
important to invite evaluation feedback about each session. These questions
are useful for assessment of the feedback design and implementation.

- Did people understand the data?
- Do they feel comfortable with the findings?
- Were there any significant surprises?
- Did they feel involved in the discussion and interpretation of the
  data?

- Did they have an opportunity to provide ideas for action priorities?
- Were they given the opportunity to nominate someone from their unit or function to serve as an action team member?
- Did the facilitator elicit feedback on the session?

This feedback data can be compared to the goals for the session to identify strengths and improvement areas. Feedback provides a continuing opportunity for learning and improvement of future sessions.

Selecting and Preparing Action Team Facilitators

Action team facilitators (Chakiris 1987) can be nominated during the feedback session. They are the link in moving to the next step in the feedback process, which is decisions and action planning. The understanding and commitment of these formal and informal leaders is critical in maintaining the momentum for change and involving people throughout the organization in decision making and planning related to change management. The criteria for choosing facilitators to help in presenting the feedback in other units include the following characteristics:

- Can link to management and all levels of the organization;
- Has a real interest in serving;
- Has the time and commitment to serve;
- Has high level of trust with management and employees;
- Can link both formal and informal communication networks;
- Has a commitment to the organization;
- Wants to learn and develop competencies in new areas;
- Is willing to perform a variety of roles;
- Is perceptive to group dynamics;
- Has an optimistic view of how the organization can achieve positive results.

It is important to work with the client and sponsor to draft an appropriate schedule for unit and departmental feedback sessions. This should be preceded by facilitation training for the action resource leaders who will conduct these feedback sessions. They should be trained in both the content and process of feedback and action planning in order to facilitate data interpretation with the groups and to brainstorm implications for possible follow-up action.

The consultation team considers how leaders and managers can most effectively be trained to facilitate feedback sessions with their work teams. After ART facilitation leaders have been identified, the consultation team can clarify roles and responsibilities and work with managers and team leaders to develop and implement feedback designs.

Monitoring and Follow-up

During feedback, it is important to identify who needs to be involved, to approve, and to be consulted regarding planning and action decisions. The consultation team must determine methods and communication channels for keeping the appropriate persons informed of progress throughout the feedback and action planning process. The team should continue to test the project priorities against management's priorities and objectives. These questions are useful in evaluating the relationship between the consultation team and the client system during the feedback process:

- Has the consultation team developed trust and openness?
- Has the consultation team created interdependency?
- Does the consultation team protect confidentiality?
- Does the consultation team express willingness to receive feedback?
- Does the client express a willingness to receive resource facilitator feedback?
- How comfortable is the consultation team in confronting issues?
- What questions are important in looking at the consultation relationship?
- How will the consultation team involve the client system in giving two-way feedback on performance?
- How will the action research team leaders be supported throughout the client system?

DECISIONS

The initial decisions on priorities are made during the feedback session. After this first session, the action research team leaders begin to meet with their individual groups. These teams must make more specific decisions related to the meaning and application of the data in their specific unit or area. They work within the existing formal or informal collaborative structure for responding to existing and emerging challenges across and within units, and with customers and suppliers. As ART members determine action strategies, they may use a teaming process for identifying challenges and opportunities, gathering data, and making action decisions based on that data.

After systematic data collection and feedback, the facilitating group may suggest that research teams, task forces, or unit teams work together on planning and diagnosis of critical challenges facing the organization. Action research teams are a unique structure for change management because of their emphasis on data based change. Clusters and project teams may also use action research techniques. The following characteristics distinguish action teams from some other types of groups and committees. Action research teams focus on these activities:

- Use data collection to define and analyze the situation and do not accept diagnosis already made;
- Examine their own function as a group with a third-party observer intervener;
- Allow for mutual influence among group members;
- Develop trust within the group;
- Promote individual involvement;
- Analyzetheir meetings and evaluate process;
- Rotate leadership through accountability participation;
- Practice a basic philosophy of collaboration among members and with other groups;
- Accept team learning and relationships among members as important;
- Evaluate and modify internal functioning;
- Freely choose areas for work and seek autonomy with ownership, commitment, and a high investment of energy.

In traditional organizations, action research teams have no formal power unless management chooses to give them power. However, when these teams are formed by senior management as part of the feedback process they are linked to power and have a definite mandate to action. The role of the team is defined and action research and the consultation process provide a ready framework for planning, facilitating, and implementing change.

The consultation team must be especially aware of the decision-making dynamics of the organization in relation to the change effort and the process of feedback, decisions, and action planning. These are some of the questions related to specific challenges and concerns:

- What feedback data is required to ensure quality interventions?
- What feedback data is needed to plan future events?

- What data is needed to uncover resistance?
- Is a pilot test necessary before going forward with feedback?
- Will feedback be generated during the design phase?
- How can the team find out differences in perception between the client and the sponsor regarding outcomes?
- What questions are important to facilitate with clients and sponsors?
- How should clients be involved in giving feedback on interventions such as programs, training, consultation, design, and needs analysis?

Facilitation Skills for Moving Data Into Action

As stated earlier, feedback sessions should provide a nondefensive climate in which openness, acceptance, and support can be experienced. The facilitators of the sessions must be able to apply the following technical process skills:

- Initiate and give helpful feedback
- Promote collaborative inquiry and interpretation
- Create trust within groups
- Gain individual involvement
- Conduct a feedback meeting that brings about positive action
- Understand both content in what data reveals and process in how to move data into action
- Use multimedia including print, charting, and visual graphs
- Be a partner and a team member working with and through others
- Gain ownership and commitment
- Keep appropriate people informed

The facilitators should create a receptive, motivational climate where people working on data can see and recognize the positive results that can occur for individuals, groups, and organizations through data-based change. Feedback can be presented from a systems perspective, allowing members to visualize the smaller parts of data within the context of the whole. Rational/behavioral, cultural/interpretive, and critical perspectives might also be recognized.

It is important to involve the client in the design of the feedback and interpretation of the data. Organizing the data in "small packages" related to driving questions helps to improve understanding, gain ownership, and facilitate action. Interpretation as a collective process for making decisions and planning action derivations can be initiated through this approach. For example, the facilitator may ask what specific trends, issues, or patterns are seen in the data to help people get involved in data applications.

Many of the initial discussions in feedback and action planning are related to getting agreements and establishing a framework for later decisions. These questions point to some information and decision needs.

- What are our goals and from where do these goals come?
- Who should be involved in the action planning?
- What are our specific roles and next steps of action?
- What is our timetable or schedule?
- What are our performance criteria ?
- What will success look like?
- How do we allocate resources?
- Do we need additional training?

The change consultation team serves a central role in helping groups to make these agreements, links follow-through action with assigned responsibilities, reminds the team of performance criteria, and designs the conceptual framework for measuring and monitoring actions.

Where Goals Come From

The starting place for understanding needs and opportunities in change management is to determine where the goals come from and how they are established. The diagnostic thinking and data collection leading up to goal setting might include these influencing factors:

- The discontent, expectations, needs, and hopes of those being served may create new goals.

- Past commitments of the organization and unrealized past goals may be good guidelines toward goals that need to be reaffirmed.

- The board, CEO, or senior executives in the system have set goals that must be related to goal setting at lower levels.

- In an environment of neighbors, peers, other competitive organizations, and various internal business units and departments, group goals and achievements are interdependent. The expectations, hopes, and needs of these groups provide important data for establishing goals.

- The successful goals of others often stimulate some to match and exceed their achievements. Individuals and groups may gain enthusiasm for and commitment to specific goals by observing the success of others.

- A person or organization may be feeling pain, discontent, and frustration with the way things are going. This may trigger a strong need to set new goals.

- Futurism is a growing discipline and many carefully derived predictions about the future are available as a resource for thinking about how teams can most effectively plan for and capitalize on opportunities for the future. This encourages imaginative goal setting.

- Goals also come from what organizational members want to happen. Many futures are possible and people can influence what will happen. It is important to clarify and to project what people want to happen to fulfill desires and needs.

- Response to competitive challenges may also promote specific goals. What is driving the global, economic, and environmental challenge? What are the best practices? What quality, service, and continuous-improvement strategy links current goals with future achievements and performance measurements? What are the various perspectives of the client, resource facilitator, sponsor, customer, and supplier?

Adapted from *"Where Goals Come From and Consulting Process in Action Skills Development Kit,"* by Gordon L. Lippitt, Ronald Lippitt, B. J. Chakiris, and Robert W. Pirsein, 1978. B. J. Chakiris Corporation.

Some Distinctions Between Futuring and Planning

After initial action plans have been made, it is useful to do some futuring to visualize where the organization might be 5, 10, or 20 years from now. This increases creativity and innovation, and puts planning into perspective. In making decisions related to feedback data and action implications, there are some clear distinctions between futuring and planning. *Futuring* is a diagnostic methodology for decision making and preparing for change based on our capacity to discover possibilities through the use of the human imagination. While *planning* serves a systematic approach to identifying where we are and where we want to go, futuring leaps ahead and creates the preferred future without the usual constraints and judgments essential to planning activities. Futuring moves beyond the problems and pain of the present and stretches the imagination in a positive direction without evaluating the results. While both planning and futuring are useful, futuring improves the team's thinking about possibilities and makes planning more innovative and connected to long-term objectives. Both are a part of change management.

The list of terms in Table 9.3 outlines the differences between futuring and planning (Lippitt and Lippitt 1982). These results were compiled from a number of seminars with executives and strategic planners from business, health care, religion, social services, government, and education.

TABLE 9.3 Futuring vs. Planning.

<u>Futuring</u>	<u>Planning</u>
Right brain	Left brain
Imagination	Decision
Predicting	Intending
Wide angle	Zoom
Creative	Methodical
Fluid	Disciplined
Free wheeling	Focused
Visionary	Structured
Conjecturing	Concluding
Nonjudgmental	Evaluative
Qualitative	Quantitative
Comprehensive	Systematic
Rainbow	Black-white-grey
Intuitive	Analysis
Free form	Priorities set
Images	Goals
Searching	Objectives
Scenarios	Limited
Expansive	Focused
Reflective	Defining
Hypothesis	Conclusion
Surveying	Organization mapping
Risking	Action ideas
Mind	Brain
Abstract	Concrete
Sensing	Selective
Mystic	Technical
Spontaneity	Discipline
Explore	Find
Stretching	Decide
Inclusive	Exclusive

Sometimes groups move too quickly from initial goals to action without taking time to explore the possibilities through futuring. Figure 9.2 illustrates the sequence from initial goals to futuring, feedback, action planning, application, and measurement. Initial goals are often established based on a rational planning perspective. Futuring stretches and enriches these roles. The feedback from a futuring exercise helps to plan more innovative and positive action and applications. Futuring helps to integrate multiple voices and perspectives in relation to change.

FIGURE 9.2 Futuring Sequence.

Initial Goals → *Futuring* → *Feedback* → *Action* → *Application* → *Measurement*

Futuring to develop an "image of potentiality" can be an exciting and rewarding experience for team members. They can begin with individual work by silently brainstorming and writing down their thoughts on what the organization will look like at some point in the future. This may be followed by group discussion and individual sharing. The group can complete a composite scenario and record this on large newsprint. If several teams are involved, the participants might view the work of other groups. Deciding on the "best" or "most realistic" scenarios is not suggested since the goal is creative strategic thinking. The following are two versions of a futuring exercise.

Scenario #1

It is the year 2001. Several managers are discussing enthusiastically how internal teaming across functions has helped them to become more responsive to their business needs and to customers. The application ART unit is collaborating with management in solving business issues. Management believes that these change initiatives have given the business a competitive advantage.

Two of the managers report that they have become more skillful in setting quality performance criteria with their direct reports. They also discuss their sense of accomplishment in using the tools of skills inventories and work design to assist individual employees in taking responsibility for personal and professional development.

Work teams in the service facility are refining their self-directed work teams, clusters, and virtual teams with new knowledge, technology rewards, cross-training, individual quality responsibility, and trained module advisors who serve as coaches and support resources. ART components are working with managers across business units to improve unit planning, setting priorities for training and development, establishing creative innovations for quality, cycle time, and cost reduction, and opening up communication among departments.

There is a notable increase in the sense of pride and satisfaction among employees as shown by the recent human resource audit, which indicated a significant improvement in areas of job and relationship satisfaction, structure and systems, and organizational effectiveness. Employees taking the audit were pleased with the feedback sessions and action plans they helped develop. Teams have been formed to work on several developmental areas. The training and education staff has taken a lead role in training change facilitators and in working closely with managers to improve their change management skills.

Managers have implemented relevant programs to enhance diversity in the work force and there is a heightened awareness of business-performance measurements, especially market share, sales, and financial measures. The organization is working in partnerships and alliances with the community and several universities.

Individual employees are taking responsibility for managing their personal and professional growth. Several career programs have been introduced and a viable succession-planning system has been developed with managers performing key consultation roles in supporting quality people and developing leadership across the organization.

This scenario is followed by the facilitator posing questions:

- Describe some of the activities that have taken place between now and the year 2001?
- What do you see and hear that pleases you?
- What else are people saying?
- What are some of the events that have taken place?
- Have any significant changes occurred?
- What is your role? How has it changed?

Team members are asked to write down their thoughts and then share them with the group.

Scenario #2

The year is 2010. Imagine yourself listening in on a conversation taking place among three people inside your organization. What are they saying about the organization? What are some of the different ways in which people are working together? What kinds of teaming are taking place? What does the organization look like? What types of structures might be most evident? Are decisions being made in different ways? How have roles changed? What are the major lessons the organization has learned?

After participants describe their future scenarios, the facilitator may ask some additional questions:

- What has happened that pleases you?
- What obstacles have been overcome to get to this future?
- What has contributed most positively to this future?

These questions should encourage creative visions of the future without analyzing and evaluating the results and dilemmas in the present context.

FIGURE 9.3 Force Field Analysis Form.

Rank	Supports		Barriers	Rank	
	1.		1.		
	2.		2.		
	3.		3.		
	4.		4.		
Strategic Objectives					
A		B		C	
Possible Next Steps of Actions					

Force-Field Analysis Form

The force-field analysis form can be used after the futuring activity to help the team visualize the driving and restraining forces that might affect change efforts in the present and moves toward future potential (see Figure 9.3). This form can also be used to determine strategic approaches and to plan next steps of action for change management.

Decision Factors

The team may find a more traditional problem-solving sequence appropriate for making decisions and planning for action based on data feedback (see Table 9.4). These questions help the group to think about driving questions in a progressive analysis process.

TABLE 9.4 Decision Sequence.

Feedback of the data related to challenge and opportunity

 What is the current situation?

 What are the most critical questions we should ask about change?

 What do we learn about the directed level? Nondirected level?

 How significant are the issues?

 What are the consequences?

 Which individuals, groups, and units are affected by the change?

 What elements can we control? Not control?

 What is the level of motivation and commitment?

 What is the timetable for decisions and actions?

Interpretation of the data

 Where should we direct our attention?

 How do we interpret this data?

 Do we have some information gaps?

 What does this data mean to us?

 What are some possible reasons for these responses?

 What procedures and policies might be related to this?

 What other information sources are available?

 What are the key decisions that must be made?

 What are the criteria for making these decisions?

Developing possible action derivations

 How many different options can we identify?

 What actions are indicated by the data?

 What would we do if we had no constraints?

 What actions do top management support?

 Are a variety of different viewpoints represented?

TABLE 9.4 (continued)

Choosing the best actions

How can we prioritize possible action derivations?

Which of these actions best meet our criteria?

What are the consequences of various actions?

Do we have the resources to implement these changes?

How are these changes related to organizational goals?

Are any of these action options compatible?

Should we consider contingency actions?

Implementing the action planning

Who has what responsibilities in change implementation?

How will results be measured?

Do we need to establish a benchmark?

Who should receive feedback?

Who should be involved in implementation?

What will be the measure of the success of specific changes?

Do we need more data?

All of the methodologies in this section including goal assessment, futuring, and force-field analysis can improve decision making for action planning and implementation in change management.

ACTION PLANNING

Diagnostic Analysis

A diagnostic analysis questionnaire (shown in Table 9.5) assumes a recommendation for change is being initiated now or in the future. These questions help the team to think about the context and implications of the change as they plan for action.

Table 9.5 Diagnostic Questionnaire.

---

1. Briefly describe the change initiative the team wants to recommend. Describe the unit of change (individual, work group, intergroup, or total organization).

2. Identify what data led the teams to conclude a change was or is needed. What was happening that indicates a need for improvement?

3. How is this change linked to a strategic goal?

4. Who is viewed as the change champion?

TABLE 9.5 (continued)

5. What are the underlying motives and values regarding this change initiative? Yours? The client? The sponsor/evaluator?

6. What are the consequences if the change is successful? Unsuccessful?

7. Looking out five years, what does the change look like?

8. Describe roles, job and career goals, visibility, organizational gains, and other areas that might be affected.

9. Since most change efforts require resources and investments often overlooked, what investment is anticipated for this change effort? Consider time, information, structure, financial and technical resources, employee training, building of client relationships, coordination and communication, goal alignment, and system integration.

10. How will you measure the change? What are the performance objectives?

Planning Step-Wise Action

After some decisions have been made, the following planning questions help define the next steps of action for change management throughout the organization.

Step 1: Establishing Roles and Responsibilities

What action is desired and in what sequence?

How will this action be completed?

Who will do it?

Where is it to be done?

When is it to be done?

What is the team's role for these action steps?

How will the team coordinate with other action teams?

Step 2: Gaining Support for Action

Who does the team need to involve or inform?

Where are the "supporting forces"?

How can this support be mobilized?

Step 3: Anticipating Barriers

What barriers can be expected?

Where are the perceived blocking forces?

How can these be reduced?

Step 4: Evaluating Results

How will the overall change action be evaluated?

How will the people know when they have completed their role?

How will the team know when this project is complete?

What support will be needed for continuity?

Success Factors for Action in Change Management

Based on empirical work and their own consulting experiences with organizational change, the Lippitts (Lippitt and Lippitt 1985; Lippitt, Lippitt, Chakiris and Pirsein 1978) have identified the key factors to which change facilitators and consultation teams should pay close attention.

Involve the work force.

People throughout the organization should have an opportunity for buy-in on the change action recommendation. This includes the participation of credible leaders at all levels. Line managers are trained as change facilitators. The consultation team anticipates "waves" of readiness and involvement.

Deal with contradictions and ambivalence about change.

The consultation team assumes a proactive posture and creates a plan for trial and revision within a limited time perspective. Some reality testing and open discussion helps uncover concerns. Effective educational designs inform, invite questions, establish understanding, and invite opposing views and different viewpoints related to change.

Assemble action teams for temporary problem solving.

Some political awareness is used to compose temporary action teams which involve key leaders and influencers at all levels. There is a voluntary matching of resource with task and sufficient time is scheduled for the start-up teaming process. These temporary teams are integrated and linked in networks throughout the organizational structure.

Establish steps toward progress.

The team takes realistic short-term steps and documents these clearly for later use and analysis. The change facilitators watch for early warning signals that might cause later problems. Appropriate steps toward performance objectives are celebrated and rewarded.

Use anticipatory practice.

The group rehearses presentations and events to adjust designs and to plan and run test development with the redesign. The task force is provided with developmental resources to encourage continuing learning and improvement as they evolve toward an interdependency model. Teams invite review and feedback on the applications of change management process.

Define accountability to ensure change results.

Teams gather periodic performance and progress feedback based on their performance measurement criteria. Report documentation is available for review and collaborative inquiry. Connections are made to outside sources of support and external resources. The organization helps maintain momentum and commitment by providing continuing training of professional development for the team members with linkage to their career management.

In any action planning related to change it is important to determine what baseline data is required. Desired outcomes related to quality, cost, productivity, customer service, and organizational, group, and individual performance and effectiveness should be identified. Other measurements or indicators needed to validate progress toward outcomes must also be established. This includes the trends that the client might seek to validate. The consultation team also determines which quantitative or qualitative measurements will be appropriate. Agreements and decisions are made around how progress will be measured as well as when, by whom, and at what frequency. The consultation team also agrees on how the client system will be involved in giving feedback or evaluating progress toward specific action goals.

CASE STUDY: STRATEGIC PLANNING IN A CHILD AND FAMILY SERVICE AGENCY

ART ensures quality feedback, decisions, and action planning and increases the application of learning and knowledge for continuous improvement and a broader sphere of ownership and participation. The following case, involving a child and family service agency (Chakiris 1993), centers on strategic planning activities and includes the participation of a core planning group made up of the planning chair, president of the board, executive director, program director for the agency, and an outside consultation resource with competence in working with social agencies in specific technical and process tasks and integrating the recommendations of diverse resources.

The core team coordinated the participation of appropriate groups for the planning process. This included facilitating what the staff and board viewed as the critical challenges for the agency in moving toward and beyond the year 2000. To involve various constituent individuals and groups, "free-form councils" were assembled to initiate data collection both inside and outside the client system. The free-form councils included panels of experts, board and committee spokespersons, and community representatives from throughout the state and local areas.

A survey was developed for gathering data from the potential market segment made up of district and state units that served in diverse roles with the agency. This included members active in voluntary leadership, member organizations serving as funding sources, and constituents that had needs served by this agency, and other competitive and noncompetitive groups and individuals.

The social concerns and needs of the agency were in areas such as family crisis, adoption, immigration, jobs and careers, skill development, adult education, and community centers for families. Their organizational needs included leadership training for committees and councils, resolution of conflicts, problem solving, facilitation skills for meetings, and cross coordination of information and resources in the community.

Several teams collected data through benchmarking "best practices" of organizations both inside and outside of the social-services field to explore innovative community service delivery systems. This activity involved a multidisciplinary population of research teams working with equally diverse groups from the community.

Each action team was composed of external experts, internal staff, voluntary board members, and members from each of the state-wide area councils. The six areas benchmarked for best practices by the action research teams were:

1. Service delivery and organization structure for the year 2000 in relation to location and decentralized vs. centralized structure;

2. Staffing for the future with new careers and the growth of new professionals;

3. Marketshare and competition in programs and products that include serving the different market segments such as senior adults, adolescents, and families, and future alliances with other organizations such as emerging community agencies, congregations, and educational units throughout the state;

5. Involvement of the users of the agency such as the congregations, judicature groups of district councils, clergy, social interest groups and others; and

6. Creative funding to respond to opportunities and the challenges of the millennium.

The role of the outside resource facilitator, who had been a former social-agency executive, was to provide process feedback to the core steering group and to the various cells of free-form groups doing the research, feedback, and first interpretations of data. During and after the study, both verbal and written reports were provided to present feedback, interpretations, and action derivations for the overall strategic plan.

The studies of these six areas helped members of each action research group to understand the challenge more thoroughly, and the outside resource facilitator also helped to strengthen their ability to work together. Before the action research teaming, consultation skills training was provided in techniques of benchmarking, clarification of the strategic planning process, the specific roles and goals of each group, how the data would be used, who would be informed, and what involvement and feedback might be presented to the individuals and organizations providing the data.

A one-day action-learning conference was conducted, attended by the board, the staff, representatives of a diverse constituency, the leaders of other social agencies, and an expert panel in the challenges being studied by the agency. A conference agenda designed by the planning and steering group included a morning session of panel presentations facilitated by a moderator with time for questions and answers with the audience. In the afternoon the executive director provided feedback results of a survey sent out to the constituent organizations asking their perspectives on current and future human services. Subgroups were organized with board members facilitating small discussions concerning the survey and the panel presentation and what implications could be derived for the future delivery system of this agency. Questions had been prepared prior to the conference. Board members had received a short training session on group facilitation, and the agency staff were briefed on their role as group historians. Group reports were documented and presented by the facilitator and group historian, with comments from other members. At the close of the conference the executive director and board president thanked everyone for their input and ideas and announced how the data would be used as input for the agency's strategic plan, with a post-conference report being made available upon request. The conference moderator distributed a form for people to write down their feedback ideas and any concerns or questions they might have. This data was analyzed and presented to the planning group as input for future meetings.

By getting involved in ART activity, people in the organization and constituent community participated actively with the action research teams

FIGURE 9.4 Planning Model.

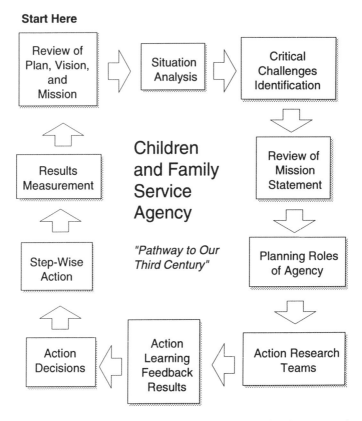

throughout the process from the initial design to the final presentation of results and discussion of their action implications (see Figure 9.6). Kurt Lewin's view is evident in that causal inferences about the behavior of human beings are more likely to be valid and enactable when the people in question participate in building and testing them. The consultation team's aim was to create an environment in which participants give and receive valid information, make free and informed choices (including the choice to participate), and generate internal commitment to the results of their inquiry.

The six ART units reported back the findings to the specific groups such as the board, staff, and other organizations that contributed to the various studies. Feedback, decisions, and actions were based on interpretations, new action recommendations, role and goal clarification, and trial and testing as appropriate for the agency during the next decade.

The followup to the strategic planning and action learning conference developed a closer relationship between the agency and its constituency. A human resource plan supported policies for staff and board development and assessment of core competencies of the agency for the present and future. This included objectives for continuous improvement with several goals related to benchmarking of other organizations to observe best practices.

10

Applications and Results Measurement

Application and results measurement are the crucial points that test the integration of directed and nondirected processes in change management. One expert suggests that through poor quality each employee may waste from $100 to $200 each day (Bhote 1988). In most cases, failure to manage the "white space" on the organizational chart is failure to effectively manage the business (Rummler and Brache 1991). The systematic improvement of performance is an ongoing application of change management in integrating directed and nondirected processes.

Once an action plan is developed by organization members, it must be implemented and the outcomes evaluated in relation to needs and performance objectives for change management. The cycle of action research in data collection, feedback, analysis, action, and monitoring continue throughout the process. This information and collaborative interpretation help to integrate directed and nondirected change activities and assess the results of specific interventions to improve performance.

Interventions are planned activities or applications by the consultation team designed to increase organizational effectiveness and facilitate change management. The focus of intervention applications is evident on four developmental levels: (1) individual, (2) small group or work group, (3) intergroup relations among groups, and (4) organization-wide systems change.

Specific interventions related to individual learning might support personal growth, career planning, leadership development, and management and communication competencies. Group interventions can include teamwork, action research, problem-solving skills, meeting management, conflict resolution, group dynamics, and continuous improvement and high-performance. Intergroup development focuses on cooperation, collaborative inquiry, information sharing, customer orientation, and creative alignment. Organizational development involves broad systems wide interventions related to performance standards, work redesign, operations research, process improvement and planning and managing change.

Phase 5 of our change-management model, emphasizes intervention applications and results measurement. Managers must apply these competencies:

- Successful action taking, converting insights and plans into motivated action, and establishing performance criteria and basic guidelines for change management;

- Ensuring quality interventions based on proven methods and techniques;

- Teaming with others to facilitate change intervention designs through application rehearsal, feedback, and observation to provide practice prior to implementation;

- Documentation of action measures while guiding this feedback into a process for planning new action, and integrating change;

- Coordinating competitive resources and designing action based on valid information collected in a voluntary manner with client system involvement, interpretation, and commitment;

- Renegotiating for necessary resources and responding to the client's sense of over-commitment when faced with the investment and risks involved in taking action;

- Celebrating steps of action and retaining the necessary momentum for change continuity; and

- Design and redesign of action based on the process of action research teaming (ART) data collection methods and continuing monitoring and evaluation of change integration.

Intervention Applications

Change management often begins with the recognition of a need that is not being satisfied or an opportunity that could benefit the organization. Satisfying the need or taking the opportunity requires changing the organization in some way. The scope of the change may involve a person, a group, or the entire organization. Since directed change is being introduced into a system, this is called an intervention. Interventions can focus on training programs, measurements, and various types of activities within the client system, from a process to organization change. Specific contexts and action may range from a two-minute phone call to a major feedback session on audit results with facilitation of action planning for systemwide change.

Planned consultation activities can include implementing new objectives for quality measurement; building research and development capacity for designing future products; increasing coordination across the organization to improve quality and reduce cycle time; improving response time and overall customer satisfaction; or conducting an image study to validate strategy required to become more competitive and to increase market share.

Interventions alter or influence the characteristics, processes, or patterns of an ongoing system, as a means to facilitate more effective change management. Thus, interventions should be intentional, coordinated, and data-based. Through these actions the facilitating system assists the client system in becoming more responsive to its environment, new situations and competitive markets in order to support survival, growth, and development. Interventions help integrate directed and nondirected change to achieve coordinated results related to issues, challenges, and opportunities.

Intervention Types

The action research teaming (ART) process involves the client system in the diagnosis, feedback, and interpretation of data, as well as action derivations and decisions about the method, design, and resources needed to bring about integrated change management. Decisions are client based, with the change facilitator's role defined only for a specified period of time relative to a program or project, with recontracting and support occurring as necessary. During this time a number of specific interventions may be facilitated by the consultation team.

Interventions are made at both the macro and microlevels to facilitate activities, programs, processes, and systems. The following list illustrates a variety of objectives, contexts, and levels of intervention used in change management.

- Conducting a human resource audit to benchmark the effectiveness of the organization as part of a total quality measurement;
- Designing a fundamental business course based on validated needs analysis and instructional design methods, and providing a related business simulation;
- Creating a self-directed career development workbook for the international sales representatives to assist them in planning their careers, help them to become a more competitive resource for job opportunities, to expand through rotating career assignments organizational global competence for future appointments;
- Conducting an environment survey for improving quality and productivity using the Deming principles;

- Developing a performance-based compensation plan for self-directed teams;

- Improving communication, unit coordination, and cooperation with training and skill competence in teaming, empowerment, and high performance;

- Using an organization simulation for an assessment that involves participants in structuring their own organization and running the enterprise with observation and process feedback;

- Using process observation in team meetings to improve overall effectiveness and productivity;

- Involving the client in the feedback sessions and interpretation of the data, setting action priorities, and facilitating nominations for temporary action teams;

- Facilitating executive conferences with predata collection, conference design, and action teaming through subgroups and post-conference follow-through on action;

- Serving as a third party in the confrontation of identified critical challenges with a senior-executive group;

- Training engineers in advanced project management using a simulation course with applications tools and technology to reduce budget and cycle time of projects and increase team coordination;

- Providing cultural-sensitivity training and career-mentoring supports for employees who are working in different continents in multinational and global assignments;

- Providing consultation to general managers of business units in cycle time, productivity, and quality;

- Facilitating work redesign, organization structure, and staffing requirements for changing from a management-centered to a team-centered culture; and

- Developing alliance and consultation with local resources of other continents to establish competency programs with a global delivery system for training and education.

Improving Interventions

During the intervention and application phase, barriers to the directed change and deliberate blockages can occur. The consultation team, which can include managers, should not create additional obstacles by ignoring these defensive responses. Anticipating and listening to the concerns of the client system can ultimately increase acceptance of the change. Appropriate intervention methods should be designed to elicit timely feedback and involve key people in the review and interpretation of information concerning change as it affects their relationships, events, work activities, and overall goals.

Interventions should be data-based to validate needs with appropriate involvement and client system ownership. However, it is often easier to make a decision about when intervention is needed than about *how* to make the intervention. "How" involves both client system readiness and facilitating system competence in change management. The following are some ways to enhance intervention competencies for change facilitators:

- Seek feedback to guide adjustments in action and approach

- Train in "how-to" skills

- Do tryouts and pilots to test results

- Team with other people

- Generate appropriate evaluation feedback data

- Appreciate and understand people's reaction to change

- Rehearse and practice in situations in which you are not "playing for keeps"

There are several methods to help develop intervention process skills for change management. Simulations and role-playing in informal learning situations can provide an opportunity for practice and feedback on process skills. An activity for skill-practice-through-rehearsal activity (Lippitt and Chakiris 1982) can be used in a subgroup of peers or in a training session. For example, the group may be asked to list examples of client behaviors or statements that sometimes puzzle them and block effective change management. In this rehearsal activity, one person volunteers to try coping with one of these circumstances, selecting a situation that is real and problematic. The change facilitator selects a colleague to take the role of the client and gives a brief description of the situation and the context in which it occurs. An example of a situation might be that the client does not feel it is necessary to meet with employee teams to discuss a new change initiative. These two people then begin a dialogue while the rest of the group listens and observes how the change facilitator copes and how the "client" reacts. The activity continues for no more than five minutes, which allows enough time to get a sense of behavior for observation and feedback. The group gives feedback on the role play, how the client reacted, and what the facilitator did in response to the client behavior. This is followed by the total group brainstorming ideas on how the facilitator might be more effective. The person practicing the behavior is given a chance to replay the scene using the suggestions. This is followed by feedback and observations on the different approaches, and planning new action to improve the effectiveness of the intervention behavior.

The facilitator may also elicit two-way feedback from the client system to guide design revisions and improve the change intervention. For example, during a feedback session the facilitator can legitimize acceptance and define barriers or concerns by using process questions to invite feedback on a crucial intervention. These questions can be used during or after feedback session to provide data for the facilitators:

- How helpful was this feedback session for you?
- Was sufficient time provided to gain understanding of the information?
- Are there additional questions you have at this time?
- What suggestions do you have for improvement?
- Are there any concerns you have ?
- How helpful was the feedback?

This information, once collected and summarized, will help the resource facilitator redesign future sessions and validate when change interventions are working effectively.

Another method for improving overall change intervention results is to use pilot tests and rehearsals. These activities can involve a representative design team from the client system in the unit receiving the service, or a cross-section constituent group of the organization. Colleagues and other professionals such as staff resources can provide helpful feedback for improving change facilitation practices. Skill competence can also be improved through practicums, mentoring activities with other professionals, and university continuing education programs.

Action-learning feedback instruments generate process data for improving action interventions. As described in previous chapters, a learning instrument is a set of statements or questions that are used to generate data for feedback, discussion, and new action. Using these instruments, change facilitators can provide a process for immediate feedback. Learning tools might be used to plan new interventions or as an evaluation format for reviewing past activities. This is followed by discussion with the client and later action implementation which may also involve work units, functions, or sponsor groups.

Table 10.1, is an example of an intervention assessment to help improve the quality and competency of the intervention in helping the facilitating and client system take effective action. This can be used following a planning

TABLE 10.1 Intervention Assessment.

Please circle the number to indicate your self-rating on each item.

Criteria	Inadequate		Average		Excellent
1. Is the action aligned with goals of client and client system?	1	2	3	4	5
2. Is the action as clear and simple as the task will permit?	1	2	3	4	5
3. Does the action involve all appropriate personnel?	1	2	3	4	5
4. Is the action based on a realistic analysis of the forces in the situation?	1	2	3	4	5
5. Does the action provide a proper balance for both change and stability?	1	2	3	4	5
6. Is the action economical in the use of human resources needed to implement?	1	2	3	4	5
7. Is the action economical in the use of financial resources needed to implement?	1	2	3	4	5
8. Will teaming provide efficient implementation?	1	2	3	4	5
9. Do methods for action meet quality standards?	1	2	3	4	5
10. Does the action provide adequate training to accomplish the results?	1	2	3	4	5
11. Does the action provide continuous review, feedback, and evaluation?	1	2	3	4	5
12. Does the action have a first step and proper sequence?	1	2	3	4	5
13. Does action provide clear time perspective and commitment?	1	2	3	4	5
14. Is the action effectively linked within the client system?	1	2	3	4	5

Adapted from "Conditions for Taking Effective Action". *Consulting Process in Action Skills Development Kit.* by Gordon L. Lippitt, Ronald Lippitt, B.J. Chakiris and Robert W. Pirsein. 1978. B.J. Chakiris Corporation.

session when action statements have already been made and approved by the client group. The questions focus on the applications and results of these actions and help the group to develop change management competencies.

RESULTS MEASUREMENT

Integrated change and mutual benefits are some of the basic outcomes or results of the change management model. However, these results should be verified through a quantitative or qualitative measurement that helps in transferring competency and maintaining effective performance. Chapter 8 on data collection describes many useful methods for measuring results. The Change Consultation Audit (Chakiris 1993) provides key questions for the facilitating system to assess results and relationships in working with the client system. This audit assesses practices of change management by looking at needs, roles, results, relationships, and culture. The sample section in Table 10.2 focuses on results.

Application and measurement are interdependent parts of the learning process related to results in change management. Organizations are evolving a broader philosophy to identify and define appropriate performance measurements (Eccles 1991). These are some of the core questions related to performance criteria.

- Given our business strategy, what are our most important performance measurements?
- How do our measurements relate to one another? How should they relate?
- What measures truly predict long-term financial success in our business?
- How are our performance objectives linked to determining strategy, promotion, compensation, bonuses, and other rewards?
- How does change management relate to effective performance?
- What role responsibility and accountability do we have for measurement?

The COmpetitive REsourcing (CORE) of Austin and Hall (1989) uses planning, identifying decision units, writing decision packages, ranking, implementation, and performance auditing to require managers to match the results of their activities to the needs of their customers. In a CORE environment the results of change management are identified and evaluated for value and benefit to the organization. This orientation coordinates and

TABLE 10.2 Sample Section of Change Consultation Audit.

	Circle One
Results	Strongly Agree / Agree / Disagree / Strongly Disagree
70. Critical challenges of the client organization are identified.	1 2 3 4
71. Strategy for improving linkage has been identified.	1 2 3 4
72. Change is investment to improve competitive advantage.	1 2 3 4
73. Contradictions in results have been confronted.	1 2 3 4
74. Business goals are visible in project results.	1 2 3 4
75. Project goals align with unit goals.	1 2 3 4
76. Performance criteria for desired results are known.	1 2 3 4
77. Accountability for measuring progress is known.	1 2 3 4
78. Frequency of measurement is established.	1 2 3 4
79. Anticipated performance deviation can be overcome.	1 2 3 4
80. Measurement reporting requiring client support is in place.	1 2 3 4
81. Change goals align with strategy of the organization.	1 2 3 4
82. Resources (finance, people, time, technology) are available to achieve results.	1 2 3 4
83. Change management is viewed as strategic investment.	1 2 3 4
84. The investment required of senior level sponsors is affirmed.	1 2 3 4
85. There is a process to communicate progress to sponsor.	1 2 3 4
86. Project contributes to strategic measurement of organization.	1 2 3 4
87. Feedback of results measurement is effectively communicated.	1 2 3 4
88. Client is involved in the results interpretation.	1 2 3 4
89. Progress measurement is used for developing new action.	1 2 3 4
90. Change goals are aligned with goals of people involved.	1 2 3 4
91. A high-level design for project measurements is established.	1 2 3 4
92. Timing is appropriate for action results to be achieved.	1 2 3 4

1992 Copyright Metrex ® BJ Chakiris Corporation.

allocates resources only to those activities that ensure strategic objectives. These activities compete for funding and the best possible resources, bringing a customer and market focus to all levels within the organization to reach an agreement on which activities should be implemented to fulfill the organization's strategy. The mixture of results and resource decisions are prioritized to satisfy the needs of the customer, and the internal organization as well as to fulfill the demands of external competition.

In order to reach performance goals and manage change, the CEO and senior executives must be committed to establishing measurement criteria, monitoring results, and rewarding success. Early in the process, a decision must be made on who is responsible for specific performance measurements. A senior executive can be assigned to different measurements or to a centralized function of measurement accountability. For example, in the area of customer service each function coordinates specific tasks and role responsibilities, but an overall executive function could monitor specific measurements across functions, such as customer service, information systems, marketing, and human resources. Teams should also be involved in measuring results and monitoring progress.

In change management, it is important that the organization align its incentives to recognize and reward people based on performance measures that are important to change management. For example, effective performance appraisals require an explanation of the criteria and the qualitative and quantitative information on which assessments are made. Clear measurement and performance criteria are especially crucial in view of the limited organizational resources for rewards, compensation, salary increases, career benefits, movement, bonuses, and stock options.

Measurement data should provide a distribution of information for the planners and the doers in change, identifying key areas for new action, and documentation of leading performance indicators. Resources outside the organization such as consultation firms, public-accounting corporations, trade and industry associations, information technology groups, and data vendors are moving into this field with a full range of performance measurement services. Some of the key performance objectives for change management measurement might include:

- Customer satisfaction for responsiveness and service
- Quality metrics in zero defects, response time, and delivery commitment
- Quality performance criteria for functions of the organization
- Financial measurements in cash flow, and leveraged recapitalization

- Market share
- Other business measures such as sales, cost, and total management information systems
- Organization fluidity and capacity for fast adaptation
- Human resources
- Manufacturing and service effectiveness
- Impact on the community
- Innovation
- Benchmarking "best practices"
- Core competencies of the organization

Program Evaluation and Measurement

Programs must have some acceptable criteria for measurement and evaluation so that there can be effective agreements, data collection, planning, action, and monitoring for effective performance. Human resources programs, for instance, can be evaluated using the criteria suggested by Lippitt (1982): relevant needs, clear objectives, criterion-based, uniqueness, flexibility, skill-based, professional leadership, future perspective, value system, evaluation, information system, organizational support, and participant commitment. Appropriate criteria help organizations to apply performance measures in a realistic and productive manner, which is consistent with the goals and values of the organization for change management.

Using these measurements, a human resource program can be evaluated in relation to its contribution toward the present and potential needs of the organization. The evaluation should be based on specific and measurable objectives that serve the current needs of the organization and yet are responsive to changing needs and future challenges. Other criteria for evaluation include the development of skills and competencies and the utilization of the competencies and leadership of internal and external resources. Data-based evaluation helps individuals and groups learn from past experience and practices. Finally, the program can be evaluated on the level of participant commitment and organizational support.

Table 10.3 shows a sample of a program evaluation format (Dokken and Chakiris 1980). This instrument first establishes a context for evaluation with identification of clear criteria. Other factors such as sources, methods, roles, timeframe, and costs are included. The evaluation team is also asked to assess the ways in which their evaluation process can be improved.

TABLE 10.3 Program Evaluation.

Program, Service, Activity Being Evaluated:

1. Why is this evaluation needed?

2. What conditions existed before the program was initiated?

3. What will be the criteria for evaluation?

☐ achievement of goals and/or objectives		☐ cost effectiveness	
☐ behavior change		☐ innovativeness	
☐ reactions and response		☐ change management	
☐ constituents served		☐ other (explain)	

4. What sources will provide information for the evaluation?

Sources   What information

☐ Executive Group _____

☐ Board _____

☐ Advisors _____

☐ Funding Sources _____

☐ Constituents _____

☐ Government/Agencies _____

☐ Documents _____

☐ Customers/Clients _____

Date of Evaluation:

5. How will the evaluation be conducted

☐ observation	☐ questionnaire	☐ interview
☐ meeting	☐ instrument	☐ other (explain)

6. Who will conduct the evaluation?

☐ internal evaluator   role: _____

☐ external evaluator   role: _____

☐ volunteer resource   role: _____

☐ various publics   role: _____

What are the training needs for these people?_____

TABLE 10.3 (continued)

---

7. **When will the evaluation take place? (be specific)**

☐ during the program   _____
☐ after the program   _____
☐ delayed   _____
☐ when will the evaluation start?   _____

8. **Where will the evaluation take place?**

9. **What will the evaluation "cost"?**

☐ time: _____   available? _____
☐ budget: _____   available? _____
☐ people: _____   available? _____
☐ materials: _____   available? _____
☐ other: _____   available? _____

Are the benefits worth the cost?

How might this evaluation be made cost effective?

10. **How will the evaluation process or design be determined?**

☐ Who needs to be involved?   role: _____
☐ Who needs to approve?   role: _____
☐ Who needs to be informed?   role: _____

11. **How will this evaluation be used?**

12. **How public will the results of this evaluation be?**

13. **Use this space for any other evaluation design items you feel are important for your particular situation:**

The questions in Table 10.4 are useful in designing a specific performance measurement for change management. They help to integrate measurement into an overall action research process and establish a clear focus for assessing results.

Table 10.4 Measurement Guidelines.

---

1. Why should we measure this?
   Does the consultation initiative, program, process, or activity need to be measured?
   What is our purpose in measuring?

2. What is the measurement of the status quo?
   What conditions existed prior to the initiative, program, process, or activity?

3. What are the areas of performance measurement?
   What are the overall goals or subgoals of this initiative, program, process or activity?
   What collective goals need to be considered in the criteria?
   What are the sponsor's expectations? Client's expectations? Team members' expectations?

4. What will be the measurement criteria?
   Reaction instrument?
   Behavior observation?
   Cost-effectiveness or cost-related factors?
   Results or goal-related factors?
   Quantitative statistical measurement?
   Qualitative anecdotal measurement?
   What indicators should the consultation team observe?

5. What method or procedure should be used for monitoring directed and nondirected change?
   Will observation, questionnaires, interviews, focus group, or documentation be used?
   What process action is needed, e.g., ART, interpretive feedback, action planning, or ad hoc task force ?
   What format is appropriate for collecting this data?
   What records need to be maintained?

6. Who will measure the results of the change initiative?
   Internal resources, external resources, volunteer resources?
   Are there various publics or relevant groups who might assist in the measurement?
   What training is needed for those who will conduct the measurement?

TABLE 10.4 (continued)

---

7. When will the measurement take place?
    Before beginning initiative, program, process, or activity?
    During initiative, program, process, or activity?
    Immediately after the initiative, program, process, or activity?
    Delayed several months or a year after the program?
    When will the measurement start?

8. Where will the measurements be collected?
    Tracking measurement through manual or computer techniques?
    Information architecture and supporting technology needed?
    Measurement at location of client? Customer? Supplier?

9. What kinds of measurement are appropriate?
    Formative process measurement? Summative results measurement?
    How frequently should measurement occur?
    How will data be used for action planning?
    How can the team assess the values, benefits, and objectives of the
       change initiative, program, process, or activity?
    How can team members assess the measurement activity itself
       through written or verbal feedback?

10. What roles will various individuals and/or teams assume?
    Who will be informed regarding the measurement?
    Who will approve how the measurement is performed?
    What is the role of the person or group who wants the measurement?
    What is the role of the person or group being assessed?

11. What should the measurements tell organizational members about
       change?
    How will positive feedback be presented? Negative feedback?
    How might individuals or groups be prepared for unexpected
       outcomes?
    How could this information be used in action planning?

12. What is the investment cost for this measurement?
    How might the consultation group explore measurements that are
       cost-effective?
    Will training of ad hoc members reduce cost and improve overall
       effectiveness of the process?

TABLE 10.4 (continued)

---

13. How will the measurement process design be determined?
    How might the measurement be linked to action planning?
    At what phase of the change process should the measurement design
    be mapped?
    Who needs to be involved in the measurement goal setting?
    What are the expectations for the person or group desiring the
    measurement?

14. What should be done about the change initiative, program, process,
    or unit of change after it has been measured?
    Who will make that decision?
    How will the measurement data be used?
    What facilitation of feedback will occur?

15. How public should measurement results be?
    Who should be involved in the feedback activities?
    What training is required for facilitation of feedback, decisions, and action?

Evaluation Model

The evaluation model adapted from the work of Swartz and Lippitt (1975) shown in Figure 10.1 is an example from a national service agency (Dokken and Chakiris 1980) that supports the arts. This model helps to visualize the elements of measurement and evaluation in a specific interrelated context. Nonprofit organizations offer some of the greatest challenges for measurement and evaluation because of the creative solutions and innovations that result from limited resources, voluntary leadership roles on boards, and accountability to constituents as well as local, state, and federal agencies. Many social-service agencies also bring together the best resources of the corporate community. This model summarizes several levels of operating relationships: Intra-agency, agency with constituents, constituents with agency, and funding sources with agency.

FIGURE 10.1 Evaluation Model.

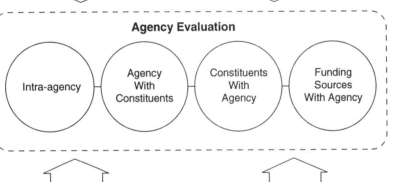

**Sources of Information
for Evaluation**
- CEO/Director
- Agency Staff
- Board/Council/Commission
- Advisors
- Funding Sources
- Constituents
- Government/Political System
- Available Documents

Methods of Evaluation
- Observation
- Questionnaire
- Interviews
- Meetings
- Statistically Valid Instrument
- Others

How will the evaluation be conducted?
Who will conduct the evaluation?
When will the evaluation take place?

Agency Evaluation

Intra-agency

Agency
With
Constituents

Constituents
With
Agency

Funding
Sources
With Agency

Evaluation Areas

Overall Agency Effectiveness
Programs, Services and Activities
Individual Performance
Relationships
Planning Process
Others

Evaluation Criteria

Achievement of Goals
Behavior Change
Reactions
Constituents Served
Cost-effectiveness
Innovativeness
Others

CASE STUDY: CUSTOMER SERVICE SYSTEMS IN DISTRIBUTION CENTERS

This case provides information from a study conducted with four distribution units in the institutional food-service industry across the United States. Customer service is a "window to the world" in any organization. These distribution units learned the true meaning of this statement. Action-based learning from this study resulted in a continuous improvement strategy, change in the information technology, revisions of policies and procedures, and teaming across functions in the organization. This change management process involved management and employees of customer service, sales, operations, purchasing, information systems, finance, and credit.

The performance-measurement methods included interviews, questionnaires, focus groups, and a customer service systems audit. At the same time, a customer service assessment was completed for the chairman of the board of the 24 distribution and manufacturing facilities of this organization.

The results provided action learning applications from various perspectives in the customer's order service cycle and how these related to total customer satisfaction. The customer service function or department was identified as the "facilitation team" for making things happen for the customer, and the total organization was viewed as a "response team" for satisfying the needs of the customer. When all of these groups worked effectively, the whole system created high performance for the customer. However, when one unit malfunctioned, the entire system was slowed down or malfunctioned, and unnecessarily placed people in a tense situation. Unfortunately, the customer received the fallout of services that were not at a high-performance level.

This study involved an inside and outside facilitation team using various methods of data collection including questionnaires, one-on-one and group interviews, a customer service audit, training and education events, targeted conflict resolutions, and team development for branch units. This change intervention was focused on how the total system served its customers. Measurements were tracked internally and with customers. The process was grounded in a specific criteria of total customer satisfaction for both internal and external customers who received services from the units.

Several system elements were researched including perceived quality of products and services, response cycle time to customer needs, system flexibility, communication and information systems, elimination of errors, support and conflict elements of the system, and employee involvement and teaming. The following statements are a sample of the findings related to performance measurement and developmental needs:

- Employees were not familiar with food-service distribution systems, and training was needed.

- Operations lacked effective integration among the warehouse, transportation, sales, and finance areas.

- Information technology needed to be upgraded to track products at any point in time.

- All functions needed to become customer-service oriented in order to serve customer needs and become an extension of the sales personnel.

- Sales personnel feared losing their personal touch with customers because they now had to go from representing 5,000 to 10,000 products rather than speciality items. Personnel required orientation and training to expand their approach and to broaden their skills and knowledge base.

This intervention brought significant data-based change to the organization. Disenchanted employees expressed their concerns openly where their ideas could provide solutions. Customer service was legitimized as a significant function of the corporation with an established senior officer at the corporate level. Figure 10.2 shows two representations of the study — the divergent model and the convergent model.

The divergent model illustrates what happens when a customer situation (need, problem, opportunity) occurs. The customer service unit reaches out to the total branch to determine who has the information, what information is available to solve the problem or need, who needs to be informed or consulted, and who makes the decision. They also examine whether the information is available and accurate, how much time will be required to resolve the situation, and who will keep the customer informed. This establishes the total cycle time needed and the priority for the customer.

The convergent model illustrates what happens when information and decisions come back to the customer service unit and they respond to the customer situation. The critical factors in this model include the level of accuracy and the reliability in the response, the consistency of the response in relation to other situations, the perception of the customer as to whether the situation or problem was solved, and the total cycle time for the response.

The customer service function provides interaction with the distribution center (functions A through G on the model), other team members of the customer service unit, and most importantly, with the customer. This includes communication skills, personal interaction with the customer, the technology

FIGURE 10.2 Customer Service Model.

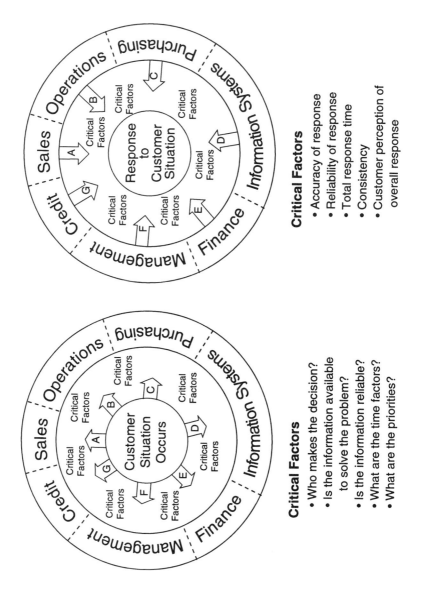

Critical Factors

- Accuracy of response
- Reliability of response
- Total response time
- Consistency
- Customer perception of overall response

Critical Factors

- Who makes the decision?
- Is the information available to solve the problem?
- Is the information reliable?
- What are the time factors?
- What are the priorities?

of information, policies, rules, and procedures of the organization, and the decision making processes of managers and staff.

Customer service contact persons act as problem solvers in customer situations. Through training, empowerment, and involvement, they are provided with a set of decisions that they can make for specific situations. Their capacity to be responsive and consultative with the customer and the distribution center is primary to role competency. They must respond to each customer episode in a professional manner to ensure quality service and value for the customer while at the same time serving the distribution center profit objectives. The customer service department often received feedback from customers. When encouraged and recognized by managers, these customer ideas flowed back into the organization as feedback to help shape vision, policy, and procedures to improve overall customer satisfaction.

Customer situations included activities that were measured with high, medium, and low frequency. These activities were monitored through the customer service systems audit, which tracked such items as a delivery truck breaking down, out-of-stock products and just-in-time delivery, COD collections that were surprises for customers and delayed drivers, orders coming in after the cut-off time, sales representatives not picking up messages, a minimum orders policy that was difficult to explain to the customer, pricing information that was not understood by customers, a "must-go" to a customer when the facility is out of the product which increases the cost for extra distribution, errors in picking products, errors from driver's trip sheets on collections, customers left holding on the telephone, being understaffed at peak business times, missed shipments, customer approving substitute products, customer rejecting substitute products that arrived without approvals, chain accounts and sales representatives approving substitutes, inquiries regarding delivery schedule, talking through the reason for COD delivery, clearing customer credit with finance and credit units, inaccurate pricing, and product returns due to quality deficiencies.

Several questionnaires were designed for the interviews as well as a Customer Service Systems Audit (Chakiris and Grill 1982) that included interviews with every function of the branch whose mission was to serve the customer. Other data collection methods included one-on-one and group interviews with the customer service work team, and phone interviews with key customers. Specific questions for the customer service unit are shown in Table 10.5.

TABLE 10.5 Customer Service Interview Questionnaire.

Questions Related to the Job

What tasks take up the majority of your time?

What do you find difficult in your job?

Do you perform other jobs outside of direct customer service such as receptionist or selecting the products?

Are you assigned to specific accounts, specific sales representatives, or a specific national accounts?

Are there particular customers and sales representatives who ask for a specific customer service person by name?

What do you like most about your job?

What do you like least?

Questions Related to Phone Usage

Does everyone in the department answer all phone calls?

Do you receive irate customer calls? How do you feel when customers display anger? Do you take this personally? How do you respond?

If you were away from your desk, who would answer your phones? How long would the customer be put on hold?

What is the content of the incoming calls to customer service?

What happens when you promise to call back a customer in a specified amount of time and you cannot resolve the customer situation in the period of time promised? Do you call the customer to give a progress report? What do you say?

Do you sell on the phone? Would you like to do phone sales?

How do you learn about the distribution of products? How do you learn about product promotions? Do you sell these promotions?

What incentives are available for selling on the phone?

How do you find out that you are doing a good job?

What decisions are you authorized to make? Not authorized to make?

When do you need to go to your manager or team leader for interdepartmental contacts?

Questions Related to the Customer

If the customer criticizes the company, how do you respond? To whom might you refer them?

Do you receive information about how this situation was handled from the perspective of the internal coordinator? From the perspective of the customer?

When there are complaints about the quality of the product, where do you go with that information or recommendation?

When you report back to the customer and you do not have all of the information, how do you report this?

What would the customer say is most important to your role?

TABLE 10.5 (continued)

Questions Related to Training Needs

What training did you receive for your position including new-entry orientation?

What additional training do you require?

Of all the materials you use for your job, such as manuals, forms, price lists, computer printouts, computer or manual inventory sheets or stock outs, and delivery schedules, which do you find difficult to interpret or understand? Does your customer understand these materials when they are available to the customer? Which materials need to be clarified or changed?

What specific information do you want to know about other departments? What information would be most helpful to you?

What other functions of the branch do you want to know more about?

Should you receive further training in customer service? What would you want to know about customer service?

Is there a manual with procedures on how to answer the phone? Is there training on phone procedures?

Is there a policy and procedure manual for customer service?

Questions Related to Teaming

Who approves credit? Are there problems associated with your informing customers about their credit approvals? About CODs with drivers and customers?

What specific policy and procedures are provided to you for contacting other departments? For transferring calls to another department?

In general, where does product feedback information go in your organization?

Are there other departments that show exceptional support for your customer service function?

Are there specific departments within the distribution center that sometimes cause slow-downs in solving customer-related issues quickly?

How would you rate your customer service unit in teaming to serve the customer? Give examples of team member cooperation?

Are there times when members lack cooperation or hold back on communication?

What constraints, if any, do you experience in working with other departments?

Do you attend regular meetings of the customer service team? What do you discuss? What other agenda items would you want to discuss?

What do you think the sales organization perceives as most important to your role within the customer service team?

TABLE 10.5 (continued)

What would other departments of this branch say is the most important part of your role or your function?

Do you have a good working relationship with sales representatives?

What additional information do you need regarding the sales organizations? About customers? About other departments? About your own customer service team?

Questions Related to Improvement

What, in your view, are improvements that you would recommend for customer service overall:

Relations in this unit?

Relations of this unit with others in this branch?

Relations with customers?

Physical layout of this department? Phone and technological resources?

Relationships among team members? Relationships between team members and leaders?

Interviews and tailored questionnaires were administered with all functions of the branch-distribution center including general management, finance, sales and marketing, information systems, and operations. A parallel customer quality audit was facilitated through the office of the chairman of the board to all the facilities across the country. As a result of this extensive feedback, tailored training and quality interventions were implemented for more effective performance and change management processes.

POSSIBLE TRAINING APPLICATIONS

The following are some examples of specific interventions of training techniques and applications that have been used by service organizations to achieve a desired outcome of total customer satisfaction. These program designs provide the methodology and tools to measure and improve performance in customer satisfaction and teamwork based on data collection, planning, and action decisions for applications and results measurement.

Training for Total Customer Satisfaction

After the diagnostic customer service assessment has provided a comprehensive snapshot of current service levels, the data serves as a baseline to measure service quality improvement by indicating where to focus future efforts and resources, identifying obstacles to service improvement as perceived at different levels within the organization, outlining employee suggestions for future steps, and validating both perceived strengths and areas of development for continuous improvement. Every person in the organization should be "in touch" with the competitive realities facing the business. Seeing the world of customers and competitors as it really is becomes a priority. As a result, customer service supports an ongoing improvement effort based on realistic data and effective change management.

A customer-satisfaction or managing-your-job training program can provide skill-based activities and processes for developing employee competency to continually find ways to improve service to internal and external customers. Program elements may include a manual for frontline employees with a facilitator guide and audio- or video-assisted modules in those areas that would give service a competitive edge. Training can also build relationship skills for increasing responsiveness in listening, communicating, and contracting with customers.

Training for Teamwork and Employee Involvement

The competitive challenge of managing change requires that employees be involved in ongoing quality improvement in products, services, and total customer satisfaction through teamwork. Training interventions can help integrate nondirected practices with directed change efforts. Interventions might include specific exercises and skill applications and provide awareness orientation for quality teams and advisory groups with performance criteria for customer-oriented role responsibilities.

Training in communication skills is useful for facilitators, managers, and team leaders to help them work more effectively. Learning about what motivates people, understanding the needs and values of team members, and applying the essential skills of group dynamics can improve teamwork and group decision making.

A feedback process can be used for an ongoing method of measurement with specific units of the organization. Action-oriented communication processes help to monitor and improve performance through employee involvement in feedback related to communication, performance, and motivation in teaming. A feedback measurement instrument and communication process also allow the manager, self-directed module advisor, facilitator, and team members to provide feedback to each other for positive change and improvement in areas such as supportiveness, dependability, attitude, innovation, job knowledge, service, and quality orientation. The impact for change is brought about by colleague or coworker feedback rather than organizational pressure. Self-development is encouraged by providing people with frequent, accurate, confidential information so they can grow and develop as professionals and as team members.

Training for System-Wide Quality Initiative and Skills Application

Technical skills using quality tools (Chakiris 1985) and techniques help organizational members manage change with training and education made available to develop quality skills:

- Planning and controlling project techniques provide productive ways of utilizing resources effectively and meeting deadlines. Simulations, action logs, and Gantt charts can be used in this training.

- Flowcharting and flow diagrams are useful in analyzing and improving a process or operation by visualizing work practices and how work is completed.

- Sampling helps the group collect data in an effective way that saves time and money and provides an accurate investigation and interpretation of the data from a representative sample.

- Survey data collection prepares the group to collect spoken or written information in an objective and organized manner by developing appropriate questions and survey processes.

- Work-measurement techniques assess work processes for operations. This methodology can improve work flow and help a department or work unit function more smoothly and efficiently.

- Work-simplification techniques assist the group in making work processes more productive and meaningful by eliminating duplication and unnecessary tasks or by combining or integrating tasks. Attitude and creativity are also emphasized as important parts of this process.

- Project benefits and cost-analysis techniques help the team track its accomplishments and determine project costs and savings. These analysis procedures include project documentation to prepare the group to present action recommendations to management.

The results of training interventions, performance measurement, and action research teaming should be monitored and supported as a part of a process of continuous learning. This links implementation with continuity and renewal in a context of ongoing change management.

11

Continuity and Renewal

Even industry giants, some of the largest and most successful businesses in the world, dominating the market in autos, retailing, and computers, can become "dinosaurs" struggling to survive. As the former CEO of one of these organizations explained, "It's a mysterious thing" (Loomis 1993). For others there is no mystery. The reality is clear, but it may have come too late.

The ability to act not only in terms of "what is" but also "what will be" is crucial for developing continuity and renewal in organizations, individuals, and groups. Organizations must be constantly renewing their commitment and competencies as they move toward the future, but the balance between stability and innovation can be precarious. Change requires learning and the transferring this knowledge and competencies throughout the system.

We are continuously influenced by our experiences with others (Hampton-Turner 1970). Since Chapter 1, we have emphasized that change is interpreted by people in their interactions and work practices. Our human experience and intuition can provide us with the capacity to manage change. This creative capacity to use the past and present for directing future action has the potential to strengthen organizational resources to respond to developing challenges and global issues. These creative resources might include the research and development of innovative products and services to serve new markets; the creation of learning systems for working with diverse functions, communities, and nations; and support for teams of people who can bring new solutions to macroproblems that face the people and environment of the planet. Change management is a continuous process that requires continuity in transferring competencies and renewal in confronting difficult issues.

Renewal and continuity are the focus of Phase 6 of the consultation process. The change management team must balance direction toward future goals with exploration of the resources, decisions, and actions required to facilitate and integrate directed and nondirected change in the present. This helps ensure continuity and increase capacity to support current and future change management activities, programs, and processes.

Cultural values and conflicting perceptions of change can affect the environment for continuity and renewal. Interventions might be viewed as successful by one client with a vision of long-term results and be perceived as less successful by another who desires a quick-fix solution. Amid the diverse goals of a client system, there is always the challenge of recognizing and coordinating philosophical and conceptual differences to gain agreement and congruence between conflicting expectations and "realities" in assessing the results of the overall change process.

This chapter focuses on the issues and implications of continuity and renewal in the change management process. These include an understanding of renewal, the career of the organization, obsolescence, and benchmarking.

CHANGE CONTINUITY

Some of the most important questions of this phase are related to the continuing success of change management. Will a major directed change have continuity or will past patterns return? How can changes be integrated at the directed and nondirected level? How can organization members stay connected to support and resources for continuing change management? The consultation team and the client should explore options for continued support, and discuss ways to create linkage for periodic follow-up and appropriate initiatives for new projects and programs.

In the agreements of Phase 2, the consultation team and client develop a plan of action relating to change continuity, but role relationships and objectives can change. The client system should become more competent and confident in facilitating data-based change. The consultation team tries not to create client dependency on expert resources but, at the same time, they do not want to pull away needed supports too soon. A proper balance of technical expertise and process facilitation is important in transferring competencies to the client system.

The classic models of leadership (Tannenbaum and Schmidt 1973) present options for the manager—from using authority to providing areas of freedom with accountability and employee participation. Change management requires consultative leadership. Directed and nondirected change activities can be integrated through employee involvement and various forms of action teams with increasing role responsibility and shared decision-making authority. This builds individual and group competency for change management.

The consultation team should work together and provide freedom for learning in a balanced intervention that builds the capacity of the organization. Success in continuity and renewal requires that the change facilitation team not go "deeper" than required for a change and not go further than the energy and resources that can be committed to bring about a specific directed change.

There also needs to be some congruency between rewards and the organizational philosophy for involving people in achieving the desired outcomes. A "trail-off" effect in motivation and participation can be anticipated if there are no provisions for celebrating milestones and dealing with changes in the context of organizational learning and development. Champion leaders may leave and the initial enthusiasm can wear off, or the organization might move rapidly in a new direction without considering the integration of a major change with current action. There is a need to build change management competencies for continuity and renewal.

At the completion of a specific project or program, both the client and the consultation team should assess their role responsibilities, performance, and outcomes, and encourage feedback from others. A helpful process for ensuring continuity is to review the process and content knowledge and the related skills for change management. The team can assess the strengths and developmental areas in action-role competencies in the client system and work through the client's concerns for support. The facilitators may encourage new action that could be implemented without investing too much additional time and money.

At completion, effective consultation teams transfer to the unit or organization the change competencies to use resources within the client system to accomplish goals and set targets for continuous renewal and development.

ORGANIZATIONAL RENEWAL

The renewal process (Lippitt 1982) provides a process for ongoing diagnosis, decisions, and action based on new data, circumstances, people, and goals. For many years effective decision making was believed to be the foundation of leadership. However, an unimplemented decision, no matter how good, is ultimately worthless. According to Lippitt, teamwork and skills training in themselves do not solve problems. Problem solving also requires that organization members take responsibility and implement decisions in relation to changing contexts, crises, and opportunities. Gordon Lippitt (1982) defines renewal in this statement:

> Organizational renewal is the process of initiating, creating, and
> confronting needed change so as to make it possible for organizations
> to become or remain viable, to adapt to new conditions, to solve
> problems, and to learn from experiences and move toward greater
> organizational maturity.

The focus of renewal is on learning and action within a continuing change
management process that facilitates an assessment of the critical challenges of
the organization on a periodic basis. With the assistance of a consultation team
and action research groups, data is collected and feedback is provided. Then
the client system interprets results and acts on key challenges.

The growth stages of an organization are an outcome of the environmental
response to external forces as well as organizational stages of development.
"Growth" in this context does not refer to an increase in shareholders' equity
or capital assets but rather implies a broader perspective. The concept of
growth in renewal refers to building the organization's capacity and internal
systems in order to adapt to the external environment. This process is similar
to the maturation of an individual but different in that organizations, unlike
people, can exist over many generations. The survival of the organization is
the most basic management challenge for businesses of all sizes and types. For
example, Ward (1987) suggests that only 13 percent of successful family businesses last through the third generation. Planning for continuity in culture,
growth and leadership helps support longer term survival. Competencies in
change management are essential as organizations grow, develop, rightsize,
redesign, merge, and reorganize throughout their existence.

An organization must cope with both its internal and external responsiveness and various crises that confront it at different stages of growth. A circular
model of continuity and renewal of organizational functioning emphasizes the
need for the organization to reexamine goals, assess performance, renew its
spirit, and demonstrate the ability to respond to both threat and opportunity in
change management.

Renewal Context: The Career of the Organization

One way to assess the changing nature and renewal stages of organizations is
to view them as human systems with "careers." Influences such as external
forces in the changing nature of technology, markets, work design, and social
systems, as well as internal leadership and vision in strategy and direction
allow the organization to be studied historically. This history can be interpreted as a career. The following activity is useful in helping managers, leaders,
and team members to understand specific types of development in the history

or career of the organization (Leach 1982).

Reflect upon the "career line" of this organization as you have observed it in your experiences, read about it in the books, newsletters or business literature, heard about it in stories from "old timers," seen it in the media, or simply as you interpret the changes from past to present. While you are thinking through the history of the organization, consolidate your thoughts by making some notes and descriptive comments on a separate sheet of paper. Then follow these directions:

- Think of the career line in stages. Categorize the stages and assign them descriptive labels or category headings. The categories selected can include any terms you deem appropriate: life cycle (infancy, adolescence, maturity); functional trends (engineering-dominated, marketing-dominated, financial-dominated, and others); evolving philosophies (high risk to varying degrees of conservatism); changing products, markets, environments (domestic, international, multinational, global), or organization structure (form, size, and coordinating elements).

  Do not feel that you must limit your career outline of the organization solely to the categories mentioned above. For example, one organization's historical development was likened to the movements of a symphony. You are encouraged to use imagination and creativity to develop the category labels that best describe the uniqueness of your organization.

- Once you have some sorting categories in mind, write a few lines that describe each career stage, including the present stage. Note how these changes in career line have affected the human resources with respect to morale, recruitment, and selection of new employees, the impact upon the careers of incumbent employees, training and development, organization development, and upgrading and "getting ahead" practices. Note both the positive and negatives associated with each career phase.

- Anticipate or predict what you think will be the next step in the organization's career line and note what impact this new organizational career phase will have for human resources planning strategies, and change management.

RENEWAL APPLICATION: OBSOLESCENCE STUDY

Another example of a renewal activity examines individual careers, deskilling and reskilling of jobs, and worker and job obsolescence in a changing organization. The following instruments can be used to assess vulnerability for an individual, a specific task, a function, an organization, or an industry. The findings provide information for action and change management related to continuity and renewal.

Obsolescence-Vulnerability Audit

The process of renewal requires awareness of present conditions and future needs. Each of these requires confrontation. Leaders and team members must confront the information related to the changing environment and internal and external forces, and recognize the gaps in their knowledge and work practices. Obsolescence studies such as those developed by Leach and Chakiris (1984) provide a systematic approach to monitoring information to help organizations guard against surprises and reactive change. People who expect secure employment may be shocked when they realize that their job, task, function, or organization could "disappear."

A vulnerability audit provides organizations with another tool for human systems renewal. This is especially pertinent to managers and team members who want to remain flexible and adaptable by building capacity for career movement across jobs, functions, organizations, and industries. This instrument looks at vulnerability prediction (Part I), provides a diagnostic grid for analysis (Part II), and charts possible courses of action (Part III). This can be used by individuals and groups for change management applications.

Part I: Prediction Grid

Consider all aspects of your career situation: Your present level of knowledge and skills; the actual work you do; how this work relates to the survival or growth of your business function and organization; and the place your organization occupies in its industry. Predict your vulnerabilities to becoming unessential or obsolete by placing an "X" in the appropriate box in the instrument found in Table 11.1, under Part I - Obsolescence Prediction Grid, for each of the areas listed. Remember that "person" refers to you; "task" refers to your present set of assignments and objectives; "function" refers to your business discipline; "organization" refers to your employer; and "industry" identifies the business of your organization.

TABLE 11.1 Obsolescence Diagnostic Instruments.

Part I - Obsolescence Prediction Grid

	Not at all	Somewhat	Possibly	Probably	Significantly
	1	2	3	4	5
Person					
Task					
Function					
Organization					
Industry					

Part II - Vulnerability Impactors

1. **Marketplace Dynamics**
   - Competitive awareness
   - Domestic economy
   - Global economy

2. **Technology**
   - R and D innovation levels
   - Leader and follower
   - Reducing costs
   - Replacing people

3. **Leadership**
   - Myopic vs. visionary
   - Communication
   - Participation
   - Change management
   - Style

4. **Culture**
   - Mission and business goals
   - Operating philosophy
   - Marketing
   - New ideas
   - Decision making

5. **Human Resource Capability**
   - Strategic planning
   - Linkage to business plan
   - Forecasting requirements
   - Management development
   - Career development
   - Organization development

6. **Customer and Market Responsiveness**
   - Customer requirements
   - Quality requirements
   - Total cycle time and responsiveness

7. **Financial Conditions**
   - Price and earnings ratio
   - Return on equity
   - Book value
   - Public vs. private ownership
   - Cash reserves

TABLE 11.1 (continued)

	Not at all Vulnerable	Somewhat	Possibly	Probably	Significantly Vulnerable
	1	2	3	4	5

AREAS OF IMPACT

IMPACTOR*	(A) Person	(B) Task	(C) Function	(D) Organization	(E) Industry
1. Marketplace Dynamics					
2. Technology					
3. Leadership					
4. Culture					
5. Human Resource Capability					
6. Customer and Market Responsiveness					
7. Financial Conditions					

Part III - Vulnerability Action Plan

Social and Technical - Professional Practice Areas

IMPACTORS	Career Development	Instructional Technology	International	Management Development	Technical Skills	Sales and Marketing	Organization Development
1. Marketplace Dynamics							
2. Technology							
3. Leadership							
4. Culture							
5. Human Resource Capability							
6. Customer and Market Responsiveness							
7. Financial Conditions							

Part II: Diagnostic Grid

Step 1: Familiarize yourself with the impactors and the areas of impact noted in Table 11.1, listed under Part II - Vulnerability Impactors.

Step 2: Rate each impactor, using the instrument in Table 11.1, under Part II - Vulnerability Diagnostic Grid, in each of the areas of impact. Place a number in each box, indicating the degree of vulnerability that the area has using the five-point scale.

If the impactor is under control, it is assumed that productivity is also under control and therefore is not an issue.

Part III: Action Plan

Step 1: Based on Part II, place an "X" in the appropriate boxes in the instrument in Table 11.1, listed under Part III - Vulnerability Action Plan, that best represent the human resource vulnerabilities for your organization in relation to social and technical change management competencies.

Step 2: Now indicate by placing an "O" in those vulnerability areas where you or your team directly have the most potential impact.

Step 3: Review your X's and O's and select the top three priorities where you, your team, or the organization need to develop action to facilitate change management competency.

Discussion questions:

- What kind of data do you need to gather? When? Where? Why?
- Which policies and goals need to be created or revised in each practice area?
- What human resource program, process, and or activity needs to be continued, changed, eliminated, and or developed?
- What internal tracking methods need to be put in place to monitor and to provide feedback for further planning and data collection?
- Which action needs to be first? What are the next steps? What personnel, budget and information resources should be allocated? Who is assigned accountability? What is the desired completion date?

DESIGNS FOR THE ORGANIZATION RENEWAL PROCESS

Organization renewal as discussed in this book refers to the process of confrontation of issues and challenges, collective search for information and understanding, and coping or transferring learning to new situations. This is an absolute necessity in effective change management. A good way to start renewal processes related to integrated change is by building a network of coordinated functioning teams within the organization. Intraunit and interunit teaming strengthens communication, coordination, and collaboration throughout the organization, builds internal strengths within the client system for renewal, and provides continuity in directed and nondirected change integration. Action teams support renewal.

In a Chapters 4 and 9, we provided case studies of executive and planning conference models, which can be used for building effective teams and increasing organizational capacity for change and renewal. For example, a management development session can be conducted as an extended meeting, an off-site session, or a one-or two-day conference every four to six months. Clearing the ground by reducing barriers and encouraging collective thinking can bring greater unity and effectiveness to groups and business units. Renewal elements might include action research teams in collecting data through interviews, and developing a summary of this data for the feedback and design of the team development session. The design of this session allows participants to imagine a vision of the future and construct a force-field analysis to consider the supports and barriers that might affect this future. The session concludes with collective action plans and goal setting in subgroups with follow-up sessions. Renewal should also involve these teams in a continuing cycle of data collection, feedback, analysis, and action taking.

Performance is enhanced by consultation skills that help manage organizational change through ongoing renewal processes. This encourages continuing learning to support change management competencies. The following questions focus on renewal through the development of the individual and group resources of managers, staff professionals, and action team members.

- What actions will be taken to achieve increased change management competence?
- What resources are available?
- What experiences will be gained, what credentials will be needed, what position will be available, and what professional organizations will be available to help people to develop these competencies?

- What action steps are most important in progressing toward these goals? List the steps that can be taken.

- What skills or other competencies related to change management are most essential in taking the above action steps? List the action steps and note the skills that must be developed to achieve each step.

For managers and team leaders, specific developmental areas might include these personal and professional change opportunities: on-the-job training, teaming with other professionals, attending university classes, serving on community boards and committees, coordinating exchange of practices with professional colleagues and staff members of other internal functions, and participating in local, regional, national, and international professional associations. However, these actions require commitment, planning, and support for integrated change throughout the system.

Action Planning Activity — Promises and Requests

This activity is useful in identifying and removing barriers that stand in the way of people taking implicit and explicit ownership of their job performance and responsibility in managing change and facilitating renewal.

After teams have identified what opportunities or changes are most important, they should consider why they are taking this action and the extent to which it supports effective change management. The next step is thinking about what commitment will be made, who will make that commitment, and what actions this involves.

For example, an action research team might state their commitment to investigate how other companies look at self-directed performance systems in order to more effectively align with their company's service delivery need. Team members must determine the "promises" and "requests" required to complete this action. This can include commitments such as "We will go to visit managers, staff, and their customers to request input information, and present this data for review in team action recommendations."

Team members should also consider these questions: What might we expect to find? By when? How could it be different than what we could have previously expected? How will the client and others know the commitment was made? What are the different options for data collection? Who will receive this input? How will the data be put into action? How can the results be measured? What are some possible pitfalls? How can consultation team resources work together? To what extent does this broaden the definition of change management? Promises and requests are a part of the informal aspects of continuity in integrated change and the need to be made explicit in agreements related to change management.

BENCHMARKING FOR ORGANIZATION RENEWAL

A major factor in organizational change management is effective benchmarking (Chakiris 1982) to establish standards of excellence and performance measurements. Benchmarking is a proven data-based learning approach to organizational change and renewal.

The formal concept began in 1979 when Xerox initiated a process called "competitive benchmarking" along with employee involvement as part of an overall change and renewal strategy. At first only a few of the operating units in manufacturing used benchmarking, but by 1981 it was adopted as a corporate-wide effort and is credited as a significant factor in Xerox's competitive survival (Kearns and Nadler 1992). Competitive benchmarking is a process designed to allow the organization to assess itself and its competition and to use that knowledge or data to develop and implement an action plan to achieve leadership and excellence in the marketplace. The Xerox competitive benchmarking process (Camp 1989) consists of five phases: planning, analysis, integration, action, and maturity. In each of these phases, specific action items need to be accomplished.

As competitive benchmarking evolved in the decades that followed, adaptations were coordinated. An early observation was the discovery that the benchmarking process of data collecting and action greatly benefitted the organization by targeting not only the competition, but also diverse functions and business units within the same organization as well as in different companies outside the industry. Innovative developments in "learning from the competition" moved the process toward achieving "best practices" and expanding beyond the competition to measure products, services, management activities, customer service, human resources, education and training, marketing, and practices of outstanding local, national, and global leaders in diverse organizational areas.

Benchmarking is a directed process of change that provides tools to help the organization become the "best in class" in delivering products and services, improving total cycle time and quality, achieving total customer satisfaction, and in becoming a preferred employer, supplier, or partner and a responsible citizen and leader in the community and the world.

Benchmarking identifies, establishes, and achieves standards of excellence based on the realities of the market place. This collaborative action research process also requires that the organization look at its vision and mission, identify critical issues, determine the customer's acceptance criteria, and ask, "Who is the best in this particular area?" Identifying the person, function, company, nonprofit agency, or local, national, and global leader as "best in class" can help the organization set a standard of excellence and learn how that excellence is achieved. As a learning experience, benchmarking looks at how others work their practices and, where these make sense, the organization adapts and builds upon these practices for its own use. This process recognizes the ongoing need for renewal and integrated change in response to a competitive global environment.

Benchmarking helps to document and communicate best-in-class products and services and improves the satisfaction of both internal and external customers. Using both quantitative and qualitative benchmarking measurement techniques to improve quality and service, the organization continues to look at its best competition for every unit of service or product. The driving question is "Who is the best?" Benchmarking is not an organizational program or campaign; it provides the function, company, agency, or country with an ongoing process for change management.

The participation of senior executives is an essential element in the success of benchmarking. The chairman of the board and chief executives must be involved. Senior officers should move from endorsement to involvement and act as role models to support benchmarking implementation, strategies, and tactics. At the macrolevel, these leaders provide the overall vision and identify the critical success factors and issues of the organization in relation to benchmarking.

The customer role is most crucial in determining the ultimate success of benchmarking as customer satisfaction criteria become known and serve as a guide for quality. Organizational vision, value, and mission should reflect the priority to become the best-in-class in products and services. Improving quality also holds costs down, reduces total cycle time, improves productivity, and delivers the best products and services for total customer satisfaction. Business measurements support long-term improvement, continuity, and renewal. Yet sufficient time and resources must be provided to achieve long-term goals through the commitment of organizational leaders and team members.

Benchmarking Components

Benchmarking may focus on a number of internal and external performance measures. The following list includes significant areas of benchmarking for change management:

- Customer satisfaction
- Quality
- Cost
- Response time

- Manufacturing technology and processes
- Product cycle time
- Just-in-time delivery
- Productivity
- Human resources
- Structure
- Self-directed teams
- Technological change
- Leadership continuity and succession
- Organizational effectiveness
- Team effectiveness
- Individual effectiveness
- Functional areas
- Work design

Accomplishment criteria are related to the organization, function, group, and individual. Many are based on financial and economic needs and cost and profit measures. Both quantitative and qualitative data are used to measure goal-related and quality-related accomplishments, developments, and renewal processes. Behavior observation, reaction, work measurement, team measurement, support service unit measurement, and productivity measurements can provide valuable data for planning, implementing, and monitoring change.

Benchmarking Sources and Methods of Data Collection

External information sourcing occurs through competitive information, customers, government officials, trade and professional associations, suppliers, other organizations, suppliers, external resources, academicians, trade shows, associations, ad agencies, auditors, consumer groups, conferences, journals, and company publications.

Internal information sourcing might come from participation, action research, problem-solving groups, ideas in meetings, study reports, creativity in other subgroups, and giving and receiving feedback on projects and new product developments. Ideas may also move internally across and among business units, functions, peers, and other sources. Some specific methods of data collection for benchmarking include observation, audits, surveys, questionnaires, one-on-one interviews, group interviews, review of research studies, documentation review, quality techniques and tools, instruments, content analysis, meetings, and pilot designs.

Integrating Benchmarking Information

Benchmarking is a complex process that requires continuity in the integration and coordination of information and resources for change management. The major elements for success are:

- Integration of benchmarking into strategic planning;
- Strategy to achieve competitive leadership position;
- Execution of change to offset competition;
- Integration of benchmarking into organizational policies and practices;
- Communication and progress orientation and documentation;
- Marketing and customer relations action decisions; and
- Rewards, recognition, and benefits for participants.

Benchmarking Competency Areas

Benchmarking competency areas include: 1) the knowledge, theories, and perspectives in understanding and application; 2) the actual benchmarking process and techniques; and 3) participation and integration into the organizational system (see Table 11.2).

TABLE 11.2 Benchmarking Competencies.

Knowledge, Theory, and Perspectives

Demonstrate basic knowledge and awareness of benchmarking.

Relate to other theories and concepts such as benchmarking definitions, historical and current applications, and macro and microchange.

Identify the critical success factors of the business that are appropriate areas for benchmarking.

Formulate effective criteria for selecting critical business areas for competitive benchmarking.

Train others in the relevant management techniques and measurement instruments.

Anticipate strategies and tactics needed for successful benchmarking implementation: scope, horizon, roles and responsibilities, and use of a change model to look at dynamics, readiness, and the systematic impact and integration of directed and nondirected change.

TABLE 11.2 (continued)

Benchmarking Processes and Techniques

Establish goals and objectives for benchmarking.

Clarify roles, responsibilities, and accountabilities.

Choose appropriate methods for benchmarking data collection.

Identify and source benchmarking information.

Develop valid benchmarking instrumentation.

Involve relevant resources when collecting information.

Identify key resources for analysis, feedback, problem solving, action planning, and change implementation.

Utilize cross-business and interdisciplinary action teaming for diagnosis, analysis, feedback, and actions for change.

Recognize progress checkpoints of overall achievements in moving toward a leadership position, while recognizing and communicating the accomplishments of others.

Establish measurable goals and targets.

Integrate a benchmarking process into the overall change management planning process.

Participation and Integration

Involve others in interpretation derivations of the data.

Provide feedback to appropriate audiences.

Initiate employee involvement practices in planning feedback and applications for improvement and change.

Gain ownership from others.

Integrate benchmarking practices into the operational and strategic aspects of the business.

Benchmarking Sponsor Questionnaire

The commitment of senior executives determines the overall success of benchmarking in organizational missions and objectives. Therefore, it is important for these leaders and managers to think in a systematic way about the requirements and implications of the benchmarking process. The executive group and the management group serve as the critical interface with the employee group and action research teams for strategy and implementation. A questionnaire for benchmarking intervention can help organizational leaders to evaluate current change contexts and competencies as well as areas that may need some development (see Table 11.3).

TABLE 11.3 Benchmarking Sponsor Questionnaire.

Values and Culture

What cultural shifts might be anticipated as the organization moves to benchmarking ?

What would motivate executives to become more interested in intelligence outside their basic business and cross-business synergy in benchmarking? What would motivate managers?

What really drives implementation plans and actions (e.g., engineering innovation vs. customer's needs; deadlines vs. quality; profit vs. market share; or short vs. long-term goals)? How should this emphasis change as managers and team members become more effective in the integration of benchmarking techniques in the future?

How will executives and managers know that employees and team members understand and accept the new benchmarking values?

What resistance might be expected from a staff person or manager in relation to some of these new values? What impact will these new benchmarking values have on executive, management, and team roles?

How important are executives and managers in passing on these quality standards? How can the executive group be linked with the management group? How can they be linked to action teams?

How can leaders communicate new values within the organization? How have values been communicated in the past? What was effective or not effective?

How will organizational leaders benefit from benchmarking? Will people be concerned about change and their jobs? How will managers benefit? How will employees benefit?

What do managers perceive as issues and concerns within their control and outside of their control? How much freedom do they have to restructure their unit to gain greater authority over control issues?

What are some ways to involve organizational members to gain acceptance of this new thinking, including benchmarking values?

How could senior executives and corporate executive leaders reduce resistance by managers and staff?

What do executives want from managers and employees in implementing benchmarking?

What is the application environment in the organization today? How does this environment impact benchmarking near-term? Long-term?

TABLE 11.3 (continued)

Architecture

What changes will have to take place in the organization to accommodate new benchmarking roles for executives, managers, staff, and team members?

How will action teams will be formed throughout the system?

How will planning for change be based on these new roles and structures?

What kind of changes in structures might be necessary to implement the benchmarking strategy (e.g., information, communication sharing, performance-appraisal feedback, quality-and production-control feedback, operating financial controls and feedback, and market-place feedback)?

What systems might need to be modified or restructured such as quality, customer service, communication, succession planning, career development, performance appraisal, and training?

How might programs be developed to strengthen organizational planning and implementation (e.g., human resource planning for the movement of people across functions and continents; cross-business career pathing, and retraining; compensation and rewards; or worker, job, function, and industry obsolescence monitoring)?

Communication

What is the manner in which executives interact with customers, suppliers, the government, the academic community, and associations? How effective has this communication been? How do managers gather information internally and externally?

What is the typical manager's competence and experience in collecting and using data in the organization's internal and external environment? How is cross-business data shared now? How do employees collect data?

What areas of communication and information are available to senior executives but not available to employees? What data will be confidential and what will be shared?

What information will need to be centralized? Decentralized?

What feedback channels will be needed to facilitate change management?

How should the benchmarking strategy be communicated to staff, managers, and team members? What is the most appropriate timing, approach, language, and media for communicating this information?

What is the best setting to discuss initial benchmarking strategy? At a conference? At staff meetings? During a training session? With a council? With a small group of managers?

TABLE 11.3 (continued)

What is the best timing for data collection, planning, and implementation?

What approach would be most effective to present the benchmarking message? Group process with each function or team? Representation from one business unit or across business or functional units?

What education and training is necessary for learning and exchanging methods, techniques, and tools?

How can management communicate new values, strategies, and possible new structures and systems?

What new communication issues will executives and managers need to attend to if this information is going to flow intelligently throughout the system?

What communication channels are used now? How effective are these communication channels?

What new channels can help to facilitate and support integrated change?

Competency

What is the readiness of executives for benchmarking given their present level of performance and development in knowledge, skills, and behavior? Readiness of managers? Staff? Team members?

What creative skills and leadership will be required for developing benchmarking practices?

How effectively are performance goals set? What are some constraints in achieving these goals?

What kinds of skills will be needed to convey changes in the culture (e.g., conflict resolution, consensus, role-modeling, recognition, feedback, rewards, or participation)?

How will employee involvement be used to help meet the benchmarking challenge? How do executives need to change their behavior to make the employee-involvement process more effective?

How can managers facilitate employee involvement in the benchmarking process?

What are the training and education needs for changes in work practices, skills, and knowledge?

How do senior executives and sponsors perceive training and education needs? Strengths and developmental areas?

How do key individuals and groups within the organization conceptualize change? What are the dominant perspectives toward change?

To what degree do people openly confront issues? Is confrontation viewed as a threat to authority, disloyalty, a sign of trust, or the first step of innovation?

Do senior executives and managers use participative processes in working with one another? How can this be improved?

What is the overall responsiveness level of executives in relation to change and innovation? How do managers respond to change opportunities?

TABLE 11.3 (continued)

Human Resource Development

What are the types of resources executives, managers, and action teams will need in order to effectively implement benchmarking to take advantage of cross-business information, synergy, and innovative practices?

What resource and staffing needs are anticipated during the various phases of the benchmarking process and during the application activities to bring about an integrated change process for competitive advantage?

What global staffing will be needed for expanding markets in local and national arenas and across continents? What are the criteria for selection of managers, team leaders, and facilitators?

Will the criteria of selection, orientation, performance, reward, and compensation be impacted by the changing direction of the enterprise in a continuous improvement effort?

AN IMPLEMENTATION MODEL FOR BENCHMARKING

Benchmarking is a systematic, data-based process for facilitating organizational change and development by learning from the individuals, groups, and organizations who do the job best. Figure 11.1 illustrates the elements in an integrated sequence of change implementation beginning with the experience-based knowledge and competence in specific organizations. Crises and challenges bring an awareness of the need to begin this process. Benchmarking is facilitated through consultation competencies in getting agreements, establishing roles and responsibilities, assessing readiness, gathering data, and developing, implementing, and monitoring action plans. Executives, managers, staff, employees, and consultation teams work together in a process of collective learning for change management.

Benchmarking Applications

The questions in Table 11.4 help executives, managers, and change facilitation teams work through this model with increased awareness for focused planning, implementation, and results monitoring for improved performance.

FIGURE 11.1 - Planning for Change Model

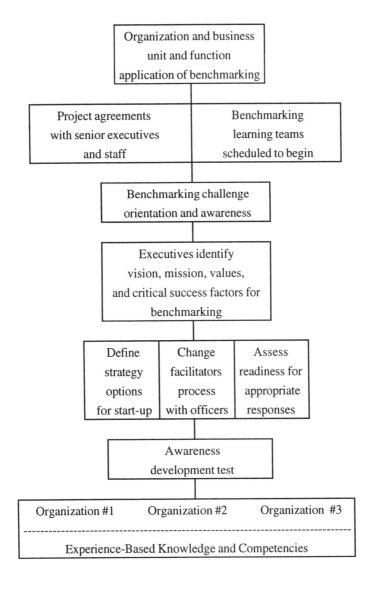

TABLE 11.4 Implementation Applications.

Definition and Orientation for Benchmarking

What is Benchmarking? How do we define it? How did our organization discover benchmarking as an important strategy?

What is the mission, purpose, and rationale for benchmarking in our organization?

What are the critical success factors for achieving productive and measurable accomplishments associated with benchmarking in our organization? In what parts of our organization is benchmarking used? Who is doing the most with benchmarking?

What are some of the premises, perceptions, goals, prerequisites, and priorities that we feel are associated with benchmarking in our organization? What are some of the assumptions associated with the application of benchmarking and its reinforcement in practices within our organization?

Formulation of Strategy and Tactics

What do we feel should be the geographic focus for benchmarking? How do we see the benchmarking process assisting us in achieving a global-leadership position?

How do we see employee involvement assisting in the application of benchmarking? How does employee involvement contribute to the success of the benchmarking process within our organization?

How do you see benchmarking helping our organization to implement operational and organizational change to offset competition?

How do we see benchmarking assisting our organization in global strategies and our ability to better serve customer-market segments and expectations?

To insure the continuity of the benchmarking process in our organization, what do we view as the key rewards, recognition, and benefits that need to be satisfied?

As the organization plans for the application of benchmarking as a strategy, what types of barriers do we anticipate? What advice or insight might we give based on our experience?

Evaluation

What are the significant accomplishments that took place as a result of benchmarking?

What was happening in benchmarking as a process? In achieving particular goals?

What should have been happening in benchmarking that has not happened? In achieving particular goals?

Table 11.4 (continued)
What were some of the reasons for the variance between what happened and what should have been happening?
Given the present state of the benchmarking program, what is happening now in benchmarking as a process? In achieving particular accomplishments?
Where do we see benchmarking going in the next year? Next five years? Next 10 years?

In implementing and evaluating benchmarking, it is important to talk to people within the organization as well as resource professionals in other organizations. Research articles, training materials, and other studies should also be reviewed before initial implementation. All these resources can help to establish critical success factors for effective change management.

Critical Success Factors

The following are some of the most significant recommendations from our study of benchmarking for organizational change and renewal.

- Involve senior executives in identifying vision, values, and critical success factors for benchmarking so that priorities become known for each business unit and or function.

- Establish an advisory council of representative senior executives including chairperson, CEO, and COO representation to gain guidance, ownership to provide a test-development climate, and to establish accountability. In a nonprofit agency, this could include the board members, executive committee chairs, and senior staff.

- Clarify role responsibilities for each function so that resources and support are given to the effort.

- Create an executive-development strategy that fits the business so that ownership, involvement, and commitment are given to the benchmarking change effort.

- Focus efforts on determining the critical success factors for achieving the strategic business plan in order to focus developmental efforts on those criteria that result in the greatest payoff for the business.

- Do not expect too much too soon, and understand the impact of change process on culture, roles, structure, and work practices.

- Provide awareness of the competitive threat so that a rationale for change and innovation is obvious.

TABLE 11.5 Benchmarking in Three Organizations.

Action Area	Organization 1	Organization 2	Organization 3
Change Initiative	Initially imposed, which created hostility; used campaign approach.	Management orientation and field testing of self-implemented training manuals. Started in manufacturing, extended to office and services.	Senior executives were the initial change initiators; gradually moved into the total organization.
Vision and Values	What business are we in and not in; enduring values provide a guide for employees' daily work.	Broad-based education and training in total quality values and skills; performance leadership in meeting customer requirements by doing the right things right the first time.	Senior executives determined strategic vision and guiding principles.
Focus of Change	Quality Innovation Best function	Profile analysis of business used factors of cost, material, labor, and cycle time.	Established internal and external customer acceptance criteria; what is important to customers.
Critical Success Factors	Determined by each business; required to successfully implement business strategy.	Global knowledge base provided understanding of customers' perceptions of values related to products and services.	Vision training, role negotiation, supplier relationships, executive education of benchmarking techniques, and communicating quality in every decision.
Criteria for Benchmarking	Best criteria with each business unit determining what to benchmark, (i.e., customer surveys, product cost, capital plans, market-share, employee ratios).	World-class leadership, customer satisfaction, and financial performance. Measurement of quantitative engineering change, value, price, cost, response time, and improvement of total quality.	Who is "best-in-class" in function, company, organization in other nations? Benchmarking success criteria from market research, audit and warranty data, comparison in one to three yea rs, test proceedings.
Role responsibilities	Line has primary responsibility; staff no authority, only influence.	Validated need for commitment to quality from push-to-pull strategy; employee involvement process for problem-solving participation.	Senior executives moved from endorsement to involvement as role models for organization.
Integration of Directed and Nondirected Process	Strategic plan with management-by-objectives program.	Regular planning, total quality improvement objectives, and training on techniques. Each work center setting objectives, world-class benchmarking knowledge base, competitive, and world sourcing to establish quality and productivity requirements.	Planning and performance review cycle, from short-to-long-term vision, strategic market responses, and data-based improvement changes.
Change Management Learning	Establish customer and acceptance criteria, visit outside sources, and use internal employee problem solving work teams.	Change perceived as threatening: need confidence "it will work." Mid-management blockages, need for ownership and involvement. If one unit became "world class," change is incorporated for rest of organization. Intimate knowledge of customer requirement.	Analyze gaps, ask what changes are needed to become "better than the best." Requires ongoing monitoring and recalibrating to anticipate market, trends, new products, and pricing strategies.

- Learn from others and find ways to transfer that learning to other parts of the business. Move beyond the "not-invented-here" syndrome and integrate outside resources.

- Start in friendly areas where success can be achieved and support gained for test development.

- Take adequate time to plan and involve key people in determining change requirements.

- Communicate the idea that change is an ongoing process, not just a program.

- Integrate the directed and nondirected elements of change.

Figure 11.2 outlines benchmarking action areas as they were documented in three major organizations. Each is based on a distinct vision with a specific implementation approach and particular pattern of organizational learning.

PART IV
Competency Development

12

Change Management Competency

Change management competencies help the organization understand, plan, integrate, implement, and monitor change processes. Consultative relationships, whether temporary or ongoing, help transfer competencies and build the capacity for change. Shared benefits result from leaders and interrelated teams working together to meet challenges and take advantage of opportunities.

Vision and leadership are essential elements in any change process. Leadership roles include ambassadors and heads of nations, boards, directors, CEOs, chief financial and human resource officers, presidents and senior-line executives, managers and supervisors, project team leaders, self-directed units, action research teams, consultation teams, technical resources, academic partners, political and community leaders, and members of various committees, councils, and steering groups.

Leaders and change facilitators can be more successful if they work with and through others using influence, collaboration, and teaming to manage change. The balancing of both technical and process skills in these relationships involves resources with diverse interests and mutual goals at the local, national, and even global level. Through change management, people agree to work together in both a formal and informal way to accomplish a mutually beneficial outcome for themselves and for the organization. Change management competencies can be focused in the following areas:

- Personal level of competence
- Career-development competency
- Core competence in change-consultation process
- Action roles for change facilitation
- Assessment of change-management competencies in practice

PERSONAL LEVEL OF COMPETENCE

The individual competence that leaders, facilitators, or managers bring to the consultation relationship includes their style of communication, facilitation, responsiveness to self and others, awareness of change dynamics, view of systems, ethics, and business knowledge.

Communication: The effective change facilitator listens in an alert and understanding way, and creates and sustains trust and openness. The managers must establish rapport, and empathize and reflect on diverse perspectives in helping groups and individuals reach a consensus for action. Competency includes being sensitive to cultural perspectives, having knowledge of group dynamics, using confronting skills when appropriate, and supporting feedback and multiple communication channels. Both written skills for writing reports, proposals and documentation, and verbal skills for presentation training and facilitation, are important in maintaining coordination, unity, and direction in accomplishing team goals.

Facilitative style: Managers and change facilitators work in both formal and informal leader roles demonstrating the capacity to lead and to follow as a team member. An effective facilitator respects the views and differences of others, is comfortable in working in a supporting role, and expresses personal views or opinions only when they are clearly identified as such. Trusting the ideas of other people, the facilitator should be both flexible and adaptable to a variety of situations. Personal strengths include the valuing mutual learning, respecting the ideas of participating members, and being comfortable with working behind the scenes and helping clients, sponsors, and other colleagues to be successful.

Self-responsiveness: Having a personal sense of mission and unity of purpose is essential to leadership in change management. The manager respects the views of others, expresses feelings when appropriate, is willing to take risks, and has the capacity to be patient in dealing with ambiguity and frustration. Change complexities demand that facilitators be perceptive, have a historical perspective on self, be aware of personal beliefs and values, have a sense of humor, develop the capacity to "transcend the moment" (Shepherd 1975), and see beyond the current situation.

Responsiveness to others: The change facilitator demonstrates teaming skills, and works with and through others without using authority to impose ideas and controls. An ability to communicate with optimism about achieving outcomes and to convey dynamism helps motivate action teams. Working effectively across units, functions, and hierarchical levels of the organization is essential. The change facilitator or manager, in being responsive to others, is collaborative, and has the capacity to think in a dialectic manner to learn about opposing ideas while suspending his or her own judgment.

Change process skills: In using process skills to bring about change, the facilitator recognizes the need for third-party observation with feedback critique. This includes being politically astute about organizational dynamics and being sensitive to the motivation and readiness of others. Appropriate diagnostic methods are used to validate need, define the situation more accurately, and explore the potential for working effectively together. Client inquiries help develop a working knowledge of the mission, strategy, desired measurement, business challenge, assessment of the cross-business synergy, and amount of cooperation. Ongoing assessment of organizational performance supports a data-based intervention strategy. Role rehearsals can be used to refine these process skills.

Systems view: The change facilitator retains objectivity, takes a systems perspective, acknowledges self-perspectives, and achieves a proper balance of distance from the client and agenda. To effectively link key sponsors and clients, the facilitator acts as an educator to communicate the change innovation with the formal and informal leaders of the organization. It is important to legitimize self-competence and confidence with the client and to define action roles of client, sponsor, and facilitator. Teaming skills maximize inside and outside collaboration with consultation partners. Clients and sponsors, and the consultation team, need to agree on the conceptual approach, methods, directions, and the action of each consultation phase. Access to information and organizational resources is critical to achieving these goals.

Ethics: Leaders, facilitators, and managers need to be aware of role limitations and of the idea that authoritarian imposition of change is not as effective as voluntary change. Each individual working on directed change projects should be knowledgeable about ethics and corporate policy. Routine assessment of professional practices with feedback from clients and colleagues is helpful for staying on target and learning from continuous improvement efforts. Taking time to consider underlying assumptions of actions, and being sensitive to cross-cultural differences and values, offers the consultation team a chance to examine its practices in terms of choices and ethics.

Business knowledge: General business knowledge is essential to change management. This perspective brings a "holistic" business view with an appreciation of finance, marketing, quality, manufacturing, operations, legal, human resources, structure, skills, systems, customer satisfaction, systems dynamics, and global practices. Technical functional knowledge and experience should be current with new technologies. Awareness of how the organization will reward and measure the change outcome is important for determining progress checkpoints.

Other areas of knowledge may be related to human resources systems, performance assessments, succession and career planning, compensation, vision and values, and leadership styles. Business information includes industry trends, best practices, competitive market data, and local and global alliances with other organizations, countries, academic institutions, associations, and suppliers. Managers and team members should understand how the change will link to the organizational strategy at all levels.

Global: Global competence requires flexibility and tolerance for ambiguity. Managers and change facilitators working in a multicultural context must be willing to learn from differences and take risks related to their career development. Mutual respect, patience, listening and observations skills are important in understanding other points of view.

Some knowledge of the specific culture is essential. This might include business practices, legal regulations, education systems, religious beliefs, political systems, and social norms related to work and family. It is important to understand cultural and global career contexts and the range of appropriate behaviors.

CAREER-DEVELOPMENT COMPETENCY

Consultation requires consideration of goals at the individual, group, and organizational level. For change to be effective, the career of the individual must be considered. Individuals taking a risk related to change often are concerned about their career. Will the change be beneficial in accomplishing a higher level of performance to move to a broader experience or challenge? Perhaps the effect of the change will provide an opportunity for global career assignment or a transfer to a new project team with greater visibility and challenge linked to corporate strategy. Often career goals do not become known — not because they are hidden, but because they are not planned (Chakiris and Fornaciari 1993) or discussed. Both the change facilitator and the client need to put career goals and development on their agenda of desired outcomes.

Additionally, there are a number of leaders and senior professionals who are not fully aware of the career context of organizational life. They may be aware of career pathing, career laddering, and career planning, but most people in organizations are not aware of the significance of managing one's own career goals, and career-development activities, programs, and processes. For example, individuals rotating in and out of global assignments would need to be cognizant of the phase of entry, completion, and reentry career phases and the contracting activities for each phase. As part of career competency there are specific dynamics that affect change management from the perspective of jobs, work, and careers. These trends include:

- Global competition with companies competing in technology, jobs, and skill competencies.

- Technology that eliminates and "deskills" jobs with labor-saving technology that requires fewer workers including managers and professionals. Monitoring worker and job obsolescence is essential. For example, being aware of technological developments should provide clues for self-development in new skills areas if a job, task, function, organization, or industry shrinks or even disappears.

- An increased number of new jobs in the service sector are providing fewer career advantages with more compressed career opportunity and increased worker job obsolescence.

- More than 76 million Baby Boomers born between 1946 and 1964 are competing for fewer jobs with more education and higher expectations, and are having difficulty matching job expectations.

- More women are in the labor force and there is an increased enrollment in law, medicine, and business schools. Many women become successful entrepreneurs in small business because they perceive fewer opportunities in large corporations. There are more competent women than there are good jobs available.

- Diversity patterns for the year 2000, indicate that 80 percent of new entry-level employees in the United States will be women and immigrants. This pluralistic surge of values, expectations, priorities, and diverse languages may profoundly affect job competition, education for global markets, and organizational roles and structures.

Distinctions Among Job, Work, and Careers

Organizations are changing and this fact affects careers. Our work in studying careers indicates that people have different ways of seeing their profession based on how they view the distinction among jobs, work, and careers. Often when people talk about careers they are referring to traditional careers within a large corporation. This is no longer a realistic option for many people.

In the past, a person started out in a good, steady, entry-level job with a big company in one industry where an explicit career path was evident and promotions came regularly until the person reached a certain age or stage and was "plateaued," either voluntarily or involuntarily, and eventually retired with a party and a pension.

This traditional career-ladder model represents a major stumbling block when individuals attempt to analyze their career development and role competency for the future. Change management in career planning provides a broader framework for defining new career forms. This is evident in the distinctions among jobs, work, and careers.

Jobs: Jobs are derived from the work of a society, a nation's agenda, and its goals. Jobs are economy-based and depend upon the economic well-being of a nation. The individual and the organization have an economy-based contract. There are good and bad jobs. Jobs flow from society, and the type of jobs are determined by what is important to that nation. All jobs imply work and jobs flow from work; however, not all work implies jobs. Jobs contribute to the gross national product (GNP) of a nation as an objective, quantitative measurement.

Work: Work is defined as a purposeful activity in that requires some physical or mental effort to perform. It can be either economic-based or noneconomic-based, paid or unpaid. Work is based on society's sociopolitical vision. Society has always used work to achieve its goals, however, not all work contributes to the nation's GNP. Jobs flow from work but not all the work has to be finalized in economic contracts. A nation can have a great deal of work but for one reason or another may have few jobs. All jobs imply work but not all work implies jobs.

Careers: Economic-based jobs set a limit to the number of jobs available even though there is almost limitless work available in society. Society has more work than careers. Careers flow from jobs. They are continuous behavioral episodes leading to a path or ladder that ends in some kind of a capstone experience. Careers are a recent concept, an invention of large corporations and government bureaucracies.

Careers are sociopsychological concepts that involve status, power, influence, and economics and traditionally make a statement regarding financial status and how important a person is in the eyes of others. Careers also influence perception of self-worth. An advanced society might calculate self-worth using new criteria such as a person's character, companionability, renaissance-like knowledge, contribution to community, and patience to enhance a pluralistic society (Leach and Chakiris 1987). Social good and citizen roles would constitute the basis for these new criteria. Today's highly competitive, high-technology industrialized society rewards upward mobility as a major "social good." Changing organizational structures are demolishing traditional career paths. The inability of a nation to generate a sufficient number of careers is not necessarily an indictment of its economic well being but an indicator of its creativity in defining work, of its vision, goals, and agenda for change in relation to the work to be done.

New Career Forms

As we move into the 21st century, we see new career forms and a framework for expanded definitions from traditional and new styles of careering. This includes linear-form, free-form, and mixed-form careers.

Linear-Form Careers: Traditional corporate career models are composed of a planned or unplanned patterns or events (Chakiris and Fornaciari 1984) with each activity leading to another in an upward movement with responsibility and pay increases as one moves up the ladder. People pursuing linear careers generally take a common route to career possibilities: they get an education to prepare for a job; they begin a career in a large organization; they find their time and energy being consumed in getting established in their careers; they interact with intermediaries or sponsors who believe in their work; they take on challenging roles and assignments; they move across and upward; ultimately reaching a peak, and then attempt to maintain that peak; and they finally disengage and retire. Some pursue a second, third, and sometimes five or more careers in a lifetime.

The employer plays a decisive role regarding this career movement. Business needs come first: "The bottom line is the bottom line," and self-actualization is largely accidental. Being competent includes fitting in and understanding the culture. People trade autonomy for career security. The growing trend is toward fewer linear careers; yet career-development professionals, human resource specialists, counselors and practitioners, outplacement firms, and researchers tend to use the linear career as the "classic" career-development model.

Free-Form Careers: The free-form career can be either an economic or noneconomic role working for pay or working at some activity for no pay. Pay-based activities include various forms of permanent or temporary part-time work, subcontracted work when personnel are "leased" for a specific period, small business activities, or entrepreneurial efforts. Free-form activities are not structured within a corporate organizational chart and may not lead anywhere in a planned sequence. People enter free-form careers for limited or extended periods of time and can combine them to form novel, opportunities for learning and development. Cooperative or collegial relationships rather than competitive careering are more often the norm. Small business and entrepreneur activities fit many of the free-form career criteria and may have economic drives, but autonomy needs are usually most important. There is a greater increase in free-form careers than in the linear corporate model. Paid free-form careerists represent about 30 percent of all workers. Including unpaid free-form people could substantially increase this number. Again, human resource specialists, counselors, outplacement groups, and research professionals allocate very little time to free-form career needs.

Mixed-Form Careers: The major characteristic of this career form is the notion of behavioral transitions as people make significant changes in their repertoire of skills, knowledge, and attitude orientation in relation to their "work." Transitions can be planned or random oscillations between linear and free form career patterns or between economic and noneconomic based roles within the free form career pattern. These people experience significant changes in their life as they plan, rehearse, and emotionally work through a mixed-form career. One women professional, for example, experienced a mixed-career form with 10 transitions:

> In her youth she prepared for a career in psychology in the field of dance therapy (1) and pursued this career until marriage (2). Upon becoming a parent (3), she devotedly worked in this new role, adding to it by nurturing several immigrant foster children. As the children grew and became able to cope for themselves, she began community-volunteer work (4). With an emerging interest in training and education in business, she became self-employed (5) as a professional contractor to large companies that led her to a full-time (6) program design leadership position with a large not-for-profit organization. While working there, she returned to the university (7) to earn an MBA degree. Shortly after completion she went to work (8) for a major corporation as an instructional designer. Ten years later, she left (9) the industry to write science fiction novels and in her spare time (10) to volunteer work with a large urban-based agency board .

The transitions involved here included some planned and some random career and life changes between the free-form and the linear-form career patterns, and also several transitions in the free-form pattern.

The temporarily underemployed and permanently unemployed can fit the mixed-form career pattern if they are in the midst of some transition such as retraining. People emotionally disengaged from either a linear or free-form career could fall into the mixed category because psychologically this is a period of transition. Transition careers involve oscillation until some decisions are made regarding "coping" strategies. The number of people in transition careers is growing. Statistics based on unemployment outplacement rates are likely gross underestimates. Change facilitators need to understand the impact of change on careers as they integrate directed and nondirected change processes.

Implications for Change Management

In the future, most jobs will be generated by people in small businesses. To eliminate the narrow emphasis on linear-career forms, change management processes should pay attention to the distinctions between job, work, and careers, and to human development patterns in transforming systems.

Linear-career people will continue to need assistance in terms of succession planning, career planning, transitions to different cultures, and technical and process skill bases, but their numbers are dwindling. This elite group will be overworked and have significant career problems. For example, the psychological dependency on the corporation is one of most challenging aspects of the linear-career form. Change management competencies can help provide resources to facilitate career redirection for younger and senior workers, people experiencing change and transition in outplacement or unemployment, and continue to research career-development issues in mixed-form careers.

The world of work is changing (Leach and Chakiris 1985). Because of these changes, traditional career-development models are beginning to lack relevance for many jobholders. More people are now working in small businesses free-lancing, working part-time or contract work, consulting, or developing home cottage industries. The transfer of competencies both within an organizational system and across linear, free-form, and mixed-form careers is a critical challenge for change management.

CORE COMPETENCE IN CHANGE MANAGEMENT - SIX PHASES

During the next decade, organizations leaders and managers will be judged on their ability to identify, cultivate, and apply the core competencies that make growth possible (Prahalad and Hamel 1990). The real source of advantage is found in management's ability to consolidate organization-wide technologies and skills into competencies that empower individual people or groups to adapt quickly to change opportunities. To illustrate the core competencies, Prahalad and Hamel suggest that we visualize these diversified organization as a large tree. The trunk and major limbs are the core products or services; the branches are the core organizational or business units; and the leaves, flowers, and fruit are the end products and services. The root system that nourishes and provides stability to the system is called the *core competence* of the organization. As Prahalad and Hamel suggest, we can miss the strength of the tree if we look only at its leaves.

They define core competencies as the collective learning of the organization, including its knowledge, skills, and technologies. Core competence involves communication, involvement, and a deep commitment to working across organizational boundaries with many levels of people and all functions. Unlike physical assets, which deteriorate over time, competencies grow as they are applied and shared. Competencies need to be nurtured and protected; since knowledge and skills fade or become obsolete if not used. A core competence based on a comprehensive pattern of internal coordination and learning creates distinctions that are difficult for competitors to imitate.

The tangible link between core competencies and end products is what Prahalad and Hamel call the core product or service, the embodiment of one or more core competencies. Core products or services contribute to the value of the end product. It is essential to make a distinction between core competencies, core products and services, and end products and services. The core service provides the revenue and market feedback that determines the pace at which core competencies can be developed and extended. A dominant position of control over core products or services is critical to allow an organization to shape the evolution of applications and end markets.

Developing "strategic architecture" helps to establish objectives for competence building. This is a road map for the future of change management. For example, how can an organization partner make decisions and act intelligently in relation to other organizations, suppliers, or nations without a clear understanding of what core competencies the system is trying to build? The change-management process provides a template both for the development of core competencies and for an action research model of collaborative inquiry and collective learning to support these competencies. Core competencies are organizational assets deployed by management as critical resources for change management.

The core competencies we have described for change management are:
- Human resources and career development
- Consultation technology
- Teaming with customer
- Industry knowledge
- Organizational effectiveness criteria
- General business knowledge
- Global intracultural resources
- Strategic alignment of goals
- Change management competence
- Trust and ethical integrity

- Image through marketing and quality of delivery of services

The core services include:

- Action research teaming
- Applications technical/process portfolio
- Quality and organizational surveys/audits
- Design for learning competencies

FIGURE 12.1 Competencies for Change Management.

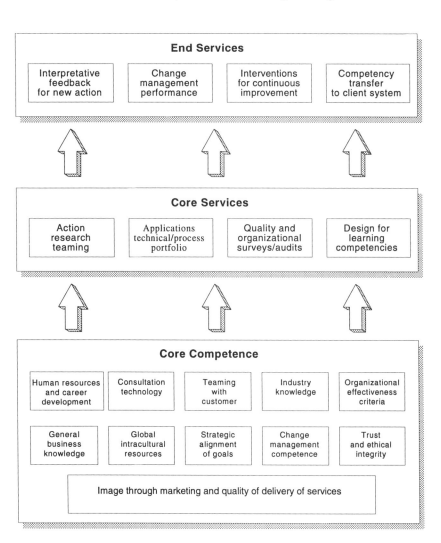

The end services include:

* Interpretive feedback for new action
* Change management performance
* Interventions for continuous improvement
* Competency transfer to client system

Career movement within the organization should allow boundary crossing among units and so that people can identify with next-generation competencies and build for the future. Assignments to cross-divisional project teams can build core competencies and loosen the bonds that tie an individual to one unit or business even when opportunities for learning and development also exist in other parts of an interrelated system.

Core competencies are the wellspring of new business development as well as the integration of directed and nondirected change. They constitute the focus for corporate strategy (see Figure 12.1) for change management. Top management can add value by establishing the strategic architecture that guides the development of core competence, core products and services, and end products and services to integrate stability and innovation in a changing organization.

The next section discusses core competencies for the change facilitator and the consultation team, which includes the client, sponsors, managers, and other internal and external resources.

Competence for Phase 1: Need and Opportunity in Change Initiatives

The first phase establishes the initial contact and entry for clarifying the work areas, roles, and outcomes for change management. A common problem in change consultation is that people move too fast through this orientation phase. The goal should be to establish a level of trust and openness, to agree on starting roles and goals, to verify expectations, to explore whether or not to move forward in working together, and to assess the nature of the change as voluntary or imposed. Relationships require time, patience, and a testing period to see if things will work out. In the beginning there is a tendency to promise too much too soon, and to agree on things that later prove impossible because of client system resistance, lack of readiness, and limited resources. Sometimes the change team moves ahead only to find out later that the persons involved did not have ownership. The following competencies support the need and opportunity initiative.

Awareness of the key decisions for contact: The first contact initiative explores the change-consultation effort. Entry may occur through an invitation to work on a project or directed change initiative, through a third-party, be imposed in an involuntary relationship, or be a self-initiated entry by the change facilitator. Entries take time to build credibility, trust, and competence legitimization. Help can be either accepted or rejected, depending on sponsor ownership, and the past experience of the client working with change consultation. This first phase explores issues and goals and clarifies the perceived need for change. There are several methods for exploring the relationship. Entry competency provides a mix of skills in areas of diagnostic analysis and discussion with the client related to a tentative definition of the work relationship, the scope of the work assignment, and possible outcomes. Classic decisions involve role and goal expectations, issues of dependency, interdependency, and counterdependency, power, and client commitment.

Capable of scouting: Scouting is the term used for gathering intelligence data of the internal and external publics and markets of the potential client system. This may include employees, suppliers, customers, competitors, and industry and global-market information. The capacity for scouting helps to position a strategy by coordinating pertinent information such as quality, performance criteria, career development, succession planning, training and education, cultural values, and leadership styles. The facilitating system becomes aware of the client system's informal and formal communication channels, the architecture or structure of the organization and its markets, and its current business challenges. Scouting information should focus on how people view measurement in terms of what they measure and why they make measurements. General business knowledge competence includes a "holistic" perspective of finance, marketing, quality, customer satisfaction, manufacturing, operations, legal, human resources, and culture. In addition, information is collected to assess current and future client system competence and present and future needs in technical, functional, global, and process skills.

Responds appropriately to the dynamics of entry hierarchy: Entry dynamics must be analyzed. Often, change facilitators and internal or external resources are brought in by one client who quickly becomes the sponsor and disappears from active involvement. The situation changes from an invited, voluntary relationship to an imposed involuntary relationship with potential counterdependency, conflict, and resistance. The challenge for change facilitators is to move from an imposed to a voluntary relationship. It is important at entry to consider using third parties when conflict is present in the system. For example, a good question to ask is: "Who would be involved should a conflict arise?" A crucial competency in this initial phase is to anticipate and respond to conflict situations.

When the change initiative is vague or hidden and goals and roles are unclear, the change facilitator must have a tolerance for ambiguity combined with the diagnostic competence to probe the issues, and find out who will be involved, what goals are expected, and by whom. It is quite helpful during the entry diagnosis to question clients and sponsors to understand their overall view of change management, and to learn about their experience in working with a consultation group. From these other change efforts, the team can identify the factors that determined success and acceptance, or rejection and resistance? These are key questions at entry.

Conducts entry diagnosis: The consultation team seeks to retain objectivity with the client. Much of the entry diagnostic data collection is facilitated in an unobtrusive manner, as the change facilitators use entry inquiry questions to clarify the need and in collecting the initial information through sensitizing interviews, observation, documentation, and analysis. The diagnostic findings are discussed for client feedback and interpretation to validate the initial need as perceived by the consultation team, client, and sponsor. In addition, the overall conceptual approach is agreed upon among all parties.

The group should be comfortable in expressing self values while not buying into the client values, pain, or agenda. Where possible, the change facilitators should work with other colleagues. The consultation team involves key sponsors and clients to create appropriate internal linkage to connect change to the power structure. They must work with these groups to plan ongoing feedback about progress, to determine how things are going, and to decide what new action is required.

During the initial diagnostic period of Phase 1, change facilitators can explore a working relationship with the client by using a phased approach for getting started. This provides ongoing validation to check client system readiness, available resources, access to data, and possible linkage with internal resources for change management. Diagnostic findings at entry also help to verify units of change—individual, group, intergroup, and organization.

Rehearses entry initiative: Entry competence can be improved by rehearsing the role and goal perspectives of the client, sponsor, and change facilitator. Role rehearsal provides practice, and understanding of the types of entry, the complexity of the start-up, and the need for linkage, clear roles, goals, and interdependency in the change management process.

Accomplishes entry targets: Target outcomes for this phase include creating an open climate of trust, role and goal clarity, interdependency, and sponsor linkage with realistic expectations that position change management as an investment to achieve strategic business goals. The allocation of appropriate resources, access to organizational resources, and awareness of self-motivation help to define roles and goals.

Competencies for Phase 2: Agreements for Establishing Working Relationships

Competencies for Phase 2 include agreeing on the conceptual approach to guide the change management process, determining what key decisions are essential to the relationship, how needs will be validated and owned by everyone involved, and what specific role differences exist within the relationship, inquiring about important measurements, and assessing measurement requirements and the types of skills required for the change continuity. Skill balance is reflected in process, technical, and functional expertise for change management.

Awareness of the key decisions for making agreements: Key decisions of this phase include methods to validate need; what type of overall process is required for gaining ownership; what role distinctions are perceived among client, sponsor, and change facilitator; what happens should the client change; whether there is an appropriate balance in technical, process, and functional skills; and how assessment of ongoing agreements with feedback might continuously improve the relationship and results. This phase validates need and determines what outcomes are desired and how they will be achieved. Through a process of thoughtful contract questions and decisions there is an agreement on time perspective, performance criteria, ongoing feedback to determine reward, measurement, and involvement. Decisions must also be made on the type of agreement—informal, formal, or technical.

Validates need and outcome with the client, sponsor, and change facilitator: From a systems perspective, the validation of needs and opportunities integrates current and desired conditions to gain consensus ownership and linkage to the power structure. Appropriate alliances are considered and the assessment of both readiness and priority are facilitated. Motivation, career development, goals, visibility, and recognition in relation to the individual needs of change facilitator, client, and sponsor are discussed.

Clarifies role distinction and role modifications for the client, sponsor, and change facilitator: An important part of the contracting phase is anticipating future clients as the change consultation continues over a period of time. Sponsors also change, and new sponsors may question and block the change initiative. Hidden sponsors also become known as they are affected by the change. Potential conflicts arising between client and sponsor, between one client and another client, and among client, sponsor, and facilitator should be resolved early. Change facilitators need competence in how to facilitate differences, conflict, and resistance to change resulting from role relationships and alternative perspectives and needs during a directed change. Priority must also be given to the importance of individual performance and the career goals of key players.

Determines results, measurement, and investment: During the contracting phase, an agreement should be reached between client, sponsor, and change facilitators about the measurement of results. This includes defining outcome in measurement terms, articulating, and aligning the goals of each unit of change including individual, group, organization, and societal/global. These measurements may relate to customer satisfaction, supplier relations, and the organization's image with various publics. During the contract phase, clients articulate the priorities of the organization, how the change management will be positioned with regard to the strategic goals of the organization, and the commitment to resource requirements to achieve specific outcomes. The change facilitators or consultation team also lends insight into how feedback information will be used to measure and to plan for new action.

Develops a mutually open relationship and agrees upon tasks: Openness and agreement are the primary outcomes of this phase. Yet contracting is a continuous process throughout the change effort. Skilled process facilitation gains agreement with appropriate teaming for effective action and linking of resources to accomplish a goal. The consultation team involves people in collecting data and openly confronting issues to coordinate action, tasks, and outcomes.

Involves the client system for change ownership and continuity: The contract phase looks ahead to change continuity and what early decisions are needed to effectively transfer technology to the client, and to establish competencies for ongoing change management. With client input, the change facilitators assess where the organization is in its overall development, what skills and training systems exist, and what will be needed to build client capacity for long-term change management.

Aware of the need to balance technical and process action roles: Action roles described later in this chapter focus on both technical and process expertise. These roles include advocate, technical expert, fact finder or diagnostic expert, trainer/educator or mentor, action research team partner, linker and alternative identifier of resources and solutions, process facilitator, and reflector or objective observer. Each role supports different aspects of the change management process. The team needs a capacity to choose the appropriate technical or process action role. Feedback provides data to develop and expand roles for the facilitating system and the client system and assists the client in developing competencies.

Rehearses contract to coordinate elements for effective relationship: To rehearse the contracting phase, the consultation team can simulate the perspectives of the client, sponsor, client system, and the role of the facilitator. For example, by reversing roles, the team members provide insight into client, sponsor, and facilitator concerns, develop new sensitivity about what is needed to introduce the change, what skills are essential, and the threats perceived around structural change. Rehearsal sessions show that imposing too much change too soon is not helpful, and increase awareness of pacing and timing in choosing appropriate inquiry questions to formulate an effective working agreement; they encourage the use of synergistic win-win negotiation language to introduce a phased-in approach with the client. Facilitation competence includes communicating understanding in written documents, honoring both verbal and written promises, and choosing the appropriate time to openly confront issues of concern with the client or team members.. Observer roles provide feedback from the rehearsal to improve action by critiquing the intervention approach, language, and results.

Competencies for Phase 3: Data Collection and Analysis

Diagnostic analysis is an important competence for the change management team, including the client, sponsor, and the client system. Linkage between data collection, analysis, feedback, decisions, and action is needed to improve client ownership and client role responsibility. There are a number of skill requirements for this phase including a basic knowledge and experience in using diverse research methods, tools, and systems of diagnosis and analysis. Questions of when to involve the client and sponsor should be answered. A support system and client readiness for looking at the data are essential for achieving a successful outcome for this phase and should be a priority.

Awareness of the key decisions for collecting and analyzing data: Design, structure, and process are required for the data collection and analysis phase. Decisions are related to overall strategy of how to involve the client system in action research teaming (ART), selecting the appropriate data collection methods, determining units of analysis, facilitating client agreement for understanding the purpose of data collection, protecting client confidentiality in the data-collection activity, and validating client need and assumptions. Client responsibility includes providing access to the data and agreeing how the data will be used.

Uses systems perspective for organization diagnosis: The change facilitators should provide a systems perspective and have the capacity to visualize the change, and both short- and long-term impact on the client system. Clients assume role responsibility as part of the consultation team in determining who collects what data in the organization, and providing knowledge of what measurements are currently being used and what measurements will be needed in the future. Clients can also provide information about the levels of power, and the historical and future vision of the organization.

Uses ART as a strategy for change: ART involves clients and members of the client system in diagnosis, feedback, and decision making. Using this approach requires training the consultation team, ad hoc task forces, committees, and advisory councils in directed and nondirected change, change integration, and data-based change. Designing effective team structure and establishing a trained sponsor and client base are important competencies to support the diagnostic findings and ensure integrated change.

Prepares designs for collecting and analyzing data: This phase provides the client with an organized design prepared in collaboration with the change facilitators and approved by the key sponsors. Quantitative and qualitative methods and both macro and microdata collection approaches are included when appropriate. A theoretical or conceptual visual model of the input and output of the data collection process is helpful. The benefits of data collection to the organization should be defined. The consultation team must also consider how the data will be put into action with future measurement linked to the goals and performance of the organization.

Demonstrates skill, knowledge, and experience in data-collecting methods: Specific skills, knowledge, and experience are essential in collecting data. The consultation team should have a wide repertoire of data-collection methods and experience in both macro and microchange. In the absence of this experience, it is important to work with other professional resources who have skills and an experience base. Different methods used in data collection have advantages and disadvantages, and it is important to be knowledgeable about measurement and organizational assessment in order to select the appropriate method for the situation. The change facilitator must get an agreement with the client on how the data will be used and design data-collection events including the facilitation of appropriate inquiry, sequencing questions, facilitating nonthreatening exploratory interviews, and retaining confidentiality. During analysis the consultation team should have the capacity to analyze and the skills to to apply useful statistical instruments, and audits for team effectiveness, readiness, human resources, quality, training needs validation, skills inventory, career development, and self-assessment.

Uses force-field analysis for change diagnosis: The force-field analysis looks at forces that drive toward the change and the forces that restrain or resist change. This visual method involves the client, sponsor, and consultation team in the diagnosis and helps to identify concerns and challenges in order to develop ways to increase support and reduce barriers to change.

Can determine appropriate unit and level for change initiative: The data collection and analysis validates the need and gives priority to the specific unit of change: individual, group, relationships between groups, or the total organization. While the focus may be on one unit, all units are interrelated and should be considered as part of the context for change management.

Facilitates interpretive feedback, decisions, and action: The investment in data collection and analysis emerges from feedback sessions. This is where the payoff begins for the client, sponsor, and the organization. Working closely with the client, the consultation team designs the feedback sessions with a process for guiding feedback, training internal facilitators, and creating collective action decisions based on the data.

Competencies for Phase 4: Feedback, Decisions, and Action Planning

Competencies for Phase 4 include essential elements for making change management effective. Feedback, decisions, and action plans move the data into a program of integrated change management.

Aware of key decisions related to feedback, decisions, and action plans: During this phase, make-or-break decisions include: designing participative feedback sessions with interpretation of data, priority setting, action derivations, and client system ownership of change. Desired goals are projected and the schedule, role responsibilities, and performance criteria are set during this phase. The consultation team needs to involve the client and sponsor in the critical decisions of this phase to determine what intervention is appropriate, what resources are required for the change, and what process is needed for goal setting, goal content, feasibility-testing of goals, and critical path decisions for successful outcomes during the change application.

Designs and coordinates intervention designs: The consultation team is involved in the design of appropriate interventions, linking the client, sponsor, and client system. As change facilitators they provide knowledge, skill, and experience, and a repertoire of change interventions including team building, conflict resolution, executive planning conferences, and the facilitation of open communication. Using skills of process consultation, this resource team provides third-party assistance to the client in managing conflict and agreements, facilitating awareness of hidden agendas, confronting collusive behavior, introducing "undiscussables" into an open agenda, clarifying roles and goals, facilitating meeting summaries and time checks, and using stop sessions in meetings to assess the process of how people are working together.

Facilitates client feedback with interpretive inquiry: The consultation team working with the client prepares data packages for understanding, gains client ownership for the action, and designs feedback sessions involving the client and the client system in data interpretation for decisions and action. Training client and internal coordinators in the facilitation of feedback helps create a supportive culture of openness and trust for feedback activities. This training prepares the client system to conduct meaningful feedback sessions, to facilitate critical and thoughtful questions, and to invite individual and group participation. Perceptive feedback identifies trends, issues, or patterns seen in the data, with the client system identifying possible action priorities. Evaluation summaries of the feedback session also provide data for the consultation group with new ideas from the participants on how to improve future team sessions.

Provides planning resources: The change consultation team works with the client system to determine who needs to be involved in action planning, and facilitates different types of meetings and agendas for information dissemination and planning, including action where challenge is known, action where challenge is unknown, orientation briefing, and other meeting designs.

Planning resources must be considered at the macro and microunit levels. Planning competence and the ability to involve the appropriate people in the process increases focus commitment to change. Training and linking people is part of action teaming. The capacity to analyze the change dynamics in terms of consequences within a particular economic, social, and political context is crucial to effective planning.

Designs and facilitates futuring activities: Futuring is a strategic competence for this phase. Clients admit they often know what they "don't want" but are not certain what they do want. The facilitation of futuring toward desired goals is helpful. Skills include knowing the difference between planning and futuring, being knowledgeable of where goals come from in the organization, collecting data and client input prior to designing futuring scenarios, facilitating futuring activities with client system ownership of the goals, priority setting, and evaluating of preferred futures. Additional methods might focus on reviewing outcomes, using force-field charting to analyze supports and blockages, facilitating strategic action to overcome blockage, and strengthening supporting forces to reach preferred futures.

Facilitates client using stepwise action: Facilitating next steps of action and using a stepwise action process for change on an improvement continuum is helpful for clients in reviewing progress steps to achieve the desired results. Clients and organizational team members need to own the results at each step. The facilitator assists in the early identification of goals and actions and what each step will look like. Feedback monitoring is used during the application phase to change the action as necessary based on new data collected.

Supports client system ownership and accountability: Client and sponsor accountability is essential to a successful outcome. The facilitation of progress milestones for the application phase, communicating the change effectively through visual charts and other media, specifying goals, roles, and next steps of action, and allocation of the necessary organizational resources helps the client, sponsor, organizational members to take ownership and responsibility, and involves people throughout the system in managing change.

Establishes client-performance criteria: The consultation team and client system must follow through with action and assigned responsibilities. The client, sponsor, and representative organization members provide input to determine what success will look like. Performance criteria and a conceptual framework for measuring and monitoring action are a part of this phase.

Competencies for Phase 5: Applications and Results Measurement

This phase puts data and decisions into action. The consultation team must be aware of needs for intervention and facilitation during implementation of directed change. Measurement of results should be made at both a directed and a nondirected level. Integrated change is an ongoing challenge. To ensure quality interventions, successful action should be based on data collected. The application and results measurement phase also continue to monitor nondirected change such as resistance and change blockages, as well as new ideas, innovations, and emerging issues from within and outside the organization. During the change application this monitoring process collects feedback for guiding new decisions and action in allocating additional resources, involving specific groups, learning from the change, and confronting challenges.

During this phase, a process must be developed to review change integration, possible "disconnects," and continuity patterns. Anticipating and planning for change continuity helps ensure continuous improvement in matching appropriate resources to emerging and existing need, and developing a supportive environment for effective action.

Supports training and development: Based on validated needs, the consultation team initiates activities and processes to educate and train members of the client system, and design applications to support change management. Workshops in data collection, strategic planning, performance measurements, and teamwork may be needed. Technical and process consultation is provided to confront collusive action and to open up the communication process. For example, there may be a need for the consultation team to recognize and discuss concerns and fears to develop greater openness and acceptance of the change management process.

Facilitates results measurement, feedback, and planning for new action: Awareness of models of measurement provides design concepts for methods, sources, and criteria for performance measurement. With input from the client, and sponsor, the consultation team can assist the client system in proposing appropriate measurement, tools, and a feedback system for monitoring progress, guiding feedback for new action, and documenting results for continuous progress and improvement in managing directed and nondirected change in an integrated way.

Feedback is used as a positive force for change continuity. The client, and client system are trained in evaluation, modifying action based on new direction and learning, and linking business results to individual, group, and organizational performance goals. People throughout the system are involved in the interpretation of the feedback, action planning, and monitoring of results.

Competencies for Phase 6: Continuity and Renewal

The recognition of change as a continuous, and often contradictory process creates a need for continuity and renewal as a part of change management. This involves not only the transfer of competencies to the client system but also rewards recognition and celebration of success. The concept of organizational renewal requires an ongoing confrontation of real issues to appropriately respond to situations that impact customers, employees, and the organization. These can be related to competitive threat, as well as the social, political and economic issues of nations, communities, and organizations.

An important competency for the change consultation team is an awareness of the need to design a plan that provides continuity and support for integrated change management. A review of what has been learned, and events for expanding role competencies are a part of this phase. The plan for diminishing support from the facilitating system is based on the transfer of competencies to the client system. The consultation team and the client should openly explore the feelings of wanting to continue as a team and the need to create linkage for periodic follow-up and new projects.

Evaluates the client and consultation team relationship: The facilitators, client, and sponsor evaluate their working relationship and opportunities for expanding each person's professional development. Assessment of their action roles, responsibility, and interaction focuses on new ways to improve these relationships.

Professional development action planning includes a review of knowledge, role competencies, career-development goals, and functional and process role competence. A part of this development is a reflection upon the ethics of the professional practices, a consideration of role responsibility of the outside resource in not creating dependency, and the role of the client, internal facilitators, and the sponsor for accountability in change management.

Completes contract and results measurement: The client and consultation team assess the level of consultation and set targets for continuous renewal and development. They track results measurements and facilitate the successful use of resources within the organization to effectively accomplish goals and transfer change management competencies. Renewal diagnosis includes measuring the continuous improvement and recycling the data collected with periodic audits for measurement, feedback, and action.

ACTION ROLES FOR CHANGE FACILITATORS

Change management provides a continuum of process and technical action roles (Lippitt, Lippitt, Chakiris, Pirsein 1978) to match the change situation, the specific phase, and the long-term results desired by the client system to build the capacity for managing change and achieving both short and long-term goals. Change facilitators choose action roles based on the task orientation, the process desired, and the integration of directed and nondirected activities. Some dimensions of these action roles are illustrated in Figure 12.2.

FIGURE 12.2 Action Roles.

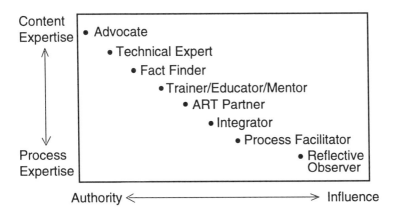

Action roles can be assessed in terms of the skill competence, frequency, and impact of the role in the outcome and the perception of the role by the key players and the client systems. Role situation, consultation phase, impact, performance level, and interest in expanding the role repertoire are some factors that may affect role choices for the consultation team.

As outlined in previous chapters, the basic roles are advocate, technical expert, fact finder or diagnostic expert, trainer educator/mentor, ART partner, integrator, process facilitator, and reflective observer.

Role-Selection Criteria

Decisions on which roles are appropriate are determined by the nature of the client, the development of the client system in current teaming and training support, the type of goals desired, the cultural norms, and the consultation relationships among client, sponsors, and facilitator. Past consultation experience in the system, the outcome of that consultation in relation to long-term goals, the professional competence of the organization, and the key positions of the client, sponsor, and others within the system also influence current roles.

The growth stage of the organization may affect the selection of roles. For example, is this a start-up, a venture project, a new function, such as self-directed work teams, or a quality initiative? What are the priorities of the organization given its challenges, organizational effectiveness, and performance dynamics? To what degree do people currently work together effectively across the organization?

The consultation team influences the client system through competence, trust, acceptance, and action roles. Each role can be appropriate for a specific situation at a particular time. The target is role flexibility in choosing the appropriate roles in relation to context, needs, and objectives. Specific dilemmas may occur if too much emphasis is placed on any particular role. Change-management competencies demand coordinated action roles.

Role Competence

The consultation team must be aware of the impact of different action roles. In what situation did they use particular roles? In what phase of the consultation process did this occur? What impact did the role behavior have? How do they view their competence in performing this role? Are there areas for improvement? Would other roles have been more relevant for a specific situation?

With one or more colleagues, consultation team members can look back at this analysis and identify key situations that show effectiveness or cause concern. They may wish to examine criteria for role choice, and discuss with a colleagues role experiences and the areas they would most like to improve. Managers can use the following exercise to assess role competence and target areas for individual performance improvement.

Directions: Select the action role you want to increase or decrease for greater impact. Write down one or two steps of action you would like to take to improve the role selected. Assess your development goals in the following four areas:

Adaptability: How easily do you adapt to each role? Do all action roles fit your self-image and style? With what action roles are you most comfortable? Which make you uncomfortable? Are new action roles needed to increase your flexibility in change management?

Performance: How frequently do you perform each role? How often are you called upon to function in a specific role? What action roles do you use with high frequency? Are there action roles you would like to use with more or less frequency? What new action roles are needed for performance in change management?

Results: When you function in each role, what results or impact do you have? Are there some action roles that have a strong and favorable impact? Are there action roles you want to increase or decrease to improve results?

Skills: How skilled are you in performing each action role? What action role do you want to perform less? What action role do you want to develop and use more? What skill development is needed to develop specific action roles?

Specific Action Roles

The Advocate:

- Actively supports what is perceived as the "best practice"
- Exerts intentional influence upon the client situation to use a high-level design and appropriate methods and techniques
- Provides focus and direction
- Proposes guidelines, persuades, and advises client on appropriate action in response to need
- Performs an authoritative role to achieve change outcome
- Provides measurement expertise for recognized performance

criteria such as Deming, Baldridge, organizational effectiveness, quality of work life, human resource and customer audits

Role challenge: Advocacy is a position of authority. Because the client may lack experience or insight in a specific situation, change facilitators may be pulled into the role of telling the client what to do or aggressively seeking to influence client decisions and actions. Long term, this may not be in the best interest of the client. This role can create dependency with the client always expecting to receive the answers from expert resource professionals. The role also may reduce ownership of the change on the part of the client and client system may not learn to solve their own problems, and meet the challenges of ongoing changes. An appropriate balance of authority and influence is the major challenge in this role.

The Technical Expert:

- Brings specialized knowledge and experience to the client system in technical and process areas
- Is recognized as a subject-matter expert, is aware of industry trends, best practices, and has an diverse experience base
- Facilitates input for policy-level decisions and organizational practices
- Designs the initial action to respond to the client need or opportunity
- Can articulate how strategic change or action will achieve short- and long-term goals of the organization
- Identifies core competencies for change management practices and career development

Role challenge: This role, like the advocate role, is performed by experts of technical and process specialization. These resources may be known for their knowledge, experience, and expertise. Early in the consultation process, this expertise may be appropriate, but later this role needs to shift to other roles that act more as a catalyst for client system development. The caution with an expert role is that the client does not learn to manage change and there is a underdevelopment to build capacity in the system to meet future challenges. It is also difficult for the change facilitator to get out of the expectations of this role. There also may be some concerns about imposing prescriptive answers and solutions in complex organizational systems. The challenge is to link this expertise with internal capability and to combine these resources for change improvement with continuity in the transfer of competencies.

The Fact Finder:

- Designs the data-collection approach for diagnosis and analysis of the need and/or opportunity
- Provides facilitation experience in the use of ART with client system involvement in data gathering and feedback interpretation for action derivations
- Uses both directed and nondirected change elements to research these
- Facilitates specific inquiry questions
- Provides third-party listening capacity to learn and respond to opposing views
- Acts as a trained observer and can provide helpful feedback on group dynamics in meetings and project-team effectiveness
- Has high-level of competence in choosing appropriate diagnostic methods for client situation and need
- Shows overall awareness of client business dynamics and goals
- Can analyze, prioritize, and present data with clarity

Role challenge: In this role, there must be a balance between technical and process competencies. The change facilitator provides expert knowledge of change dynamics, competence in how to collect and use data, and information on how to involve people to gain interpretation and decisions for action. The expertise of the change facilitator recognizes resistance as a force and appreciates the need to collect data in the least disruptive manner. The change facilitator performs process advocacy when recommending methods and process for data collection, feedback, interpretation, and collaborative inquiry for data-based integrated change.

The consultation team uses the trainer and education role to develop fact-finding skills of the client, sponsor, and client system. The process of contracting with the client about the use of the information, the design for appropriate feedback, and specific needs for confidentiality are also part of the challenge of this role.

The trainer/educator or mentor:

- Facilitates and supports client system learning for understanding the change process
- Is knowledgeable in how people learn and can educate clients
- Facilitates knowledge of how to transfer change technology through learning hierarchy of instructional design competence
- Trains individuals and groups in change management skills

- Designs with client a strategy for educating sponsors in change process
- Designs specific change events with client such as executive conferences, training sessions, and group discussions

Role challenge: The trainer and educator role helps bring process and technical competence to the organization. This role supports organizational learning and manages the change process through client involvement and competence-development events for the client system. The challenge for achieving long-term results is that training and educating require an investment in time and resources. Learning technology demands awareness of development patterns and expertise in design with a balance of both content and process. Another challenge is integrating training and education with other operational needs and activities for change management.

The ART Partner:

- Designs the architecture with temporary or matrix structure for ART
- Facilitates client system perception of critical challenges
- Facilitates mutual testing of assumptions about what can and cannot be controlled in the process
- Facilitates perception of confidence level in ordering of client challenge priorities
- Facilitates decisions that need to be made, and closes information gaps for achieving desired action

Role Challenge: This role also blends the competence of both process and technical expertise. The change facilitator collaborates with action research teams to solve problems, and shares skills and techniques to measure change. The challenge is to clarify who is responsible for a decision, when to confront an issue appropriately, and how to involve the client and key sponsors to increase ownership, and reduce conflicts around approaches, outcomes, timing, investment, and other areas.

The Integrator:

- Involves client, sponsor, and client system in all phases of consultation
- Facilitates linkage to integrate directive and nondirected change
- Helps client to identify resources of internal and external environment

- Locates specific information and assists client system in linking to needed resources
- Is culturally sensitive to linkage across continents or borders
- Provides skills for developing networking and alliance-building capacity throughout the system
- Facilitates the identification of alternatives and consequence evaluation
- Facilitates client system in developing a strategy for continuous improvement and change integration

Role challenge: In this role, teaming as well as the capacity to find and link resources is an important orientation. Leadership emerges on both an informal and formal level. People who are trusted by others in the organization become candidates for feedback-session leaders. Change facilitators both within the client system and from the outside should be comfortable supporting others and letting the client gain recognition for success in change management. The challenge is to anticipate natural alliances, find known and unknown resources available to the organization, and to determine and assess the culture of the organization related to the rewards and support for linkage and collaborative inquiry.

The Process Facilitator:

- Develops client system capacity to observe change dynamics while raising issues during discussion and feedback
- Brings systems perspective for integrating directed and nondirected change
- Facilitates change ownership through appropriate process of client system involvement during data collection, feedback, decisions, and action
- Confronts collusive or closed behavior, and groupthink, to improve reality-based communication

Role challenge: The role competence of process facilitation is a challenge for technical resource people. It is important to be aware of different approaches to change including rational/behavioral, systems, cultural interpretive, and critical assumptions about process and outcomes. Change management requires some agreements about process. The process action role facilitates understanding and communication for effective consultation. Often, technical experts team with a process specialist in delivering services to the client. In this role, the consultation team is more comfortable in confronting clients who are avoiding issues. This role is also helpful in clarifying the role responsibility of the client through the change process. One of the challenges is the need to train clients in the practice of process consultation and to legitimize internal resources for performing the process facilitator role.

The Reflective Observer:

- Facilitates reflective questions to help people look at the situation from different perspectives

- Anticipates change impact legitimizing resistance as a creative force for gaining acceptance

- Facilitates client sensitivity with diplomacy, flexibility, and patience during the change process

- Reflects client needs, using appropriate timing, pacing, and sequence for change action

- Remains descriptive rather than prescriptive

- Helps client to view the need to balance change with stability

Role challenge: This reflective process role resource facilitates through nonthreatening process questions to clarify issues of client responsibility for decisions. In this role the facilitator remains neutral, suspending judgment, and informing the group when giving "personal" beliefs or opinions. The challenges are in how long to wait for the client and the sponsor to make decisions, the amount of tolerance the facilitator has for living with the unknown or ambiguity at the moment, and the intuition and experience to know when to confront issues, and when to merely observe. The change facilitator competent in this role has the capacity to ask effective questions and design interventions to bring about effective resolutions to conflict and differences of perspectives. This role brings both objectivity and a realistic "mirror" to the client system.

ASSESSMENT OF CHANGE MANAGEMENT COMPETENCIES IN PRACTICE

The following self-assessment instrument (see Tables 12.1 - 12.6), provides an overview of key questions pertaining to each phase of the change consultation process. Change facilitators, managers, consultation teams, and staff professionals can use this as a check list and a learning tool for change management.

Table 12.1 Need and Opportunity in Change Initiative.

	Strongly Agree	Agree	Disagree	Strongly Disagree
Phase I: Need and Opportunity in Change Initiative				
Initial Need Validation				
Objectivity is perceived by all parties.	1	2	3	4
Reasons why client came to resource person are known.	1	2	3	4
Facilitator's competence is legitimatized with the client.	1	2	3	4
Data was collected prior to contracting phase.	1	2	3	4
Values - Norms have been established for:				
a. openness	1	2	3	4
b. confrontation	1	2	3	4
c. commitment	1	2	3	4
d. cultural sensitivity	1	2	3	4
Resource is client sensitive but does not agree to unknowns.	1	2	3	4
Sponsor is known and committed to change initiative.	1	2	3	4
Hidden agendas are shared.	1	2	3	4
Expectations				
Client and resource facilitator expectations are clear.	1	2	3	4
Unrealistic expectations are not a problem.	1	2	3	4
Expectations are within defined parameters.	1	2	3	4
Goals are appropriate for available resources.	1	2	3	4
Relationship Interdependency				
Action is voluntary.	1	2	3	4
The relationship is perceived as temporary by all parties.	1	2	3	4
Counterdependency is not an issue.	1	2	3	4
Relationship will not create dependency for either party.	1	2	3	4
Power and Authority				
Power is appropriately shared.	1	2	3	4
Source of power of change has been clarified.	1	2	3	4
Empowerment is observed in consultation relationship.	1	2	3	4
Sponsor is appropriately involved in the start-up.	1	2	3	4
Readiness and Commitment				
Assessment of client system readiness is positive.	1	2	3	4
Action consequences have been probed adequately.	1	2	3	4
Examination of client concerns have been reviewed.	1	2	3	4
Client is ready to move from present to the future.	1	2	3	4
Self Analysis and Motivation				
Self-searching took place prior to getting involved.	1	2	3	4
Project success motivation has been reflected upon.	1	2	3	4
Self-motivation is mutually shared.	1	2	3	4
Client and facilitator are aware of mutual career goals.	1	2	3	4

Circle One

Table 12.2 Agreements: Establishing Working Relationships.

	Strongly Agree	Agree	Disagree	Strongly Disagree
Reward				
Rewards in situation are clearly recognized.	1	2	3	4
Nature of rewards are discussed and agreed upon.	1	2	3	4
Rewards that accrue to client have been discussed.	1	2	3	4
All parties share information about rewards.	1	2	3	4
Performance Measurement Criteria				
Proper attention is being paid to measuring results.	1	2	3	4
Performance objectives have been established.	1	2	3	4
External resources are being used to measure progress.	1	2	3	4
There is an appropriate balance of quantitative and qualitative measurement.	1	2	3	4
Time Perspective				
There is a realistic time span for reaching each goal.	1	2	3	4
Image of potentiality process is used for goal setting.	1	2	3	4
Unrealistic time expectations are confronted.	1	2	3	4
Budget restraints affecting outcome are removed.	1	2	3	4
Commitment and Readiness				
Effectiveness of relationship is frequently examined.	1	2	3	4
Action consequences are being probed adequately.	1	2	3	4
Client concerns are reviewed regularly.	1	2	3	4
Readiness exists to move from present to future.	1	2	3	4
Involvement				
Who to involve has been adequately addressed.	1	2	3	4
Involvement encourages risk-taking initiative.	1	2	3	4
Employees affected by the change are involved.	1	2	3	4
Training prepares employees for involvement.	1	2	3	4
Transfer of Technology to Client				
Training will take place for client to internalize change.	1	2	3	4
Change-management skills shared with client system.	1	2	3	4
Intervention design decisions are client-based.	1	2	3	4
Client is comfortable with change management design.	1	2	3	4

Table 12.3 Data Collection and Analysis.

	Strongly Agree	Agree	Disagree	Strongly Disagree
Causal Assumptions				
Single cause mindset has been challenged.	1	2	3	4
Perspectives on problem reasons have been expanded.	1	2	3	4
Client as part of the cause or problem is known.	1	2	3	4
Causal factors are adequately examined.	1	2	3	4
Advocacy				
Consequence of taking expert role is known to facilitator.	1	2	3	4
Facilitator balances advocacy and process roles.	1	2	3	4
Facilitator is aware of advocacy lessening objectivity.	1	2	3	4
Facilitator advocacy is preventing client ownership.	1	2	3	4
Data Collection Objectives				
Rationale and purpose for data is known.	1	2	3	4
Futuring is used to help the client identify goals.	1	2	3	4
The client is unclear about desired outcomes.	1	2	3	4
Client and sponsor agree on data collecting objectives.	1	2	3	4
Action Research Teaming				
Client is committed to employee involvement.	1	2	3	4
Data collection involves client system.	1	2	3	4
Training for feedback and action planning is provided.	1	2	3	4
Client participation in feedback sessions is planned.	1	2	3	4
Time Perspective				
There is a realistic time span for reaching each goal.	1	2	3	4
Image of potentiality process is used for goal setting.	1	2	3	4
Unrealistic time expectations are confronted.	1	2	3	4
Budget restraints affecting outcome are removed.	1	2	3	4
Confrontation				
A process is used to "open up" relevant data.	1	2	3	4
Critical issues are raised without arousing defensiveness.	1	2	3	4
Concerns are sufficiently raised.	1	2	3	4
Confrontation is accepted without becoming defensive.	1	2	3	4
Objectivity				
The facilitating system is objective.	1	2	3	4
Outside resources are available to validate objectivity.	1	2	3	4
Assumptions are examined regularly.	1	2	3	4
There are some concerns about personal biases.	1	2	3	4
Openness and Access				
The facilitating system has access to the needed data.	1	2	3	4
The client system is responsive to inquiry questions.	1	2	3	4
People are not holding back.	1	2	3	4
A sense of confidentiality is encouraging openness.	1	2	3	4

Circle One

Table 12.4 Feedback, Decisions, and Action Planning.

	Strongly Agree	Agree	Disagree	Strongly Disagree
Process Intervention				
Relationship dynamics are assessed periodically.	1	2	3	4
"Stop sessions" are used for process improvement.	1	2	3	4
Attention is given to improving ineffective work patterns.	1	2	3	4
Feedback is used to continuously improve relationship.	1	2	3	4
Competitive Resourcing				
Appropriate resources are selected for action.	1	2	3	4
Alternative resources are considered.	1	2	3	4
Increase or decrease in facilitator services is determined.	1	2	3	4
Allocation of resources is regularly assessed.	1	2	3	4
Critical Path				
There is a process to discuss "keeping on track."	1	2	3	4
Client has a contingency plan.	1	2	3	4
Alternative paths are explored.	1	2	3	4
Sufficient progress checkpoints are provided.	1	2	3	4
Process of Goal Setting Process				
There are effective methods to establish goals.	1	2	3	4
Lack of appropriate involvement is confronted.	1	2	3	4
Client is choosing action goals.	1	2	3	4
Client performance criteria for measurement is established.	1	2	3	4
Goal Content Advocacy				
Goal and value linkage is reviewed by client and facilitator.	1	2	3	4
Facilitator is comfortable in critiquing client goals.	1	2	3	4
Questions of feasibility are not imposing goal content.	1	2	3	4
Consequences are being adequately assessed.	1	2	3	4
Feasibility Testing				
A process for consequences analysis has been used.	1	2	3	4
Feasibility doubts are openly discussed.	1	2	3	4
Questions about resource adequacy are raised.	1	2	3	4
Consequence is looked at without inhibiting risk-taking.	1	2	3	4
Collaborative Inquiry				
The client system is involved in data interpretation.	1	2	3	4
The facilitator asks interpretative questions.	1	2	3	4
The client identifies action derivations.	1	2	3	4
A repertoire of change interventions are explored.	1	2	3	4
Alternative Exploration				
People are not making premature closing on one option.	1	2	3	4
There is a pressure to agree to common goals.	1	2	3	4
There is a healthy questioning of ideas.	1	2	3	4
New alternatives are regularly explored.	1	2	3	4

Circle One

Table 12.5 Applications and Results Measurement.

	Strongly Agree	Agree	Disagree	Strongly Disagree
Performance Criteria				
Attention is paid to monitoring results measurement.	1	2	3	4
Performance-based objectives is established.	1	2	3	4
External resources are used to measure progress.	1	2	3	4
Both quantitative and qualitative measurements are used.	1	2	3	4
Involvement				
Who to involve has been adequately addressed.	1	2	3	4
Involvement has encouraged risk-taking initiative.	1	2	3	4
People affected by the change are involved.	1	2	3	4
Training is provided for employee involvement.	1	2	3	4
Consultation Technology Transfer to Client				
Training is taking place for client to internalize change.	1	2	3	4
Change-consultation skills are being shared with client.	1	2	3	4
Intervention design decisions are discussed with client.	1	2	3	4
Client is comfortable with application design.	1	2	3	4
Confrontation				
A process is used to "open up" relevant data.	1	2	3	4
Critical issues are raised without arousing defensiveness.	1	2	3	4
Concerns are sufficiently raised.	1	2	3	4
Confrontation is accepted without becoming defensive.	1	2	3	4
Process Intervention				
There is a process to assess dynamics of the relationship.	1	2	3	4
"Stop sessions" are used to improve process.	1	2	3	4
Attention is given to improving ineffective work patterns.	1	2	3	4
Feedback is used to plan for new action.	1	2	3	4
Alternative Exploration				
People are not making premature closing on one option.	1	2	3	4
There is a pressure to agree to common goals.	1	2	3	4
There is healthy questioning of ideas.	1	2	3	4
New alternatives are regularly explored.	1	2	3	4
Resources				
Appropriate resources are selected to work on issue.	1	2	3	4
Resources are adequate to problem solve.	1	2	3	4
Increases or decreases in resources are questioned.	1	2	3	4
Performance of resource is regularly assessed.	1	2	3	4
Critical Path				
There is a process to "keep on track."	1	2	3	4
The client has a plan that provides for contingencies.	1	2	3	4
Alternative paths are explored.	1	2	3	4
Milestones are celebrated.	1	2	3	4

Circle One

Table 12.6 Continuity and Renewal.

	Strongly Agree	Agree	Disagree	Strongly Disagree
Performance Measurement Criteria				
Attention is given to monitoring results measurement.	1	2	3	4
Performance measurement has been established.	1	2	3	4
External resources are used to measure progress.	1	2	3	4
Both quantitative and qualitative measurement exists.	1	2	3	4
Consultation Technology Transfer to Client				
Client has internalized the change competence.	1	2	3	4
Consultation skills are practiced by client system.	1	2	3	4
The client has acquired the skills of change management.	1	2	3	4
A process is in place for periodic skills assessment.	1	2	3	4
Evaluating the Client and Facilitator Relationship				
Feedback is elicited for client and facilitator relationship.	1	2	3	4
Action is taken to continuously improve relationship.	1	2	3	4
Action roles are assessed.	1	2	3	4
Client is comfortable with relationship.	1	2	3	4
Professional Development Plan				
Team members have developed a professional development action plan.	1	2	3	4
Action is planned for exchange of practices to continue role competency learning.	1	2	3	4
Effective confronting skills are used for ongoing renewal.	1	2	3	4
Career development competence is being applied.	1	2	3	4
Continuity Planning				
Options for support continuity are discussed.	1	2	3	4
Realistic timeframe for continuity is planned.	1	2	3	4
Transition actions are developed to sustain change.	1	2	3	4
Ethical questions of dependency are raised.	1	2	3	4
Contract Completion				
Project completion or beginning anew is discussed.	1	2	3	4
Questions of completion are asked.	1	2	3	4
Facilitator plans to encourage without giving direct support.	1	2	3	4
Feelings about wanting to continue are confronted.	1	2	3	4

Assessment of Change Competencies In Practice, adapted from *Consulting Process in Action Skills Development Kit*. "Looking at Dilemmas of the Phases" by Gordon L. Lippitt, Ronald Lippitt, B.J. Chakiris and Robert W. Pirsein. 1978. B.J. Chakiris Corporation.

13

Exchange of Practices

One of the greatest challenges of change management is encouraging organizations to open up and look at themselves in a realistic way. This requires a recognition of change as a continuous, sometimes contradictory process interpreted by organization members and facilitated through collaborative inquiry and teamwork. Part of this challenge is helping the organization to legitimize information sharing as integral to individual, group, and organizational development. People need to talk together about their successes and failures, to transfer knowledge and benefit from the experience of others in integrating directed and nondirected change processes. For example, to build core competencies, Prahalad and Hamel (1990) suggest bringing "competence carriers" across the organization together to share ideas.

The rich insights and innovations of creative professionals and outstanding managers and leaders may go unnoticed if their achievements are not made visible and validated or adapted by others. Some experienced and talented managers and senior practitioners may feel burnout and boredom within the sometimes rigid routines of traditional organizational structure and procedures, which may not always recognize or encourage new or innovative practices. For beginning professionals full of energy and optimism, the challenge is making up for limited experience on the firing line and a lack of seasoned insight and knowledge that only years of practice can bring.

An exchange of practices, is a designed session in which two or more colleagues, managers, or a community of professionals discuss and analyze a variety of factors related to consultation and change management including applications, knowledge, and feelings. This supportive learning group helps professionals to integrate their experience, applications, and concerns. When members of these groups listen, discuss, critique, analyze, and brainstorm ideas, they help one another to learn about innovative practices and to develop new organizational competencies for facilitating change management.

While professionals may at times reflect on past practices and the knowledge that they have gained, Schon (1983) suggests "reflection-in-action," an inquiry that occurs in the present while thoughtful action can still make a difference in the outcome. This individual process can be expanded and enriched through an exchange of professional practices. Those who are involved in a challenging project or intervention can benefit from the knowledge, experience, and skills of other organization members and outside resources in a process of collective learning related to the change process.

The work of Ronald Lippitt and Gordon Lippitt and others introduced the idea of professional development through various techniques of exchange of practices. Ronald Lippitt (1966) believed that this could help remedy the lack of documentation about creative new practices. He developed professional action-learning groups in which formal or informal information could be exchanged regarding case applications. This allows assessment and learning through peer feedback and open sessions for critique, discussion, and assessment. The model also includes practicum designs for university graduate schools, business organizations, and nonprofit and community groups.

Within an organization, the exchange of practices may take place in a specific unit, among different units, with an outside resource, or between various organizations within an association, alliance, or symposium. Exchanges may also occur within learning institutions and universities and in internships and practicums. These interactions provide knowledge, legitimize assumptions and feelings, and encourage the continuous improvement of consultation competencies and interventions for change management. Participants discuss the types of practices that are being used as well as specific designs and interventions. Possible traps or dilemmas are also identified and explored so that people can learn how difficulties are being overcome and also develop the skills needed to adapt new practices.

KEY COMPONENTS AND OUTCOMES

Competencies discussed in the exchange sessions might relate to developing strategies to market internal consultation, designing, and evaluating interventions, exchanging information, and creating a resource support network. Some needs and concerns could be satisfied in a phone consultation with colleagues; others require more extensive interaction and benefit from collective analysis in exchange of practices sessions.

Develop a Marketing Strategy

Developing a marketing strategy for internal consultation services is an area that is often underdeveloped in organizations. Staff professionals and management resources try to connect their services to client needs and develop new services to meet the growing demands of internal and external customers. In exchange of practices, managers, resource professionals, and change facilitators can brainstorm ideas to help them to develop visibility and attract internal or external clients for the change management process.

Role-playing client responses to proposals may be a basis for revision and improvement of the proposal to better meet the needs and expectations of a current or potential client. Participants may help one another in documenting strategies for budget development and presentation. Collective experience and insight can also help to establish the appropriate mix of educational and marketing ingredients in a proposal to a specific unit.

Improve Interventions

Interventions are critical at each stage of the consultation process from the initial need and opportunity in initiative to the completion stage of continuity and renewal. The exchange of practice session allows exploration and brainstorming of alternative intervention ideas with colleagues before selecting a strategy. An exchange might focus on developing a design for feedback from clients and prospective clients or recontracting with the client around shifting needs. Examining the results, resource alignment, consultation technology, and context can increase understanding and improve specific consultation competencies in strategic change management interventions.

Exchange Information

These sessions are also an opportunity for documenting and exchanging training designs, successful exercises, and consultation procedures. Trading reprints, copies of articles, and other resources may be included in the session. Participants might review and discuss abstracts from professional journals, research studies, and other specialized publications on current issues. Participating in regular sessions to share knowledge and discuss new projects encourages more effective resource utilization and involves managers and other professionals in collective learning for change management.

Create Support Networks

One of the most important outcomes of an exchange of practices is the development of a network of professional resources. Participants may create a directory listing network members with specific areas of expertise and interest. They may establish dyad or triad support relationships for brainstorming, testing ideas, and critiquing alternative approaches to change management. By "contracting" with a facilitator or mentor, an individual or group can receive assistance on papers, proposals, action recommendations, and intervention designs with some reciprocal agreement or shared risk formula for stipend payoff. The group can create strategies for developing and maintaining a local colleague team and support clusters in their area. This network can also draw on the resources of graduate programs and other professional development opportunities.

GUIDELINES FOR EXCHANGE OF PRACTICES

An exchange session does not just happen when a group of managers or staff professionals get together to talk about their work. This learning process must be carefully designed and supported within the organizational culture as a part of change management. These are the general guidelines for the effective exchange of practices:

- Take time to stop and assess practices
- Legitimize sharing
- Use available resources
- Develop a design or structure for exchange

Take Time to Stop and Assess Practices

"We must be able to have some sort of space in which thought can slow down and we can all look at it" (Bohm and Edwards 1991). In their plea for a changed consciousness that recognizes the impact of individual and collective thought, Bohm and Edwards call for a shared dialogue and a more active process of thinking about our assumptions, decisions, and actions. An exchange of practices offers an opportunity for a shared dialogue about the way we think as professionals and interact as members of organizations.

In the deadlines and daily crises of organizational life, it is important to take some time together to reflect and reevaluate individual, group, and organizational practices. This interactive communication can help build quality change consultation and transfer competencies for change management. The reporting of "war stories" related to success and failure in real consultation situations can help professional practitioners and managers to learn from actual experiences and make more realistic and competent change interventions in their unit or organization.

Some of the questions that might be used to begin this discussion relate to the overall need for change and development in relation to individual, group, and organizational objectives:

- How do units work together?
- How do we serve one another?
- How can we serve our customers better?
- Where are the gaps in our practices?
- How do we think about what we do?

This sharing process also clarifies change management practices, and decisions and the variety of techniques and tools being used in different units or organizations. Analyzing some of the major barriers related to improving quality, productivity, and service can lead to exploration and assistance in how to overcome blockages and meet the challenges of integrating directed and nondirected change through innovative interventions. This is an opportunity to test individual and group assumptions and examine how these thoughts can affect the diagnosis of a situation. Feedback and ideas from others help to determine if a particular intervention or directed change is realistic and appropriate. Participants explore assumptions that may be influencing the situation, identify the issues, evaluate alternative options, and recognize gaps and developmental needs.

Assessing different change-consultation styles can help others visualize a variety of process and technical roles and reflect on the boundaries of responsibility and interaction in change management. Taking the time to stop and assess practices can be a positive individual and group development experience. Participating in this peer support system can increase competence and commitment through a continuing team-learning process.

Legitimize Sharing

The power relationships and structures within organizations do not encourage a cooperative team culture. In a competitive environment, individuals and groups may withhold information in order to maintain a position of control and advantage in a changing environment. There is often a fear of making mistakes and admitting failure. In some cases there may even be a penalty or implied weakness in asking for help. Collective remembering and forgetting (Middleton and Edwards 1990) help to reinforce and constitute the dominant organizational culture. It is not always easy to suddenly open up an organization and say that it is now alright to share and talk about specific practices, challenges, and sensitive issues that have not been openly discussed in the past.

The need to show evidence of effective performance to superiors and to outperform other peers can be strong. Without an effective facilitator, exchange of practice sessions can become elaborate "brag" sessions with little opportunity for the assessment of individual and group developmental areas. The goals for learning, critique, and realistic discussion must be clear from the beginning. Participants should be encouraged to share failures as well as successes.

One way to facilitate sharing and teamwork in the exchange of practices is to have "shadow" consultation groups who can develop trust and cooperation to help one another through complex change processes and difficult interventions. For example, one person or a small group of people might serve as an unofficial resource and sounding board for a colleague. This can be a reciprocal role that helps all sides to learn together in a supportive relationship that encourages open communication and integrated change.

Part of this relationship is establishing mutual trust and respecting confidentiality. This is both an individual attitude and a cultural value related to listening and respecting each person's experience and values. The early studies of Lippitt (Lewin, Lippitt, and White 1939) document six points that characterize a democratic organization that encourages free expression and group participation:

- *Open-mindedness,* freedom of speech, listening receptively to the point of view of the other person, sharing in the other person's goals and ideas;
- *Self-acceptance* and self-confidence based on achievement that reflects pride and humility simultaneously;
- *Realism* in respect for the facts and a continuous reorientation to the present and to the possible reality of the future;
- *Freedom* from status-mindedness in a spirit of equality without loss of dignity or authority;
- *Fairness* or equality of rights and opportunities; and
- *Simple friendliness* and goodwill toward others.

These are ethical and practical obligations that support a more effective and cooperative organization in the process of continuous collective learning and development. They provide some general guidelines for exchange of practices sessions based on trust, respect, and openness in facilitating team learning for effective change management.

Use Available Resources

Maximizing resources is a stated goal of many organizations, yet much of the knowledge, experience, and insight of individual organization members and an extended client system is not used. For example, a valued supplier or a long-term customer may have substantial information that can lead to improved practices and interventions. An internal professional could present a self-assessment learning instrument, a role-play exercise, or a provocative training video that triggers new understanding and application. A manager may have experience and insight that can help other managers integrate change and improve teamwork.

The following questions can be useful in identifying and integrating internal and external resources for change management:

- What are the model behaviors in this organization?
- Which outside resources should we bring in?
- Which units have the most successful programs?
- Which units have had the greatest challenges?
- What can we learn from one another?
- Who should we get together with for this exchange?
- What information resources do we have?
- What training resources might be helpful?

Exchange-of-practice sessions work best when different points of view and alternatives are explored through a variety of resources. This prevents groupthink and encourages change, innovation, and learning beyond routine solutions and procedures.

Different learning rhythms (G. Lippitt 1982) and patterns should also be considered in selecting resources to help facilitate directed and nondirected change. Why do some specific events in group sessions become "peak learning" experiences? For instance, a prominent professional received a phone call from one of his clients with whom he had facilitated a team-development work session several years before. The caller said, "Do you remember that great team-building session we had about 10 years ago? Well, it really changed my whole life and made a difference in the direction of my career and my profession."

What made this group exchange so significant for this individual? According to Lippitt, specific learning rhythms such as climate, readiness, substance and content, facilitation, methodologies, and supporting relationships may combine to create a profound learning experience. Those who work with change consultation recognize similar reports from clients and colleagues. Something comes together at a point in time, "a cherished moment" when we leap ahead in our learning. An application, a group discussion, an insightful thought, or an innovative methodology can make a real difference in attitudes and practices.

A variety of effective resources—from training materials to the account of a skilled practitioner facilitating a complex change process, or the story of a new staff resource professional dealing with a difficult client—can help foster the conditions that encourage individual and collective learning experiences in exchange of practice sessions. Development opportunities based on these shared resources help the participants to let go, forget, remember, analyze, synthesize, or just "make sense" out of conflicting patterns and actions related to change and change management.

Develop a Design or Structure for Exchange

It is obvious that the exchange of practices is not just the simple process of getting together to talk about consultation, change management, clients, and client systems.   An exchange of practices is a sophisticated learning process that requires an experienced facilitator, someone who can encourage honesty and openness, mediate conflicts, and identify major learning points. A senior manager or practitioner can be especially valuable in this role. For change facilitators there are many crucial questions related to the preparation and implementation of an effective learning session:

- How do we prepare an agenda for exchange of practices?
- How can we orient the participants?
- How can we handle information during the session?
- How can additional resources be integrated?
- What should be the role of the facilitator or leader?
- How do we make closure in the sessions?
- What kind of follow-up might be required?

An exchange of practices demands a structure to facilitate sharing and learning as an ongoing process within a professional group. Creating conditions for learning requires an understanding of the strategies of training and development. These must be mobilized to help develop competencies for new organizational roles for managers and employees. Ronald Lippitt makes these suggestions for local network clusters:

- *Be linkage-oriented* to connect information to applications.
- *Set growth objectives* as a learning contract.

- *Use colearner teams* in small subgroups or dyads.

- *Practice* with supervised observation and analysis including guided fieldwork with reporting and interview analysis.

- *Provide tutorial modeling* and apprenticeship using mentors, advisors, senior managers, and retirees.

- *Design laboratory practice* and "repractice" opportunities with feedback, simulations, and role-play rehearsals.

- *Prepare learners* with support linkage for risk taking, including activities for training and education designs where peer dyads take risks together, debrief in discussions, maintain phone contact for support, and do anticipatory rehearsal in preparation for on-the-job application.

- *Develop membership* in a peer support group or network that includes the creation of support groups from within the work organization or with resource people outside the system. Telephone, fax, and computer networking can be used among different locations.

- *Celebrate accomplishments* in action initiatives and performance improvements by defining the criteria of progress toward goals and developing plans for celebrating progress and getting recognition for successful efforts.

DEVELOPING AN AGENDA FOR EXCHANGE OF PRACTICES

An agenda should integrate results, coordination, technology, and context into an action-learning model that helps participants to think about what they do and how they could be more effective in change management. A representative agenda would include preparation for participants, specific exchange and applications, and linkage and closure.

A typical exchange session begins with participants signing in with their name and address. Name badges are also available on which participants can write their role, function, and organization or location. Most people then move to the resource table and take copies of materials that interest them. If members want consultation brainstorming or discussion on a specific intervention or project, they write down the need or challenge, which will be discussed during the session depending on the amount of time and the number of requests.

The interaction and discussion may include individual brainstorming or "internal dialogue" related to a current challenge and the forces that are supporting or creating barriers to change. Members may choose some of the individual needs and do cluster brainstorming in groups. They may also exchange designs and new ideas for change management.

Cluster Brainstorming

Small-group brainstorming may be conducted in clusters with a specific interest or need. The topics may come from a specific question or challenge that someone has expressed or written down at the beginning of the session. In one recent session, the following question was explored: What are some ways to get my organization to understand, internalize, and use research?

Some of the answers from the cluster-brainstorming session for this question included: conduct formal and informal needs assessment; develop retreats for primary persons; use practitioner advisors; create feedback teams; implement reward systems and celebrate accomplishments; publish a newsletter; have staff and participants determine implications of research for organization; demonstrate results of research; demystify "research" and use other terms; work on a grant project for dissemination and use of knowledge; use customers as researchers; encourage staff to be researchers; survey clients; have "influentials" define areas for research and draw out implications; travel to conferences to present and publish research; adapt market-research techniques; develop personnel-exchange arrangements; try contests; connect research findings to practices fast and early; cultivate localism in research and funding; build inside and outside advisory networks; use competition; show results to community; build cosponsorship of research; and make a claim of the organization's leadership in research.

This exchange session also included some internal dialogue questions to help individuals think about their own assumptions and interventions related to the use of research and performance objectives for change management.

Internal Dialogue

An internal dialogue allows individuals to explore their own supporting and resisting "voices" in perceptions, attitudes, and assumptions related to specific interventions and accomplishments. For example, our change management model can help facilitators, consultation teams, managers, action research teams, and employee groups to work more effectively by providing a holistic pattern for linkage and integration of knowing, feeling, and doing in different ways of defining and implementing change. This process of linkage and integration can focus on the disconnections, paradoxes, and contradictions related to directed and nondirected change. For instance, effective customer service requires some linkage (R. Lippitt and Schindler-Raiman 1978) among thinking, feeling, experiencing, and intuiting. During an exchange of practices, individuals can learn to identify and link all four dimensions for a more realistic picture of individual, group, and organization thinking and action in relation to change. As Jung suggests, both integration and differentiation of these elements are the foundation of individual development. In an exchange of practices, each of these dimensions might include the following competencies:

- *Thinking:* sharing concepts, clarifying schemes, premises and assumptions, inferences, metaphorical images, and visualizing change;

- *Feeling:* dealing with confidence and anxiety, confronting conflicts, feeling threatened and secure, acknowledging trust and lack of openness, anger and joy;

- *Experiencing:* taking risks, activating, demonstrating, simulating, and creating results through skill practice, application initiatives, and role-modeling; and

- *Intuiting:* making new connections and creating ideas, futuring the image-of-potential exercise, and finding new directions and innovations in the here-and-now.

The internal dialogue helps individuals to understand and apply these different ways of gathering data about the world and making decisions based on that data. For example, a senior executive concerned about improving productivity and quality might be asked to describe his organization as he imagines a customer might see it, walking through the hallways and observing employees at work. Through an internal dialogue, this executive can link the knowing aspects of these various perspectives, hear the positive and negative voices, recognize possible feelings of reaction and concern, and perceive more clearly the actions and possible consequences of change.

The purpose of an internal dialogue is to encourage the free flow of ideas and to provide self-knowledge that may be useful. The following activity uses individual brainstorming alternated with inner-dialogue.

1. Choose the subject you want to brainstorm: How I could improve _____. Ways to be a better _____. Brainstorming also could be on "Topics I might brainstorm" or "Things I want to do."

2. This exercise requires two pages. The first page is for individual brainstorming with the topic written at the top. The second page documents the internal dialogue related to these actions or ideas. This includes two columns, one titled "Forces driving me toward

doing this action or improvement" and another with "Forces keeping me from completing this action or improvement."

3. Begin brainstorming on the first sheet. As soon as you run out of ideas or your mind begins to wander, record the voices you hear in your head in one or the other columns of the inner-dialogue sheet on the second page. You may be ambivalent about what you do, and there are internal voices saying things to you alternately pulling you toward and pushing you away from your goal. For example, if you are brainstorming about how to get going on a project that you have not worked on for a long time, at certain points in the brainstorming process, you get stuck. When this happens, turn to the inner-dialogue sheet and record some of the reasons you are getting struck, and why you are not working on the project.

Experience with this technique in practice suggests that the following thoughts may be typical in an internal dialogue related to this stalled project:

As I write the first ideas down I feel some excitement return about this project. I really care what happens on this. I have been avoiding writing this list for a long time and I'm not sure I want to go ahead now even though I'm doing it. Now I know why I balk at doing it–I cared so much about it but got no support at a critical time. This is the force that is keeping me from moving forward on the project. This may be why I stopped work on it and I now feel disappointed. I'm being connected into starting again.

There are a number of variations on the internal dialogue exercise. The following example is adapted from cluster sessions of the Lippitt Group professional network:

Prior to starting a project, working with a client, facilitating a problem-solving session, conducting a planning session, or making other interventions, consider brainstorming with yourself on the following questions, writing down your inner-dialogue and thoughts.

- What are your current ideas regarding this client, activity, or process?
- What assumptions do you have about what is going on?
- Is there anything in your past experience that reminds you of this situation?
- Do have any negative thoughts about this situation?
- What positive ideas come to mind?

This dialogue helps to clarify assumptions, bias, emotions, and perceptions that might affect relationships and interventions. This is also a useful exercise to check individual feelings at various points in the change management process.

CASE APPLICATIONS AND PRACTICES

An exchange session identifies the practices that the participants in the session have developed or adopted that are successful for them and would be useful for others. Everyone collects and scans the practices and identifies the "inventor" or person who is sharing the idea or practice. There is a brief discussion period to probe further those practices the group finds most interesting to adopt or adapt. Several learning and exchange clusters may evolve to bring together multidisciplined professionals who want to learn from one another, need support for their work, and place high value on the input and critique of others who listen to the case-application stories.

In another exchange group each person who has a practice to volunteer identifies it. The group chooses the practices they want to document for those in other groups. Participants use an interview schedule to question the person presenting the case. A recorder or resource person documents the information and these materials are duplicated. Typically each group documents two or three practices for the resource table. The following are examples of some activities to elicit information for exchange of practices related to specific change management interventions.

Activity #1–Which Intervention Should Be Chosen?

This activity helps identify and share experiences with a group of individuals that have some experience in consultation practices and action interventions for change management. This activity also can be built into conferences when managers or internal practitioners gather for discussion and planning. Before starting the exchange, a facilitator is appointed or nominated by the group. This activity revolves around answering and discussing these questions:

- What is your experience with change efforts?
- What action interventions do you use?
- What are your most successful activities?

A sample of activities might include creating action teams, temporary groups, and resource councils to study issues; benchmarking "best practices" within and outside of the organization and industry; business education and training; career development; self-directed team planning; third-party intervention in a confrontation situation; data collection for a conference; a system-wide survey for measurement of organizational effectiveness; needs validation instruments to administer across cultures and continents; pilot on a new course for design collaborators; facilitation of a feedback session with various units of the organization; or a retreat conference for management teaming and action planning for change management.

At the group level, each person takes a few minutes to respond to the three questions by sharing some action she or he is currently using or planning to use to facilitate change management. This is not a discussion time and participants simply state their answers. Someone in the group volunteers to chart the statements on an easel flipchart so that everyone can see.

After all of the interventions have been listed, participants identify the three skills they view as being the most important for effective change management. Each person writes down two or three skills on a note card. The facilitator then collects these cards and charts the choices. The group takes 15 minutes to probe and more fully document the interventions. They may select any activity on the list that they are curious about or want to get a clearer picture of in relation to action possibilities. Questions are asked and participants share their experience and knowledge. At the end of the session the group records their top three priority skills for change interventions.

The lead facilitator brings the several subgroups back together and collects data from each group by asking these questions:

- What are the three priority skills?

- How much agreement is there about these priorities?

- How competent do people feel in using these skills?

- What are some possible development actions to increase, improve, and expand these skills?

Activity #2–How Can We Measure Outcomes?

This activity targets measurement criteria in change management practices including cost and profit, organizational effectiveness, behavior, observation, and reaction to "hard" and "soft" measures. These are considered in relation to the client preference for quantitative or qualitative data, (See Table 13.1).

Subgroups select the evaluation area most relevant to their practice. Each person completes the worksheet. In column (a) they describe the desired outcome; in columns (b) and (c) they identify the measurement their client expects. Each person gives a brief example of an evaluation expectation from the client perspective indicating the quantitative or qualitative measurements

---

TABLE 13.1 Measuring Outcomes.

(a)	(b)	(c)
Criteria	**Hard measure**	**Soft measure**
Cost and profit ratio		
Organizational effectiveness		
Total customer satisfaction		
Quality		
Other		

---

that are required or expected by the client or sponsor.

After initial sharing, the group begins to discuss the following questions in relation to measurement and evaluation:

- Why do we measure?
- What concerns do we have about measurement?
- What data will be used to establish measurement?

The group also considers ways in which the change facilitator or consultation team can work with the client in stepwise measures and provide effective feedback on measurement. Issues such as interdependence, trust, and confidentiality are discussed. Is the client open to receiving feedback? How comfortable is the change facilitator in confronting issues with the client? What involvement does the client have in giving feedback on performance?

Action interventions are affected by how data and feedback are used in planning action. Some interventions might include pilot workshops to get feedback on training designs. Group members may discuss how they work through the different perceptions of the client and sponsor regarding desired outcomes. Participants may consider ways to involve others in the client system in measurement and feedback on needs validation, actions, programs, and training related to change management.

Group members can also examine goal measurements and what baseline data might be used related to quality, productivity, customer satisfaction, and financial and organizational effectiveness.

- What outcome indicators do we look for?
- How do we measure progress? How often?

- How do we integrate qualitative and quantitative data?

Activity #3–How Do We Develop More Teaming?

Several questions related to small groups, including structure, maintenance, and process questions, are important in this activity. For example, discussion questions might include:

- What are some of the new team formations in your client system?
- What patterns do you find in teams and small groups?
- What opportunities exist for professional and peer teaming?
- How does diversity of functions, gender, age, and ethnicity affect teaming?
- What forces maintain continuity of a group even when one or more parties may desire a change in the pattern?
- Why don't creative innovations for teaming and group processes become more widely utilized?

The discussion of trends and issues affecting teaming can be documented and presented to the larger exchange group. Specific consultation case studies may also add insight and information. The following list of challenges related to teaming was developed by members of one subgroup as a resource handout for all the other participants in an exchange session.

- A right-sizing environment with increased pressure for quality and continuous improvement with internal job transfers and outplacement creates goal conflicts. *How can we establish and maintain loyalty in the face of insecurity and reduction of resources in a major systems change?*

- Shared power and responsibility create expectations as the organization hierarchy is flattened. The initiatives of self-directed work teams demand new leader roles for improving linkage and quality. At the same time managers and supervisors are feeling a loss of control in staffing report relations. They are trying to meet the new challenges and roles of empowerment for which new skills, supports, and resources are required. *How can we prepare managers for new facilitative consultation roles?*

- There are new norms of interdependence, collaboration, and more free flow of communication with an increased need for feedback within and between units of the organization to discover and transfer innovative practices. At the same time there remains a culture of individual contributors, competitive resources, and autonomous units. *How do we integrate both individual and team contributions within the organization?*

- The diversity patterns of global organizations require linkage across markets and borders to increase the cycle and coordination of new products and to involve local global markets. There is also a corresponding need to stay close to the customer while the organization acquires cross-cultural competencies. The skill transfer of core competencies across borders is combined with other challenges relating to job rotation, dual career couples, spouse and family relocations, new models of networking, and a flexible team facilitation style that can access diverse resources in different combinations. *How do we build flexible teams with unity and diversity?*

Closure

The exchange of practices closes with members summarizing the activities and their memories and learning from the session. There may also be some discussion of agenda elements for the next session. The facilitator gives some summary observations, calls for any additional feedback, makes comments or suggestions, and closes the meeting.

The statements of participants at the end of an exchange-of-practice session are often very positive. They enjoy hearing about other designs and interventions and appreciate the opportunity to learn more about their own change management. Participants appreciate the brainstorming and group activities that have a direct relationship to their practices.

An effective facilitator is necessary for a successful exchange of practices. This person must be positive and nondomineering yet keep the participants "honest" regarding the agenda, specific objectives, and critical evaluation. While there is often a lead facilitator, this role can be shared. In later sessions, other members might lead modules and share their designs through participative experiences, handouts, and supporting materials.

MANAGEMENT COMPETENCIES IN EXCHANGE OF PRACTICES

Technical and process training, as well as research and development can be facilitated through an exchange of practices. One basic challenge for change management is moving the roles of leaders, managers, and resource professionals away from independence and autonomy, toward collaborative inquiry and pride in interdependence and recipient help. This shifts the hierarchy and expertise of authority-based roles to relationships that share competitive resources that mutually benefit from their complementary differences. These new consultative roles require specific competencies that can be enhanced by exchange of practices:

Facilitating directed and nondirected responses to change. This includes reviewing priorities, reassessing the benefits of current programs, exploring the exchange and resource sharing, benchmarking for innovative "best practice" in new models of service and production, examining different interpretations and applications of change, and restructuring roles to make use of the interface between people and technology.

Networking resources for the individual. Managers are feeling stress as they work with reduced authority, fewer staff people, and more responsibility. Clusters of skilled resources for self and others can help. These skills involve asking peers for consultation, linking resources for support, forming alliances of loose federation for action, and involving others in brainstorming ideas for responding to needs and developing new role competenc.ies

Recognizing the self as a resource. This includes listening to the internal dialogue within the self that expresses hidden feelings and needs, supports risk taking and caution, and reflects on different action alternatives and consequences. Listening to and using these internal resources requires a reflective perspective and allocated time to think about what is truly important in individual, group, and organizational development.

Achieving a balance of diversity and commonality through participation. This means providing sufficient participation close to the action. The proper balance for change initiatives is to seek other perspectives from across and outside the system. In the desire to arrive at consensus and unit, there needs to be a complementary of inviting different views, beliefs, and values. This type of leadership requires facilitation competencies.

Using feedback groups to modify action. This may occur several times a year in a senior executive conference session that brings leaders together to discuss key issues that have been identified through data collection and interviews. Based on this initial feedback the group integrates the data into new action that may change their relationships, and action. They choose to move from detached to responsible problem solving and from closed agendas to an open agenda that confronts topics relevant to all members as they develop their competencies for responsive leadership and integrated change management.

Improving effectiveness with process feedback. The National Training Laboratory, and other institutions for group and organizational research have shown that groups significantly improve their productivity and effectiveness if a focus on the process of how people interact with one another as they engage in various group tasks. For example a brief "stop session" in meetings allows members to share data and feedback about how things are going and what might be done to improve the quality of their interaction and practices. Ongoing feedback is a crucial part of any change management process.

Facilitating diverse teams. To insure that people of different backgrounds, specialities, and disciplines work effectively together is one of the leadership challenges of the coming decades. The technology of resource sharing, the concept of "creative compromise" in finding win-win approaches, and the extensive use of free-flow, nonevaluative brainstorming and dialogue should become a part of the manager's facilitative competencies.

Integrating people and technology. Managers and facilitators must help technology-oriented and people-oriented team members understand and appreciate one another. This involves establishing procedures for teaching and learning from one another and for cooperative trial runs or simulations where people can explore new perspectives in a no-risk environment. Team members learn to accept and respect different viewpoints and competencies in shared leadership. Action research teams might combine a technically sophisticated staff professional with a senior manager who has experience and skills in the tradition, history, and human side of the enterprise.

Recognizing neighbors and outsiders as potential resources. There is a temptation to define boundaries and "turfdom" in a "rightsizing" world where the goal is to do more with less. The leaders, managers and change facilitators of the coming decades must actively explore, share, and exchange resources and successful practices that help organizations to survive, grow, and profit in a changing environment. This challenge requires a continuing linkage with internal and external resources in facilitating change management.

CASE STUDY: INTERNATIONAL INSTITUTE FOR THE STUDY OF SYSTEMS RENEWAL (SRi)

The Institute's Program (Figure 13.1) was conceptualized and founded by Donald Swartz (1982) based on theories of action learning and systems renewal. The initial program was sponsored in the early 1980s by Organization Renewal, an international consortium that included Gordon Lippitt, Ronald Lippitt, B. J. Chakiris, Oscar Mink, and Jerry Harvey.

This model represents the ideas of that institute and the work of its founders in exchanging practices as a mode for action learning and continuous

FIGURE 13.1 International Institute for the Study of Systems Renewal.

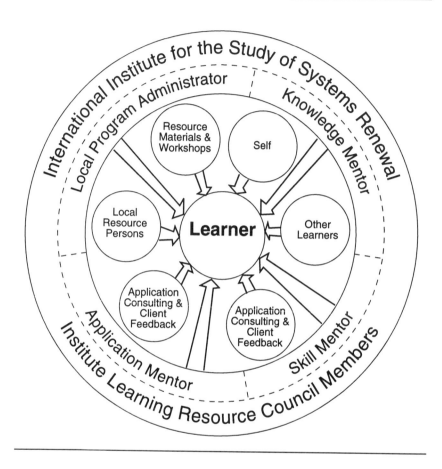

improvement. This learning practicum, used in the graduate and corporate programs, applies action learning in combination with real situations and interventions with theory-into-practice and action research teaming (ART).

In university graduate programs, business organizations, and community agencies, people are searching for ways to link conceptual theory to realistic applications. The implication for practitioners is the challenge to think theoretically, confront intervention decisions, mix theory and practice, gain colleague support, and participate in a collective learning community.

The Institute Learning Resource Council members include the local program administrator, a knowledge mentor, a skill mentor, and an application mentor. The goal is to integrate resources for the learner including self, other learners, co-leaders in knowledge and skill components, application consultation, client feedback, and local resource people.

The consultation practicum can be both formal and informal. The formal model exists within institutes such as The International Systems Renewal Institute and university graduate schools. Informal learning sessions may occur within corporate settings in career mentoring, sponsorship processes, and application teaming with internal partners. Professional associations may also promote exchange of practice clusters and cell study groups.

Participants in the practicum are working professionals and graduate students. The practicum organizes diverse members of the program into a consultation-training team to scout and make contracts with selected systems including groups, organizations, and communities. These practicum members participate in a variety of exercises, theory discussions, and intervention designs. They also secure feedback from their clients and peer groups within their organizations.

The core content in the practicum methods and process is change consultation, which includes specific theories of human-system renewal and voluntary contracting between learners and mentors or facilitators who function collaboratively as co-learners with joint responsibilities for overseeing the practicum design. The practicum is based on the following values for learning and exchange of practices in consultation:

- Learning is most effective when applied to client work;
- Effective consultation includes learning how to work with others for both support and feedback;
- Effective intervention design links values, concepts, and skills;
- Tasks should be combined with process designs for individuals and groups;
- Skill practice improvement does occur through role rehearsals; and
- Two-way communication is essential for practicum advisors and members.

Goal Setting

Individual goals in a practicum come from a variety of sources including professional practice and experiences the individual wants in the practicum, specific skills and knowledge desired for application and learning, and career-development goals including life and work goals (Swartz and Chakiris 1978) the person wants to achieve (see Table 13.2).

TABLE 13.2 Life and Work Goals Exploration.

Introduction

Presents an overview and objectives of the Life and Work Goals exploration process.

Preparation

To build a helpful working relationship between you and other learners in this action-learning program.

Taking Charge

To gain an understanding of how your can take charge of your own life and grow.

Mind Stretching

To exercise the mind so your can view the future as if it were real.

Self Inventory

To collect information about yourself in the areas of successes, abilities, desires, goals, and personal and external constraints and resources.

Interpretation and Analysis

To identify life and work goals and a set of values, needs and wants that will help you to make your life and work goals plans.

Action Planning

To provide help in developing a realistic life and work goals action plan.

The design should also incorporate the goals of the client in the organization served during the practicum. The client can be a member of a unit or work team, serve on a board of directors, participate in an ad hoc committee or action team, or contribute to a specific subunit of the organization structure as part of a project, matrix, or supplier group.

The sponsor or the individual who empowers the work may be the client's boss, the initiator of the overall project who has handed off specific responsibilities to clients in the organization, the leader of a functional area, a product manager, or the customer who receives the client's product or services. The goals and expectations of the sponsor should also be considered.

The participant's practicum goals link with other learning and knowledge, to demonstrate professional practices going beyond the traditional classroom into training sessions and seminars related to specific day-to-day work and life activities.

Contract Elements of the Practicum

The following elements are the basis of the practicum contract between the mentor, advisor or facilitator, and the professional or graduate student working in the practicum:

- Roles and goals;
- Goal setting with sponsor and client feedback;
- Intervention design, events, activities, and processes;
- Consultation project analysis and outcomes;
- Schedule with progress checkpoints;
- Result measurement;
- Review of data-collection methods;
- Documentation in journal notes and reports;
- Practicum completion schedule.

The practicum report documentation is coordinated within the organization or learning institution. For example, university requirements can involve a contract between the student and the advisor and specific documentation of activities and processes including goal statements, theory and conceptual models being used, measurement and feedback process methods, learner and advisor evaluations, ideas and suggestions for future practicum participants, and how the practicum experience integrates with career and professional practice areas.

Practicum Project Work Outline

The practicum takes place within the context of consultation practices in projects and work situations with clients, sponsors, and team members. A work outline is developed by the change facilitator taking the practicum, and shared among the key players in the project. Table 13.2 is a sample of a practicum project work outline.

TABLE 13.3 Project Work Outline.

I. Practicum Overview
    Start-up planning
    Individual attends Life and Work Goals Exploration
    Six phases of consultation
    Initial start-up
    In-progress checkpoints
    Completion

TABLE 13.3 (continued)

II. Resources to support practicum

Practicum purpose and guidelines
Procedural outline–Who does what, when, why, how?
Panel of resources–linkage with peers and other resources

III. Practicum Events

Orientation to practicum
Formation of learning partners
Grounding practicum outcomes and evaluation criteria
Learning contracts
Measurement and feedback
Practicum types
Professional practice areas: human resource management system, organizational development, instructional design, sales and marketing, career development, technical skills, international, manufacturing, operations
Association and learning institutions
Other resources

IV. Exchange of Practice Sessions

Discussion groups
Brainstorming consultation
Reality testing
Simulation practice session
Internal dialogue
Presentations
Consultation groups
Advisory panel

V. Follow-up Consultation in Scheduled Appointments With Practicum

Advisor and team members

When the practicum is part of a formal process of graduate work in a university, specific procedures must be integrated along with the practicum experience. This might include submitting a proposal to an advisor describing the practicum, including start and completion dates and progress checkpoints. Participants also have consultation sessions with the advisor and exchange of practices with others taking the practicum. The advisor serves as a mentor and an advocate during the practicum experience, providing process and structure and facilitating learning.

Those taking the practicum keep a journal recording practices, theories, intervention designs, their personal reflections on learning, and feedback notes. This information is also used prepare any final reports. Some programs also require an oral examination with one or more faculty or resource mentors discussing the practicum experience, theory, and related study topics.

Participants are expected to have taken a consultation course or to have some consultation experience before taking the practicum. The practicum should relate to on-the-job assignments and stretch the person beyond present job responsibilities.

14

Global Contexts

Some experts suggest that economic and political transformations are creating a world in which there are no national products or technologies and no national corporations (Reich 1993). Others see the technology and financial structures of organizations around the world becoming more uniform as information and resources move across continents in an increasingly "borderless" world economy (Ohmae 1990). There can be a corresponding assumption that the corporate cultures and relationships within and among those multinational, transnational, and global organizations are gaining some consensus and uniformity in practices, but cultural differences cannot be ignored or standardized. They represent a diverse and challenging context for change management.

In many instances, with the exception of what has been a sometimes obsessive commentary about Japan, culture is relegated to an almost invisible factor in the global economic market. However, the majority of people still live within national borders and maintain their unique cultural identity. This is often true of organizations. In a "global" organization, the unique cultural values of nations may be hidden or subordinate to strategic alliances, cooperative agreements, negotiations, and decision-making processes; yet inside organizations, relationships among managers, employees, customers, suppliers, and stakeholders can be affected by specific national, ethnic, and cultural values and priorities. Within and across nations, organizational practices and cultural standards can influence opportunities for employee development and participation, government and business cooperation, and social responsibility. In head-to-head competition the "individualistic" capitalism of the United States and Britain is different from the "communitarian" capitalism of Germany and Japan, which is based on team success and cooperative business groups (Thurow 1992). Comparing these systems by economic figures alone may be misleading if underlying cultural elements are not understood.

Even as organizations move into a global world, cultural stereotypes and conflicts are not easily dismissed. Executives may travel to three different countries in one day, but developing a truly global perspective for cross-cultural change management and development requires a learning approach to gather data, clarify misunderstandings, recognize differences, and respect alternative ways of thinking and organizing. Within a global organization made up of widely dispersed geographic locations, there also may be many different cultures based on functional disciplines and ethnic, gender, and racial diversity. A global perspective encourages transcultural synthesis within a shared corporate culture. Leaders, managers, resource facilitators and team leaders with consultation competencies for change management can help create a dynamic network for support, collaboration, and mutual learning in a global system.

Both Germany and Japan have developed business groups and cooperative relationships among interdependent domestic companies. The Mondragon cooperatives in Spain have encouraged employee-owner entrepreneurship and governance in a network of mutually supporting relationships (Whyte and Whyte 1988). American corporations have established innovative partnerships with employees, customers, and suppliers in order to improve product quality and increase technical competence. While the long-term mutual benefits of a collaborative relationship are easier within a common culture, teaming relationships must be extended across borders with traditional economic and cultural barriers removed to build and maintain multicultural global alliances. Consultation skills are becoming increasingly valuable for multicultural managers and emerging global business units in managing change.

RECOGNIZING CULTURAL DIFFERENCES

Several years ago a popular novel, described a protagonist who wrote travel guides for tourists who wanted to travel the world and feel as though they had never left home. While most individuals and organizations have grown beyond this narrow view, organizations still run the risk of approaching other cultures in an "armchair" fashion, with decisions and practices based on what is "normal" to the home office with little active interest or commitment to understanding cultural differences and alternative ways of working and organizing in a changing world.

Closed systems and ethnocentric thinking can lead organization members to generalize about the characteristics of Asian, African, American, or

European culture. As the "Eurocentric" view of the world is being transformed, the current trends in "political correctness" discourage the use of
universal cultural categories as inaccurate and manipulative, and encourage an
affirmation of ethnic diversity and unique contributions of specific groups.
However, in the extreme the "cult of ethnicity" can encourage ethnocentrism
and drive wedges between races and nationalities and dilute or destroy
national identity (Schlesinger 1992). At a historical time when nations are in
need of a competitive advantage with unity and shared visions to manage
change and create strategic alliances and policies to promote global strengths,
a limited focus can easily shift to differentiation, mistrust, and narrow domestic objectives. The challenge is to establish respect for different cultures and
nations with reciprocity and cooperation in achieving mutually beneficial
goals across borders and continents.

Organizations that recognize this need are educating leaders, boards,
managers, and employees to appreciate the value of cultural diversity. They
are encouraging collaborative inquiry and creating alliances to integrate this
energy into shared goals that develop individuals, groups, organizations, and
nations. Global organizations are delegating authority to the local unit and
focusing more on developing "people resources" to meet the needs for developing products and services in diverse markets. However, the management of
diversity—whether it is race, gender, age, nationality, or lifestyle— begins with
recognizing and respecting differences within the organizational workforce.
While organizations strive to respond to global challenges, they cannot neglect
the changes related to diversity within their own local and national work
groups.

There is a growing need to focus on broader economic cooperation and
strategic alliances among many diverse nations. An increasing number of
people are working for foreign-owned companies and subsidiary operations,
negotiating new ventures to build technology transfers, and developing global
alliances through licensing, distribution, and agreements for participation in
global projects.

Basic cultural consensus and synergy is an economic necessity for global
organizations. To gain consensus means working through others and integrating goal priorities in technical and process competencies as well as agreements
to respect and integrate some alternative ideas. For example, an Italian bank
manager explained the differences between the Italian and American approach
to establishing business relationships: "Americans want to get to business
right away, but we Italians feel the need to talk and get to know you and
discuss how we might work together." The manager then quoted a translation
of an old Italian proverb "The person who goes slowly goes healthy and far."

Making "progress" by moving slowly may be an adjustment for an American manager concerned with rapid change, efficiency, production schedules, and impending deadlines.

Recognizing and using cultural differences in managing change is a major challenge for global organizations. Hampden-Turner (1991) suggests that the American approach is often based on "universalism" that assumes that good American management practices work everywhere. In multicultural contexts management styles and perceptions of change vary based on different social values and organizational priorities. French managers, Egyptian managers, and Japanese managers should not be expected to work together according to a universal management theory.

A number of researchers have documented differences in national values and work and management styles. These differences not only affect internal relationships and alliances, but also teams of multicultural groups working together to make decisions and negotiate agreements and manage change across continents. Cultural factors can have a substantial impact on contact, contracting and agreements, and roles and relationships in change management and collaborative inquiry. For example, in some countries there is strong agreement that managers should have precise answers to all employee questions. In other countries there is disagreement with the role of the manager as the expert. These contradictory views of management style can range from absolute power, knowledge, and authority to the facilitation of knowledge and employee participation in the coordination of work practices.

Hofstede (1991) has referred to culture as the "software of the mind." The layers of mental programming include national, regional, ethnic, religious, linguistic, gender, generational, socio-economic, and organizational learning. In his global research, Hofstede (1980, 1991) has investigated national values and "central tendencies" in different countries around the world and identified five dimensions of organizational culture: power distance, individualism vs. collectivism, task orientation, uncertainty avoidance, and long-term vs. short-term orientation. Hofstede cautions that traditional American management theory cannot be imposed on other cultures. While some models may seem evident in other nations, the motivation and interpretation of meaning behind the working theory may be entirely different.

Hofstede characterizes *power distance* as involving to the inequality and distribution of power in superior-subordinate relationships. Less powerful members expect and accept this unequal distribution of power (Hofstede 1991). High power distance reinforces hierarchical relationships and may affect the success of changes related to participative management, team consultation, self-directed teams, and codetermination, which all deal with redistributing power and influence and adjusting power distance.

The perception and reality of power distance also affects formality and responsibility in consultation relationships. In a more authoritarian, hierarchical organizations, people might not always see participation in the change process as a positive benefit if it goes against cultural values, which have been traditionally based on a rigid class system that determines appropriate behavior and position in society. More subtle social differences are also evident in other countries where it can be inappropriate to call someone by their first name in a formal business setting. The power distance in the position and authority of the person should be recognized in role relationships and agreements.

Uncertainty avoidance relates to risk and the amount of perceived threat in uncertain or unknown situations. High uncertainty avoidance may be evident in formal rules, technology, structure, and greater emphasis on hierarchy, order, and low risk-taking. High uncertainty avoidance often supports bureaucracy and signals less willingness to make extensive or rapid changes. These organizational cultures are often more closed, with an emphasis on long-term relationships and stable structures. Power distance and uncertainty avoidance affect the way the organization deals with problems and issues related to change management.

Organizational values are also affected by the amount of *individualism* in the culture or the perceived relationship between the individual and the collective group. Rather than viewing the team, group, or nation as the collective hero, an individualistic culture recognizes and celebrates individual heroes, and may prefer a quick, decisive approach to solving problems rather than a slower and more collective consensus model. Collaborative inquiry and teamwork can bring some contradictions in an individualistic culture.

According to Hofstede, gender roles are also a cultural element affecting *task orientation* and values. A culture with less task-orientation concentrates on quality of life, service, caring, and consensus. A culture with a high task-orientation focuses on ambition, achievement, and decisiveness. This assertive, task-orientated productivity stance reinforces rigid gender roles as opposed to an emphasis on nurturing, quality of work life, interpersonal context, and goals. These different task values may be evident in management style, work goals, cooperation, and teamwork.

Hofstede's most recent work (1991) includes a comparison of *short-term* and *long-term orientation* in life as a cultural value evident in *differences* between Western and Eastern thinking. A short-term orientation respects tradition and social obligations and pressures, expects quick results, and seeks

truth. The long-term orientation is more adaptable, with thrift and persever-
ance toward slow results, willingness to be subordinate for a purpose, and
concern with virtue.

Global consultation teams should be sensitive to these broad cultural
values and different ways of thinking and working. They also must learn to
recognize and appreciate a range of behaviors and options within a single
culture and allow for broad integration and acceptance. Some cultures may
appear to be more open to change than others, but "change" is interpreted and
valued in different ways. These orientations create different ways of looking at
the world and interpreting behavior and action.

Major differences in values have been summarized in the classic model
developed by Kluckhohn and Strodtbeck (1961), as shown in Table 14.1. This
model is vigorously debated, especially when it is used to make broad general-
ities about a particular culture or group. It is useful, however, in establishing
some understanding of contradictory and potentially conflicting worldviews
that may influence change management.

TABLE 14.1 Differences in Values.

ORIENTATION		BELIEFS	
Human nature	Basically evil	Mixture	Basically good
Man-and-nature relationship	Subjugation	Harmony	Mastery
Time	Past	Present	Future
Action	Being	Becoming	Doing
Social relationships	Authoritarian	Collective	Individualistic

Adapted from Kluckhohn and Strodtbeck. *Variations in Value Orientations.* (Evanston, IL:
Row, Peterson & Co., 1961).

These orientations can affect how members of different cultures view
authority, career development, teamwork, trust, motivation, and recognition
within an organizational system. These values may also determine many
aspects of behavior from the degree of formality in a business meeting to relationships with family, friends, and colleagues. For example, some companies
may depend on a lawyer to complete an agreement while other cultures might
consider this an expression of lack of trust and depend more on a personal
commitment and developing long-term relationships.

According to the Kluckhohn-Strodtbeck model, "action" can be interpreted on the basis of three different concepts or beliefs: being, becoming, and doing. The idea of "being" emphasizes who you are, which is often rooted in tradition and history with little motivation toward change. "Becoming," on the other hand, focuses on self-development and finding harmony and integration; there is a focus on change but it is a slow, continuing process of growth and learning. "Doing" stresses direct action and showing results; change is a sign of progress and achievement under this belief system. Thus, a manager with an active "doing" orientation may try to move too fast in a "being" or "becoming" culture, which could create misunderstandings.

While it is important to avoid stereotyped national characteristics, this model does establish an initial awareness of broad cultural views. However, it is essential to take each situation as a new opportunity to learn about differences and commonalities that stretch across "created" cultural boundaries. Developing a global change management perspective requires a fundamental awareness of and respect for different values and ways of living and working. To think and act globally demands flexibility, and challenges old systems and ideologies that create artificial, defensive walls between different cultures. Differences should not be barriers.

DEVELOPING A GLOBAL PERSPECTIVE

A global perspective on change management moves toward integration and synergy among different cultures. Individuals and groups bring unique knowledge and understanding of organizations, social systems, and cultures to the team effort. Often the greatest barrier to developing a global perspective is a traditional mindset and a limited horizon in thinking about the equivocality of change, and the amount of control individuals and groups have in change management. Indeed, a traditional change perspective most often works from rigid blueprints for structured, directed organizational change and overall improvement controlled through a centralized structure. This change model assumes that it is possible to know and measure any differences and make appropriate and logical adjustments based on the facts. However, "facts" may be interpreted in different ways even in the same culture.

A global approach requires a process model of development that is organic, systemic, and based on changing, flexible models of interdependence that engage local stakeholders and provide multiple options for decisions and action. Ohmae (1990) suggests that a true global organization must be "denationalized" as the center is "decomposed" and replaced by regional headquarters with local members as employees and managers. The global organization is unified by shared values and mission rather than an overriding national identity. It is not control and authority, but rather networks of cross-cultural communication and coordination that provide for integration and change.

Change management skills that *start where the client is* and *where the culture is* are essential in establishing relationships, creating agreements, gathering and sharing information, making collaborative action plans, and working together to monitor results. The global organization defines a new balance of people and resources in what one successful top executive has characterized as "global localization" (Ohmae 1990).

The evolution of the global organization is a slow process and many organizations only evolve to a limited international market or a somewhat broader multicultural level, but never achieve the true state of denationalization that characterizes a global organization. Adler (1991) suggests four stages of development in changing to a global market: domestic, international, multinational, and global.

In the *domestic* stage, the organization is concerned primarily with products and services in one national market. There can be some parochialism in not recognizing an international market and seeing only "one way" of doing business. At this stage, change management is focused on internal units and the development of alliances among customers and suppliers in a domestic marketplace.

In the *international* stage of development, the organization recognizes an international market and adapts its product to the local needs of a specific market or nation. This may still be an ethnocentric stage with the emphasis on headquarters mentality and "our way" as the best model for how things are done. International organizations often use their own internal managers and resources, who attempt to export specific procedures and practices to other countries rather than hiring local managers and workers whom they believe may not have the necessary skills and training. Within this organization an international assignment creates distinct challenges for leaders, managers, and staff professionals. Working in a foreign country requires specialized training prior to departure and a commitment to integrating and applying the international skills and knowledge of the returning managers. Consultation teams at this level may be limited to a bicultural focus with only one representative member of another culture, perhaps visiting headquarters to report on the international operations. Action research techniques and cultural development centers can facilitate broader cross-cultural involvement in the data collection, feedback, action planning, and decisions.

A *multinational* approach focuses on a competitive global economic market with "local leader" participants to gain insider intelligence, ownership, and market position. People of other nations around the globe bring cross-cultural skills and ethnic and cultural diversity to assist the organization in becoming more innovative, responsive, and effective. Multicultural teams are used throughout the global market and across nations to facilitate and manage change.

According to Adler (1991) a true *global* organization involves diversity within and between the organization and the global environment. There are no "other-nation" corporate sites run by the home office. The organization is no longer identified with a particular country because the organization is an interdependent network of regional operations run almost entirely by local nationals in a variety of countries. Global organizations are transnational.

Wendt (1993) describes the difference between transnationals and multinationals as the difference between a globe and a map. Multinationals still place the home market and headquarters in the center of the map; for transnational corporations, the world is a seamless market.

Our model of team dynamics from Chapter 7 can be applied to global organizations. Figure 14.1 illustrates this perspective on transnational teaming. Diversity becomes the dominating element in this global model. Commonality is less defined because of increased differences. This increases the challenges and demands greater change management competencies in communication, coordination, confirmation, and renewal.

FIGURE 14.1 Global Applications of Teamwork.

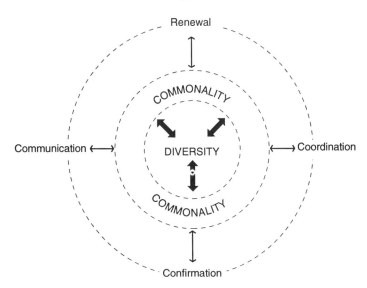

There is a growing need to improve interaction and partnerships through multicultural teams, task forces, boards, advisory committees, project teams, and temporary and permanent work groups as organizations move toward a global perspective on change management. A multicultural consultation team with diverse specialties can bring multiple perspectives, innovation, and more effective solutions for the integration of complex global change.

This diversity offers a variety of knowledge and skills to energize creative team synergy. These differences and alternative worldviews make multicultural groups less likely to fall into groupthink. This also means that multicultural change consultation teams require more time for orientation, information processing, value comparisons, and testing of assumptions and perceptions in exploring work relationships and agreements to establish commonality related to a specific project or change. Misunderstandings and conflicts may be caused by a lack of cultural context and experience, limited language ability, unclear roles and role relationships, value and priority differences, and excessive influence by dominant ideologies and personalities.

Communication and coordination are essential to effective global performance. In this process there is no substitute for language fluency and experience in the culture. This helps establish some commonality. Speaking the language and interacting within the culture is also a confirmation of the value of that partnership. When working in multicultural contexts it is impossible for one person to have all the necessary language and cultural skills. Teaming with local managers and resources is essential in effective global consultation and change management.

Renewal is a continuing challenge for global teams and a part of every interaction because of the diversity and differences among members. There needs to be a willingness to take time to look at relationships and ask questions: Is the team achieving its goals? Are members sensitive to each other? Should other people be involved? Asking for feedback and checking assumptions and perceptions is a part of this process. People may not be comfortable in talking directly about how they feel or what they need, unless the team finds a way to let people express honest feelings. If renewal and questioning are not a part of every meeting, the team may soon find they have been replaced. It is important to facilitate a continuous inquiry process to assess if the team is helping others to reach their goals.

Steiner's (1972) group-process formula can be applied to understanding problems in multicultural groups and project teams: actual productivity equals potential productivity minus losses due to faulty process. Nondirected elements must be recognized. Much of the potential of a diverse multicultural group can be dulled by ignoring the importance of process facilitation in clarifying and understanding roles and relationships, establishing trust, and defining common objectives and agreements on how the group will work together. Multicultural team leaders and managers must have consultation and change management competencies to help reduce faulty processes and improve overall cultural synergy and performance.

The global presence of organizations also may require that managers change their assumptions and modify their management style as they learn to work effectively in more than one culture. While organizations can move technology, financial assets, resources, and information across borders, they often find greater difficulty in effectively moving people across and within different cultures. Cultural orientation, training, and support for personnel are crucial parts of a multicultural and global business operation. This might include area studies, language programs, simulations, sensitivity training, and family orientation. Yet no amount of laboratory training can substitute for direct experience in the culture. On an international assignment, cross-cultural entry and reentry can cause culture shock. This is manifest in feelings of confusion and helplessness in a culture that seems unpredictable and strange to an outsider. In many cases, this is the first time the manager has felt the isolation and stress of being a "foreigner" in an unfamiliar culture. Because of this, the home office team may remain in the "tourist" mode if it does not form partnerships and alliances with local managers and workers. These local experts could be technical, business, and academic professionals with multicultural knowledge and experience as well as bilingual language skills. Change management requires an effective global team based on local resources.

This network should support flexible team structures and mobility, and build competence that transfers across continents. Organizations assign managers abroad because of specific technical knowledge, skills, or expertise. The goal may be to monitor foreign operations, provide support, transfer technology, implement new procedures, establish direct contact, negotiate agreements, or improve control and coordination. Managers returning from these international assignments—whether for a few months or two or three years—bring valuable information and insight that can benefit the organization in planning and implementing a global strategy linked to local needs in other nations.

Yet one of the greatest challenges for those working abroad for an extended period of time is reentry into the home culture. In some organizations, the global assignment is not integrated into a overall development plan for the organization and for the managers and professionals involved in these projects. In an ethnocentric corporate culture, the valuable multicultural skills obtained in foreign assignments may be ignored and not applied as part of the organizational knowledge and skill competencies. Global professionals should be recognized and rewarded for their cross-cultural career development, and have opportunities to share their experience in feedback sessions and participation in action planning based on data from multinational assignments. Many managers and resource professionals return to a changed organization and a less dynamic job compared to the excitement and autonomy of their global assignment. A lack of career planning by the individual and the organization may result in the loss of personnel, and with them global competencies that could be essential to the organization in a changing social, economic, and political environment.

Managers and staff professionals with experience in different cultures bring valuable resources to the organization. They can help in developing more effective design and content for cross-cultural training programs. Their management skills, tolerance for ambiguity, multiple perspectives, ability to work with others, and cultural sensitivity are essential assets for change management in a global organization. One important goal in moving toward a global organization is to integrate and expand the skills and experience of multicultural managers and to maintain networks of communication and support for people across continents.

Cultural learning goes beyond appropriate conversational distance or meeting protocol. Change management skills help in understanding the context, developing agreements for working together, and checking interpretations through feedback and data collection. Collaborative inquiry and action planning helps multinational teams to find options that develop capacity and skills for management change within a complex global organization.

UNDERSTANDING AND APPRECIATING CONTEXTS

As Hofstede (1991) explains, the basic skill for surviving in a multicultural world is first understanding the cultural values and identity that influence your thoughts and actions, then understanding the cultural values of those with whom you must cooperate. Awareness is where learning starts; knowledge and skills follow. This is why we emphasize the importance of understanding different perspectives toward change, and starting where the client system is.

While internal office environments and information technologies may look familiar in other cultures, the norms, attitudes, and working styles may not be the same. The objectives and daily dilemmas may also look different. Some international managers can be caught between the incompatible goals of the home office and the local operation, which may be thousands of miles away. Understanding and appreciating different contexts supports collaboration and change consultation in the global organization. This cultural awareness includes not only business decisions and practices, but also social interactions, manners, and relationships.

Cultures have clear boundaries for intimate, personal, social, and public distance (Hall 1966). Appropriate behavior related to personal space and touch may vary from the nose-to-nose conversations in Arab and Mediterranean cultures to the extended conversational distances in the United States and Western Europe. Understanding and appreciating "contexting differences" (Hall 1976) is the beginning of developing trust and cultural synergy in global teams. Recognizing and discussing cultural differences in a supportive learning environment increases understanding and helps clarify working roles and relationships. Consultation and development teams should include local nationals who know the rules of the culture and can help in understanding contextual meaning.

Culture can be a "control mechanism" (Geertz 1973) of learned behavior and attitudes that facilitate social interaction and promote unity and identification. In many ways, culture involves taken-for-granted behavior and thought patterns. Hall (1976) makes an important distinction between *high-context* cultures in which meaning is implicit and limited to insiders, and *low-context* cultures in which explicit meaning is available to a larger group. A low-context culture uses language and signs to present a more complete explanation of meaning. A high-context culture may operate with a kind of shorthand communication based on shared experiences and knowledge. This happens in different countries; it also happens in different departments such as accounting or marketing. Insiders may consciously use a private code to exclude others, but in many cases it is simply an efficient and habitual way of facilitating communication within a specific unit or function. This exclusion based on specialized language and intrinsic group norms may occur within a domestic system as well as in multilingual global contexts.

Cultural blindness often comes from a lack of understanding of contextual, historical, and situational meanings. However, even those who have experience in many cultures still face the challenges and contradictions of cultural contexts. As a seasoned foreign correspondent explained, "In Moscow, one knows nothing but understands everything. In Rome, one knows everything, but understands nothing" (Barzini 1983).

A high-context culture, such as those in Asia and Africa, is based on implicit authority and responsibility. Information in the physical environment is internalized in collective history and cultural experience. Little information is coded and presented in an explicit message. Many high-context cultures are based in the past, and they change slowly and maintain long-term stability. In social and economic spheres there is a private, restricted code that only "insiders" understand. Japanese corporations have been described as not always integrating foreign managers as equals (Thurow 1992). Learning the complexities of the Japanese language may help, but most outsiders still do not comprehend the subtle dimensions of this high-context culture. The rules are internalized and based on collective experiences, historical values, and ritualized manners. Outsiders experience more culture shock as the foreigner in a high-context culture. Every day in this new culture becomes an intense learning experience, both frustrating and rewarding.

In the beginning, outsiders have difficulty in knowing what to pay attention to and how to act in relation to specific people in a high-context culture. Meaning may be in tone of voice or nonverbal elements such as use of silence, space, touching, dress, symbols, and ceremony. There are critical questions for the global consultation or negotiation team: Who has power in this group? What is the time orientation for making decisions? How do we know that we have agreement? How do we interpret resistance? Language may have subtle alternative meanings in regional interpretations and local dialects that do not appear in a well-worn bilingual dictionary. Knowing about history, art, and culture may help, but much is not written but rather experienced by members of the culture. High-context cultures demand a team approach to consultation and development that includes partnerships and alliances with natives who understand both cultures.

A low-context culture, such as that in the United States, ideally makes the rules on behavior and procedures available to everyone, both insiders and outsiders. The code is often explicit and direct as information is widely shared through signs, directions, instructions, and explanations. A low-context culture empowers individuals and allows more people to participate as equals. Since responsibility is diffused, a low-context culture is often more open to change as well as manipulation and power plays by groups and individuals inside and outside the culture.

A low-context culture can still be confusing and misinterpreted by outsiders. For instance, Americans are often seen as gregarious, energetic, and friendly. Yet one French characterization of Americans is that they show an almost "promiscuous" excessiveness in their smiles and open conversations with strangers. To the French, conversation is a "commitment" to another person and a "commentary on their relationship" (Carroll 1988) rather than an empty ritual. Are the French more likely to build long-term relationships in business? Do Americans focus more on superficial, short-term business objectives? It is impossible to avoid stereotypes and generalizations. They are generated and reinforced in language and social interactions. These "created" assumptions can bring conflict and misundertanding to multinational relationships.

CLARIFYING INTERPRETATIONS AND MAKING AGREEMENTS

On all sides there are many stereotypes to overcome in initial cross-cultural and multicultural contexts. In the absence of data and experience, individuals and groups may rely on "war stories" and outdated generalizations. As groups work together to identify problems, analyze information, and make decisions, they need some "DOS-level" system (Quennell 1992) for guiding their discussions and developing fundamental structures for agreements of expectations, role relationships, shared roles, and ways of working together.

Part of this framework can be assessed according the Jungian categories discussed in Chapter 3. Jung distinguishes between two major approaches to perceiving and gathering data about the world (sensing and intuiting) and two approaches to processing that data (thinking and feeling). In collecting information about the world, some may rely on their current experience and senses in knowing their environment. Others may depend less on these observations and more on intuition based on past experiences and perceptions and hunches about the future. The first approach deals more with physical facts and the second with images and imagination. A manager's dominant way of perceiving or analyzing data can be influenced by cultural values and beliefs about the world.

One approach to recognizing and understanding differences in processing information during negotiation, decision making, and planning related to change management is to consider whether the information is processed primarily from a thinking perspective, a feeling perspective, or both. The thinking perspective often focuses on whether the information is true, logical, or practical. The feeling perspective might be an emotional assessment of whether this action is good or bad and how it affects people.

Managers don't make decisions in the same way, even within the same culture. In certain languages, "compromise" does not have a positive connotation. In some cultures, being decisive is considered an individual asset. In other cultural contexts decision making is slower and more interactive. A number of studies on national styles of persuasion and negotiation suggest that individuals from some cultures might use fact and logic while those from other cultures might appeal to emotion and subjective feelings. There are many factors affecting decisions that go beyond conventional "logic" and stereotypes. Values such as saving face or preserving dignity and honor might be the most important concerns. Understanding these perspectives helps facilitate agreements.

Decisions are most often made in response to a problem, challenge, or opportunity, yet in different cultures there may be conflicting definitions of what constitutes a "problem." How do we respond to a problem? Is this situation a problem or not? When does something become a problem? If cultures are more tuned to the past or more willing to accept small discrepancies as part of the total pattern and current harmony with nature, they may not be as proactive in identifying issues and problems and planning for the future. Whereas one manager may identify a potential problem early, another manager may be more willing to wait and see what happens. In some cases large problems are ignored as attention is given to nurturing small details. Cultures may perceive problems and issues in a conflicting ways, gather alternative information, and consider different strategies and priorities in making decisions and managing change. Understanding and working through this, is a part of an effective global perspective. Consultation competencies in clarifying expectations and getting agreements are essential to collaboration and alliance in reaching global business goals, and managing change across cultures and continents.

CREATING SYNERGISTIC SOLUTIONS

Global change management is a challenging process that requires sensitivity to context and different ways of gathering and interpreting data. Multicultural decision guidelines should be flexible and allow for a wide range of mutually beneficial options that create complementary situations for participants and stakeholders. This means recognizing the skills and knowledge of local nationals and developing multicultural relationships and partnerships. Team and organizational learning can be enhanced through collaborative inquiry in action research, interpretive feedback, and planning for change. These collective processes involve people in identifying problems and issues, gathering data, and defining solutions and implementing and monitoring change. Data-based change management increases coordination and integration among different systems and provides more synergistic solutions.

Hiring and developing local nationals, as well as establishing partnerships and alliances with local community leaders and experts should be a priority for the global organization. This is especially important in developing and maintaining contracts and agreements across cultures. Interpretations and assumptions can differ. There is an ethical and professional responsibility to clarify and understand expectations among all parties. By recognizing differences and working with options that provide for ranges of behavior acceptable in the contributing cultures, the team can learn to work together more effectively.

One example of a synergistic solution is the holistic systems approach to large-scale change and structural change management developed by Peter Quennell (1992) and his colleagues in the Management Systems Change Research Project of the United Nations Development Programme. This process begins with a carefully chosen multidisciplinary team that pilots systems development in a specific area such as planning or quality control. Later this team is integrated with other teams within an organization or system. Next, the systems change teams at each horizontal level are vertically integrated across broad sectors to make the sectors more efficient and help them work together with other sectors. These team arrangements are aligned throughout a country and this national network begins to work jointly with systems change teams in other countries. This structured change effort uses a framework of incremental change principles to grow the managerial, technical, and economic strength of systems over a period of time from baseline capacity to self-sustainable change capacity.

STRATEGIC ISSUES IN GLOBAL CONSULTATION AND DEVELOPMENT

The International Professional Practice Area of the American Society for Training and Development (ASTD) has created a formative document on strategic global issues (Chakiris and Murrell 1993). They list these five issues as the most critical for change management and cooperative development:

- Creating local empowerment with a global perspective;
- Involving resources of local cultures in the design and implementation of global training and development programs;
- Coordinating mutual recipient societies;
- Developing executive education East and West; and
- Establishing global career development.

Local Empowerment

Local empowerment is defined as the development process by which managers, employees, customers, and suppliers are assisted in increasing their skill levels and developing the capacity to share responsibility as individuals and groups for the operation and development of their organization and community.

The challenge to multinational professionals and consultation teams is not only to create learning systems that encourage empowerment and collaboration, but also to model a fluid, culture-sensitive structure in training designs. In a multinational setting this requires an understanding of local cultural assumptions about authority and participation as well as cultural patterns in perception, learning, and approaches to change Professional competence also demands an appreciation of the fundamental nature of the empowerment process as it relates to an interdependent global economy. How do people talk about empowerment? What are the frames for organizational participation and empowerment? How do local organizations view change and development?

The skills and resources necessary to accomplish empowerment activities are extremely limited. A sponsor group of senior executives, training professionals, and academics with experience and knowledge about global empowerment could serve as the core of this process and develop linkages and alliances with other groups and organizations to facilitate and support local empowerment with a global perspective on change management.

Involving Local Resources in Program Development

In a competitive market, corporations recognize the importance of timely and consistent training and development programs for employees worldwide. To provide culture-sensitive and relevant programs, representatives from the local culture–including professionals, suppliers, managers, and academics–should be involved early in the design. Design activities may include adapting, customizing, and translating training programs for different languages and cultural contexts. It is also important to develop consultation, design, and development competencies worldwide for application in local markets.

This process empowers local professionals who participate in the creation and application of training programs and develops local ownership and commitment. Corporations need to provide the same training opportunities to all international units so that organization members have the competence and empowerment to work in a world-class system.

Developing a network of professionals worldwide supports the consultation, training, and development necessary to accomplish corporate change strategies. Participants must understand the relationship between technology and culture, instructional design, and the technology of training and development.

Mutual Recipient Societies

There are many clusters of development needs worldwide and there are no absolute providers and receivers of development. Each country has strengths and developmental areas that encourage shared learning and improvement. This involves transferred competencies in change consultation and collaborative inquiry, rather than the traditional exportation of expertise. Global synergy can bring a transformation to facilitate increased coordination and responsibility as well as the recognition of new options, relationships, and worldviews.

The current notion of the United States being the provider of global development is outmoded. The global economy suggests that there are pockets of development and underdevelopment throughout the world. For example, the former Soviet Union is highly developed in technical and scientific areas but less developed in other areas. A mutual-recipient perspective provides an opportunity for shared and transferred competencies across national, ethnic, and cultural boundaries to benefit all participants in a holistic relationship.

Executive Education East and West

The participants in an ASTD Executive Development Seminar (Odenwald 1993) described the current traits of executives as "alone at the top," all-knowing and powerful, dictating goals and methods, predicting the future from the past, and valuing order. Many of these executives are also seen as monolingual and more focused on a domestic vision. The future traits of executives were defined as "leader as learner," someone who intuits the future and facilitates the visions of others, and accepts the paradox of order amid chaos. This future executive is characterized as multicultural with a global vision.

Alliances in a global context among corporations, business schools, governments, universities, and community organizations can facilitate innovative approaches to continuing education and learning for executive and organizational leadership development and change management competencies. Exchange programs, internships, grant research, conferences, and development projects can provide opportunities for professionals and executives to learn in different cultural contexts and to share knowledge and practices. Participation in action research projects that explore cultural differences and promote global cooperation are especially needed in relation to critical economic, political, and social issues affecting all organizations.

Global Career Development

Understanding traditional and emerging forms of careers from the perspective of the American, European, and Asian career cultures is essential as organizations become more diverse and move into an interdependent global market. Cultural diversity may be influenced by the demographics of gender, age, and race; personal and religious values; opportunity to participate in education, training, and development; current and future practices in career activities; formal and informal mentoring, job rotation, and career movement; performance systems and performance feedback; organizational communication channels; cultural economic perspectives related to rewards and expectations; and variations in government regulations and organizational cultures.

Global change management competence requires a balanced mix of both technical and process skills. Growing business activities across cultures increasingly requires skills for building relationships with partners, alliances, and networks at the local and global levels. These practices include how to work with and through others, how to be a mutually recipient culture in giving and receiving from others, how to involve people at the local level, and how to recognize the cultural meaning of local accountability, pride, quality, competition, and continuous improvement in change management.

Global career competence also includes an ethical perspective on relationships, trade transactions, and personal and corporate values, as well as methods of resolving ethical dilemmas and conflicts across cultures. Some of the most essential aspects of global competence are flexibility, respect for other cultures, and a willingness to learn. Language skills, cultural knowledge, and business skills are all part of this capacity. The major questions related to global career development are: What future global career competencies are needed to conduct effective business strategies across cultures? What are the competencies being defined now and in the future? What process is being used to define these competencies? What organizations and cultures are growing global consultation competencies for executives, managers, team leaders, and change facilitators?

The "global embrace" (Wendt 1993) of transnational corporations increases cultural, political, and social interdependence. As with many change paradoxes, these interrelationships can also bring greater freedom and diversity. Wendt explains that when a company becomes a global system, responsibility moves down and more decisions are delegated to a local level.

Global experience supports more diversified careers and opportunities for learning and development throughout the system. Change management must include the development of competencies for getting agreement and facilitating collaborative inquiry to identify issues, solve problems, and meet the challenges of the present and future. The transfer of information and technology through collaborations and strategic alliances is built on trust, reciprocity, respect for national and ethnic values, and openness for mutual learning.

Change management competencies can help managers and consultation teams to meet the challenges of a global world with greater competency and responsibility for facilitating change and multinational development.

CASE STUDY: A TRANSCULTURAL DEVELOPMENT CENTER

An example of global synergy (Moorthy 1992) comes from an electronics organization, an industry leader in global applications with a vision of world-class quality and teamwork. This organization has created a transcultural development center which translates training into as many as 13 different languages for near simultaneous presentation to personnel in the United States, Europe, Asia, and Japan. Each employee throughout the world receives a minimum of 40 hours of training each year and some receive as many as 200 hours of technical training. The goal is to get the "right training to the right people at the right time at the right cost."

The organization uses advanced technology and cultural relationships around the world to maximize learning for their personnel by transferring technology and allowing locals to take ownership in developing and presenting training materials. The development teams include translators, interpreters, technical writers, instructional designers, trainers, local translators, local instructors, administrative support personnel, and project managers.

The foundation of this unique multilingual training program is a glossary of key words, phrases, and concepts. These are translated into the targeted languages by contract translators in the native country working with an international development team. The local translator is trained to better understand the business before the translation is made. There are at least three verifications of the translation including a content expert within its facilities. The results are sent back and forth for review and feedback. The translator, proofreader, and editor work together to ensure the best possible product.

The local translator becomes an important part of the team. When an experienced trainer goes into the country to train the native instructors, the translator is also present. Training designs are developed to suit the cultural context. Some approaches are more interactive and others are more holistic. In the pilot, 24 to 30 students are trained by the local instructor with the master trainer and the translator observing.

Teams of this type also can be used for change management in creating a multilingual technology glossary and developing culture and language programs, cultural sensitivity programs, orientation programs, and various training tools. The clients for these global products may include corporate training centers, regional boards, customers, suppliers, manufacturing groups, and business partners. The result is greater collaboration and coordination in a unified global system with a shared vision of excellence in quality, training, and performance.

15

Ethics

We have throughout this book, placed emphasis on face-to-face communication in everything from project teams to global alliances. A group of people work together with trust, competence, and commitment developed through dialogue and direct interaction. What happens to these personal connections as we move toward the "virtual" corporation?

In many cases agreements, planning and implementation can be completed through a sophisticated computer system which links a geographically dispersed group around the city or around the world. The "ephemeral" structures and "edgeless", continually changing interfaces of the virtual corporation are designed for speed and flexibility to provide products "instantaneously" in response to demand (Davidow and Malone 1992). Managers, engineers, suppliers, distributors, retailers, employees and customers around the globe may soon join in a "perpetual mix" of people and competencies, to create a new kind of organization, which can be both powerful and elusive.

There are many challenges related to participation and empowerment that have not been addressed by changing organizational structures. The virtual corporation brings new ethical dilemmas. Where is accountability in this system? What responsibility does the organization have to this mix of employees for training, benefits, and involvement? What is their obligation and loyalty to the organization? What are the new competencies required to deal with ambiguous and conflicting roles, goals, and priorities? What will be the quality of these new relationships? In the absence of regular face-to-face communication, how will people confront and resolve differences?

In the fast paced, high tech environment of the virtual organization, it seems almost anachronistic as we shift the scene to a mid-career manager sitting at his desk and worrying about employees. Rapid and sometimes contradictory change can bring challenging ethical dilemmas for organizations. The future will present thorny ethical questions. Yet ethics is often a more personal and timely decision as this internal dialogue illustrates.

I don't know what to do. Who can I talk to? This change initiative doesn't seem right to me. It's not fair to our long-term employees. I disagree with this decision, but what can I say? My job could be on the line. I'm supposed to implement this change.

This manager is caught in an ethical dilemma. Does he stand against "innovative change" and "progress," designed to increase overall performance? He cannot confront critical issues affecting the organization because of internal political pressures that control data and power. Effective consultation competencies can help organizational members confront ethical dilemmas related to change management by involving people in the process, recognizing and respecting differences, and transferring knowledge and learning throughout the system and allowing codetermination in managing change. Part of this process is "driving out the fear" (Deming 1982) so that people can express their ideas and build trust and cooperation for managing change. Organizations that are successful over the long term make ethics a part of their mission and approach to change management on both a global and a local level. Balancing individual, group, and organizational needs is at the core of ethical challenges related to change and community.

DEFINING ETHICS

Sometimes people do the right things for the wrong reasons, or the wrong things for the right reasons. There are many conflicts and ethical dilemmas related to change. Some of the greatest conflicts in history have been caused by different definitions of right and wrong. In some cases "legal" and "ethical" may be in direct contradiction. Ethics must be continually defined as a dynamic part of change management in responsive and effective organizations. Wendt (1993) suggests that transnational corporations often operate at the highest common denominator and level of responsibility rather than the lowest. Countries with stringent standards of corporate behavior are often most successful in transnational and global business.

The term "ethics" (McCoy 1985) comes from the Greek term *ethika* and the term "moral" derives from the Latin term *mos* or *moris*. In either language, these terms refer to cultural customs, conduct, and character valued as good or appropriate in a particular society or organizational system. Ethics and morality are related on different levels and they are often used interchangeably. Some traditional approaches might describe morality as a general, more universal code of conduct based on cultural and religious values. Ethics has most often been characterized as a discipline that studies the judgments and actions related to this moral code in specific contexts. While moral codes can establish an ideal for behavior, ethics involves daily choices about what people want to be and what they want their organizations to be.

Today, ethics is often the more general term referring to a variety of both ethical and moral dilemmas. For example, Jacobs (1992), in her dialogue on the moral foundations of commerce and politics, distinguishes between two contradictory ethical systems–a "guardian syndrome" related to organizing, managing, and protecting, and a "commercial syndrome" based on trading, producing, and changing. The guardian syndrome respects tradition, hierarchy, loyalty, and expertise, while the commercial syndrome encourages collaborations, novelty, efficiency, and productivity. Both have value, but the problems come in confusing one with the other.

There has been continuing debate over the existence of an overriding universal ethical or moral standard. Immanuel Kant provides a powerful and controversial maxim, the Categorical Imperative, in which individuals are asked to consider what might happen if their behavior became a universal law followed by everyone. This supports fundamental moral rules of right and wrong. However, relativists contend that there is no absolute "right" or "wrong," but simply different beliefs, that are practiced in diverse contexts and cultures. One relativist perspective might contend that all options are equal and make no moral judgment. Ultimately there are few true relativists, and most fall back to a pluralist perspective that respects many options but does judge some to be better than others.

The president of one major corporation described his basic rule for an ethical organization: "You have to stand for something." An organization's values serve as its foundation for ethical decisions and actions. Ethics is generally considered from one or more of these fundamental perspectives:

- Virtuous idea of a good person or ethical organization;
- Legal and social principle or contract; and
- Consequential and utilitarian value comparison.

While these ethical foundations are related, each reflects a different emphasis or perspective on ethical behavior in change management.

Virtue Model

The virtue perspective often supports moral ideas of a good life based on human dignity and worth as well as the moral rights and duties of a good person. This perspective, influenced by Greek philosophy, focuses on an ideal self as a model for behavior and change. Would a good person or an ethical organization do this? How will this action or decision affect the image that we have of ourselves as good people and a good organization? Some organizations may embody a model of the ideal in the founder or some prominent person in the history or narrative of the organization. However, the individual model of the good person or ethical organization is fundamentally based on social and religious learning within a specific culture. Some proponents of ethical management (Blanchard and Peale 1988) apply this test: How would you feel if your decision or action were published in the newspaper or described to your family? The virtue model is both a personal and a public ideal or image, related to appropriate change management.

Indeed, the information, learning, and "rules" of the virtue model are often found in organizational narratives and stories that recount the cultural history of the organization. These are the stories that organization members tell about change to celebrate models of loyalty, courageous risk, devastating loss, and the hard work that leads to exemplary success. These tales often reflect the values and the unwritten ethical code of the organization. In some organizations, the more recent organizational virtue model is defined in striving for excellence and total quality. Have the Baldridge Award and the Deming Prize set a new model for judging the "good" organization? Ethics in change management involves not only a personal code but also accepted organizational standards for behavior, which establish a context for actions as well as a means of interpreting those actions.

Contract Model

Ethics, as one top executive observed, is ultimately a "matter of trust" among management, employees, suppliers, customers, and the community. Part of this trust is based on standards of performance and agreements within a particular culture or context. These are developed through communication and collaborative inquiry. The opportunity for feedback, dialogue, and recognition increases commitment to quality performance measures and integrity around agreements. The contract model can affect change management decisions on multiple levels.

The social contract or rule-based approach is perhaps the most explicit in organizational practices and procedures. A multitude of laws and regulations affecting organizations are established and enforced through our legal system. Organizational rules are also documented in a code of ethics, policies, and performance measures and maintained through monitoring, evaluation, and feedback. The social contract, as articulated by Hobbes, Rousseau and others focuses on the agreements that people make, formally or informally, in order to live together in a community. Essentially the contract requires that individuals do not harm others and that they honor their agreements with one another. Some ethical questions related to change management in a contract approach might be: How does this action relate to the rules in this organization? How does it fit the standards and codes of the industry? Is this a required rule or an optional rule? How do we make agreements for change? How do we know that organizational members understand or accept the "contract"?

Members of an organization are working with an implicit social contract whether it is formally recognized or informally supported. Interpretations of change may be affected by this assumed relationship. Lippitt (1982) discussed this agreement or "psychological contract" (Levinson 1966) based on the employee's expectations of the organization and the employing organization's expectations of the individual worker. Some of the terms are expressed in formal job descriptions and performance measurements, but most are unwritten manifestations of behavior. Participation, employee involvement, and self-directed teams bring new dimensions to this psychological contract in changing roles, structures, and responsibility for change management.

Utilitarian Model

A utilitarian approach focuses on a rational assessment of values and the consequences of actions and changes on relevant stakeholders such as employees, management, customers, suppliers, and community. Stated in a simplistic manner as "the greatest good for the greatest number," this is essentially the principle of utility as described by John Stuart Mill, one of the greatest advocates of utilitarianism. The core of this approach is an understanding of values and a determination of which actions best maximize those values for the people affected. The ethical questions are: Who are the people that will be affected by this decision, action, or change? What are the essential values involved? Which of these values are most important for the majority of people affected by the change? Which action maximizes our dominant values? Which change will bring the most positive benefit to the greatest number of individuals?

Yet how do we define the "common good" in a world of diversity with valid conflicting interests? This model requires a thoughtful assessment of values. While some aspects of utilitarianism might be quantified in a hard-nosed objective manner, many aspects of values are qualitative and ultimately subjective. For example, the CEO can look at the economic forecasts and the cost and profit margins that demand layoffs and plant closings, but the ethical dilemma comes in maximizing core values in relation to these numbers. From this perspective, the CEO must answer this key question: How do we accomplish the downsizing that will help insure the survival of the organization in accordance with our values and concern for people?

Utilitarian approaches must also deal with broad issues of justice and fairness. How do we best serve the interests of stockholders and employees? Which is most important? The North American Free Trade Agreement (NAFTA), for instance, brings up many of the dilemmas of a utilitarian approach in balancing broad economic advantages of a directed change with the needs of people and jobs. Involving people in decision making and collaborative inquiry based on common goals encourages ethical decision making and helps integrate change in complex systems.

Many approaches to ethics do not fall easily into one of these categories but are related to all three. Most ethical decisions come back to values. However, values are often tested by rules or ideal models. Does this decision, action, or change reflect the core values of this organization? Is this action legal? How does this action make me feel about myself as a person, as a team member, as a professional, as a manager, and as a change facilitator?

ETHICAL DEVELOPMENT

Ethical codes are learned and modeled in the family, the community, the work place and in religious activities as part of a cultural and social heritage. Within organizations, senior-level executives define and communicate ethical behavior for the organization. Consultation in change management also shapes and is shaped by ethical practices. Increasing ethical awareness and improving assessment, problem solving, and judgment in resolving ethical dilemmas related to change management are part of a process of individual, group, and organizational development.

Some studies indicate that adults in professional schools can significantly improve their ethical consciousness and learn problem solving and reasoning strategies to help resolve ethical dilemmas. However, there is much debate as to whether ethics can be effectively taught in a university or corporate classroom. Developing ethical awareness and judgment is a gradual process that must be related to everyday experiences and work practices.

Kohlberg (1972) provides a classic and sometimes controversial model describing the structural stages in the moral development of individuals. According to Kohlberg, the three major stages of moral development are: preconventional, conventional, and postconventional.

In the *preconventional* stage, "good" behavior is based on authority and threat of punishment. Rules are followed only when they are in the individual's self-interest. In this stage, avoiding criminal charges, liability, and lawsuits might be a prominent self-interest and the major influence on behavior. The next, *conventional* stage is grounded in group norms and the expectations of others and the need to maintain social relationships and fulfill duties to individuals, groups, and society. The negotiated or implied contract has the most prominent influence in this stage. In the final, *postconventional* stage, decisions and actions are based on internalized principles that recognize relative rules, diversity, and a variety of values with a universal perspective of justice and respect for others. This development combines sensitivity to values, rules, and virtues with a macroperspective on change management. Behavior at this stage represents rational moral judgment and effective problem solving and analysis of complex moral conflicts. Sophisticated ethical understanding and application are part of a data-based approach to change in which participants move out of their own self-interest and recognize diversity and creative alternatives beyond traditional rules and structures.

Some business ethicists and management theorists suggest that many managers are at the rule-based, conventional stage while CEOs tend to be closer to the postconventional principled stage with a more universal perspective on ethics. Classical approaches to management can keep organization members at the conventional stage of moral development and might even stall ethical development at a preconventional level. At the preconventional level, and often at the conventional level, people follow the rules of others and avoid excessive thinking about the ethical implications. Participative approaches and collaborative inquiry in change management can help individuals and groups to move to a more principled stage of development at the postconventional level. This often occurs when they take a more critical approach to change and realize that there are dilemmas that the standard rules and procedures will not answer. People begin to examine their values and their reasoning processes as they consider new opportunities and consequences as part of a realistic learning process. Consultation competencies can help move organization members toward a higher level of ethical development with equity and trust in working together to manage change, and create the future.

Ethical development can also be affected by individual, group, and organizational perspectives toward change as discussed in Chapter 3. From a rational perspective, the utilitarian approach has been applied to support individual integration into the organization and the good of the organization over the individual. The social contract is also used as a performance measurement and a norm for individual and group behavior. In the systems approach to change, ethics are more complicated with conflicting, interrelated webs of action and consequences that may not be immediately evident. Transformational systems change raises many ethical dilemmas. In many ways the systems emphasis has been more utilitarian in emphasizing a macroperspective and creating a balance of benefits. This perspective most often maintains the conventional level of ethical behavior. The cultural approach to change depends on an understanding of communication interactions and the creation of rules and agreements. However, predetermined rules and practices are often simply accepted as part of expectations and norms within a specific social, economic, or political environment and never questioned. A cultural perspective may support both the virtue model and the contract or agreement model, but the result is most often a more conventional view of moral development. The critical perspective encourages reflection on these taken for granted rules for ethical behavior. Why do we accept these rules? Are they valid? Are these ethical standards appropriate? What is their impact on directed change? Nondirected change? What are the consequences for individuals, groups, and organizations? The critical perspective might also reject authority and rules as a base for ethics and encourage a more relativistic perspective or a postconventional view. Each of these perspectives is evident in the overall context of organizational change and ethical development in change management.

ETHICAL CONTEXTS WITHIN ORGANIZATIONAL SYSTEMS

From the perspective of change management, we see these major principles as establishing a context for the discussion of ethics:

- Corporations are moral agents as well as legal entities.
- Organizational ethics is a policy science reflected in organizational decisions related to multiple constituencies and change issues.
- There is a direct relationship between ethics and performance, because ethics legitimizes the need to formulate criteria for performance measurement and feedback.
- Ethical reflection integrates experience, information, and performance criteria related to the individual, group, and the organization.

Organizational ethics are most often defined by groups and interrelated social relationships and obligations. While the organization may present a formal statement of beliefs, values, and purposes, it is also a community of individuals and groups with a variety of expectations, values, objectives, and ethical perspectives. The actions and interactions of managers and teams within the organization have specific consequences and results that may affect others in the organizational system, including those in the wider community. Ethics help guide change management in relation to values and performance by focusing on consequences as well as respect for the dignity of individuals and groups in organizational systems.

An ethical corporation recognizes and appreciates the whole person. A national conference focusing on "The Family, the Corporation, and the Common Good" was recently sponsored by the Center for Ethics and Corporate Policy and several major companies including AT&T, Ameritech, and Continental Bank. Business executives, human resource professionals, social service directors, clergy, and academics explored the ethical challenges of balancing work life and family responsibilities, and restoring a sense of community in the workplace. For example, the Work and Family Initiative at DuPont supports a sense of community as a core value. With many second and third generation employees, they include the children of employees as stakeholders in their organization. Employee benefits are part of this support.

A two year project by researchers from the University of Chicago (1993) studied the impact of the wide range of employee benefits offered by Fel-Pro, a diversified manufacturing corporation. Family benefits include on-site child care, family leave, elder care resources, subsidized tutoring, college scholarships and summer camp for employee's children, a health and fitness center, and flexible work hours. The results showed that "family responsive" policies did make a significant contribution to individual job performances and openness to change. The more workers use and appreciate Fel-Pro's benefits, the more they support and participate in quality improvement and other changes taking place in the organization.

Ethical management involves people throughout the organization in planning for their collective future. However, this process must be based on performance goals and agreements that clearly and appropriately establish expectations and obligations.

Determining the responsibility of individuals, groups, and organizations surfaces other ethical dilemmas. As Werhane (1985) explains, corporations are "secondary" moral agents dependent on a collection of primary actions by individual people. This collective action is often impersonal, goal-oriented, and intentional. According to Werhane, organizational ethics is the "sum of decision-making procedures" of managers, teams, and boards. These decisions should be based on facts as well as the consideration of ethical issues, stakeholders, alternatives, implications, and constraints.

Donaldson (1982) states that the sources of corporate misconduct come from the need for profit and productivity, and from system-oriented problems related to decision making and goal-rational behavior. He suggests that moral goals be considered along with profit goals and that decision making also be concerned with ethical behavior. This is not an easy task for executives, managers, boards, and teams struggling to manage change and help the organization survive in a competitive global economy.

Organization leaders, managers, and consultation teams do have ethical responsibilities as they facilitate change, confront issues, and resolve conflict in complex systems. The consequences of change are enormous. Directed changes are transforming the organization, reducing the work force, and redesigning the work place, developing competitive products and services, changing the organizational "architecture" in fundamental structures and relationships, and increasing dependence on technology and information.

Ethics in Relationships

Throughout this book, we have encouraged collaboration and open communication to help executives, managers, and teams to learn more about their interdependent work and the integration of directed and nondirected change to reach mutually beneficial goals. Successful consultation in change management grows from ethical guidelines that are based on a fundamental respect for people and the contributions they can make to the organization in their daily work practices.

The following list includes some basic ethical responsibilities that managers and change facilitators have to people throughout the organizational system including employees, suppliers, customers, and community:

- Share information
- Promote equity and fairness
- Be honest and open
- Make and keep agreements about how data is used
- Respect privacy
- Recognize multiple options and solutions
- Listen to opposing views
- Ensure freedom of choice
- Consider consequences of actions
- Take responsibility for behavior
- Be willing to live with your own rules
- Promote development of the individual, group, and organization

These responsibilities create challenges for leaders, change facilitators, managers, and teams in planning, influencing, and implementing change.

Dilemmas of Change Management

Some of the major dilemmas of change management are related to the use of data, differing expectations and opportunities for learning, and problems with routinized processes in changing structures.

Dilemma: How do we anticipate, prepare for, and resolve the conflict and power issues associated with data?

Participation and employee involvement support greater awareness and access to information to help organization members understand contexts, alternatives, and consequences related to directed and nondirected change. An open access to data can create ethical dilemmas and potential conflicts within traditional organizations. As Zuboff (1988) explains, the "informating" process of technology and computer-mediated work puts knowledge and traditional bureaucratic authority on a direct "collision course." Increased possibilities for producing and disseminating information places power in the hands of those who control this knowledge base, traditionally the domain of the manager. The new learning environment expands this knowledge to employees and other organization members. Thus, information increases responsibility and extends empowerment and influence in the learning organization. Ethical change management helps to increase access to knowledge and encourages collaborative data collection, analysis, planning, and implementation as a result of that data. This also implies an ethical responsibility to help managers learn new competencies and see options and opportunities for themselves within new organizational structures.

From an ethical change management perspective, this situation requires clear agreements about how data will be used while respecting privacy and encouraging voluntary sharing and openness. The underdeveloped areas in many organizations are in not preparing people for the opportunities to influence and the responsibility associated with data, as well as the need to receive and confront data. This process can give rise to conflicts and hidden agendas that must be discussed and resolved. Ethical consultation practices can help facilitate the change process based on collective learning and shared data.

Dilemma: How do we ground the change process in where the client is, so that we begin at the right place in order to learn together and reach mutual goals?

Ethical responsibilities in change consultation also include transferring competencies and developing people within the client system starting where they are. Carl Rogers (1961) provides insight to consultation in his "client-centered" approach to individual and group change and development. Rogers' concept of "significant learning" is not based on the accumulation of facts but rather on learning that "makes a difference" in behavior and action and integrates knowledge and experience. Some current approaches focus only on application without content and theoretical foundations. From our perspective, change management should deal with significant mutual learning, which integrates both process and content, and theory and application. This increases understanding and grounds the process in a more realistic way.

Sometimes the facilitating system and the client system start in different places and nothing they wanted to happen really happens because of their different expectations. It is essential to start where the client system is to avoid this misunderstanding and conflict. This requires collaborative inquiry and clear agreement on current and future expectations.

Dilemma: How do we keep from falling into routine management practices, which discourage innovation and new learning?

The "reflective practitioner" described by Schon (1983) helps managers and change facilitators to gain perspective and reflexive self-knowledge throughout the change process. Schon's concept of "reflection in action" involves discovering, discussing, critically analyzing, testing, and restructuring those basic assumptions, intuitions, and understandings of experience and practice that have become routine and reactive. According to Schon, many professionals can fall into the trap of being the "expert," knowledgeable and competent. Perhaps they are so confident that they do not question their own judgment and prescriptions. This lack of reflexivity can foster an empty, sometimes mechanical application of practices, which does not transfer competencies to the client system nor adequately serve the needs of the employees or customers .

Change facilitators should encourage free thought from the consultation team as well as from individuals and groups within the organization. Yet many pressures toward conformity and groupthink can lead to an assumed consensus and no real commitment or responsibility to change. Old rules and policies don't always fit current needs. Change management must encourage a sense of ongoing discovery and innovation, which involves people throughout the system in creating and recreating their own collective future.

CONVERSATIONS AND GUIDELINES FOR ETHICS

While there is some discussion among members of the organization and the community about morality and ethics within complex social and organizational systems, other social observers express a postmodern pessimism that, appearances aside, the basic substance and meaning of morality have been fragmented and lost (MacIntyre 1984). Organizations and professions may have codes of ethics but the contexts are vague, and ethical statements are often only formalities and not living documents. Directed and nondirected elements must be integrated to connect ethics to practice.

There are a number of critical questions that should be discussed and analyzed in developing a collective, reflective view of the ethics of change management.

- Do individuals, groups, and the organization have accountability for change? What does this mean?

- Are ethics connected to the everyday decisions and actions of people in organizational systems? How is nondirected change related to directed change?

- How do ethical practices reflect organizational values? Are people honest with each other? Do they trust each other?

- How does ethics affect consultation methods that support individual, group, and organizational development in the context of global and local change?

- How does a change management team most effectively "help" an organization deal with momentous changes in roles, structure, and control?

- Can ethics be taught to managers, change facilitators and organization members?

- How does the process of collaborative inquiry encourage discussion and analysis of ethical dilemmas in the work place and in the organization's relationship with a larger community?

After a "60 Minutes" interrogation or a revealing article in the *Wall Street Journal,* a senior manager may ask, "How did we get to this?" Schein (1987) suggests the importance of historical "reconstruction" in looking at the decisions and actions that led to a specific condition or situation. In many cases ethical and legal problems within an organization reflect the lack of a long term perspective built on a "living" code of ethics with personal commitment, openness, and accountability based on what has been learned from the past and what will be encountered in the future.

In recent years organizations have been called to a greater accountability and responsibility by employees, customers, suppliers, stockholders, and the community. These stakeholder groups are taking a more critical perspective and asking new questions that force some reflexive assessment of organizational practices. Public opinion and pressure from consumers, special-interest groups, and the media, as well as global competition, multinational operations, and advances in technology have changed the way organizations operate and extended the boundaries of their responsibility. Organizations must recognize the need to be more responsive to a variety of publics and more socially responsible in their decisions and actions related to change management.

Many organizations are developing ethical codes and statements of value in confronting the challenging issues related to ethical business conduct. Others have well-established ethical codes that have served as models for other organizations. Johnson & Johnson first published its credo in 1944 and has continued to refine and develop the ethical code as a "living document" with credo challenge meeting among top managers, a credo survey of all employees, and feedback meetings to encourage participation in ethical discussions throughout the organization.

To be effective, corporate ethics over the long term should be institutionalized throughout the structures, patterns, and operations of the entire corporation. In many ways, ethics comes from the CEO's office as a history, a vision of the future, and a way of doing business in the present. A Business Roundtable Report on Policy and Practice in Company Conduct (Keogh 1988) states three major factors that contribute to ethical conduct:

- The CEO and those around the CEO need to be openly and strongly committed to ethical conduct, and give constant leadership in tending and renewing the values of the organization;

- A code of ethics is important to clarify company expectations of employee conduct in various situations and make clear that the company intends and expects its personnel to recognize the ethical dimensions of corporate policies and actions; and

- Compliance with company standards of conduct can be ensured through mechanisms such as management involvement and oversight, attention to values and ethics in recruiting and hiring, emphasis on corporate ethics in education and training, communication programs, auditing, and enforcement procedures.

There has been considerable discussion of the value and significance of ethical codes. These codes would seem to create a more ethical climate, yet a study of over 200 major manufacturing corporations (Mathews 1988) concluded that the code of ethics does not necessarily result in fewer violations. According to Mathews, few of the codes have specific compliance and enforcement procedures, and most focus on the corporation's fear of "victimization" by employees in areas such as proprietary information, conflict of interests, bribery, embezzlement, and theft. There is little mention of the responsibilities of the organization to the community, customers, and employees. In this respect the code helps to protect the organization against litigation and loss but does not always reflect the specific social responsibility of the company to various stakeholders.

Interpretations of what is "good" or "out of bounds" may vary from one company or nation to another. Expectations must be clarified and agreements made relative to goals, roles, and responsibilities concerning change management. Still the questions are difficult to answer: Should a consultation team identify managers with developmental needs knowing these people may be terminated rather than retrained? Do organization members have a right to see confidential data about changes that affect them and their department? When do consultation roles step over the line in controlling a situation or using inappropriate intervention? How are ethics determined in a multicultural organization with conflicting national and cultural standards of conduct?

Ethics begins with data collection that opens up the change management process and maximizes organizational resources. Ethical issues such as national and local laws, corporate policies and rules, and cultural standards and values should be identified. The perspectives and consequences for the people affected by the change action must be considered. Whenever possible they should be involved in the process. Ethical actions demand a realistic examination of alternatives and options that attempt to integrate different points of view and reduce the conflict created by change. The ethical implications of specific changes should be clearly understood and analyzed. What precedent will this set? Is this consistent with company policy? How will concerned people be affected by this change? Is this decision congruent with our values?

Often, organizational restraints and roadblocks such as lack of time, resources, information, or political pressures have a direct effect on decisions. The ethical implications of these factors have to be recognized. The final decision or action should meet the test of both values and rules in collective analysis of the change management process.

ETHICAL ISSUES IN CHANGE CONSULTATION

Many competent change facilitators and internal and external specialists in a growing number of areas offer a variety of services in the global marketplace. However, "consultation" has sometimes been applied in cases where the process, technology, and quality of services and skills vary widely. These factors can lead to some skepticism and confusion about consultation practices. One critic, for example, suggests Machiavelli as the "patron saint" of organizational consultants and describes their "sins" as pandering to employer's prejudices and thriving on "truisms, hyperbole, and gimmicks" (March 1991). Another characterization focuses on consultation as the "archetype of hyper-emphasis on style, brevity and intensity" (Browning and Hawes 1991). Indeed one of the three major job categories of the future has been termed "symbolic-analytic services" in identifying and solving problems and brokering strategic activities through the "manipulation of symbols" in data, words, and images that can be traded in the world market (Reich 1992).

With the growing emphasis on internal consultation, managers as change facilitators, and internal and external consultation teams, process consultation is becoming more important in facilitating responsible organizational change and development. We might conclude that the harsh characterizations in the previous paragraph simply reflect a lack of positive experiences with the collaborative process consultation as practiced by competent, ethical professionals. However, these statements may more accurately present an ethical challenge to all those who work with change management to critically assess their own intentions and practices in relation to their values and the personal and professional codes of conduct that they follow. Change management can be distorted and misused within the organizational system to serve narrow political agendas rather than developmental and learning goals. This reinforces traditional bureaucracy and does not encourage the data-based, collaborative, innovative spirit of effective change management, which can energize, develop, and renew the organization in a way that benefits everyone involved in the collective process.

Developing consultation competencies for change management encourages learning on the part of executives, change facilitators, managers, consultation teams, and the client system. This process requires a collaborative approach to the facilitation of change that supports ethical decisions and stakeholder involvement in gathering data and making the decisions that affect them. From the perspective of the change management team, these are some of the ethical questions and dilemmas affecting decisions and actions at each of the six phases of change consultation.

Phase 1: Need and Opportunity in Change Initiative
- What is the level of openness in the organization?
- How open is the client in discussing issues?
- Do we trust the client? Does the client trust us?
- What are the client's expectations? Change facilitators' expectations?
- Do consultation team competencies match client system needs?

- What is the level of commitment and readiness to change?
- What are the power relationships related to change?
- Are there hidden agendas for the client or sponsor?
- Will there be equity in the client and consultation team relationship?
- Does the team have appropriate skills and expertise?
- What is the team's intent in working with this client?

Phase 2: Agreements for Establishing a Working Relationship

- Are there clear performance criteria with evaluation and measurement?
- Is the time perspective realistic? Appropriate?
- Are both the consultation team and the client committed to the project?
- Will people who are affected by the directed change be involved in the process?
- Will consultation skills be transferred to the client system?
- How can the change facilitators avoid being the "expert" with all the answers?
- What are the "standards for quality" in this process?
- What responsibility does the consultation team have for the interventions made?

Phase 3: Data Collection and Analysis

- Can team members confront the client on sensitive issues?
- Are they objective in collecting and analyzing data?
- Are team members available and accessible as resources?
- Is the client attempting to manipulate data?
- Does data reflect the diversity and variety of viewpoints within the organizational system?
- Has the team taken the time to understand the organization? Unit?
- Are representative members of the client system involved in data collection?
- Is information balanced to reflect opposing views?

Phase 4: Feedback, Decisions, and Action Planning
- Do the facilitators make appropriate process interventions?
- Are resources used effectively?
- Are decisions realistic and data-based?
- Is data presented in an accurate and straightforward way?
- Do decisions support organizational values?
- Do decisions reflect organizational policies?
- Are decisions collective? Is there consensus?
- Are alternatives explored?
- Are consequences considered for relevant groups?
- Are action plans realistic in relation to market needs?
- Do organization members understand all dimensions of the issue?
- What are the consequences of change interventions?
- Are people allowing for multiple options?
- Is the team avoiding a prescriptive approach?
- Is there equity in the relationship with the client?
- Is the team creating a passive dependency rather than allowing the client and client system to learn to solve problems?

Phase 5: Applications and Results Measurement
- Are those affected by the change involved in implementation?
- Are feedback channels established?
- Is feedback on results shared throughout the system?
- Does this application recognize diversity within the organization?
- Are there any long-term factors that might affect this change?

Phase 6: Continuity and Renewal
- Are competencies transferred to the client system?
- Is adequate follow-up established?
- Are all parties satisfied with the results?
- Are all requirements of the agreement or contract completed?
- How do team members feel about the decisions and actions?

Ethical Concerns for Change Management

There are a number of basic ethical issues related to change management including expertise, intent, consequences, equity in relationships, freedom of choice, and openness and truth.

Expertise and Competence

Consultation teams, change facilitators, managers, and staff professionals have a responsibility to keep up-to-date on developments in organizational thinking and practice, to be continually learning and improving competence and specialized skills, and to be open to new ideas and approaches.

The traditional expert approach to consultation is often characterized as: "You give me a problem; I give you the answer." While this may appear to be an efficient approach with immediate results, it is not always an appropriate developmental approach from a human resource or an ethical perspective. The "expert" role raises ethical dilemmas related to competence, equity in relationships, consequences, and responsibility. The expert role is most damaging when it creates a dependency on the part of the client rather than allowing the client and client system to develop competency and independence in change management.

Intent

The motivation of the manager, the change facilitator, consultation team, and the client and sponsor should be understood before the process begins. All parties are moving toward conscious goals and these should be integrated so that expectations and responsibilities are clear in formal or informal agreements. Hidden agendas should be opened up and explored so that they do not cause difficulties later in the process.

The process model of change management demands caring and committed people with professional competence and experience. This includes external resources as well as internal managers and staff professionals. The intent is on "influence" rather than "authority" and "helping" rather than "controlling" in a participative, collaborative model of change management.

Consequences or Impact

The consequences of decisions and actions in a change initiative can be profound. Change facilitators must consider how change affects employees, customers, the community, the supplier, and other stakeholders. In this process the manager can model behavior and set an ethical standard for collaborative inquiry, feedback, and action planning. Effective change management makes the organization better by increasing individual and group influence and participation in the change process. Action research and planning helps organization members understand their responsibility as well as the consequences of change. The transfer of specific competencies to the client and the client system can have lasting effects within the organization as the client "learns to learn" and applies action-research cycles to everyday challenges in integrating nondirected change in routine practices with broad directed change efforts.

Equity and Fairness

Change management is based on developing and nurturing partnerships and learning alliances throughout the organization. The consultation relationship among managers, change facilitators, and the client should be a partnership rather than a one-up or one-down situation. Ethical decisions and actions are perceived as fair and balanced when there is respect for individuals and the group. Equitable actions help to develop a win-win situation for members of the consultation team, and the organization. Decisions are more balanced and democratic when participants feel a sense of teamwork and equality in both contributions and benefits.

Freedom of Choice

Ethical approaches to individual, group, and organizational development should be based on voluntary choices rather than imposed demands for change. Participation, empowerment, and teamwork cannot be "commanded." Those who are involved in creating the rules are more likely to respect and follow those rules. Those who participate in data collection, analysis, planning, and action implementation will be more knowledgeable and committed to the process. Organizational members must freely choose to take some part in developing the collective future of the organization with the knowledge and data necessary to recognize options and consequences. The client must also choose to recognize and "own" the situation and show readiness for change. Otherwise, as Gibb (1961) explains, the help and consultation will not be perceived as "helpful."

Openness and Truth

Organization members have a right to timely, accurate information that helps them increase their understanding and effectiveness within the organization. Action research and collaborative inquiry are based on access and openness to gather and process data that can benefit everyone. Closed systems cannot survive rapid social, economic, and political change. Ethical change management requires honest communication among leaders, managers, team members, employees, suppliers, customers, and community. This openness should begin at the top of the organization.

Ethics is a process of continuing development, assessment, and learning that encourages thoughtful action as a result of reflection and analysis of the moral significance of specific decisions and behaviors. In change consultation, ethics is involved in every aspect of the process from initial contact and agreement to interventions and completion of the project. Change management should build on a consistent ethical code based in professional knowledge and competency, with respect for individuals and diverse organizational cultures. Effective organizational performance is supported by ethical change management. Table 15.1 is a model ethical code used by one management consultation firm that has built long-term relationships with many systems based on these core values. These guidelines can apply to both internal and external change facilitation teams working toward the future.

TABLE 15.1 Model Code of Ethics.

We work with and through our clients.

We avoid the creation of client dependency on us.

We endeavor to increase our clients internal resource capabilities.

We align our objectives to organizational strategy and measurements.

We involve employees, managers, and staff in the overall design.

We test, develop, and modify based on feedback and evaluation.

We base our action and designs on the actual data we collect.

We prefer to assist clients in measuring results.

We work where senior management and employee sponsorship and commitment exist.

We reject techniques and methodologies that could embarrass or degrade persons in the client's system.

We adhere to the principle of "no surprises" for our clients and their personnel.

We prefer to work closely with an internal person or management team in the work of data collection, diagnosis, analysis, and interpretation of the data, feedback, decisions and actions, and establishing of performance criteria, accountabilities formation, and monitoring of action implementation.

We take on only those assignments in which our competence has been established and where we can guarantee high-quality performance.

TABLE 15.1 (continued)

We tailor interventions and materials to fit the organizational culture.

We manage projects effectively and efficiently to deliver the highest quality resources at the lowest investment cost and expense.

We view our role as helping organizations to maximize their internal organizational strengths to take advantage of the competitive external environment.

We believe it is possible to accomplish three types of goals: individual (career planning, performance, and learning); group (coordination, outcomes, and growth); and organization goals (direction, unity, and internal and external responsiveness).

1993 Copyright. B.J. Chakiris Corporation.

References

Adizes, I. (1988). *Corporate Lifecycles: How and Why Corporations Grow and Die and What To Do About It.* Englewood Cliffs, NJ: Prentice Hall.

Adler, N. J. (1991). *International Dimensions of Organizational Behavior* (2nd ed). Boston: PWS-Kent Publishing.

Agor, W. (1984). *Intuitive Management: Integrating Left and Right Brain Management Skills.* Englewood Cliffs, NJ: Prentice-Hall.

Argyris, C. (1970). *Intervention Theory and Method: A Behavioral Science View.* Reading, MA: Addison-Wesley.

Argyris, C. and Schon, D. A. (1974). *Theory in Practice: Increasing Professional Effectiveness.* San Francisco, CA: Jossey-Bass Publishers.

Argyris, C. and Schon, D. A. (1978). *Organizational Learning.* Reading, MA: Addison-Wesley.

Argyris, C. (1985). *Strategy, Change, and Defensive Routines.* Boston: Pitman.

Ashby, W. R. (1956). *An Introduction to Cybernetics.* London: Chapman and Hall.

Aubrey, C. A. and Felkins, P. K. (1988). *Teamwork: Involving People in Quality and Productivity Improvement.* Milwaukee, WI: Quality Press and White Plains, NY: Quality Resources.

Austin, L. A. and Hall, Dean G. (1989). *Competitive Resourcing.* New York: AMACOM.

Bales, R. F. (1950). *Interaction Process Analysis: A Method for the Study of Small Groups.* Reading, MA: Addison-Wesley.

Barnard, C. I. (1938). *The Functions of the Executive.* Cambridge, MA: Harvard University Press.

Barrett, W. (1978). *The Illusion of Technique: A Search for Meaning in a Technological Civilization.* Garden City, NY: Anchor Books.

Barrett, W. (1986). *Death of the Soul: From Descartes to the Computer.* New York: Anchor Books/Doubleday.

Barzini, L. (1983). *The Europeans.* New York: Penguin Books.

Beckhard, R. and Harris, R. (1987). *Organizational Transitions* (2nd ed.). Reading, MA: Addison-Wesley.

Bennis, W. G. and Slater P. E. (1968).*The Temporary Society*. New York: Harper and Row.

Berger, P. L. and Luckmann, T. (1966). *The Social Construction of Reality: A Treatise in the Sociology of Knowledge*. Garden City, NY: Doubleday.

Bertalanffy, L. (1968). *General System Theory*. New York: George Braziller.

Bhote, K. R. (1991). *World Class Quality: Using Design of Experiments to Make It Happen*. New York: AMACOM.

Blake, R. R. and Mouton, J. S. (1978). *The New Managerial Grid*. Houston, TX: Gulf Publishing.

Blanchard, D. and Murrell, K. L. (1982). *OrgSim*. Pensacola, FL: ByteSize, Inc. and Chicago: B. J. Chakiris Corporation.

Blanchard, D. (1993). *Nexus: Work and Family Simulation*. Pensacola, FL: ByteSize and Chicago: B. J. Chakiris Corporation.

Blanchard, K. and Peale, N. V. (1988). *The Power of Ethical Management*. New York: William Morrow and Company.

Blumer, H. (1969). *Symbolic Interactionism: Perspective and Method*. Englewood Cliffs, NJ: Prentice-Hall.

Bohm, D. and Edwards, M. (1991). *Changing Consciousness: Exploring The Hidden Source of the Social, Political, and Environmental Crises Facing Our World*. San Francisco: HarperCollins.

Brissett, D. and Edgley, C. (Eds.) (1990). *Life as Theatre: A Dramaturgical Sourcebook* (2nd ed.). New York: Aldine de Gruyter.

Brody, E. W. and Stone, G. C. (1989). *Public Relations Research*. New York: Praeger.

Brown, S. R. (1986). Q Technique and Method: Principles and Procedures. In W. D. Berry and M. S. Lewis-Beck (Eds.). *New Tools for Social Scientists*. Beverly Hills: Sage.

Browing, L. D. and Hawes, L. C. (1991). Style, Process, Surface, Context: Consulting as Postmodern Art. *Journal of Applied Communication Research*. 19, (1-2), 32-54.

Burke, K. (1966). *Language as Symbolic Action: Essays on Life, Literature, and Method*. Berkeley: University of California Press.

Camp, R. C. (1989). *Benchmarking*. White Plains, NY: Quality Resources.

Carroll, R. (1988). *Cultural Misunderstandings: The French-American Experience*. Volk, C. (Trans). Chicago: The University of Chicago Press.

Chakiris, B. J. (1981). *Action Research Teaming Feedback Worksheets*. Project Journal from International Action Research Team Project in Ornskoldsvike, Sweden. Chicago: B. J. Chakiris Corporation.

Chakiris, B. J. and Grill, J. P. (1982). *Customer Service Systems*. Project notes. Chicago: B. J. Chakiris Corporation.

Chakiris, B. J. (1982). *Benchmarking As Change Intervention.*. Unpublished notes. Chicago: B. J. Chakiris Corporation.

Chakiris, B. J. and Fornaciari, G. M. (1984). Career Integration: An Understanding of Employee Roles, Work Group Relations and Organizational Structures. In *Career Development, Current Perspectives.* Alexandria, VA: ASTD Career Development Professional Practice Area.

Chakiris, B. J. (1985). *Employee Quality and Productivity Program.* Chicago: B. J. Chakiris Corporation.

Chakiris, B. J. and Leach, John (1985). *Rusting Out of America Obsolescence Study.* Project Reports. Chicago: B. J. Chakiris Corporation.

Chakiris, B. J. (1987). *Human Resource Audit Facilitation Manual.* Chicago: B. J. Chakiris Corporation.

Chakiris, B. J. (1991). *ART: Action Research Teaming Workbook.* Chicago: B. J. Chakiris Corporation.

Chakiris, B. J. (1992). *Human Resource Audit.* Chicago: Metrex® Division of B. J. Chakiris Corporation.

Chakiris, B. J. (1992). *Environment Survey for Quality and Productivity Improvement.* Chicago: Metrex® Division of B. J. Chakiris Corporation.

Chakiris, B. J. (1992). *Metrex® Process Guide.* Chicago: BJ Chakiris Corporation.

Chakiris, B. J. and Murrell, K. L. (1993). *Globalization Issues.* Working paper prepared for International Professional Practice Area of ASTD National Conference. Chicago: B. J. Chakiris Corporation.

Chakiris, B. J. (1992). *Change Consultation Audit.* Chicago: Metrex® Division of B. J. Chakiris Corporation.

Chakiris, B. J. and Fornaciari, G. M. (1993). Self Development. In W. R. Tracey (Ed.), *Human Resources Management & Development Handbook.* New York: AMACOM.

Chakiris, B. J. (1993). *Lutheran Child and Family Agency of Illinois. Strategic Planning Model.* Project notes. Chicago: B. J. Chakiris Corporation.

Cohen, M. D., March, J. G. and Olsen, J. P. (1972). A Garbage Can Model of Organizational Choice. *Administrative Science Quarterly,* 17 (1), 1-25.

Davidow, W. H. and Malone, M. S. (1992). *The Virtual Corporation: Structuring and Revitalizing the Corporation for the 21st Century.* New York: HarperCollins.

Deal, T. C. and Kennedy A. A. (1982). *Corporate Cultures: The Rites and Rituals of Corporate Life.* Reading, MA: Addison-Wesley.

Deetz. S. A. (1992). *Democracy In An Age of Corporate Colonization.* Albany, NY: State University of New York Press.

Deming, E. (1986). *Out of Crisis.* Cambridge, MA: Massachusetts Institute of Technology.

Dokken, D. and Chakiris, B. J. (1980). *People In Planning*. National Endowment for the Arts and The National Assembly for the State Arts. Chicago: B. J. Chakiris Corporation.

Donaldson, T. (1982). *Corporations and Morality*. Englewood Cliffs, NJ: Prentice-Hall.

Drucker, P. F. (1985). *Innovation and Entrepreneurship*. New York: Harper and Row.

Drucker, P. F. (1992). *Managing For The Future: The 1990s And Beyond*. New York: Truman Talley Books/Dutton.

Eccles, R. G. (1991). The Performance Measurement Manifesto. *Harvard Business Review*. 69 (1), 131-137.

Elden, M. and Chisholm, R. F. (1993) Emerging Varieties of Action Research. *Human Relations*. 46 (2), 121-141.

Elden, M. and Levin, M. (1991). Cogenerative Learning: Bringing Participation into Action Research. In W. F. Whyte (Ed.), *Participatory Action Research*. Newbury Park, CA: Sage.

Fayol, H. (1949). *General and Industrial Management*. London: Pitman.

Felkins, P. K. and Chakiris, B. J. (1981). *Managing Your Job*. Chicago: B. J. Chakiris Corporation.

Felkins, P. K. and Chakiris, B. J. (1985). *University Image Study*. Project Reports. Chicago: B. J. Chakiris Corporation.

Ferguson, M. (1980). *The Acquarian Conspiracy: Personal and Social Transformation in the 1980s*. Los Angeles: J. P. Tarcher.

Fisher, B. A. (1980). *Small Group Decision Making* (2nd ed.). New York: McGraw-Hill.

Fornaciari, G. M. and Chakiris, B. J. (1985). Organization Development and The Consulting Sociologist. In J. M. Iutcovich and M. Iutcovich (Eds.), *The Sociologist As Consultant*. New York: Praeger.

Freud, S. (1961). *Civilization and Its Discontents*. J. Strachey (Ed.). New York: W. W. Norton.

Geertz, C. (1973). *The Interpretation of Cultures*. New York: Basic Books.

George, Carl F. (1991). *Prepare Your Church for the Future*. Grand Rapids, MI: Fleming .

Gergen, K. J. (1991). *The Saturated Self: Dilemmas of Identity in Contemporary Life*. New York: Basic Books.

Gibb, J. R. (1961). Defensive Communication. *Journal of Communication*. 11, 141-148.

Giddens, A. (1984). *The Constitution of Society: Outline of the Theory of Structuration*. Berkeley, CA: University of California Press.

Gleick, J. (1987). *Chaos: Making A New Science*. New York: Penguin Books.

Glidewell, J. C. (1959). The Entry Problem In Consultation. *Journal of Social Issues.* 15 (2).

Goldman, I. (1990). Abductory Inference, Communication Theory and Subjective Science. *Electronic Journal of Communication. La Revue Electronic de Communication.*, 1. (Troy, NY: Computer access Via E Mail "send GOLDMAN VIN 90" COMSERVE @ R PIECES.)

Goffman, E. (1974). *Frame Analysis: An Essay on the Organization of Experience.* Cambridge, MA: Harvard University Press.

Hall, E.T. (1966). *The Hidden Dimension.* Garden City, NY: Anchor Books/Doubleday.

Hall, E. T. (1976). *Beyond Culture.* Garden City, NY: Anchor Press/Doubleday.

Hampden-Turner, C. (1970). *Radical Man.* Cambridge, MA: Schenkman.

Hampden-Turner, C. (1991). The Boundaries of Business: The Cross-Cultural Quagmire. *Harvard Business Review*, 69 (5), 94-96.

Handy, C. (1989). *The Age of Unreason.* Boston, MA: Harvard Business School Press.

Harris, P. R. (1983). *New World, New Ways, New Management: Metaindustrial Organizations.* New York: AMACOM.

Heath, R. L. and Nelson, R. A. (1986). *Issues Management: Corporate Policymaking in an Information Society.* Newbury Park, CA: Sage.

Heisenberg, W. (1958). *The Physicist's Conception of Nature.* London: Hutchinson.

Hofstede, G. (1991). *Cultures and Organizations: Software of the Mind.* London: McGraw-Hill.

Ishikawa, K. (1985). *What is Total Quality Control? The Japanese Way.* D. J. Lu (Trans.). Englewood Cliffs, NJ: Prentice-Hall.

Jacobs, J. (1992). *Systems of Survival: A Dialogue on the Moral Foundations of Commerce and Politics.* New York: Random House.

James, W. (1907). *Pragmatism.* Cleveland, OH: World Publishing.

Janis, I. L. (1982). *Groupthink: Psychological Studies of Policy Decisions and Fiascoes* (2nd ed.). Boston: Houghton Mifflin.

Jung, C. G. (1971). *Psychological Types.* H.G. Baynes (Trans.). Princeton, NJ: Princeton University Press.

Jung. C.G. (1989). *Analytical Psychology.* W. McGuire (Ed.). Princeton, NJ: Princeton University Press.

Kanter, R. M. (1983). *The Change Masters: Innovation for Productivity in the American Corporation.* New York: Simon and Schuster.

Kanter, R. M., Stein, B. A., and Jick, T.D. (1992). *The Challenge of Organizational Change: How Companies Experience It and Leaders Guide It.* New York: The Free Press.

Kaplan, A. (1964). *The Conduct of Inquiry: Methodology for Behavioral Science.* Scranton, PA: Chandler Publishing.

Kearnes, D. T. and Nadler, D. A. (1992). *Prophets In The Dark: How Xerox Reinvented Itself And Beat Back The Japanese.* New York: Harper Business.

Keogh, J. (Ed.). (1988). *Corporate Ethics: A Prime Business Asset.* New York: The Business Roundtable.

Kelley, R. E. (1992). *The Power of Followership.* New York: Doubleday.

Ketchum, L. D. and Trist, E. (1992). *All Teams Are Not Created Equal: How Employee Empowerment Really Works.* Newbury Park, CA: Sage.

Kets de Vries, M. F. R. and Miller, D. (1984). *The Neurotic Organization: Diagnosing and Revitalizing Unhealthy Companies.* New York: Harper Business.

Kluckhohn, F. and Strodtbeck, F. L. (1961). *Variations in Value Orientations.* Evanston, IL: Row, Peterson.

Koestler, A. (1967). *The Ghost in the Machine.* London: Arkana.

Kohlberg, L. (1984). *The Psychology of Moral Development: The Nature and Validity of Moral Stages.* San Francisco, CA: Harper & Row.

Kotter, J. P. (1990). *A Force for Change: How Leadership Differs from Management.* New York: The Free Press.

Korzybski, A. (1958). *Science and Sanity: An Introduction To Non-Aristotelian Systems and General Semantics.* (4th Ed.). Lakeville, CT: International Non-Aristotelian Library Publications.

Lawler, E. E. III (1992). *The Ultimate Advantage: Creating The High-Involvement Organization.* San Francisco: Jossey-Bass.

Leach, J. (1982). *The Career of The Organization.* Chicago: University of Chicago Industrial Institute.

Leach, J. and Chakiris, B. J. (1984). *R.O.I.A.: Rusting Out Of America Obsolescence Study.* Unpublished Conference Paper. Chicago: B. J. Chakiris Corporation.

Leach, J. and Chakiris, B. J. (1985). The Dwindling Future of Work in America. *Training and Development Journal.* 39 (4), 44-46.

Leach, J. and Chakiris, B. J. (1988). The Future of Jobs, Work and Careers. *Training and Development Journal.* 42 (4), 48-54.

Levinson, H. (1966). *Men, Management, and Mental Health.* Cambridge, MA: Harvard University Press.

Lewin, K. (1951). *Field Theory in Social Science.* D. Cartwright (Ed.) New York: Harper and Row.

Likert, R. (1967). *The Human Organization: Its Management and Value.* New York: McGraw-Hill.

Lippitt, G. L. (1982). *Organizational Renewal: A Holistic Approach to Organizational Development* (2nd ed.). Englewood Cliffs, NJ: Prentice-Hall.

Lippitt, G. L.; Lippitt, R.; Chakiris, B. J.; and Pirsein, R. W. (1978). *Consulting Process In Action Skill Development Kit.* Chicago: B. J. Chakiris Corporation.

Lippitt, G. L. and Chakiris, B. J. (1980). *Executive Conferences.* Unpublished notes. Chicago: B. J. Chakiris Corporation.

Lippitt, G. and Lippitt, R. (1982). *Futuring and Planning.* Lippitt network meeting notes.

Lippitt, G. and Lippitt, R. (1986). *The Consulting Process in Action.* (2nd ed.) San Diego, CA: University Associates.

Lippitt, R. (1966). Processes of Curriculum Change. In R.R. Leeper (Ed.), *Curriculum Change: Direction and Process.* Washington, DC: Association for Supervision and Curriculum Development, NEA.

Lippitt, R. and Schindler-Rainman, E. (1978). Beyond The Scientific: A Comprehensive View of Consciousness: Knowing, Feeling, Doing. In A.W. Foshayad and I. Morrissett. (Eds.). *Proceedings of 1975 Annual Conference of SSEC.* (Publication No. 214). Boulder, CO: Social Science Education Consortium, Inc.

Lippitt, R., Hooyman, G., Sashkin, M. and Kaplan, J. (1978). *Resource Book for Planned Change.* Ann Arbor, MI: Human Resource Development Associates.

Lippitt, R. (1979). *Kurt Lewin, Action Research and Planned Change.* W. Germany: Kindler Verlag Ag Zurich.

Lippitt, R. and Chakiris, B. J. (1981). *Organizational Climate Survey.* Unpublished paper. Chicago: B. J. Chakiris Corporation.

Lippitt, R. and Chakiris, B. J. (1982). *Organization Renewal Consortium Cluster Meetings.* Unpublished notes of Network Cluster Meetings. Chicago: B. J. Chakiris Corporation.

Loomis, C. (1993). Dinosaurs? *Fortune.* 127 (9), 36-42.

Lyman, S. M. and Scott, M. B. (1975). *The Drama of Social Reality.* New York: Oxford University Press.

Maccoby, M. (1988). *Why Work: Motivating and Leading the New Generation.* New York: Simon and Schuster.

MacIntyre, A. (1984). *After Virtue* (2nd ed.). Notre Dame, IN: University of Notre Dame Press.

March, J. G. (1991). Organizational Consultants and Organizational Research. *Journal of Applied Communication Research.* 19, (1-2) 20-31.

Maslow, A. (1954). *Motivation and Personality.* New York: Harper and Row.

Mathews, M. C. (1988). *Strategic Intervention in Organizations: Resolving Ethical Dilemmas*. Newbury Park, CA: Sage.

Mayo, E. (1933). *The Human Problems of an Industrial Civilization*. New York: Macmillan.

McCoy, C. S. (1985). *Management of Values: The Ethical Difference in Corporate Policy and Performance*. Boston: Pitman.

McGregor, D. (1960). *The Human Side of Enterprise*. New York: McGraw-Hill.

McWhinney, W. (1992). *Paths of Change: Strategic Choices for Organizations and Society*. Newbury Park, CA: Sage.

Mead, G. H. (1962). *Mind, Self, and Society*. C. W. Morris (Ed.). Chicago: University of Chicago Press.

Middleton, D. and Edwards, D. (Eds.) (1990). *Collective Remembering*. Newbury Park, CA: Sage.

Miller, D. C. (1991). *Handbook of Research Design and Social Measurement*. (5th ed.). Newbury Park, CA: Sage.

Miller, R. (1989). *Government Contracts*. Conference paper. Brisbane, Australia: International Consultants Foundation.

Mills, C. W. (1959). *The Sociological Imagination*. London: Oxford University Press.

Mills, D. Q. (1991). *Rebirth of the Corporation*. New York: John Wiley and Sons.

Mink, O. G., Shultz, J. M. and Mink B. (1979). *Developing and Managing Open Organizations: A Model and Methods for Maximizing Organizational Potential*. Austin, TX: Learning Concepts.

Mintzberg, H. (1973). *The Nature of Managerial Work*. New York: Harper and Row.

Mintzberg, H. (1989). *Mintzberg on Management: Inside Our Strange World of Organizations*. New York: The Free Press.

Mintzberg, H. (1990). The Manager's Job: Folklore and Fact. *Harvard Business Review*, 68 (2), 163-175. .

Mintzberg, H. (1993). *Structure in Fives: Designing Effective Organizations*. Englewood Cliffs, NJ: Prentice Hall.

Mitroff, I. I. and Kilmann, R. H. (1978). *Methodological Approaches to Social Science: Integrating Divergent Concepts and Theories*. San Francisco, CA: Jossey Bass.

Moorthy, R. S. (1992). *Global Design and Delivery System*. Unpublished paper presented at 1992 ASTD Conference. Schaumberg, IL: Motorola University.

Morgan, G. (1986). *Images of Organization*. Newbury Park, CA: Sage.

Morgan, D. L. (1988). *Focus Groups as Qualitative Research.* Newbury Park, CA: Sage.

Mumby, D. K. (1988). *Communication and Power in Organizations: Discourse, Ideology, and Domination.* Norwood, N.J.: Ablex.

Murrell, K. L. and Chakiris, B. J. (1992). *OrgSim Global.* Chicago: B. J. Chakiris Corporation.

Nadler, D. A. (1977). *Feedback and Organization Development: Using Data-Based Methods.* Reading, MA: Addison-Wesley.

Nadler, D. A., Gerstein, M .S. and Shaw, R. B. (1992). *Organizational Architecture: Designs for Changing Organizations.* San Francisco: Jossey-Bass.

Naisbitt, J. and Aburdene P. (1990). *Megatrends 2000: Ten New Directions for the 1990's.* New York: William Morrow and Company.

Neuhauser, P. C. (1988).*Tribal Warfare In Organizations.* New York: Harper Business.

Odenwald, S. B. (1993). *Global Training: How To Design A Program For the Multinational Corporation.* Alexandria, VA: American Society for Training and Development.

Ohmae, K. (1990). *The Borderless World: Power and Strategy in the Interlinked Economy.* New York: Harper Business.

Orsburn, J. D., Moran, L., Musselwhite, E., and Zenger, J. H. (1990). *Self-Directed Work Teams: The New American Challenge.* Homewood, IL: Business One Irwin.

Parsons, T. (1960). *Structure and Process in Modern Societies.* New York: The Free Press.

Pearce, W. B. and Cronen, V. (1980). *Communication, Action, and Meaning.* New York: Praeger.

Pearce, W. B. (1989). *Communication and the Human Condition.* Carbondale, IL: Southern Illinois University Press.

Peters, T. J. and Waterman, R. H., Jr. (1982). *In Search of Excellence: Lessons from America's Best-Run Companies.* New York: Harper and Row.

Peters, T. (1987). *Thriving on Chaos: Handbook for Management Revolution.* New York: Alfred A. Knopf.

Prahalad C. K. and Hamel, G. (1990). The Core Competence of the Corporation. *Harvard Business Review.* 68 (3), 79-87.

Quennell, P. M. (1992). *Structural Change Management.* Project United Nations Development Programme. Project Notes. New York: Management Systems Change Research.

Reich, R. C. (1992). *The Work of Nations: Preparing Ourselves for 21st-Century Capitalism.* New York: Vintage Books/Random House.

Roethlisberger, F. and Dickson, W. (1939). *Management and the Worker.* Cambridge, MA: Harvard University Press.

Rogers, C. R. (1961). *On Becoming a Person.* Boston: Houghton Mifflin.

Rothenberg, A. (1979). *The Emerging Goddess: The Creative Process in Art, Science, and Other Fields.* Chicago: University of Chicago Press.

Rowan, R. (1986). *The Intuitive Manager.* Boston: Little, Brown.

Rummler, G. A. and Brache, A. P. (1990). *Improving Performance: How to Manage the White Space on the Organization Chart.* San Francisco: Jossey-Bass.

Ryle, G. (1949). *The Concept of Mind.* London: Hutchinson.

Ryan, K. D. and Oestreich, D. (1991). *Driving Fear Out of the Workplace.* San Francisco: Jossey-Bass.

Scheidel, T. M., and Crowell, L. (1979). *Discussing and Deciding: A Desk Book for Group Leaders and Members.* New York: Macmillan.

Schein, E. H. (1987). *Process Consultation: Lessons for Managers and Consultants* (Vol. II). Reading, MA: Addison-Wesley.

Schlesinger, A. M., Jr. (1992). *The Disuniting of America: Reflections on a Multicultural Society.* New York: W.W. Norton.

Schon, D. A. (1983). *The Reflective Practitioner: How Professionals Think in Action.* New York: Basic Books.

Schultz, B. L. (1992). Shifting to Self-Direction. *Target,* 8(3), 36-38.

Schutz, W. C. (1966). *The Interpersonal Underworld.* Palo Alto, CA: Science and Behavior Books.

Senge, P.M. (1990). *The Fifth Discipline: The Art and Practice of the Learning Organization.* New York: Doubleday.

Shaw, M. E. (1981). Group Dynamics: *The Psychology of Small Group Behavior.* New York: McGraw-Hill.

Shephard, H. (1975). Rules of Thumb For Change Agents. *OD Practitioners.* Seattle, WA: Network newsletter for consultants.

Singh, J. V. (1990). *Organizational Evolution: New Directions.* Newbury Park, CA: Sage.

Srivastva, S. and Cooperrider, D. L. (1990). *Appreciative Management and Leadership: The Power of Positive Thought and Action in Organizations.* San Francisco: Jossey-Bass.

Steiner, I. D. (1972). *Group Processes and Productivity.* New York: Academic Press.

Stephenson, W. (1953). *The Study of Behavior: Q-Technique and Its Methodology.* Chicago: The University of Chicago Press.

Stephenson, W. (1967). *The Play Theory of Mass Communication.* Chicago: The University of Chicago Press.

Swartz, D. and Lippitt, G. L. (1975). Evaluating the Consulting Process. The *Journal of European Training,* 5. Bradford, England: Publications, Ltd.

Swartz, D. and Chakiris, B. J. (1978). *The Life and Work Goals Exploration.* Chicago, IL: B. J. Chakiris Corporation, and Seattle, WA: Effectiveness Resource Group, Inc.

Swartz, D. (1982). *Institute Documents.* International Institute for the Study of Systems Renewal. Seattle, WA: SRi Nonprofit Educational Corporation.

Swartz, D. (1985). *Consultation Contracting.* Working documents. Seattle, WA: Effectiveness Resource Group, Inc.

Tannenbaum, R. and Schmidt, W. H. (1986). How to Choose a Leadership Pattern. *Harvard Business Review.* 64 (4), 129.

Taylor, F. W. (1911). *Principles of Scientific Management.* New York: Harper and Row.

Terkel, S. (1974). *Working.* New York: Avon Books.

Thurow, L. C. (1992). *Head to Head: The Coming Economic Battle Among Japan, Europe, and America.* New York: William Morrow and Company.

Tichy, N. M. and Sherman, S. (1993). *Control Your Destiny or Someone Else Will.* New York: Currency /Doubleday.

Trimble, V. H. (1990). *Sam Walton: The Inside Story of America's Richest Man.* New York: Dutton.

Trujillo, N. (1987). Implications of Interpretive Approaches for Organizational Communication Research and Practice. In L. Thayer (Ed.), *Organization Communication: Emerging Perspectives.* Norwood, N.J.: Ablex.

Tuckman, B. (1965). Developmental sequence in small groups. *Psychological Bulletin* 63, 384-399.

Turner, V. (1986). *The Anthropology of Performance.* New York: PAJ Publications.

University of Chicago (1993). *Added Benefits: The Link Between Family Responsive Policies and Job Performance.* A Study of Fel-Pro Incorporated. Chicago: The University of Chicago School of Social Service Administration.

Vogt, J. and Murrell K. L. (1990). *Empowerment in Organizations: How to Spark Exceptional Performance.* San Diego, CA: University Associates.

Walton, S. with Huey, J. (1992). *Sam Walton: Made in America.* New York: Doubleday.

Ward, J. L. (1987). *Keeping the Family Business Healthy: How to Plan for Continuing Growth, Profitability, and Family Leadership.* San Francisco: Jossey-Bass.

Waterman, R. H., Jr., (1990). *Adhocracy: The Power to Change.* New York: W.W. Norton.

Watzlawick, P., Beavin, J. and Jackson, D. (1967). *The Pragmatics of Human Communication: A Study of International Patterns, Pathologies, and Paradoxes.* New York: W. W. Norton.

Watzlawick, P., Weakland, J. H. and Fisch R. (1974). *Change: Principles of Problem Formation and Problem Resolution.* New York: W. W. Norton.

Webb, E. J., Campbell D. T., Schwartz, R. D. and Sechrest, L. (1966). *Unobtrusive Measures: Nonreative Research in the Social Sciences.* Chicago: Rand McNally.

Weber, M. (1947). *The Theory of Social and Economic Organization.* A.M. Henderson and T. Parson. (Trans.). New York: Oxford University Press.

Weber, M. (1958). *Max Weber: Essays in Sociology.* H. H. Gerth and C. W. Mills (Eds.). New York: Oxford University Press.

Weick, K. E. (1979). *The Social Psychology of Organizing* (2nd ed.). New York: Random House.

Wendt, H. (1993). *Global Embrace: Corporate Challenges in a Transnational World.* New York: Harper Business.

Werhane, P. H. (1985). *Persons, Rights, and Corporations.* Englewood Cliffs, NJ: Prentice-Hall.

Westinghouse Electric Corporation (1985). *Total Quality: A Westinghouse Imperative.* Pittsburg, PA: Westinghouse Productivity and Quality Center.

White, R. K. and Lippitt, R. (1960). *Autocracy and Democracy: A Experimental Inquiry.* New York: Harper and Row.

Whyte, W. F. (Ed.). (1991). *Participatory Action Research.* Newbury Park, CA: Sage.

Whyte, W. F. and Whyte, K. K. (1988). *Making Mondragon: The Growth and Dynamics of the Worker Cooperative Complex.* Ithaca, NY: ILR Press Cornell University.

Whyte, W. H. (1956). *The Organization Man.* Garden City, NY: Doubleday.

Winter, S. G. (1990). *Survival, Selection, and Inheritance in Evolutionary Theories of Organization.* In Jitendra. V. Singh (Ed.) *Organizational Evolution: New Directions.* Newbury Park, CA: Sage.

Xerox Corporation (1984). *Competitive Benchmarking: What It Is And What It Can Do For You.* Stamford, CT: Xerox Corporation Quality Office.

Zuboff, S. (1988). *In the Age of the Smart Machine: The Future of Work and Power.* New York: Basic Books.

Index

Communication *(continued)*
monocultural, 202; openness and
truth in, 452-453; in rational and
behavioral approaches, 66-68; in
stop session, 201; in teams and
teamwork, 188, 191, 192, 196,
197-203; in transcultural development center, 431; undiscussable
topics in, 196-197, 233
Communication management model,
173-174
Community sense, in workplace, 441
Competencies, 17, 21, 23, 36, 349-
384; in action planning, 268, 367-
369, 382; in action research
teams, 98-100; in action roles, 99-
100, 372; assessment of, 378-384;
in benchmarking, 335-336, 339; in
career development, 352 -357; in
continuity of change, 370-371,
384; core, 164, 357-371; in data
collection and analysis, 226, 361,
362, 365-367, 381; in decision
making, 367, 382; in entry phase,
360-363, 380; in ethical issues,
351; ethical issues in, 439, 451;
in exchange of practices, 401-403;
in feedback process, 21, 273,
367, 382; in global consultation,
35, 352, 430-431; in interventions,
296, 299, 369-370, 383; personal
level of, 98, 350-352; in renewal
process, 330-331, 370-371, 384;
in results measurement, 296,
369-370, 383; in teams and
teamwork, 183-184, 187-189;
transfer of, in consultation
process. *See* Transfer of
competencies; in working
agreement formulation,

Competencies *(continued)*
148-149, 172, 363-365; working
agreement on, 164
Competitive benchmarking, 332
Competitive resourcing (Core), 302-
304
Compulsive organizations, 84
Confederation form of organizations,
182
Conferences, action learning, 111-
114, 231, 293
Confirmation, in teams and
teamwork, 191, 192; in Wal-Mart,
204-205
Conflicts, 27; competency in, 361;
tribal, 198
Confrontation, 268, 269, 271, 330
Consultation, 23-25, 36-45; action
research teams in, 91-121;
approaches to, 37-38; audit of,
302, 303; change facilitators in.
See Change facilitators; in change
management model, 28, 36-45,
58, 59, 216; client in. *See* Client;
system; collaborative inquiry in,
16-18, 38; competencies in, 23,
349-384; completion of project,
45, 171, 371; cost of. *See* Cost of
project; customers of client in, 49,
139-140, 156, 168; data collection
and analysis in, 42-43, 211-264;
definition of, 23, 36; dependency
in, 133, 171, 322; differing
perspectives on change in, 62-64,
86-87; doctor-patient model of,
37; entry into, 137-146; ethical
issues in, 443-444, 447-454;
exchange of practices in, 385-409;
expert model of, 37-38; facilitation of change in, 24-25, 27-28,

Olsen, J. P., 11

Openness, agreement concerning, 161, 170-171, 172, 364; ethical issues in, 452-453

Operating core of organization, 7, 73

Opportunity and need for change, 38-41, 125-146. *See also* Need and opportunity for change

Organization shock, 34

Organizational change, 3-21; action planning in, 43-44, 265, 268, 288-291; action research teams in, 29, 42, 59, 91-121; application of plans and intentions in, 44-45, 295-302; approaches to, 60-85; benchmarking in, 332-345; challenges of, 52-53; consultation process in, 20-21, 36-45; context of, 30-36; continuity of, 45, 321-323; as continuous process, 12-14; contradictory aspects of, 9-12, 290; data collection and analysis in, 42-43, 211-264; decision making in, 43-44, 265, 268, 278-288; directed, 5; exchange of practices in, 385-409; feedback process in, 43-44, 265-278; global perspective of, 34-35, 411-432; in growth stages, 31-32; interactions of organizational members in, 14, 15-16; need and opportunity for, 38-41, 125-146; nondirected, 5-6; perceptions on, 14-15, 16, 57-58; proactive orientation to, 18, 19, 35; rate of, 19-20; renewal process in, 45, 321-322, 323-345; results in, 25, 45, 50-52, 295-296, 302-310; role of management in, 25-28; social responsibilities and obligations in, 35-36; sources

Organizational change *(continued)* of innovations in, 32-34; system-wide, 320; teams and teamwork in, 16-18, 181-208; working agreements on, 41-42, 147-180

Organizing process, 89

Orientation to change, 18-20, 35, 57-58; to task, 189, 193, 200, 415; to time, 415-416, 424

Panels and focus groups, interviews with, 251-252

Paranoid organizations, 84

Parsons, T., 71

Participation, 17, 18, 21; in action phase, 290; in action research, 92, 113, 114, 118, 119, 293-294; in change management, 189-191; contradictory aspects of, 10; cultural differences in, 428; in data collection and analysis, 224-226; in directed and nondirected change, 8; in global organizations, local empowerment in, 427-428; in group model of management, 66, 67; in rational and behavioral approach, 64-65; in recognition of need for change, 127; results of, 51; role of management in, 25, 26; task orientation in, 193; in teams and teamwork, 181, 182, 184, 185, 188, 189, 190; training for, 319-320; voluntary, 24, 148, 452

Pattern maintenance function of organizations, 71

Payment for services, working agreements on, 176-177

Pearce, W. Barnett, 77, 202-203

Perceptions on change, 21, 56, 57-58; of organizational members, 14-15, 16